# TRADE AND NAVIGATION BETWEEN SPAIN AND THE INDIES

## DEDICATORIA

Á ELENA

C. H. H.

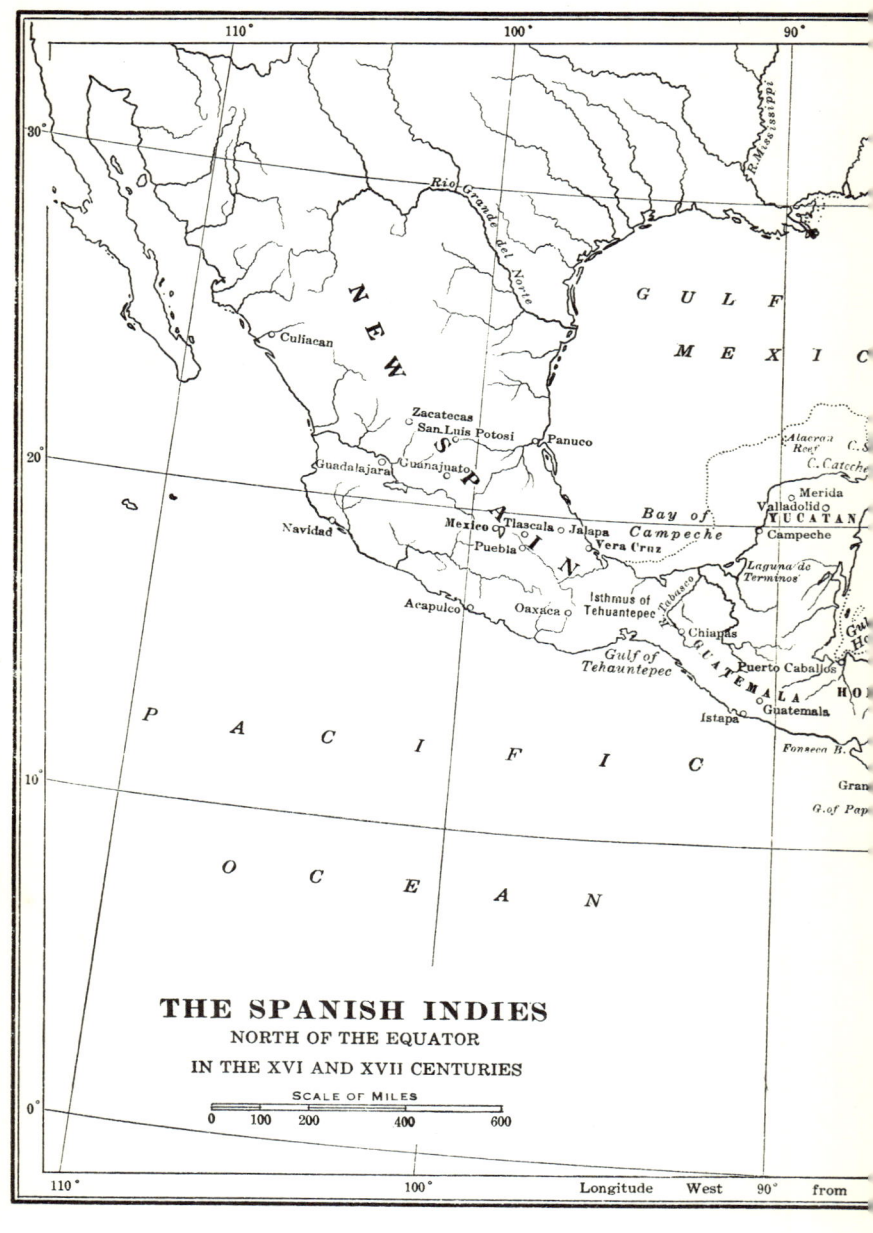

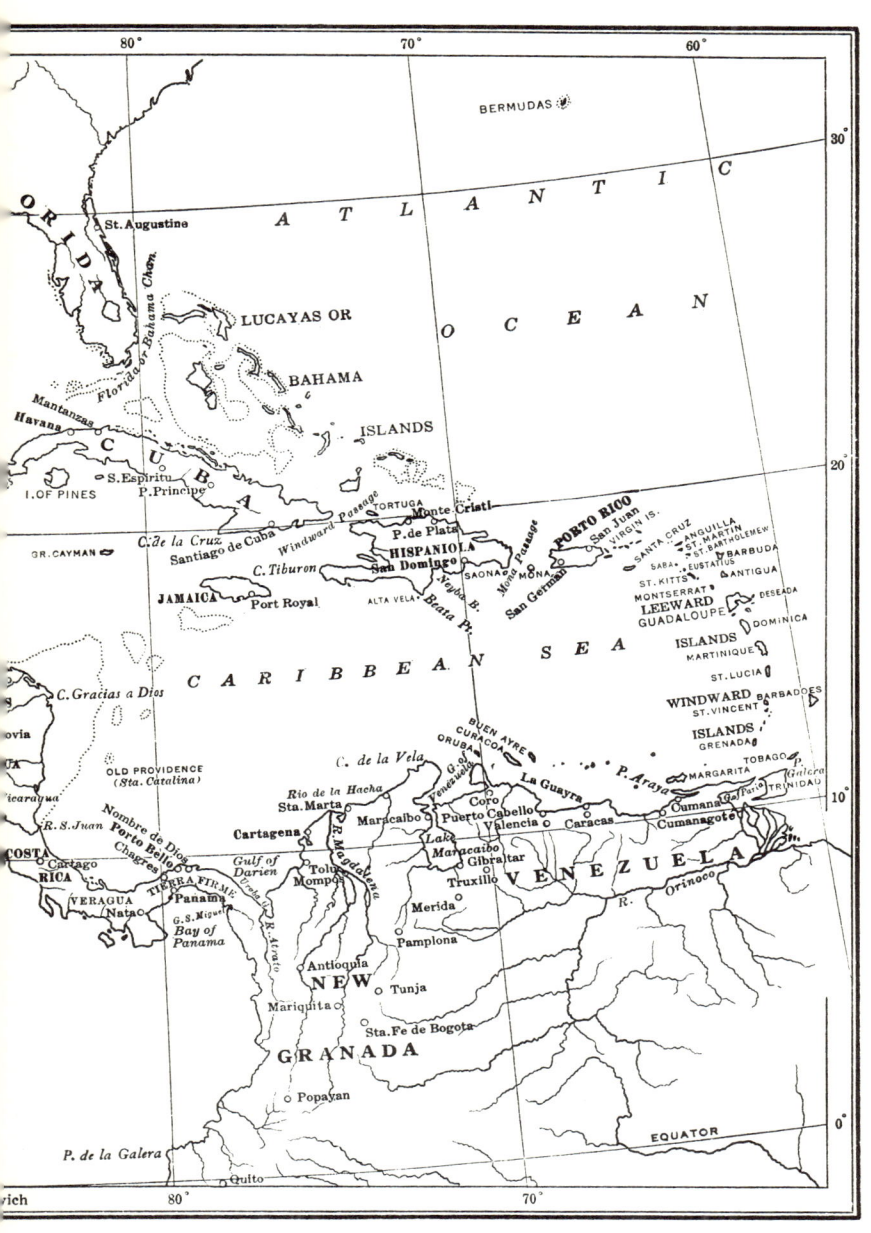

# TRADE AND NAVIGATION BETWEEN SPAIN AND THE INDIES

## IN THE TIME OF THE HAPSBURGS

BY

CLARENCE HENRY HARING, PH.D.
ASSISTANT PROFESSOR OF HISTORY
IN YALE UNIVERSITY

GLOUCESTER, MASS.
PETER SMITH
1964

Copyright, 1918
Harvard University Press

Reprinted, 1964 by Permission of
Harvard University Press

# CONTENTS

|  | PAGE |
|---|---|
| PREFACE | xi |
| BIBLIOGRAPHY | xv |

## PART ONE

### CHAPTER I

THE SEVILLE MONOPOLY . . . . . . . . . . . . . . . . 3
    Beginnings of American trade. The Seville monopoly. The ordinance of 1529. The Canary Islands.

### CHAPTER II

THE CASA DE CONTRATACIÓN . . . . . . . . . . . . . 21
    Its original purpose. The ordinances of 1503, 1510, and 1552. Hydrographic bureau and school of navigation. The Casa as a court of law. The Consulado.

### CHAPTER III

ORGANIZATION VS. EFFICIENCY . . . . . . . . . . . . 46
    The President of the Casa. New duties for the Treasurer. The Purveyor-General. Artillery. Quicksilver. Deputy Auditor and Tribunal de la Contaduría de Averías. Alguacil Mayor. Supernumerary Officials. Alcaide y Guarda Mayor. Sala de Justicia.

### CHAPTER IV

REGISTERS AND CUSTOMS . . . . . . . . . . . . . . . 59
    Avería. Almojarifazgo. Derechos de Toneladas. The royal accounts.

### CHAPTER V

EMIGRATION AND THE FOREIGN INTERLOPER . . . . . . 96
    Policy of Isabella. Of Charles V. Of Philip II. Licenses. Jews and heretics. Early efforts to promote emigration. Trade restricted to Spaniards and naturalized foreigners. Evasion of the law. Clandestine trade at Seville and Cadiz. Contraband trade in America.

## CHAPTER VI

THE SPANISH MONOPOLY . . . . . . . . . . . . . . . . 123
    Paternalism of the government. Measures affecting agriculture. Textiles. Carácas tobacco. Effect of the social and ecclesiastical policy of the Crown. Articles forbidden to be carried to the Indies. Restriction of trade to the wealthier merchants. Major and minor ports in the Indies. The "question of Buenos Aires." The Philippine commerce. Trade between Peru and New Spain. Corruption of colonial officials. Failure of the Spanish system.

## CHAPTER VII

THE PRECIOUS METALS . . . . . . . . . . . . . . . . 155
    Royalties from American mines. Use of quicksilver. Remittances of bullion. Seizure of private treasure by the Crown. "Benevolences" from Sevillan merchants. Evil results of these practices. Compradores de Oro y Plata.

## CHAPTER VIII

THE ISTHMUS OF PANAMA . . . . . . . . . . . . . . . . 180
    Portage between the two oceans. Nombre de Dios and Porto Bello. The city of Panama. The isthmian fair. The project of a canal.

# PART TWO

## CHAPTER IX

GALLEONS AND FLOTAS . . . . . . . . . . . . . . . . 201
    Early regulations for fleets and convoys. Armadas de la Guardia de la Carrera de las Indias. Size of the fleets. Their decline. Cargoes on men-of-war. Captains general and other officers. Course of the fleets to and from the West Indies. Mail boats.

## CHAPTER X

CORSARIOS LUTERANOS . . . . . . . . . . . . . . . . 231
    Frenchmen in the West Indies in the sixteenth century. Captain William Jackson. The Dutch West India Company. Piet Heyn. Jacques l'Hermite. Cornelius Joll. Cromwell's West Indian enterprise. Blake at Santa Cruz. English policy after the Restoration. The buccaneers. Armadas de Barlovento. Spanish privateers.

## CONTENTS

### CHAPTER XI

SHIPS AND NAVIGATORS (I) . . . . . . . . . . . . . . . 258
    Ownership and origin of vessels in the India navigation. Crews. Size and types of Spanish ships. Alvaro Bazan. Pero Menéndez de Avilés. Shipbuilding in the colonies. Its decline in Spain. Ordinances relating to the equipment, manning and armament of Atlantic vessels. Rations. Licenses. Freight contracts. Marine insurance. Inspection of ships and cargoes. Disregard of the regulations. Shipwrecks.

### CHAPTER XII

SHIPS AND NAVIGATORS (II) . . . . . . . . . . . . 298
    Nautical instruction and examinations at the Casa. Maps and mapmaking. Nautical science in Spain in the sixteenth and seventeenth centuries. Pilots, masters, and captains. Wages of Spanish seamen. Universidad de los Mareantes de Sevilla.

### APPENDICES

I. THE CASA LONJA . . . . . . . . . . . . . . . . 325

II. "LIBRO DE SITUADOS," OR SALARIES AND PENSIONS PAID OUT OF THE FUNDS OF THE CASA DE CONTRATACIÓN . . . . . . . . . . . . . . . . . . . . 326

III. AVERÍA COLLECTED ON THE CARGOES OF THE INDIA FLEETS, 1537–61 . . . . . . . . . . . . . . . . 327
RATE OF THE AVERÍA PAID ON ARTICLES IMPORTED FROM THE INDIES, 1557–64 . . . . . . . . . . . 328

IV. RECEIPTS OF THE TREASURERS OF THE CASA DE CONTRATACIÓN, 1503–90 . . . . . . . . . . . . . . 329

V. REMITTANCES OF BULLION FROM NEW SPAIN, 1522–1601 . . . . . . . . . . . . . . . . . . . . . 332

VI. ROYAL "QUINTO" OF THE SILVER EXTRACTED FROM POTOSÍ, 1556–1640 . . . . . . . . . . . . . . . 333

VII. VALUE IN MARAVEDIS OF THE ROYAL TREASURE ON THE PRINCIPAL FLEETS RETURNING FROM THE INDIES BETWEEN 1538 AND 1556 . . . . . . . . . . . . 336

## CONTENTS

- VIII. REGISTERED VESSELS SAILING TO AND FROM THE INDIES, 1504–55 . . . . . . . . . . . . . . . . . 339
- IX. WAGES ON VESSELS IN THE INDIA NAVIGATION. SIXTEENTH CENTURY . . . . . . . . . . . . . . . . 342
  SCHEDULE OF MONTHLY WAGES ON A GALLEON OF 500 TONS IN THE ARMADA REAL—XVII CENTURY? 343
- X. ORDINANCES OF THE CONSULADO OF SEVILLE RELATING TO MARINE INSURANCE . . . . . . . . . . . 344

INDEX . . . . . . . . . . . . . . . . . . . . . . . . 355

# PREFACE

It is an historical commonplace that with the discovery of the western hemisphere and of the Portuguese route to the East, European trade expanded from a continental and Mediterranean into a world commerce. The mapping of new sea routes revolutionized the conditions of mercantile traffic. Till then coasting and overland trade had predominated; about Europe galleys and clumsy sailing barges of a hundred tons or less were generally sufficient to meet the demands of the contemporary merchant. But from the end of the fifteenth century ocean trade assumed the first place, and galleons and carracks challenged the secrets of the outer seas. The shores of the Atlantic became the centre of international exchange, and the commercial hegemony of Europe passed from the cities of Renaissance Italy to the maritime states in the west. With the capture of Constantinople, moreover, and the destruction of the Mamelukes in Egypt, the Ottoman Turks were masters of all the routes to India. The explorations of the Portuguese freed Europe from this thralldom to the Infidel, and the discoveries of the Spaniards revealed a new world with riches undreamed of in the countinghouses of Venice. In Spain and Portugal suddenly flowered the age of their greatest material prosperity, and the powerful influence they exerted in the sixteenth century on the political fortunes of Europe was in no small measure made possible by their conquests in the eastern and the western Indies.

In the two centuries before Columbus, the lack of precious metals to meet the requirements of an expanding mercantile activity came to be felt with increasing severity. The production of bullion in the few mines worked in Europe was small and uncertain. A variety of circumstances, such as trade with Asia, the transforming of gold and silver into plate and jewels, and the accumulation of ecclesiastical treasure, had so far offset the output of the mines as probably to deplete the stock of money in circulation. It was the crying need for gold which fostered an increase of alchemy toward the end of the Middle Ages; and one of the principal motives which led to the discovery of the New World was the conviction that by sailing westward might be found Marco Polo's golden land of Zipangu. The precious commodity was not obtained from Zipangu, but in the barbarian empires of Peru and Mexico. The masses of gold and silver brought from America in the sixteenth and seventeenth centuries were out of all proportion to the actual needs of the moment, and became the most important cause of the price revolution of that era.

It was Spain, the discoverer, which first engrossed the entire New World, and through Spain in the sixteenth century passed virtually all the commerce with the west. Not till toward the end of that century did the northern maritime nations, France, Holland, and England, turn their thoughts to the possession of colonial states in America, or seriously dispute with Spain her exclusive trade and dominion there. And the Spanish government accepted the task of colonization with the most painstaking seriousness. With high ideals of order and justice, of religious and political unity, it extended to its ultramarine possessions its faith, its language, its law, and its administration; built churches and monasteries; founded schools and universities; in short, endeavored to make its colonies an integral part of the Spanish monarchy.[1] Emigration was carefully watched to keep them free from the contamination of heresy and foreigners; and trade and navigation were organized with the same infinite care for detail that characterized social and political activities.

If the actual results of Spanish colonial policy fell far below these ideals, yet they were results by no means to be despised. A Spaniard could write, little more than a century after Columbus:

. . . (en las Indias) se han edificado 70,000 iglesias, 500 conventos de las religiones de Santo Domingo, San Francisco, San Agustín, la Merced, y Compañía de Jesus . . . que tenian . . . mas de 3,000 religiosos en conventos y doctrinas, á los quales da el Rey para vino y azeite, y curar los infermos, 47,000 pesos de limosna, y les haze el gasto hasta ponerles en

[1] P. P. Leroy Beaulieu, *De la colonisation chez les peuples modernes* (ed. of 1908), i, pp. 4 f.

# PREFACE

Indias. Hanse erigido para le enseñanza dellas y buen govierno muchas doctrinas, un patriarchato, seis arcobispados, treinta y dos obispados, tres inquisiciones, dos universidades, dos virreynados, once audiencias, muchos gobiernos, corregimientos, y presidios para defensa de aquellas costas; y se han fundado mas de 200 ciudades, y muchas villas, colonias de nuestra España, que tienen el mismo traje, lengua, costumbres y leyes . . . Reynos tan opulentos que pone asombro considerar de espacio la immensidad de riquezas que han venido de aquel Orbe á nuestra España, que passan, conforme á un memorial que yo ví, de 1,500 millones de oro y plata, hasta el año de 1617 con registro, sin los que han venido sin esta razon. Y consta que de solo el cerro de Potosí se han sacado de las venas de su cuerpo, desde el año de 1545, 260 millones de plata; y no entran en esta cuenta las piedras preciosas, açogue, mermellon, cochinilla, grana fina, grana silvestre, añir, açucar, cueros, almizele, palo de campeche, palo brasilece, clavo de comer, choculate, çarçaparilla, cañafistola, topar, tabaco, cobre, y otras infinitas cosas. . . .[1]

It is a description of the trade and navigation between Spain and the New World, of the commerce which made possible the creation of this Spanish-American civilization, that will be attempted in the following pages. Part of the material in Chapter VII was embodied in an article printed in the Quarterly Journal of Economics, in May, 1915, and the second half of Chapter VIII is largely an adaptation of another article, "España y el Canal de Panamá," which appeared in Hispania (London) in December, 1912. I take the opportunity here to acknowledge the kind offices of D. Pedro Torres Lanzas, Director of the Archivo de Indias at Seville, and of Captain Arias, Chief of the Hydrographic Bureau in Madrid. I also desire to express my indebtedness to Professor E. F. Gay of Harvard University for certain very useful suggestions, to G. W. Robinson, who very kindly checked the bibliography and footnotes, and to Professor R. B. Merriman for his helpful criticism and unfailing sympathy throughout the course of the present work. To Professor Merriman, indeed, I am under the very deepest obligation, for to him I owe my initial interest in things Spanish and Spanish-American.

YALE UNIVERSITY, NEW HAVEN,
    March, 1917.

[1] G. Gonzalez Dávila, *Teatro de las grandezas de la Villa de Madrid* (Madrid, 1623), pp. 471 f.

# BIBLIOGRAPHY

THE goal of all investigators of Spanish colonial history is the great collection of state papers comprised in the Archivo de Indias, and preserved in the old Merchants' Exchange, or Casa Lonja, of Seville. For the first two centuries of colonization, the period covered by this monograph, the collection includes most of the documentary sources of an official or semi-official character. The organization of a separate Archivo de Indias was not undertaken till near the close of the reign of Charles III (1784), most government papers, including those relating to America, having been sent to the general repository at Simancas. And although it was intended that all colonial records should be removed from Simancas and elsewhere to the new office, the separation and transfer of documents for a long time fell far short of the exactness and completeness desired. Many remained behind, and later many more of the same class continued to be sent to Simancas. If things move slowly in Spain, however, they do move, and eventually the oldest legajos or bundles of MSS. were in great part forwarded to Seville. Apparently there are between 600 and 700 still in the north, almost all belonging to the eighteenth and nineteenth centuries, and most of them of little importance for the history of trade and navigation. This does not include some thousands of legajos of financial papers and accounts emanating from the Council of the Hacienda and from the various tribunals of the Contaduría which composed the elaborate financial machinery of the monarchy. In these legajos may be found scattered many documents relating to the colonial exchequer.

In Madrid, the Archivo Histórico-Nacional contains little of importance, apart from the minutes of the Council of the Indies, for the period before the eighteenth century. The Hydrographic Office (Dirección de Hidrografía) possesses the transcripts of Navarrete, the Vargas y Ponce collection, useful for the history of the Spanish marine, and a few late financial and economic papers. But one may very well study the colonial trade of Hapsburg Spain without seeing Madrid.

While Spanish scholars in the nineteenth century have produced few works of capital interest relating to their splendid colonial past, none have been more assiduous in the publication of collections of historical sources. Carelessness and inaccuracies are not infrequent in these great "colecciones," but the American student is grateful notwithstanding for the means they afford of studying Spanish colonization without having recourse in every instance to Spain. A great many of the documents preserved in Seville, especially for the first half of the sixteenth century, may be found in the

> *Colección de los viajes y descubrimientos que hicieron por mar los Españoles desde fines del siglo XV.* Madrid, 1825-37. 5 vols.

printed by the government for that indefatigable scholar, Martin Fernandez de Navarrete; also in the extensive

> *Colección de documentos inéditos relativos al descubrimiento, conquista, y colonización de las posesiones españolas en América y Oceanía.* Madrid, 1864-84. 42 vols.

and in its continuation, published with a slightly different title under the direction of the Royal Academy of History:

> *Colección de documentos inéditos relativos al descubrimiento, conquista, y organización de las antiguas posesiones españolas de ultramar.* Madrid, 1885-1900. 13 vols.

To supplement one's researches in the later Hapsburg era, there are happily several other printed collections also available. The

> *Colección de documentos inéditos para la historia de España.* Madrid, 1842-95. 112 vols.

includes some interesting materials for the years after 1550. But much more valuable are the four folio volumes of

> *Provisiones, cédulas, capítulos de ordenanzas, instruciones* [sic], *y cartas . . . tocantes al buen govierno de las Indias, y administración de la justicia en ellas. Sacado todo ello de los libros del dicho Consejo por su mandado,* etc. Madrid, 1596. 4 vols.

gathered and published by Diego de Encinas, clerk in the Secretariat of the Council of the Indies. Books i and iv are particularly useful for studying the development of trade and navigation. They may be supplemented by reference to

> Aguiar y Acuña, R. de. *Sumarios de la recopilación general de las leyes y ordenanzas, provisiones, cédulas, instrucciones . . . para las Indias Occidentales.* Madrid, 1626.[1]

and

> Puga, Vasco de. *Cedulario.* Mexico, 1563.[2]

---

[1] Brit. Mus., 501. y. 10.
[2] There is a copy of this very rare collection in the Harvard College Library.

the latter comprising all the decrees in force in New Spain at the date of its publication. The ordinances of the Casa de Contratación and of the Council of the Indies were frequently printed in the course of the sixteenth and seventeenth centuries; the former at Seville in 1552, Madrid, 1585, Valladolid, 1604, and Seville, 1647; the latter sometimes in conjunction with those of the Casa, and separately in 1603, 1636, and 1681. Ordinances of the gild merchant, or Consulado, of Seville were also published, first in 1556, and again in 1585. Copies of one or more of these imprints may usually be found in the more important libraries.

Two collections of sources published in Paris may also be used with profit: the

> *Recueil des voyages, relations et mémoires originaux pour servir à l'histoire de la découverte de l'Amérique.* 20 vols.

taken mostly from the Muñoz MSS., and printed by Ternaux-Compans in 1837–41; and the group of French documents edited by Pierre Margry, called

> *Relations et mémoires inédits pour servir à l'histoire de la France dans les pays d'outremer.* Paris, 1867.

Other printed materials consulted, referring especially to Central and South America, are in the following:

> *Memorias de los vireyes que han gobernado el Perú durante el tiempo del coloniaje español.* Lima, 1859. 6 vols.
> *Memorias de vireyes. Marqués de Mancera y Conde de Salvatierra.* Lima, 1899.
> *Nueva colección de documentos inéditos para la historia de España y de sus Indias.* Madrid, 1892–96. 6 vols.
> Peralta, M. M. de. *Costa Rica, Nicaragua, y Panamá en el siglo xvi.* Madrid, 1883.
> *Relaciones de los vireyes y audiencias que han gobernado el Perú.* Lima, 1867–72. 3 vols.
> *Relaciones históricas y geográficas de América Central.* Madrid, 1908. (*Colecc. de libros . . . referentes á la historia de América.* Vol. viii.)
> Ruidíaz y Caravia, Eugenio. *La Florida: su conquista y colonización por Pedro Menéndez de Avilés.* Madrid, 1893. 2 vols.
> Serrano y Sanz, M. *El Archivo de Indias y las exploraciones del istmo de Panamá en los años 1527 á 1534.* Madrid, 1911.

An extraordinarily valuable work, and one for all intents and purposes a 'source,' is the *Norte de la contratación de las Indias Occidentales*, published by Joseph de Veitia Linaje in 1672,[1] the only treatise

[1] The English translation by Capt. John Stevens, published in London about 1700, is very much abridged from the original.

on the organization of Spanish colonial commerce before the eighteenth century. Veitia Linaje was for thirty years a member of the Casa, and from 1659 its treasurer. He therefore possessed an intimate knowledge of the mechanism of the trade in all its infinite and meticulous details. This fact, indeed, accounts for the principal shortcomings of his book. As pointed out in the suggestive essay by J. M. Piernas y Hurtado (*La Casa de la Contratación de las Indias*, Madrid, 1907), it is the faithful testimony of a zealous functionary, more concerned with the formulas of administration, and the particulars of official precedence and etiquette, than with the life and spirit of the institution to which he belonged and its influence for the common weal. While, therefore, the machinery is well explained, there is little or no commentary, where commentary would be most welcome and illuminating. Yet the work is based upon a detailed study of the voluminous archives at the writer's disposition, and is extremely well documented, at least for the years following 1550. With the period of the Catholic Kings and of their grandson the Emperor, Veitia Linaje for some reason shows little real acquaintance. Yet the documents were still in existence, for they survive to-day in Seville for those who care to go and read. It is likely that they were then hidden away in the old castle at Simancas, therefore to a Spanish gentleman and scholar of the leisurely seventeenth century for all practical purposes inaccessible.

One of the sources most used by modern writers on this subject — Roscher, Bourne, Dahlgren, and others — is the entirely natural and obvious one, the *Recopilación de leyes de los reynos de las Indias*, published by command of Charles II in 1681 (Madrid, 4 vols.). But for the study of historical development these Laws of the Indies are a very slender reed to lean upon. The marginal notes giving the dates of the promulgation of the laws are untrustworthy, in that they frequently do not go back to the time when the ruling was originally issued. Some of the laws, referred to early cédulas, were altered in wording to fit the situation in 1680, though no indication is vouchsafed of the change. Others as they appear in the *Recopilación* are a compilation of several earlier decrees published at widely different times; and it is impossible to distinguish from the text alone the clauses due to one decree from those due to another. Whenever possible, therefore, I have avoided the Laws of the Indies as a sole authority, and as a rule have referred to them only for lack of a better source.

The early chroniclers of Spanish American history, such as Peter Martyr, Las Casas, Gómara, Oviedo, and Herrera, all except the last more or less contemporary, are too well known to warrant lengthy comment here. Except in so far as they pause to describe the natural products and conditions of the New World, their interests are not generally those of the economic historian. Yet they yield here and there scraps of information extremely valuable in tracing the agricultural and industrial growth of the colonies. Herrera's great work, which partakes least of the nature of a chronicle, is based either on the narratives of his predecessors or on official documents which for the most part still survive. He is chiefly useful, therefore, to students to whom the printed and manuscript sources are unavailable. Of contemporary narratives of a more purely descriptive character, records of travel and observation in the western hemisphere, the following are the most noteworthy and are generally available in the larger libraries:

Acosta, José de. *Historia natural y moral de las Indias*. Seville, 1590. (Tr. for the Hakluyt Soc., 1880.)

Benzoni, Girolamo. *Historia del mondo nuovo*. Venice, 1565. (Tr. for the Hakluyt Soc., 1857.)

Cieza de Leon, Pedro. *Crónica del Perú*. Part I. Seville, 1553. (Tr. for the Hakluyt Soc., 1864.)

Gage, Thomas. *The English American, or a new Survey of the West Indies*. London, 1648.

The *Geografía y descripción universal de las Indias* (Madrid, 1894), compiled in 1571–74 by Lopez de Velasco, Coronista Mayor of the Council of the Indies, is a dictionary of geographical information, extremely useful for the sixteenth century, as is the gazeteer of Alcedo, *Diccionario geográfico-histórico de las Indias Occidentales ó América* (Madrid, 1786–89. 5 vols.),[1] for a later time. The fragment of the Jesuit Bernabé Cobo's *Historia del Nuevo Mundo* (Seville, 1890–93. 4 vols.), written presumably in Peru about 1653, comprises a systematic description of climate, minerals, flora, fauna, etc., the most complete and painstaking that the early Spaniards have left us. The *Política Indiana* of Juan de Solórzano Pereira, published originally in Latin in 1629–39 under the title *De Indiarum Jure*, is first of all a legal treatise, only less ponderous than most legal writings of that day and generation; but it is also largely historical, and very valuable for the institutional side of Spanish colonial society.

Of secondary accounts, the best and most comprehensive in many ways, though open to much the same criticism as that of Veitia Linaje, is the *Memorias Históricas* published by Rafael Antuñez y Acevedo at

[1] Published in English translation in London, 1812–15.

the end of the eighteenth century (1797). It is an intelligent historical description of the mechanism of the trade, under the five captions, Ports, Ships, Cargo, Imposts, and Persons, with little comment or discussion, and for the sixteenth and seventeenth centuries is based upon Encinas, Veitia Linaje, the Laws of the Indies, and Herrera. Later Spanish scholarship has nothing to offer so informative as these *Memorias*. The short treatise by J. M. Piernas y Hurtado, already alluded to, is very stimulating, and whets one's appetite for more from the same distinguished author; but it has remained little more than a programme for subsequent development. Danvila y Collado's essay, *Significación que tuvieron en el gobierno de América la Casa de la Contratación de Sevilla y el Consejo Supremo de las Indias* (Madrid, 1892), lacks every quality which makes that of Professor Hurtado notable. A. M. Fabie's *Ensayo histórico de la legislación española en sus estados de ultramar* (Madrid, 1896) is a reprint of the introductions to certain volumes in the *Colección de ultramar*, but it presents little more than a résumé or paraphrase of the documents of which Señor Fabie was editor. There is no European background for this colonial legislation, and no attempt at historical synthesis. The volume published in 1888 by M. Blanco Herrera, *Política de España en ultramar*, is without any particular value for the early stages of Spanish colonization. Book viii of Robertson's *History of America*, though published in 1777 and somewhat antiquated, is still one of the most readable English descriptions of the Spanish colonial administrative and commercial system. Noteworthy modern descriptions, all of them comparatively brief, are found in the following:

Bourne, E. G. *Spain in America*. New York, 1904 (*American Nation Series*, vol. iii.)
Dahlgren, E. W. *Les relations commerciales et maritimes entre la France et les côtes de l'océan Pacifique*. Vol. i. Paris, 1909.
Lannoy, Charles de, and Linden, Herman vander. *Histoire de l'expansion coloniale des peuples Européens*. Vol. i, Portugal et Espagne. Paris, 1907.
Leroy Beaulieu, P. P. *De la colonisation chez les peuples modernes*. 6th ed., Paris, 1908. 2 vols.
Roscher, W. *The Spanish Colonial System*. (Tr. by E. G. Bourne.) New York, 1904.
Scelle, G. *La traite négrière aux Indes de Castille*. Vols. i and ii. Paris, 1906.[1]

---

[1] Zimmermann's *Die Kolonialpolitik Portugals und Spaniens* (Berlin, 1890) touches but very lightly the economic side of Spanish colonization.

A Peruvian Jesuit, Ricardo Cappa, has written a series of studies on early Spanish American society, *Estudios críticos acerca de la dominación española en América* (Madrid, 1889-97. 20 vols.), volumes vii to x of which treat of the beginnings of manufacturing industries in the colonies. They include many details which it is difficult or impossible to find elsewhere. For Dutch activities in the Caribbean and on the coasts of Brazil, see the articles by George Edmundson in volumes xi-xix of the *English Historical Review*. Earlier accounts, almost entirely military and political, are those of Netscher (*Les Hollandais au Brésil*, Paris, 1853) and Varnhagen (*Historia das lutas comos Hollandezes no Brazil desde 1624 a 1654*, Vienna, 1671). Most of the sources available in print relating to trade between New Spain and the Philippines may be found in English translation in the 55 volumes of Robertson and Blair's *The Philippine Islands, 1493-1898* (Cleveland, 1903-09). For a discussion of the production of gold and silver in the New World in the sixteenth and seventeenth centuries, see

Duport, St. Clair. *De la production des métaux précieux au Mexique*. Paris, 1843.

Haring, C. H. "American gold and silver production in the first half of the sixteenth century." In *Quarterly Journal of Economics*, xxix (1915), pp. 433-474.

Humboldt, Alex. von. *Essai politique sur le royaume de la Nouvelle Espagne*. 2d ed. Paris, 1825-27. 4 vols.

Lexis, W. " Beiträge zur Statistik der Edelmetalle." In *Jahrbücher für Nationalökonomie und Statistik*, xxxiv (1879), pp. 361-417.

Restrepo, Vicente. *Estudio sobre las minas de oro y plata de Colombia*. 2d ed. Bogotá, 1888.

Soetbeer, Adolf. *Edelmetall-produktion und Werthverhältniss zwischen Gold und Silber seit der Entdeckung Amerikas bis zur Gegenwart*. Gotha, 1879. (Petermann's Mitteilungen.)

The following general histories of certain of our Latin American neighbors deal more or less adequately with the colonial period, and do not altogether neglect economic matters:

Baralt, R. M. *Resumen de la historia de Venezuela . . . hasta el año de 1797*. Paris, 1841.

Barros Arana, D. *Historia jeneral de Chile*. Santiago, 1884-1902. 16 vols.

González Suárez, F. *Historia general de la república del Ecuador*. Quito, 1890-1903. 7 vols.

Milla, José, and Gomez Carillo, Agustín. *Historia de América Central*. Guatemala, 1879-97. 4 vols.

Pezuela, Jacobo de la. *Historia de la isla de Cuba*. Madrid, 1868-78. 4 vols.

For information about the state of Spanish nautical science in the sixteenth and seventeenth centuries, recourse may be had to such works as those of Martin Fernandez de Navarrete,[1] Picatoste y Rodriguez,[2] Puente y Olea[3] and Fernandez Duro.[4] In all except the last, however, indiscriminate eulogy is too often allowed to usurp the place of genuine criticism. The documents printed by Fernandez Duro in his *Disquisiciones naúticas* are especially illuminating. The writings of Henry Harrisse, notably *The Discovery of North America* (London, 1892) and *John Cabot, the Discoverer of North America, and Sebastian, his Son* (London, 1896), contain a great deal of information on this topic, but are in some ways disappointing. A careful perusal of Harrisse's works leads to what is more than a suspicion that he had little familiarity with the Spanish language. Among other books useful for the history of navigation in that age are:

> Albertis, E. A. d'. *Le costruzioni navali e l'arte della navigazione al tempo de Cristoforo Colombo.* Rome, 1893. (*Raccolta Colombiana*, pt. iv, vol. i.)
> Bensaude, J. *L'astronomie nautique au Portugal à l'époque des grandes découvertes.* Berne, 1912.
> Harrisse, H. *Fernand Colomb: sa vie, ses oeuvres.* Paris, 1872.
> Mayer, E. *Die Hilfsmittel der Schifffahrtskunde zur Zeit der grossen Länderentdeckungen.* Vienna, 1879.
> Oppenheim, M. *Naval accounts and inventories of the reign of Henry VII, 1485-88 and 1495-97.* London, 1896. (Navy Records Soc., vol. viii.)
> Oppenheim, M. *The naval tracts of . . . Sir William Monson.* Vols. i-v. London, 1902-14. (Navy Records Soc., vols. xxii, xxiii, xliii, xlv, xlvii.)
> Ravenstein, E. G. *Martin Beheim.* London, 1908.

For a treatment of early forms of maritime associations and partnerships, one must turn to

> Schmoller, Gustav. "Die Handelsgesellshaften des Mittelalters und der Renaissancezeit." In *Jahrbuch für Gesetzgebung . . . des Deutschen Reiches*, 2d ser., xvii, 2, pp. 1-33.
> Wagner, R. *Handbuch des Seerechts.* 2d ed. Leipsic, 1906.

In describing the history and organization of Spanish colonial trade, a comparison with the situation in the contemporary Portuguese

---

[1] *Disertación sobre la historia de la naútica* (Madrid, 1846); *Biblioteca maritima española* (Madrid, 1851), 2 vols.

[2] *Apuntes para una biblioteca científica española del siglo xvi* (Madrid, 1891).

[3] *Los trabajos geográficos de la Casa de la Contratación* (Seville, 1900).

[4] *La Armada Española* (Madrid, 1895-1903), 9 vols.; *Disquisiciones naúticas* (Madrid, 1876-81), 6 vols.

empire naturally suggests itself. Unfortunately there is no work which deals in any adequate fashion with this important subject. Zimmermann [1] and Lannoy and vander Linden are extremely cursory and unsatisfactory. Danvers [2] and Whiteway [3] confine themselves mainly to a chronological narrative of voyages, conquests, and political administration. Some idea of the beginnings of the Portuguese East India trade may be gleaned from the opening chapters of Haebler's *Die überseeischen Unternehmungen der Welser und ihrer Gesellschafter* (Leipsic, 1903). But the field of Portuguese colonial history, even more than that of Spain, still awaits the conscientious modern investigator.

An adequate account of the course of Spain's economic decline in the sixteenth and seventeenth centuries has yet to make its appearance. Gounon-Loubens,[4] writing over fifty years ago, although still very good, approaches the subject from the administrative point of view. Haebler [5] must be used cautiously, and corrected by reference to the article of Bernays.[6] Something may be gleaned from Ranke [7] and from Colmeiro; [8] Weiss [9] tries to cover the ground systematically, but is rather antiquated. Of writers contemporary with the Hapsburgs, Pedro Fernandez Navarrete,[10] Martinez de la Mata [11] and Alvarez Osorio y Redin,[12] Spanish publicists of the time of Philip III, Philip IV, and Charles II, reflect in their works the progressive moral and economic ruin of the Spanish state. The elaborate and scholarly monograph of Georges Scelle on the Assiento, referred to above, becomes but a running commentary on this same theme.

In spite of the volume of gold and silver from the American mines, the Hapsburgs could not have played the political rôle to which they aspired in the sixteenth and seventeenth centuries without the assist-

[1] *Op. cit.*   [2] *The Portuguese in India* (London, 1894), 2 vols.
[3] *The rise of Portuguese Power in India*, 1497-1550 (Westminster, 1899).
[4] *Essais sur l'administration de la Castille au xvi$^e$ siècle* (Paris, 1860).
[5] *Die wirtschaftliche Blüte Spaniens im 16. Jahrhundert* (Berlin, 1888).
[6] " Zur inneren Entwicklung Castiliens unter Karl V," in *Deutsche Zeitschrift für Geschichtswissenschaft*, i (1889), pp. 381-428.
[7] *Die Osmanen und die Spanische Monarchie* (3d ed., Berlin, 1857).
[8] *Historia de la economía política en España* (Madrid, 1863), 2 vols.
[9] *L'Espagne depuis Philippe II jusqu'aux Bourbons* (Paris, 1844), 2 vols.
[10] *Conservación de monarquías*, etc. Madrid, 1626.
[11] *Los ocho discursos* (1656). In *Apéndice á la Educación popular*, edited by Pedro Rodriguez de Campomanes (Madrid, 1775-77), 4 vols.
[12] *Extensión política y económica*. In *Apéndice*, etc., of Pedro Rodriguez de Campomanes.

ance of foreign capitalists. The ubiquitous Italian or German banker was constantly resorted to for long or short time loans at usurious interest, and generally recouped himself from the treasure on the India fleets, with assignments of royal revenues, with monopolies of mines, or with trading or banking privileges. The activities of the great German commercial and banking houses of that age have come in for their due share of attention at the hands of modern scholars. They may be studied to advantage in the following works:

> Daenell, Ernst. "Zu den deutschen Handelsunternehmungen in Amerika im 16. Jahrhundert." In *Hist. Vierteljahrschrift*, xiii (1910), pp. 183–191.
> Ehrenberg, Richard. *Das Zeitalter der Fugger. Geldkapital und Creditverkehr im 16. Jahrhundert.* Jena, 1896. 2 vols.
> Haebler, Konrad. *Die Geschichte der Fugger'schen Handlung in Spanien.* Wiemar, 1897.
> Haebler, Konrad. *Die überseeischen Unternehmungen der Welser und ihrer Gesellschafter.* Leipsic, 1903.
> Jansen, Max. *Jakob Fugger der Reiche. Studien und Quellen*, i, Leipsic, 1910.

Other works consulted in the preparation of this treatise were the following:

> Alberti, L. de, and Chapman, A. B. W. *English Merchants and the Spanish Inquisition in the Canaries.* London, 1912. (Camden Soc. Public., 2d ser., vol. xxiii.)
> Arántegui y Sanz, José. *Apuntes históricas sobre la artillería española en la primera mitad del siglo xvi.* Madrid, 1891.
> Beazley, C. R. *John and Sebastian Cabot.* London, 1898.
> Beazley, C. R. *Prince Henry the Navigator.* New York, 1895.
> Beer, Adolf. *Allgemeine Geschichte des Welthandels.* Vienna, 1860–84. 5 vols.
> Blok, P. J. *History of the People of the Netherlands.* Tr. by C. A. Bierstadt and R. Putnam. New York, 1898–1912. 5 vols.
> Bodin, Jean. *Discours sur les causes de l'extrême cherté qui est aujourd'huy en France. 1574.* (Archives curieuses de l'histoire de France. Paris, 1835.)
> Bonn, M. J. *Spaniens Niedergang während der Preisrevolution des 16. Jahrhundert.* Stuttgart, 1896. (Münchener volkswirtschaftliche Studien, no. 12.)
> *Cartas de Indias. Publicalas el Ministerio de Fomento.* Madrid, 1877.
> Champlain, Samuel de. *Narrative of a Voyage to the West Indies and Mexico in the years 1599–1602.* Tr. by Alice Wilmere. London, 1857. (Hakluyt Soc. Public., 1st ser., no. 23.)
> Corbett, J. S. *Drake and the Tudor Navy.* London, 1898. 2 vols.
> Corbett, J. S., ed. *Fighting Instructions, 1530–1816.* London, 1905. (Navy Records Soc. Public., vol. xxix.)

# BIBLIOGRAPHY  XXV

Corbett, J. S., ed. *Papers relating to the Navy during the Spanish War, 1585–1587*. London, 1898. (Navy Records Soc. Public., vol. xi.)
Corbett, J. S. *The Successors of Drake*. London, 1900.
Cortes, Hernando. *Letters to the Emperor Charles V*. Tr. and ed. by F. A. MacNutt. New York, 1908. 2 vols.
*Cortes de los antiguos reinos de Leon y de Castilla (1020–1559)*. Madrid, 1861–1903. 5 vols.
Cuevas, M., ed. *Cartas y otros documentos de Hernan Cortes*. Seville, 1915.
Cuevas, M., ed. *Documentos inéditos del siglo xvi para la historia de México*. Mexico, 1914.
Daenell, E. *Die Spanier in Nordamerika von 1513 bis 1824*. Munich, 1911.
Diaz del Castillo, Bernal. *Historia verdadera de la conquista de la Nueva España*. Madrid, 1632.
Dumont, Jean, ed. *Corps universel diplomatique*. Hague, 1726–39. 13 vols.
Elhuyer, F. de. *Indagaciones sobre la amonedación en Nueva España*. Madrid, 1818.
Enriquez de Guzman, Alonso. *Life and Acts, 1518–1543*. Tr. by C. R. Markham. London, 1862. (Hakluyt Soc. Public., 1st ser., no. 29.)
*Extracto historial . . . sobre la forma en que se ha de hacer y continuar el comercio . . . de las Islas Philipinas*. Madrid, 1736.
Fernandez de Navarrete, M. de. *Colección de opúsculos*. Madrid, 1848.
Firth, C. H. *The last years of the Protectorate, 1656–58*. London, 1909. 2 vols.
Gallardo Fernandez, F. *Origen, progresos y estado de las rentas de la corona de España, su gobierno y administración*. Madrid, 1805–08. 8 vols.
Gelpi y Ferro, G. *Estudios sobre la América*. Havana, 1864–70. 2 vols.
Goldschmidt, L. *Universalgeschichte des Handelsrechts*. Stuttgart, 1891.
Greenhow, R. *Memoir on the Northwest Coast*. Washington, 1840.
Hakluyt, R. *The principal Navigations . . . of the English Nation*. Ed. for the Hakluyt Soc. Glasgow, 1904. 12 vols.
Haring, C. H. *The Buccaneers in the West Indies in the Seventeenth Century*. London, 1910.
Harrisse, H. *Christophe Colomb: son origine, sa vie, ses voyages*. Paris, 1884. 2 vols.
Heiss, Aloiss. *Descripción general de las monedas Hispano-Cristianas*. Madrid, 1865–69. 3 vols.
Humboldt, A. von. *The Fluctuations of Gold*. Tr. by W. Maude. New York, 1900.
Laiglesia, F. de. *Los caudales de Indias en la primera mitad del siglo xvi*. Madrid, 1904.
Lea, H. C. *The Inquisition in the Spanish Dependencies*. New York, 1908.
Lowery, Woodbury. *The Spanish Settlements within the present Limits of the United States*. New York, 1901–05. 2 vols.

Madero, Eduardo. *Historia del puerto de Buenos Aires.* Vol. 1. Buenos Aires, 1892.
Marcel, Gabriel. *Les corsaires français au xvi siècle dans les Antilles.* Paris, 1902.
Markham, Sir C. R. *Life of Christopher Columbus.* London, 1902.
Markham, Sir C. R. *Reports on the Discovery of Peru.* London, 1872. (Hakluyt Soc. Public., 1st ser., no. 47.)
Marsden, R. G., ed. *Select Pleas in the Court of Admiralty.* London, 1894-97. 2 vols. (Selden Soc. Public., vols. vi, xi.)
Martinez de Zuñiga, J. *Estadismo de las Islas Filipinas.* Ed. by W. E. Retana. Madrid, 1893. 2 vols.
Medina, J. T. *Historia . . . de la inquisición en Chile.* Santiago, 1890. 2 vols.
Merivale, H. *Lectures on Colonization and Colonies.* New ed. London, 1861.
Montero y Vidal, J. *Historia general de Filipinas.* Madrid, 1887-95. 3 vols.
Navarrete, Adolfo. *Historia maritima militar de España.* Madrid, 1901.
Novoa, Matias de. *Historia de Felipe IV, rey de España.* (Colecc. de doc. . . . de España. Vol. lx ff.)
Nuñez de Castro, A. *Solo Madrid es Corte, y el cortesano en Madrid.* 2d ed. Madrid, 1669.
*Ordenanzas de la Junta de Guerra de Indias.* Madrid, 1636.
*Ordenanzas reales para el gobierno de los tribunales de contaduría mayor en los reynos de las Indias.* Valladolid, 1606.
Pardessus, J. M., ed. *Collection de lois maritimes antérieures au xviii siècle.* Paris, 1828-45. 6 vols.
Rezabal, J. *Tratado del derecho de medias anatas y lanzas.* Madrid, 1792.
Ripia, Juan de. *Práctica de la administración y cobranza de las rentas reales.* Ed. by D. M. Gallard. Madrid, 1795-96. 5 vols. and Index.
Roberts, Lewes. *The Merchants' Mappe of Commerce.* London, 1636.
Saco, J. A. *Historia de la esclavitud en los paises Américo-Hispanos.* Barcelona, 1879.
Sapper, K. *Wirtschaftsgeographie von Mexico.* Halle a. S., 1908.
Schmidt, U. *Voyage to the Rivers La Plata and Paraguai.* (In *The Conquest of the River Plate, 1535-1555.* London, 1891. Hakluyt Soc. Public., 1st ser., no. 81.)
Sentenach, N. (Articles on Spanish coinage in the *Revista de Archivos, Bibliotecas y Museos,* 1905-06; 3d ser., xii, pp. 195-220; xiii, pp. 180-199; xiv, pp. 329-345.)
Solórzano Pereira, J. de. *El discurso y alegación en derecho sobre la culpa que resulta contra el general D. Juan de Benevides Bazan,* etc. Madrid, 1631.
Tapia y Rivero, A. *Biblioteca histórica de Puerto Rico.* Porto Rico, 1854.
Wangüemert y Poggio, J. *El almirante D. Francisco Diaz Pimienta y su época.* Madrid, 1905.

Wiebe, Georg. *Zur Geschichte der Preisrevolution des xvi. und xvii. Jahrhunderts.* Leipsic, 1895. (Staats- und Socialwissenschaftliche Beiträge, ed. by A. von Miaskowski.)
Wieser, F. R. von. *Die Karten von Amerika in dem Islario General des Alonso de Santa Cruz, Cosmógrafo Mayor des Kaisers Karl V.*, Innsbruck, 1908.
Williamson, J. A. *Maritime Enterprise, 1485–1558.* Oxford, 1913.
Winsor, Justin, ed. *Narrative and Critical History of America.* London, 8 vols.

# ABBREVIATIONS

| | |
|---|---|
| A. de I. | Archivo de Indias (Seville). |
| A. de I., Patr. | Archivo de Indias, section Patronato Real. |
| Antuñez y Acevedo. | Antuñez y Acevedo, Rafael. *Memorias históricas sobre la legislación y gobierno del comercio en las Indias Occidentales.* Madrid, 1797. |
| B. M. | British Museum. |
| Bibl. Nat. | Bibliothèque Nationale (Paris). |
| Colecc. de doc., 1st ser. | *Colección de documentos inéditos relativos al descubrimiento, conquista, y colonización de las posesiones españolas en América y Oceanía.* Madrid, 1864–84. 42 vols. |
| Colecc. de doc., 2d ser. | *Colección de documentos inéditos relativos al descubrimiento, conquista, y organización de las antiguas posesiones españolas de ultramar.* Madrid, 1885–1900. 13 vols. |
| Colecc. de España. | *Colección de documentos inéditos para la historia de España.* Madrid, 1842–95. 112 vols. |
| Encinas. | Encinas, Diego de. *Provisiones, cédulas, capítulos de ordenanças,* etc. Madrid, 1596. 4 vols. |
| Extensión política. | Alvarez Osorio y Redin, Miguel. *Extensión política y económica.* Printed in *Apéndice á la Educación popular,* ed. by Pedro Rodriguez de Campomanes (Madrid, 1775–77). 4 vols. |
| Herrera. | Herrera y Tordesillas, Antonio de. *Historia general de los hechos de los Castellanos en las islas i tierra firme del mar oceano.* Madrid, 1601–15. 4 vols. |
| N.M.C. | Manuscript collection of Martin Fernandez de Navarrete (Hydrographic Office, Madrid). |
| Ord. of the Casa. | *Ordenenzas reales para la Casa de la Contratación de las Indias.* Seville, 1552, Madrid, 1585, etc. |
| Recop. | *Recopilación de leyes de los reynos de las Indias, mandadas imprimir y publicar por rey Carlos II.* Madrid, 1681. 4 vols. |
| Veitia Linaje. | Veitia Linaje, Joseph de. *Norte de la Contratación de las Indias Occidentales.* Seville, 1672. |
| Viajes. | Fernandez de Navarrete, Martin. *Colección de los viajes y descubrimientos que hicieron por mar los Españoles desde fines del siglo xv.* Madrid, 1825–37. 5 vols. |

# PART I
# TRADE

# TRADE AND NAVIGATION BETWEEN SPAIN AND THE INDIES

## CHAPTER I

### THE SEVILLE MONOPOLY

"DIVINE Providence having permitted, in the year 1492, the beginning of the discovery of the Western Indies, by Christopher Columbus . . . in the name and at the expense of the Catholic kings of Leon and Castile, Don Ferdinand and Doña Isabel, . . . the affairs relating to the provinces and islands so discovered were governed by various commissions entrusted by the Catholic kings to particular individuals, especially for many years to D. Juan Rodriguez de Fonseca, dean of the Holy Church of Seville, afterwards bishop of . . . Burgos . . . until Queen Joanna, by her cédula issued at Alcalá de Henares on the 14th of February of 1503," established in Seville the Casa de Contratación.[1]

Such was the epitome in 1672, by the royal councillor, Veitia Linaje, of the governance of Spain's trade with the New World before 1503. Veitia Linaje in composing his elaborate and learned work, *The Pole-star of American Trade*, the sole treatise on the subject before the eighteenth century, began his discussion with the creation of the celebrated India House. But the first decade after the voyage of Columbus cannot be disposed of so summarily as this would imply, nor does the foundation of the Casa de Contratación mark the inauguration of mercantile relations with the newly discovered hemisphere. It is true that American trade was then first put upon a definitely organized basis. But even before 1503, export to the Western Indies, the name by which America was always officially designated in Spain, was permitted to private individuals, rules were promulgated for

[1] Veitia Linaje, lib. i, cap. 1, par. 1.
It was really Isabella who issued this cédula, as her death did not occur till the following year, 1504.

the regulation of commerce, and a customhouse set up on American shores.

As the first voyage of Columbus was mostly at the expense of the Castilian queen, all potential profits were expressly reserved to the Crown, save one tenth of the net proceeds which went to the discoverer. Columbus, however, was allowed in addition to contribute one eighth of the cost of the cargo, and receive one eighth of the returns of the venture.[1] A similiar provision was made for the second voyage in 1493. In the instructions issued by Ferdinand and Isabella to the admiral in May of that year, private individuals of any degree or condition were expressly prohibited from carrying merchandise on that or any other fleet for purposes of trade. All persons and goods accompanying the expedition had to be registered before an agent of the royal exchequer; and on arrival in the Indies be presented a second time for comparison with the original register. Anything found over and above what was declared in Castile was confiscated to the Crown. It was also provided that a customhouse (casa de aduana) be immediately erected for the receipt of the royal merchandise, and that every commercial transaction take place before the treasurer, comptroller and a representative of the admiral, or deputies, and be entered in a book set apart for such business.[2]

Thus in the very first regulations laid down for the guidance of Columbus and his companions, we find the germs of the most characteristic features of the Spanish commercial system as it evolved in the succeeding century. There is the control exercised by a treasurer, comptroller, and royal factor, and there is the minute provision for the registration of every sailor, officer and passenger, every piece of ordnance, every package of munitions, merchandise or provisions, carried to and from the New World.

The royal monopoly, however, was of short duration. Within two years trans-Atlantic trade was thrown open to all of Isabella's subjects. Spaniards were clamoring for permission to cross the seas, some to emulate the achievements of the great discoverer and find gold and new lands to conquer, others to settle in the

[1] *Viajes*, ii, p. 7.  [2] *Ibid.*, p. 66.

colony already established on the island of Hispaniola. In response to these desires an ordinance, issued on April 10, 1495, extended to all Castilian subjects liberty to go to America for settlement, exploration or trade, under conditions prescribed.[1] Ships must register at, and sail from, the port of Cadiz, and return thither on the homeward voyage. A tenth part of the tonnage was reserved for the use of the Crown without payment of freight, whether the vessel was bent upon trade or exploration, and one tenth of everything secured by barter or other means was likewise a perquisite of the king,[2] except gold obtained on Hispaniola. Mines, by the ancient law of Spain, were crown property, and only one third of their produce was by royal grace awarded to the miner.

Eight years, therefore, before the foundation of the Casa de Contratación, trade and navigation between Spain and America were freer than they were destined to be during the next three centuries; for very soon regulations and restrictions upon ships, passengers and cargoes were to increase at an extraordinary rate. As early as 1501, Ferdinand and Isabella sent a letter throughout Spain, reversing their policy, and strictly enjoining any one from going to the Indies, either to the settlements or for discovery and exploration, without royal license.[3] And even before this date the voyages of Ojeda, Niño, Lepe and Pinzon were made only on the basis of special capitulations with the Crown. Moreover, such was the eagerness of Spanish mariners, that the government soon found it could make better terms than those provided in the liberal decree of 1495. In the agreements with these companions

[1] *Viajes*, ii, p. 165.
[2] Apparently in the trade carried on earlier with northwest Africa and the coast of Guinea, the Crown reserved to itself double the above proportion, or one fifth of the cargoes brought to Spain. *Ibid.*, iii, p. 465.
[3] *Ibid.*, ii, p. 257.

Bourne intimates (*Spain in America*, pp. 45, 46) that the concessions of 1495 were soon revoked at the instance of Columbus, because they clashed with his privileges. He is evidently referring to the royal order of June 2, 1497 (*Viajes*, ii, p. 201). The Crown, however, declares merely that these concessions shall not be understood as prejudicing rights previously accorded to the admiral. And none of the rights assured him in 1492 could be construed to interfere with freedom of trade and navigation. Other documents of the same year, 1497, used by Bourne, make it clear that as yet no specific restrictions were contemplated.

and pupils of Columbus, the Crown was guaranteed from a half to a fourth or a fifth of the profits of their voyages.[1]

In the very beginning, the American navigation was exempt in the peninsula from the payment of tolls, taxes or dues of any sort.[2] This would obviously be so for the earliest expeditions, which were equipped at the royal charge. It was also true after 1495, when the Indies were thrown open to all properly accredited Spaniards. Royal decrees in the spring of 1497 excused all goods imported from the West from the payment of almojarifazgo, portazgo, almirantazgo or any other duties, and also from the payment of the alcabala on the first sale in Spain. Merchandise shipped to the Indies "for their maintenance and support" was similarly exempt at the port of embarkation.[3] In all these early decrees the rule was made contingent on the pleasure of the sovereign. It was reiterated in 1501 in connection with the expedition which Nicolas de Ovando was preparing, to go and assume the governorship of Hispaniola.[4] In 1504 it was extended for a specified period of ten years, and was reissued in 1519 by Charles V.[5] Not till 1543 were any customs dues levied in Spain on American trade. This exemption, however, did not apply to ports in the colonies. It seems that from the first, goods brought to Hispaniola paid a duty of $7\frac{1}{2}$ per cent, equal to the combined import and export rates customary in Andalusia. Instructions of March 20, 1503 to Governor Ovando expressly empowered him to tax such merchandise, and the decree of 1504 exempting American trade at Seville clearly stated that goods on reaching the Indies should pay almojarifazgo at the ordinary Sevillan rates.[6]

[1] *Viajes*, ii, pp. 244, 247; *Colecc. de doc.*, 1st ser., xxxi, pp. 1, 187.
[2] *Viajes*, ii, pp. 16, 39; iii, p. 493; *Colecc. de doc.*, 1st ser., xix, pp. 461, 507; xxxviii, pp. 110, 135, 294.
[3] *Viajes*, ii, pp. 190, 196; *Colecc. de doc.*, 1st ser., xxxvi, p. 146; xxxviii, p. 380.
[4] *Colecc. de doc.*, 1st ser., xxxi, p. 61.
[5] *Ibid.*, p. 233; 2d ser., ix, p. 98.
[6] Bourne says (*op. cit.*, p. 18) that Columbus, in the original compact with the Spanish sovereigns in 1492, was granted a royalty of ten per cent of the net proceeds of all trade with the regions discovered. This is a bit misleading. As the wording of the Capitulation indicates, a tenth of the profits of the Crown alone was contemplated. And this interpretation is borne out by later documents of 1497, 1501, and 1508 (*Viajes*, ii, pp. 202, 275, 325). On the strength of this agreement,

## THE SEVILLE MONOPOLY    7

Columbus' momentous voyage, with its three small boats and ninety men, was undertaken from Palos, a tiny seaport directly west of Seville at the mouth of the Rio Tinto. His second fleet sailed in September, 1493, from the larger port of Cadiz; and Cadiz remained for a decade the usual place of departure for expeditions sent to America. A special customhouse was established there, in charge of Juan de Soria, secretary to the king's son and deputy of the exchequer, where was registered all merchandise passing to and from the New World. The large fleet of Ovando, however, in 1502, sailed from San Lucar de Barrameda, a town below Seville at the mouth of the Guadalquivir.

As the islands and mainland revealed by the explorers became more extensive, the Crown determined to create a "casa de contratación," or House of Trade, for the regulation and encouragement of commerce with these new regions. And Seville was chosen as its residence, not because of superior maritime facilities, for Cadiz had much the better harbor, but probably because Seville happened to be the wealthiest and most populous city of

Columbus and his son, Diego, enjoyed a tenth of all royal revenues in the West Indian islands.

It is possible, however, that the discoverer and his successors levied an admiralty duty in American ports by virtue of their office as admirals of the Indies. In the first agreement, Columbus received, for himself and his heirs and successors forever, the title of admiral of all the islands and mainland discovered by him, with all the "preëminences and prerogatives" exercised by the admirals of Castile. The latter exacted at Seville and Cadiz, from skippers who were not natives of Andalusia, a payment for the right of lading and unlading (almirantazgo), as well as anchorage dues. These admiralty duties were never paid by vessels engaged in the India trade, and whether the Columbus family collected them in America is doubtful. At least I have found no mention of them. Veitia Linaje says that they were levied (lib. ii, cap. 22, par. 2); but he is probably arguing from the later cédula of revocation.

The concessions of 1492 were confirmed in 1497, and again in 1536. In 1547 D. Luis Columbus, grandson of the discoverer, renounced forever all but the mere title of admiral, and received in recompense an annuity of 7000 ducats on the revenues of the Indies. *Viajes*, ii, pp. 7, 191; Antuñez y Acevedo, pp. 259 f.; *Recop.*, lib. ix, tit. 43, leyes i, 12, 13.

In 1518 the admiral of Castile was granted a pension of 400,000 maravedis, paid out of the funds of the Casa de Contratación, 270,000 by way of *merced*, and 130,000 as equivalent to the tax he declared was due him from ships sailing to America. But this ceased with the death of the then admiral, D. Fernando Enriquez, in 1543.

Castile, of which the Indies were considered to be the exclusive possession. The city was favorably situated, moreover, as an interior port, nearest to the central regions of the kingdom. Foreign merchants, especially Genoese, had enjoyed privileges there since the time of St. Ferdinand, and the traffic and movement incidental to the war of Granada had increased its prosperity and importance.[1] As all trade with the New World was to pass through the Casa, the control of this commerce was from the outset restricted to a single port for the whole of Spain. And for two centuries, in spite of the claims of other cities, in spite of protests from the colonies, and the well-intentioned efforts of Ferdinand's grandson the emperor, Seville retained her high distinction. The vested interests of the merchants whose prosperity depended upon the preservation of this monopoly were sufficient to bear down all opposition; and for the Crown it was much easier to maintain in a single port that rigid supervision of every detail of trade and navigation which was the Spaniard's ideal.

At first ships might receive their cargoes elsewhere, but before crossing the Atlantic were required to ascend the Guadalquivir and register with the officials of the Casa. But it was soon found impossible to compel all vessels to submit to this formality. Mariners were not long in complaining that the city lay twenty leagues from the sea, that the bar at San Lucar was dangerous to cross, and the channel narrow and tortuous. Moreover ships increased in size, so that where formerly they were scarcely of a hundred tons burden, within a generation there were many of over two hundred. The larger vessels, even in the first half of the sixteenth century, before the river had silted up to the extent it did later, were unable to ascend it without unloading half of the cargo eight leagues below the city. Sometimes captains were delayed a month or more, sufficient time to make the entire Atlantic voyage. As the traffic grew heavier this became a serious disability.

The colonists, too, in the beginning often complained of the impediments to trade presented by the Seville monopoly. In 1508

[1] *Viajes*, i, introduction; Piernas y Hurtado, *La Casa de la Contratación de las Indias* (Madrid, 1907).

the settlers on Hispaniola petitioned that natives of Castile and Aragon might ship commodities from any port of the peninsula directly to America. The request was repeated by the Hieronymite governors of the Indies in 1517, and by the municipality of San Domingo ten years later. In 1540 the royal audiencia in Hispaniola protested to the emperor that the island was understocked with wine, flour and other necessities, and the freights excessive, because of the scant supply of ships from Seville.

If the approach to Seville was dangerous and uncertain, Cadiz, situated on a deep, commodious bay and close to the metropolis, was the obvious alternative. In 1508, in response to the colonists' address, vessels were given permission to load and register there and at San Lucar, under the eye of an inspector or " visitador "; and a few months later Pedro de Aguila was appointed by the Crown to that post.[1] Ships on the homeward voyage, however, or at least those which carried treasure, must still return to Seville. Though Aguila was theoretically subordinate to the officials at Seville, his appointment was bound to cause friction, if only because of the intense jealousy of the two cities. So ten years later, in 1519, Charles V, recognizing the inconvenience of such a division of authority, ordered that thereafter the visitador be appointed directly by the officers of the Casa.[2]

This step did not improve matters, for the Casa, having now full control of the situation in Cadiz, often neglected to appoint any one at all, thus forcing vessels to call at Seville. The emperor consequently in 1530 transferred the nomination of the visitador to the lately organized Council of the Indies; and this body in the following year decided that the three officials of the Casa themselves each reside in Cadiz four months of the year, aided by two deputies representing the colleagues who remained at home.[3] But experience soon showed that these periodical absences brought confusion into the Casa's affairs, and it was finally agreed in 1535 to appoint a permanent resident at Cadiz, to act in conjunction with deputies of the three Sevillan officials. Later in the same year, Pedro Ortiz de Matienzo was nominated

---

[1] Veitia Linaje, lib. i, cap. 25, par. 1; A. de I., 139. 1. 4, lib. 2, fol. 30.
[2] Veitia Linaje, lib. i, cap. 25, par. 1.
[3] *Ibid.*, par. 2; A. de I., Patr. 2. 5. 1/6, ramo 28.

by royal letters " juez oficial " of that port.[1] Matienzo, in spite of his title, was given no judicial powers such as were exercised by the Casa;[2] but on the other hand, ships from America might thereafter unload at Cadiz, even if they carried gold and silver, provided that the cargoes and registers were transported intact to Seville.

So was established the " Juzgado de Indias " of Cadiz, the source throughout the sixteenth and seventeenth centuries of constant disputes and irritation. The Casa de Contratación tried to confine the exports from Cadiz to local products, such as wine and wax, and later when trade was restricted to annual fleets, to keep the proportionate tonnage assigned to the city as small as possible. In quiet opposition was the Cadiz resident, subject to the Casa's authority, but always alert to extend his own jurisdiction and influence, and allied with the inhabitants in importuning the Crown for greater privileges. The merchants of Seville contended that the harbor of Cadiz, being open to the sea, afforded no shelter from gales and pirates. Drake without the least difficulty destroyed all the shipping in the port in 1587, and his exploit was emulated by other Englishmen in 1596 and 1625.[3] The protagonists for Cadiz replied that the 'levante' there was never so dangerous as the current at San Lucar when the river was at flood; and that vessels at Cadiz might retire behind the forts for protection from corsairs, while the latter in pinnaces could easily enter San Lucar. At the mouth of the Guadalquivir the largest ships became entangled with one another, often lost cables and anchors, and drifted on to the rocks. The sand bar was an added danger, captains sometimes waiting weeks for a proper conjunction of tides, winds and daylight, finally in despair taking a chance and often losing their vessels.[4] All of which is perhaps also a commentary on Spanish seamanship.

[1] *Colecc. de doc.*, 2d ser., x, pp. 287, 303; *Recop.*, lib. ix, tit. 4, leyes 1, 4.
[2] Minor judicial functions were later attached to the office. *Recop.*, lib. ix, tit. 4, ley 3.
[3] In 1596 the English took prisoner the president of the Casa de Contratación, Dr. Pedro Gutierrez Flores, and the Cadiz resident, D. Pedro de Castillo, and held them for ransom. Veitia Linaje, lib. i, cap. 25, par. 20.
[4] B. M., Add. mss. 13, 975, fol. 182.

The Juzgado in the form established in 1535 continued for twenty years, till 1556, the year of Charles' abdication. The officers of the Casa still declined to nominate deputies, whether from neglect or jealousy, or fear of responsibility, is unknown; and so in December, 1556, Philip II decreed that henceforth the resident appointed by the Crown should exercise his authority alone. The order provided, however, that when the vessels or fleets were of sufficient importance, one of the Sevillan trio or his deputy might come down to inspect and dispatch them; and that if any of these officials happened to be in Cadiz, they should perform the duties of the Juzgado in company with the regular resident.[1] Passengers, moreover, had all to be cleared by the Casa itself, registers of outgoing vessels had to be sent to Seville, and ships returning from the Indies had all to go directly to San Lucar, thus rescinding the grace extended to Cadiz in 1535. But again it was found impossible to maintain so unnatural a rule, and within two years, in April, 1558, an exception was made in favor of vessels from Hispaniola or Porto Rico laden with hides or sugar, which were permitted to discharge their cargoes in Cadiz harbor.[2] This dispensation was extended in 1560 to any vessels in distress or such as were unable to negotiate the bar at San Lucar, the treasure they carried to be shipped overland with the registers to Seville.[3]

So the rule oscillated back and forth during the rest of the sixteenth and through the seventeenth century. For those who care to read, the arguments pro and con are detailed by Veitia Linaje in his *Norte de la Contratación*, with a strong bias in favor of Seville. Sometimes the fleets were ordered to sail from the Guadalquivir, sometimes, because of the increasing tonnage of ocean-going ships, from the neighboring port. But the headquarters of the Casa de Contratación and of the great exporting houses remained at Seville. Even when the galleons set out from the Guadalquivir, however, a certain proportion of the tonnage was always reserved to the Gaditanos, the amount being fixed each year by the Council of the Indies. In the early part of the seven-

---
[1] Veitia Linaje, lib. i, cap. 25, par. 5; *Recop.*, lib. ix, tit. 4, leyes 13, 14.
[2] A. de I., 139. 1. 11, lib. 23, fol. 325, 345.   [3] *Recop.*, lib. ix, tit. 4, ley 18.

teenth century it was usually a fourth or a fifth; from the thirties onward it was one third.¹ Sevillan merchants seem generally to have had permission to lade vessels at Cadiz if the shipping in the Guadalquivir was insufficient, but ship captains at Cadiz might not solicit freights in Seville in competition with Sevillan mariners. There seems to have been some ground for the fear that if traders in either city sent goods to be shipped from the other, the privilege might be the means of defrauding the customs. By the second half of the seventeenth century, however, trade in Seville had fallen off so sadly that ships were unable to lade a third of their capacity unless they resorted to Cadiz exporters. This development was inevitable, for, apart from the selfish interests of the Seville monopolists, Cadiz harbor was in every respect more convenient and desirable; and when the fleets were fitted out there either wholly or in part, foreign traders were sure to follow, in order to avoid the expense and delays of carrying their goods twenty leagues inland to the Casa de Contratación. We find an augury of this change as early as 1633, when owing to the late arrival of the ships from Italy and Flanders, the *Flota* was ordered to proceed to Cadiz to receive its cargoes, and so obviate bringing the imported stuffs to Seville for reshipment.²

The duties of the Cadiz resident extended to the admission of vessels to the American trade, the bonding of shipmasters, and the inspection of cargoes. His authority ceased the moment the vessel sailed from the harbor. He was apparently allowed jurisdiction over minor infractions of the ordinances of the Casa, and took the preliminary depositions in more important criminal cases. But all correspondence with the Council of the Indies had to pass through the hands of the president of the Casa, especially regarding the amount of tonnage to be assigned annually to the Gaditanos. And the president must be informed in writing of all important matters touching the resident's activities. The latter from time to time endeavored to dignify his office by urging the appointment of a fiscal or judicial prosecutor, or of a special inspector for the ships, or of a public residence where he might hold

---

[1] Veitia Linaje, lib. i, cap. 25, par. 22, 23, 28.
[2] *Ibid.*, lib. ii, cap. 4, par. 35.

a regular court or audiencia. But no such concessions were ever vouchsafed him.

Whatever the port of departure, the rule became fairly constant that all vessels and fleets must return to the Guadalquivir. In the seventeenth century the penalty for noncompliance was a fine of 6000 ducats. The reasons were the solicitude of the government for the payment of customs and other dues, and the fear that elsewhere gold and silver from America might more easily be spirited away to foreign lands. Yet in this respect, too, there were frequent exceptions. Fleets put into Vigo, Coruña, Santander, Lisbon, Gibraltar or even Malaga, sometimes by order of the Crown to avoid hostile squadrons cruising about Cape St. Vincent, but more often owing to accidents of wind and weather. In the emperor's reign, when trade and navigation were left much freer than under the rule of his son, nearly every year vessels from the West appeared at Gibraltar or at towns on the Portuguese coast. But even after his time, their arrival at other ports than San Lucar was not unusual. Thus in the year 1590 the flagship and another galleon of the fleet of Alvaro de Flores entered the Tagus, and the silver, amounting it was said to over three million pesos, was conducted in galleys to Seville. In 1598 the flota from New Spain touched at the same place before making San Lucar. In 1600 the galleon, *San Marcos*, appeared at Malaga, having parted from the fleet soon after leaving Havana and picked her way alone across the Atlantic. Why she chose to pass through the strait into the Mediterranean, instead of going to Cadiz, is not told us. But as she was in unseaworthy condition, the bullion, cochineal and indigo she carried were transported overland to the Casa de Contratación. In 1616 the entire fleet commanded by Tomas de la Raspuru put into Lisbon, and again the Crown ordered the treasure to be sent to the Casa by land, although the merchants violently protested because they had to pay an extra assessment of one per cent to cover the expense of protecting the transport. Four galleons entered the harbor of Gibraltar in 1636, and in 1643 the whole fleet of D. Pedro de Ursua. In 1657, what was saved of the bullion on the ships of D. Diego de Egues, burnt in the harbor of Santa Cruz by Admiral Blake, was conveyed on small vessels from the Canaries to Gibraltar, and then overland to the Andalusian metropolis. Many such instances might be cited, but more generally the government insisted upon obedience to the law. In 1610, when the galleons from Porto Bello appeared in Cadiz harbor, they were peremptorily ordered to proceed immediately to the Guadalquivir without touching the cargoes. And in 1623, when the "capitana" and another vessel of the Mexican fleet entered the bay, the general and the owner of the merchantman were each mulcted of 2000 ducats.[1]

From about 1630 onward repeated representations were made by the Casa that the Juzgado de Cadiz be either transferred to San Lucar or abolished altogether, on account of the frauds practiced in the matter of registration. By 1664 pressure on the Crown was so strong that ship captains and the generals of flotas and armadas were ordered to sail under all circumstances to and from the Guadalquivir, on pain of heavy fines, loss of rank and exclusion from the India navigation, although for nearly thirty years the fleets had been universally despatched from Cadiz.[2] Two years later, in September, 1666, the Juzgado was entirely extinguished. The jealousy of the Casa was so intense that in 1671 D. José Centeno, general of the *Flota*, was sentenced to six years imprisonment at Oran and a fine of 6000 ducats because, finding his flagship too heavy to cross the San Lucar bar, and having news of hostile ships in the Strait of Gibraltar, he sailed for security into Cadiz harbor. His instructions had ordered him in case of danger to make for a port in Galicia or Cantabria. The captain of a galleon which followed the flagship into Cadiz waters suffered a similar punishment.[3]

The rival port remained closed to American commerce till 1679, when the king, mollified by a gift of 80,000 crowns from the Gaditanos, restored the Juzgado on its former basis. In fact in the next year the wheel of fortune had so completely turned that all the fleets were *required* to make Cadiz the beginning and end of their

---

[1] Veitia Linaje, lib. ii, cap. 4, par. 14, 23, 31. After the abolition of customs duties on American imports in 1660 (see Chapter IV) the requirement to bring goods overland to Seville was no longer insisted upon.

[2] A. de I., 139. 1. 16, lib. 41, fol. 148.

[3] Fernandez Duro, *Armada Española*, v, p. 170.

voyages. And Cadiz succeeded in retaining her privileges without notable change until the clairvoyance of a new dynasty made possible the transfer in 1717 to her port of the Casa de Contratación entire. So in the end the two cities exchanged rôles. All the tribunals and departments of the Casa were set up in Cadiz, and to her fallen adversary was left the Juzgado de Indias.[1]

Neither Seville nor Cadiz, the major seaports of Andalusia, were necessarily fitted to acquire a monopoly of American commerce. Barcelona on the Mediterranean, since the thirteenth century one of the great mercantile cities of Europe, possessed a commercial position and experience unique in the peninsula. Malaga vied with Seville in the industry and maritime enterprise of her inhabitants. Bilbao and the other ports of Biscay were busily engaged in the great fisheries, and had with the north, especially with Flanders, a rather extended trade.

Charles V, with a range of vision continental rather than Castilian, in order to facilitate emigration and trade, in January, 1529, issued a cédula allowing vessels to sail directly to the Indies from certain other ports of the peninsula: Coruña, Bayona, Avilés, Laredo, Bilbao and San Sebastian on the Biscayan coasts, Cartagena and Malaga on the Mediterranean, and Cadiz on the Atlantic. The ships might register in these ports before the royal judge and certain officials of the municipality, but were obliged always to make their return voyage to Seville, and report their cargoes to the officers of the Casa. A copy of the register must within three months of the departure of the vessel be forwarded to the Council of the Indies.[2]

Strangely enough, there is little evidence that this liberty was made use of. Indeed the historian Herrera, and Veitia Linaje, are entirely silent regarding it. The cédula appears only in the collection of decrees and ordinances published by Diego de Encinas in 1596.[3] It is odd, too, that Cadiz should have been included, when that city already possessed the privilege of clearing vessels for the Indies. If, moreover, by the general terms of this cédula

---
[1] Antuñez y Acevedo, pp. 9 f.
[2] *Ibid.*, appendix i; *Colecc. de doc.*, 2d ser., x, p. 3.      [3] Encinas, iv, p. 133.

ships sailing from Cadiz had only to register before the ordinary municipal authorities, without the intervention of Sevillan officials or their representatives, why did the city, always impatient of her subordinate position, not take advantage of this freedom ? And why the concern of the Crown in 1530 and 1535 over the regulation of the Juzgado de Indias ? Yet that such an ordinance was published by Charles V is confirmed by decrees of December 1 and 21, 1573, forbidding the Biscayan ports to send vessels to America except in company with the fleets from Seville or Cadiz, and after registration and inspection by the officers of the Casa.[1]

From the negative tenor of certain other cédulas affecting the India navigation, between the years 1543 and 1564, it would appear that the ordinance had been revoked even earlier. Yet in the *Book of Registers* of vessels plying between Spain and the Indies in the years 1504–79,[2] we find a ship sailing from Malaga as late as 1551. The cédulas of December, 1573, too, relate that the towns of Galicia were then sending vessels to America independently of the fleets, and speaks of the practice as " la costumbre que se ha tenido hasta agora." It is clear, however, in spite of such testimony, that the license granted by Charles V remained for the most part a dead letter. Although the year 1529, in which it was issued, saw also the conclusion of the second war between the emperor and Francis I, the peace between sovereigns did not restrain the activities of the French corsairs, who were becoming every year a graver menace to the merchant marine of Spain. It was this menace which forced upon the Spanish Crown the establishment of a system of great merchant fleets protected by powerful convoys, sailing periodically between Spain and her ultramarine possessions. If the danger was a frequent one on the coast of Andalusia, it was ever present in the Bay of Biscay. Ships sailing to the Indies alone from Coruña, Bilbao or other ports near the French coast ran a difficult and perilous course; and there was probably little incentive to Biscayan merchants to take advantage of the privilege offered them. It was safer to have a share in the Seville trade, and join the flotas which already in the late twenties and the thirties were being organized for the naviga-

[1] Antuñez y Acevedo, appendices 2, 3.   [2] A. de I., 30. 2. 1/3.

tion to America. As for Malaga and Cartagena on the Mediterranean, these ports in the days when ships were small, slow and clumsy, were much farther from America than they are today, and they could scarcely compete on equal terms with the Andalusian towns to the west. Some few vessels must have sailed, however, both from Biscay and from the Mediterranean, and if the registers are missing in the archives of Seville today, it is perhaps because, by the law of 1529, these registers had to be sent to the Council of the Indies and not to the Casa de Contratación. It seems likely that in the sixties the Galician ports resurrected the old rule and proceeded to act upon it.[1] Thereupon the merchant gild of Seville protested to the king that such an infraction of their monopoly was a source of fraud and a loss of trade; and Philip II, realizing that to avoid being cheated of his dues on import and export it was best to confine traffic to a single port, issued the revocation of 1573.

A century later, in 1667, the citizens of Malaga appealed to the Council of the Indies for permission to resume this commerce with America. They pleaded that the right had never been withdrawn, and offered among other evidence a judgment obtained in 1553 against the officials of the Casa, restraining them from interference. In 1794 this writ still existed in the archives of the municipality. The appeal was refused, although no proof was produced that the Malagueños had ever lost their privilege. As a matter of fact the revocation of 1573 makes no mention either of Malaga or of Cartagena.[2]

Whatever the real story of this generous provision of the young emperor, it is unquestionable that from 1574 onwards the only ports in the peninsula qualified for the India trade were Seville and Cadiz. And they remained so till the second half of the eighteenth century.

Outside the peninsula there was one region permitted to enter into mercantile relations with the New World. As early as De-

[1] A. de I., 139. 1. 11, lib. 24, fol. 148: "Orden á los gobernadores de la Coruña y Bayona en Galicia para que envien relacion de los navios que han salido de esos puertos para las Indias en seis años y cargazones que han llevado."

[2] Antuñez y Acevedo, p. 24, note; and appendices 4, 5.

cember, 1508, in order to encourage trade with the struggling colony on Hispaniola, Spanish merchants were given the right to buy in the Canary Islands and carry to the Indies any class of merchandise not generally prohibited by the Crown; and the Casa de Contratación was ordered to send a person there with sufficient authority to take charge of the matter.[1] That this liberty continued is evident from a series of later ordinances. Two royal decrees of September 20, 1518, warn the local authorities on the islands not to levy any duties on the goods of merchants or ship captains trading with America.[2] And in 1534 the islanders themselves were allowed to send their products other than luxuries (mantenimientos), without any formality except declaring them before the notary of the port from which they were shipped.[3] Whether the Casa neglected to keep a representative there, as had happened in the case of Cadiz, does not appear. It seems that at first vessels intending to carry goods from the Canaries had to start from Seville with a license from the officers of the Casa.[4] In the *Book of Registers*, however, after 1548 when the ports of departure and destination are indicated, we find nearly every year vessels sailing directly from certain of these islands. Twenty-five ships were registered from Santa Cruz in 1550, and thirty-one in 1551–52. In 1551 seventeen sailed from Tenerife, nineteen in 1552, and ten in 1553.[5] In capitulations of 1556 and 1561 renewing the privilege to the islanders of Tenerife, they were required to deposit with the Casa de Contratación a bond of 5000 ducats in gold, as security that they would remit the registers each year to Seville, and that ships in returning would sail to the Guadalquivir. As the government was informed that foreign merchants and goods found their way to the colonies under cover of this concession, in 1561 the islanders were required to give a similar bond to the royal court in Tenerife to abide by all the conditions of the grant. In this same year it was specified that only foreigners who had property and a ten years residence, and had married a woman of Spain or the Canaries, might share in the

---

[1] *Colecc. de doc.*, 2d ser., v, p. 159.    [2] N.M.C., xxi, no. 1.
[3] A. de I., 139. 1. 8, lib. 16, fol. 140. Neither Veitia Linaje nor Antuñez y Acevedo was aware of any license extended to them before 1556.
[4] Veitia Linaje, lib. ii, cap. 25, par. 10.    [5] A. de I., 30. 2. 1/3.

trade. As by that time the system of annual fleets was under way, Canary ships were forbidden to return from the Indies unless properly armed and convoyed.[1] The Canaries from their position formed a very convenient watering and victualling station for ships sailing either to the West or to the East Indies. Columbus on his first voyage tarried at Grand Canary and Gomera to refit, and after the discovery of America these islands became a regular port of call. If they were convenient for Spaniards they were equally convenient for other nations. Traders were attracted there from the maritime countries of northern Europe, Bretons, Flemings, Scotch and English. The Canaries were a usual stage in Hawkins' slaving voyages to Guinea and the Caribbean; and in 1538 permission to traffic with them was formally allowed to the Bristol merchants by Charles V.[2] The commerce of the islands was therefore considerable. Of their chief exports, wine and sugar, the former was the only one demanded in the Indies. But the presence of foreign merchants opened loopholes for other and prohibited commodities, especially as the islands were far from the metropolis and their trade difficult of control. In the early part of Philip II's reign the Crown saw fit to set up a regular institution similar to the Juzgado of Cadiz. Ordinances of January, 1564, and October, 1566, provided for resident judges, "jueces de registros," appointed by the Council of the Indies, in the three islands of Grand Canary, Tenerife and La Palma; and a long series of decrees from 1566 onwards defined the authority and jurisdiction of these officials.[3] They exercised all the powers of the officers of the Casa de Contratación, including those of a judicial nature. There was an appeal to the Casa, except in cases involving 40,000 maravedis or less, when the appeal went to the local audiencia. If the sentence was one of mutilation, banishment or death, the case might be reviewed by the Council of the Indies.[4]

[1] A. de I., Patr. 2. 1. 1/18, no. 61; Antuñez y Acevedo, pp. 26 f.; *Recop.*, lib. ix, tit. 41, ley 15.
[2] Alberti and Chapman, *English Merchants and the Spanish Inquisition in the Canaries*, p. xiii.
[3] *Recop.*, lib. ix, tit. 40, 41; Veitia Linaje, lib. ii, cap. 25.
[4] *Recop.*, lib. v, tit. 12, ley 5.

The favorable situation of the Canaries as an entrepôt for contraband trade made the islands a never-ending source of irritation to the authorities in Spain. From the time the resident judges were established, and especially in the seventeenth century, there was a stream of complaints by the Casa of irregularities. After repeated representations to the Crown, it was decided in 1612 that the Council of the Indies should indicate each year the tonnage allowed to the islands in the Indian trade, that the Casa select the American ports to which Canary ships might sail, and that only vessels of inferior size be employed.[1] In the beginning of 1649 the traffic was entirely prohibited; but only for a few months, the privilege being partially renewed again for a term of six years. In 1657 the three jueces de registros were abolished, and a superintendent judge appointed from among the members of the Casa to reside in Tenerife, with subdelegates in Grand Canary and La Palma. At the same time the annual allowance of trade was fixed at five ships with a total of not over 1000 tons; and Canary boats which did not carry treasure were permitted to make their return voyage to the islands without resort first to Seville.[2] In this form the concession was repeatedly renewed until the more liberal times of Charles III.[3]

[1] Veitia Linaje, lib. ii, cap. 25, par. 15. A later cédula, of May, 1621, directed that vessels from Seville be preferred to Canary boats in the assignment of cargoes in American ports. *Ibid.*, cap. 17, par. 35.

[2] *Recop.*, lib. ix, tit. 40, leyes 22–30.

[3] Antuñez y Acevedo, pp. 34 f.

## CHAPTER II

### THE CASA DE CONTRATACIÓN

THE initial step, one may say, in the development of an administrative system for the control of trade and navigation between Spain and the Western Indies, was taken in May, 1493, when Ferdinand and Isabella chose a member of their council, Juan Rodriguez de Fonseca, archdeacon of Seville and the Queen's chaplain, to coöperate with Columbus in preparing for the second voyage.[1] Fonseca, a man of noble family and an administrator of considerable ability, held in his hands virtually complete direction of colonial affairs till the creation, ten years later, of the Casa de Contratación. He may, indeed, have been in some measure responsible for the organization of that institution and the ideas it embodied. Although jealous of his equals and an implacable enemy, as Columbus and Cortes found to their cost, he succeeded in retaining the favor of the sovereigns, and was promoted in turn to the bishoprics of Badajoz, Palencia and Burgos. After the establishment of the Casa had taken from him the immediate superintendence of commercial matters, he continued to be practically the colonial minister, till the evolution of the Council of the Indies under Charles V diverted the responsibility to a group of ministers.

The first ordinances for the Casa de Contratación were issued from Alcalá de Henares on January 20, 1503,[2] and on February 14 three officials were appointed to take charge of the new institution. They were a treasurer, Dr. Sancho de Matienzo, canon of the cathedral of Seville; a comptroller and secretary (contador), Jimeno de Briviesca; and a business manager or factor, a Genoese named Francisco Pinelo.[3] Pinelo and Briviesca had acted in

---

[1] *Viajes*, ii, pp. 48, 78.
[2] *Ibid.*, p. 285; *Colecc. de doc.*, 2d ser., v, p. 29; xxxi, p. 139.
[3] Pinelo died in 1509, and was succeeded by Pedro Ochoa Isasaga. Jimeno de Briviesca survived him a year, and was followed by Juan Lopez de Recalde. The

similar capacities in connection with the preparations for Columbus' later expeditions.

The Casa de Contratación was the first administrative body created in Spain to take care of the new discoveries in America. As its name indicates, it was an establishment essentially commercial in character. But if we are to judge from the tenor of the first ordinances, it was intended to be primarily a "house of commerce" in the sense of any private business house, an organization for carrying on the trade of the Crown with the Indies. It was to gather in its warehouses merchandise and naval stores of every sort required for the American trade, and receive there all brought back in exchange to Spain. Its officers were expected to keep in correspondence with royal factors in the colonies, to study with closest attention the needs of the new settlements, the things most seasonable for shipping, and the vessels most convenient to send. They were to watch the state of the market, buy and sell only when most advantageous for the Crown, and keep systematic and detailed record of all their transactions.

It is clear that this is no mere bureau of the government designed to exercise a general supervision over the commercial activities of private individuals. Either the Crown, if it did not revert to its earliest policy of engrossing the American trade, still took an active share in it,[1] or it was intending to compete for such a share. Ferdinand V was no less shrewd than his contemporary, Henry VII of England, and both sovereigns resorted to mercantile adventure to help fill an exchequer which was feeling

priestly treasurer, Matienzo, lived till December, 1521. His nephew, Domingo de Orchandiano, acted as treasurer ad interim, till the appointment of Nuño de Gumiel in May, 1523.

[1] A year earlier, in December, 1501, when Ovando was preparing to leave for Hispaniola, he received warning from Ferdinand and Isabella that the people crossing with him had "adorned themselves with clothes and other articles" beyond what was necessary, and presumed to be for purposes of sale or exchange. No such transactions were to be permitted, although he was to keep the order secret until the fleet reached Hispaniola. The cédula makes especial mention of the ship "of our factor." *Colecc. de doc.*, 2d ser., v, p. 22.

See instructions to the Casa of July 28, 1503, regarding licenses to private persons to carry provisions, etc., to Hispaniola, provided that on arrival they deliver a certain proportion of their goods to the factor of the Crown; also, instructions to Juan de Ampies, royal factor in Hispaniola, October, 1511. *Ibid.*, pp. 61, 336.

the strain of an over-ambitious diplomacy. It is likely that Ferdinand had in mind an eventual monopolistic control such as his Portuguese cousins were evolving for the trade with the East Indies. Manoel, king of Portugal, after the return of Vasco da Gama from his celebrated voyage in 1498–99, confined the new communications with India and the Malabar coast to fleets chartered and equipped under his direction. There was also a Casa da India, where the ships were fitted out and the oriental cargoes, when received, sold or stored as the king saw fit. In the very beginning, Portuguese subjects, and even Italian and German merchants, were sometimes permitted to assist, by contributing vessels and sending their own factors for the purchase of spices. But their action was very circumscribed. The minimum purchase price in the East and selling price at Lisbon were settled by the Crown so as not to compete with the royal trade. And from about 1512, although the Portuguese still obtained special licenses to share in this commerce, traffic in spices seems to have been exclusively a royal monopoly, the king disposing of his stocks by contract to groups or corporations of merchants organized for that specific purpose.

The earliest ledgers of the Casa de Contratación reveal a somewhat similar situation in Spain. Trade by royal factors was evidently anticipated, and many of the ships bound for America were royal ships, the Crown receiving the passage money for passengers and cargo. If this was Ferdinand's purpose, however, we may conclude from the silence of later records that it was not long persisted in. The circumstances of the two cases were so different as to make such a policy toward America scarcely practicable. The Portuguese were trading with old countries, densely populated, governed by organized, long-established institutions. Their colonies in the East were merely "factories," stations on the coast where were received the native products of the interior, and whither repaired the fleets to carry these products to the markets of Europe. They were so many excrescences upon the oriental body politic, their governors exercised no permanent influence on the fortunes of eastern nations, and they were the germ of no extensive or enduring colonial empire. The task of Spain was a much more difficult and more glorious one. The greater part of the western hemisphere was sparsely peopled by a nomad and primitive race, depending for sustenance on the game of streams and forests. Even the so-called empires of Peru and Mexico, when divested of the glamor of Prescott's style, assume a barbarian complexion which bears no comparison with the civilizations of India and China. The Spaniards had two continents to explore and conquer. In a wilderness they laid the foundations of civilized, European communities. It was a task too great for a government unassisted by the inducements and initiative of private enterprise. If the expense of Columbus' voyages was borne by the Crown, later explorers, Ojeda, Pinzon, Bastidas and Solis, and colonizers like Arriaga and Pedrarias Davila, had to undertake expeditions at their own cost. The settling and provisioning of the colonies was a sore problem in these early years, and it was not to be expected that their growth would be fostered by a government monopoly of trade.

If a monopoly was intended, it was not the last time that the suggestion was brought forward. In 1556 Nicolás de Cardona was urging upon the Crown to undertake alone the "contratación" of the colonies, and the proposal evidently received some consideration in the Council of the Indies. The king, he said, needed a capital of one million ducats. He should keep factors resident at the fairs in Castile, and in Antwerp, Rouen and Florence, and should put the business in Seville in charge of a group of wealthy, experienced men.[1] But Philip II in 1556 had excellent uses for every ducat he could lay hands on, and to meet the necessary expenses of government was seizing the gold and silver remitted to private merchants on every fleet that reached the shores of Spain. Perhaps some of the dispossessed persons felt that if the government took over the entire American trade, its profits might be no less and they could lose no more.

In the ordinances of 1503, the officials of the Casa were instructed to use great care in the choice of captains for the India navigation, and to send with each ship a clerk (escribano), before

[1] A. de I., Patr. 2. 1. 1/18, no. 59; N.M.C., no. 48.

## THE CASA DE CONTRATACION

whom must be registered every article of the cargo put on board.[1] The registers or manifests, signed by the ship's master, were to be delivered to the royal factors in the Indies, and receipts brought back on the return voyage to Seville. All goods coming from America must be similarly registered, and the captains and escribanos be given full written instructions as to their duties on the voyage and in American ports. Once a year the officers of the Casa were to send the king their ledgers of credit and debit complete, for royal examination.

The India House was not concerned solely with the commerce of the New World, although that was soon so overwhelmingly important that any other is generally lost sight of. It also had supervision over trade with the Canary Islands, with Barbary and the Spanish stations on the African coast, subject to the same rules as governed the India traffic. Until 1508 the accounts for these regions were kept distinct from "cosas de Indias." After that date they were completely merged. But even before 1508 the receipts from Africa and the Canaries amounted to less than two per cent of the whole, and in later years their effect was inappreciable.[2]

The first residence provided for the Casa was in the Atarazanas, or arsenal of Seville; but in June of the same year Isabella issued an order transferring it to apartments in the Alcazar Real

[1] This *escribano*, an ancient institution in the history of navigation, was provided for as far back as April, 1495, in the royal orders permitting free trade and emigration to the west. The appointment, at first belonging to the master of the ship, after 1533 devolved upon the Casa de Contratación, and later upon the merchants' gild or Consulado of Seville. In the seventeenth century at least, the post was usually put up for sale.

[2] The Casa, at least in the beginning, seems also to have collected the government tax on the tuna fisheries of the Andalusian coast.

Another Casa de Contratación was erected at Coruña in December, 1522, after the voyage of Magellan, for the dispatch of fleets to trade with the Moluccas. It was established in the north probably to be closer to Antwerp, which after Lisbon was the principal emporium for the spice trade. It never assumed any importance, however, for the voyage round South America proved too long and difficult, and the Portuguese stubbornly maintained their claim to the islands. In 1529 Charles V, urged by financial necessities, ceded all political and commercial rights to the Moluccas for 350,000 ducats in gold. *Viajes*, iv, p. 389; Colecc. de Vargas y Ponce (Hydrographic Office, Madrid), leg. i, no. 9.

formerly occupied by the admiralty court. The building, with some additions after a fire in 1605, continued to house the Casa till the eighteenth century.[1]

The Casa established, Ferdinand and Isabella were soon forced to return to their earlier, more liberal, policy regarding trade and navigation in American waters. The freedom conceded in 1495 had lasted only a few years. After the autumn of 1501 special licenses from the Crown had in every case been required. And the ordinances of the Casa in 1503 revealed a desire to make American commerce a monopoly of the government. But any restrictions were prejudicial to the welfare and expansion of the colony in Hispaniola. The settlers complained that they suffered from lack of provisions and other supplies from the mother country. It was necessary to let down the bars, and in response to petitions from the island a new order was issued in February of 1504. For ten years any inhabitant of Hispaniola or any other subject of Castile might export to the colony without special license articles necessary for its provisioning and maintenance, provided they were carried on Spanish ships, and did not include slaves, arms, horses, or gold or silver in any form.[2] It is interesting to note that this decree distinguishes clearly Castilians from other subjects of the Crown, in limiting the privilege of free trade with the New World.

In March, 1503, two months after the creation of the Casa de Contratación, instructions had been sent to Nicolás de Ovando, governor of Hispaniola, to set up an analagous institution there, which was to maintain a correspondence with that in Spain. It

[1] *Colecc. de doc.*, 2d ser., v, p. 53; Veitia Linaje, lib. i, cap. 1, par. 2.

It seems that at first the officers were permitted to live in the building of the Casa. In October, 1518, however, Charles V peremptorily ordered them to leave, for the Casa, continued the cédula, was intended, not as a dwelling for officials, but as a place of meeting for the administration of Indian affairs, and for the receipt of gold and other commodities from the colonies, A. de I., 139. 1. 5, lib. 7, fol. 86, 114. This policy continued till August, 1543, when the treasurer, contador, and factor were obliged to live in the Casa. Later certain other employees were also provided with apartments there. Veitia Linaje, lib. i, cap. 1, par. 4.

At present the buildings, situated on a small square which preserves the name of Contratación, are converted into dwelling houses belonging to the royal patrimony.

[2] *Colecc. de doc.*, 1st ser., xxxi, p. 233; *Viajes*, iii, p. 523.

was an obvious development of the purpose originally expressed in the Casa, that there should be royal "factories" in the Indies to manage the king's trade there. Indeed the instructions are but a reiteration of the orders issued to Columbus for his second voyage in 1493, that a customhouse be immediately established in the New World, in charge of representatives of the Crown and the Admiral, for the deposit of royal merchandise. The Casa de Contratación of Seville was evidently but the coping to a system to be applied generally to the newly-discovered lands. But as the idea of a monopoly was gradually lost sight of, the Casas in America became little more than customhouses in the ordinary sense of the term. Like the Casa in Seville, they were under the supervision of a treasurer, factor and contador, three officials who came to be known specifically as the " royal officials " (oficiales reales), and composed what may be called the administrative organization of the colonial treasuries. Even in the seventeenth century, these officers in the principal cities of America were sometimes referred to collectively as the Casa de Contratación, and given the same title, " jueces oficiales," as had been applied to the three in Spain.[1] As most of the tribute from the Indians was in kind — wheat, corn, cloth, cocoa, honey, wax, cotton, etc. — and this tribute disposed of in public auction, to that degree they constituted a "house of trade." But their duties related chiefly to the general superintendence of the exchequer, and in so far as they touched over-seas trade, were confined to the collection of customs and the registration of cargoes. The oficiales reales had nothing to do with the regulating of commerce, and little occasion for " correspondence " with the India House.

There is also evidence that when a colonial Casa de Contratación is spoken of in letters and decrees, a material building is meant, and not an institution like that of Seville. Ferdinand wrote to Ovando in July, 1508: " . . . en lo de la casa de contratación que alla se ha de hacer, se debe dar mucha prisa, pues

[1] *Colecc. de España*, lii, pp. 527 f. In the beginning there was often a fourth official, the ' veedor de fundiciones y rescates,' but this office soon disappeared, and in some places that of factor as well.

ay recaudo de los aparejos, por la mucha necesidad que ay de la dicha casa." And in a letter of instructions to the Audiencia of Mexico in March, 1532, there is an approval of expenditures "para construir la casa de contratación labrada de adobes y tejas en la ciudad de Vera Cruz." This casa was either not completed or its adobes very impermanent, for a cédula five years later (July, 1537) orders the justices of Vera Cruz and the deputies of the treasury to see that a casa is built as soon as possible.[1]

Queen Isabella died in November, 1504, just after Columbus' return from his last voyage, and it was probably a short time before her death that the two sovereigns issued a second series of instructions to the India House. There seems to be no surviving copy; but Ferdinand speaks of them in a letter written in the summer of 1509, directing the Casa to publish them abroad for the information of the public;[2] and their content may be gathered from a transcript which the new factor, Isasaga, brought with him from the king for that purpose. They were inscribed in an abridged form on a tablet on the walls of the Casa, probably in the same year, 1509. The regulations applied to all who were in any way concerned with the Indies, whether as traders, ship captains, explorers or colonists. They included office hours of the officials, classes of prohibited merchandise, rules regarding emigration, mines and registration, and regulations for the disposal of the property of those dying *en voyage* or in the Indies. They seem to have been a sort of résumé of all the dispositions, economic and administrative, made up to that time with regard to Castile's ultramarine possessions.[3] In April, 1505, Ferdinand, acting as regent in the absence of Isabella's daughter and heiress, Joanna, formally renewed the powers of the officers of the Casa.[4]

The years 1506–1507, in contrast with those which immediately preceded and followed, were a time of almost complete quiescence in American legislation, at least so far as it affected the activities of the India House. It was also a time of political uncertainty in the peninsula, when Joanna and her husband Philip came from

[1] *Colecc. de doc.*, 2d ser., x, p. 379.    [2] *Ibid.*, v, p. 196.
[3] *Ibid.*, p. 94. A copy printed in the first series (xxxi, p. 323) is dated wrongly 1505.
[4] *Ibid.*, 1st ser., xxxi, p. 294.

the Netherlands to claim their Spanish heritage, and Ferdinand unwillingly retired to his Italian kingdom of Naples. Philip died within a few months, however, and the return of Ferdinand in the latter part of 1507, made it possible to give to colonial matters the attention their importance warranted. In the meantime the Casa found itself in conflict with the law courts over its claim of jurisdiction in cases involving its rules, and in collision with the municipality over questions of tolls and the privileges of its officials. The colony on Hispaniola, moreover, was increasing in size and importance, and the vast extent of Spain's new dominions becoming every day more apparent. From 1508, therefore, Ferdinand began to intervene actively in the general current of American affairs, attempting on the one hand to define the Casa's judicial powers, on the other planning to issue a new set of ordinances for its guidance in the administration of trade. In November, 1509, he commanded the members of the India House to send him for examination a faithful copy of all the rules and instructions then in force; and in February, 1510, directed the factor Isasaga, as the least occupied of the three, to come to court and inform him by word of mouth of things which could not be adequately discussed in writing.[1]

The new ordinances, thirty-six in number, were issued from Monzon in Aragon, June 15, 1510, and were amplified and explained by seventeen additional articles in the following May.[2] In the main they constitute little more than a codification or restatement of earlier regulations and scattered decrees. But it is significant that very little is said about commercial projects of the Crown, and a great deal about inspection and registration of the ships and goods of private traders, and the activities and conduct of the three officials.

The officers of the Casa were to come together twice every day except holidays, at the hours 10-11 and 5-6 in winter, and 9-10 and 5-6 in summer. For nonattendance without valid excuse they were fined a half real of silver, to be devoted to the

[1] *Colecc. de doc.*, 2d ser., v, pp. 187, 197. As the royal factor was the least occupied of the three officials, evidently the king's trade was not very flourishing.

[2] *Ibid.*, 1st ser., xxxvi, p. 296; xxxix, p. 191 (dated March 18); 2d ser., v, pp. 211, 250; *Viajes*, ii, pp. 337, 345.

repair of their official quarters, and as much again for each day of nonpayment of the fine. In public utterances as well as in letters to the king they were to speak in their corporate capacity, and not as individuals. They must conduct all general business, receive and answer dispatches, issue licenses and contracts, etc., in session together, and were held jointly responsible for all the acts of the Casa. In a matter of doubt or disagreement, if it was of importance and admitted of delay, they were to confer with the king; otherwise a majority vote was sufficient for a decision.[1] Every important transaction had to be countersigned by all three officials.

Rules were laid down in minutest detail for the keeping of ledgers and other records, not only concerning the receipt and release of royal treasure from America, but also for the purchase and accounting of artillery, munitions, and ships' stores of every sort. A transcript must be kept of official communications passing through the House to the Indies, so that its officers might be conversant with all colonial affairs; and if there was discovered in the dispatches anything prejudicial to royal interests or the India trade, they must report it at once to the king. Officials in America corresponding with the Crown about trade or finance were to send copies of their letters to the Casa for its enlightenment; and thereafter must also forward to Seville complete accounts of all receipts and expenditures of the colonial treasurers for preservation in the Casa's archives. It is owing to this rule that some of the most valuable and interesting of early Spanish-American records are available for us today.

Regulations regarding emigration, registration of cargoes, instructions for sea captains, etc., were renewed from the earlier ordinances of 1504. No shipowner or captain might freight for the Indies until his vessel had been examined, and its fitness and tonnage certified, by the Casa's officers. And any one loading his vessel beyond the limit officially set was liable to severe penalties. Gold brought from America unregistered or without

[1] To prevent undue influence from the example of the older members, votes were always cast in the inverse order of seniority. Veitia Linaje, lib. i, cap. 5, par. 17.

## THE CASA DE CONTRATACIÓN 31

the royal stamp,[1] was confiscate, the smuggler fined four times the amount seized, and his person placed at the mercy of the sovereign. Any one purchasing such bullion, or registering under his name the bullion of another, was subject to similar punishment. Of the treasure confiscated, one third went to the informer. It is evident that such practices, so notorious in later years when the shipments of treasure became very heavy, were already a source of difficulty to Spanish authorities.

It was also provided in these ordinances, as in 1504, that the property of persons dying in America be carefully inventoried, converted into money, and forwarded to Seville, to be kept in a special repository of the Casa until the rightful heirs could be found. The effects of those dying at sea were to be inventoried by the " escribano " of the vessel, and returned for similar disposal in Spain. The care which the home government devoted to the protection of the estates of its intestate subjects in the New World continued to be a characteristic feature of Spanish administration, and the rules regarding it form some of the most important sections of the Laws of the Indies.[2]

Of all these ordinances, only two, or at most three, concern trade for the profit of the Crown. The officials were directed, if they ventured any merchandise in the Indies, to keep separate account of it, and send word to the king — a sufficient indication that such trade was unusual, or at least very slight. They were also to endeavor to make profitable contracts with persons desirous of exploiting newly-discovered lands, subject to royal approval. And the importation of brazil or dye-wood, forbidden

[1] See Chapter VII.
[2] The records of the Casa, and the sums entrusted to its care, were kept in iron coffers provided with three different locks and keys, one key remaining in the possession of each of the three officials. There were four of these coffers: one for the preservation of correspondence and the official seal of the institution; one for the gold, silver, precious stones, and other royal revenues coming from the Indies; one for the property of deceased colonists; and one for unclaimed money or goods consigned to private individuals, and property sequestered awaiting the determination of some civil suit. An interesting specimen of these coffers may still be seen in the Archivo de Indias.

As the receipts from America grew larger, such coffers were of course insufficient to hold everything, and the overflow went to the Atarazanas, the Casa's warehouse, to which were attached three locks in similar fashion.

from any region save Spanish America, they were to take in charge and foster with the greatest diligence.

The ordinances of 1510 do not include all the rules then in force touching mercantile and political communications between Spain and the New World. For the minutiae of detail regarding qualifications of emigrants, manner of inspecting vessels and registering cargoes, conduct of masters and pilots, etc., attention was directed to various earlier pragmatics and instructions. The functions and general administration of the Casa, however, were clearly defined by this set of regulations. It gave to the India House the character and complexion it was to retain until the eighteenth century, made it the institution which is familiar to historians. Thereafter the Casa de Contratación was definitely not a business house run for the private profit of the Crown, but a department of the government, a ministry of commerce, a school of navigation, and a clearing house for colonial trade.

Subsequent legislation was in most cases only a logical and necessary expansion of these rules of 1510. New decrees which appeared from time to time need not be discussed in chronological sequence. Important regulations were issued in 1534, 1536 and 1543, but they had more to do with the armament, provisioning and manning of ships, than with the administration of commerce.[1] In 1552 were again brought together all the laws for the India House promulgated up to that time, not only general rules of administration, but every regulation concerning the duties and qualifications of merchants, passengers, masters, sailors, bankers, etc., connected with the American navigation. In November of that year license was granted to Andrés de Carvajal to print and sell copies of the work for four years, on presenting fifty to the Council of the Indies and its subordinate tribunals.[2] It is the most comprehensive collection we possess for the sixteenth century, was reprinted in Madrid in 1585, and became the basis of Book Nine of the Laws of the Indies.[3]

From these ordinances we learn that the Casa possessed a private chapel and chaplain,[4] and also in the same building a prison,

[1] See Chapter XI.   [2] A. de I., 139. 1. 10, lib. 22, fol. 453.
[3] The edition of 1585 is in the Harvard Library.
[4] The chapel of the Casa de Contratación was established and endowed by the

and a prison keeper who discharged all the functions of common janitor. The office hours were considerably longer, every morning from 7 to 10 in summer and 8 to 11 in winter, and on Monday, Wednesday and Friday afternoons after 3 in winter and 5 in summer.[1] On the other hand, each of the three officials, treasurer, contador, and factor, had now the assistance of deputies and clerks, for the keeping of books, inspection of ships, making out of registers, issue of licenses, and in fact for the performance of every important duty assigned to the Casa. In other words, the India House already by the middle of the sixteenth century had expanded into an elaborately organized institution, the original officers being the executive heads of departments, and enjoying honors, privileges and exemptions as high as those of the supreme courts and chancelleries of the realm.[2] Nothing might be sent to

Spanish kings for the celebration of masses for the souls of those who died on the India voyages. Veitia Linaje says in one place that there was such a chapel from the very beginning (lib. i, cap. 36, par. 1); in another that the post of first chaplain was created in 1550 (lib. i, cap. 15, par. 11). A second chaplain was added in 1622. The first was a nominee of the Crown, and after 1644 of the Count of Castrillo, who in that year was appointed hereditary "alcaide juez oficial" of the Casa. The patronage of the second chaplaincy was vested in the president and three officials.

[1] The afternoon sessions were for the issuing of licenses to merchants and passengers. Later, when annual fleets became the rule, while the fleet was preparing the officials were busy at all hours of the day, even on holidays or at Easter! Moreover, for the receipt and answering of royal dispatches they were apt to be called together at any time of day or night. Because of these extraordinary hours, when there was no special business the afternoon rule was not observed.

In the early years of the Casa, when there were only the three officials, none could obtain leave of absence without securing royal permission and leaving an approved deputy in his place. In the seventeenth century, when the Casa was more elaborately organized, the president could grant thirty days' leave to any of its officers without requiring a deputy. Veitia Linaje, lib. i, cap. 4, par. 11, 12.

[2] Veitia Linaje believes that each of the three officials had from the beginning a deputy or "oficial mayor," to take charge of the routine peculiar to his particular office or department. No early ordinance to that effect survives, although the first treasurer, Matienzo, seems to have had an assistant at the time of his death in 1522, his nephew Domingo de Ochandiano, who was temporarily appointed to his uncle's place. Whatever the date of origin, from a very early time there were three oficiales mayores, superior in rank to any other employees of the Casa. According to the ordinances of 1552, the contador's office already had four other chief clerks, to look after the registers, "bienes de difuntos," passengers, and sequestered or unclaimed moneys.

the Indies without the consent of the Casa, nothing might be brought back and landed, either on the account of merchants or of the king himself, without its authorization. Bullion from the colonies consigned to Spanish merchants belonged to them only when the Casa permitted its release. It controlled and regulated the character of ships, crews, and passengers. In short, it saw to the execution of all the laws and ordinances relating to trade and navigation with America. As it received all the revenues remitted by colonial officials, it was becoming one of the principal outposts of the royal exchequer, and its archives one of the richest in historical interest in Spain.[1] As a consultative body, it had the right to propose to the king anything it deemed necessary to the organization and extension of American commerce. Its officers or their deputies or servants were strictly forbidden to trade with the Indies, directly or indirectly, openly or in secret, on pain of heavy fines, forfeitures, and loss of office.[2] They might not receive gifts, write letters of recommendation, or sell licenses for the embarking of persons or goods prohibited by the statutes.

One officer, not mentioned in the code of 1552, had in the meantime been added to the Casa's staff. In May, 1514, had been created a postmaster-general (correo mayor) for colonial dispatches, and Dr. Galindez de Carvajal, a distinguished jurist and member of the Council of Castile, was appointed to the new dignity. In the beginning the correo mayor looked after the transmission, not only of letters between Spain and the Indies, but also of intercolonial posts and of those between Seville and the Court. His supervision over trans-Atlantic mails, however, whether official or private, continued only a short time. Perhaps at most it had amounted to little more than the collection of a fee.

[1] After 1591, the treasurer, factor, and contador, as officials of the exchequer, on entering office had each to give bond for 30,000 ducats to the royal Audiencia of Seville. In case of defalcation, the bondsmen of the treasurer were first held liable, and afterwards those of the factor and contador. The "oficial mayor" of the treasurer had to give bond to his superior for 10,000 ducats. Veitia Linaje, lib. i, cap. 11, par. 2, 3.

[2] The penalty was confiscation of the goods involved and loss of half of one's property. In 1591 it was changed to dismissal for the principal officers, and for subordinates ten years' banishment from the kingdom. *Ibid.*, lib. i, cap. 4, par. 13.

## THE CASA DE CONTRATACIÓN 35

The heirs of Carvajal exercised the Spanish functions of this office till 1627, when D. Fernando de Medina sold it to the Count-Duke of Olivares. And soon after, the king permitted the new incumbent, his favorite and chief minister, to collect a fee on all outgoing mail to the Indies. In 1633 the Count-Duke resold the office in perpetuity to the Count of Oñate, for 10,000 ducats in silver. Oñate was already correo mayor for the Spanish kingdoms. The office was served by a deputy in Seville, who apparently resided in the Casa de Contratación, and on presentation by the proprietor, took oath as one of the subordinates of the institution. The family of Carvajal seems to have retained control of some of the South American posts till 1768.[1]

Such was the character of the India House as an administrative institution at the end of the reign of Charles V. Its functions were clearly determined, and its place in the political economy of the Spanish monarchy justified by fifty years of continuous and efficient service. The Crown had never ceased to consider it an object of especial solicitude, had consolidated its powers, and maintained its independence of other authorities in the kingdom. Changes introduced in succeeding reigns concerned chiefly the elaboration of its personnel. In all essentials the Casa de Contratación was complete when the ageing Emperor decided to lay aside a heavy crown and retire to end his days in the monastery of Yuste.

In the first half of the sixteenth century, the Casa also developed a Hydrographic Bureau and School of Navigation, the earliest and most important in the history of modern Europe. At its head was a pilot major (piloto mayor), whose office was created apparently in the early part of 1508, and first bestowed upon Américo Vespucci. Two cédulas of March 22, 1508, assigned to Vespucci as pilot major 50,000 maravedis salary, and 25,000 more annually for "ayuda de costa."[2] It was at about that time that Ferdinand the Catholic, just returned to Castile after

---

[1] Veitia Linaje, lib. i, cap. 32; Solórzano, *Política Indiana*, lib. ii, cap. 14; Moses, *Spanish Dependencies in South America*, i, pp. 388-391.

[2] *Viajes*, iii, pp. 297 f. The instructions to Vespucci are dated August 6. *Ibid.*, p. 299.

the death of his son-in-law, Philip I, called to the Court at Burgos Juan Diaz de Solis, Vicente Yanez Pinzon, Juan de la Cosa and Américo Vespucci, to confer on the furtherance of maritime enterprise in the western seas, which had virtually ceased during the unsettled conditions of Philip's short reign. It was resolved that an expedition be sent to seek a passage to the East " á la parte del Norte hacia Occidente," a quest on which Pinzon and De Solis set out a few months later. And probably at this same conference it was decided that one of the four should remain in Seville to construct charts of the American discoveries, and teach and examine pilots for the navigation to the New World.[1]

The India House also very early retained the services of other experienced mariners to assist the pilot major in his various functions. De Solis, Pinzon and Juan de la Cosa apparently received stipends from the Casa as royal pilots at the time they were making their voyages of exploration along the American coasts. Pinzon and De la Cosa, indeed, had been entrusted with cartographical labors by the Casa before 1508, although "pilotos reales" as such seem to have been first appointed in that year. In 1512 Andrés de San Martin and Juan Vespucci, nephew of Américo, were added to the number; and in 1515 there were at least eight, including in addition to the two just mentioned, Juan Serrano, Andrés Garcia Niño, Francisco Cotto, Francisco de Torres, Vasco Gallego and Sebastian Cabot. Cabot received his first appointment as pilot in that year, although he had entered the service of Ferdinand in 1512.[2] In 1519 Nuño Garcia Torreño was given the title of "maestro de hacer cartas," and Diego Ribero that of "cosmógrapho y maestro de hacer cartas" in 1523. Presumably "maestro de hacer cartas" was in the beginning almost synonymous with cosmographer, the principal duty being that of chart making. But very shortly the cosmographers began to give their attention also to the manufacture and improvement of nautical instruments. And as both Nuño Garcia and Ribero are in other connections referred to merely as pilots,

---

[1] Puente y Olea, *Los trabajos geográficos de la Casa de la Contratación*, pp. 60–63.
[2] *Viajes*, iii, pp. 306, 307; Harrisse, *John Cabot*, p. 154. It is possible, as Harrisse suggests (*ibid.*, p. 277), that these appointments had to be renewed every year.

## THE CASA DE CONTRATACIÓN

they were doubtless navigators of practical experience as well as skilled in hydrography. The title of pilot, however, which persists for some time in the early history of the Casa, becomes in that connection slightly misleading; for many of these mariners never navigated again after their appointment at Seville, and were really rather geographers than pilots. And later in the century, cosmographer is the only title employed.

Américo Vespucci, the first pilot major, died in Seville, February 22, 1512, and on March 25 Juan Diaz de Solis was appointed in his place.[1] In 1516 De Solis was killed by Indians on the banks of the Rio de la Plata, which he was exploring in search of a passage to the East Indies; and there was an interim of two years, till February 5, 1518, when the vacant post was bestowed by Charles on Sebastian Cabot, just after the new king's arrival in Spain. Cabot has been made out by Harrisse to have been somewhat of an imposter, if not worse; but although engaged in traitorous correspondence with the Venetian Council of Ten in 1522–23, although sentenced in 1532 to four years banishment in the African penal settlement of Oran, because of misconduct during his voyage to La Plata, and although later accused of irregularities in his office of pilot major, he apparently had so firm a hold on the confidence and esteem of the Emperor, that he retained his post till 1548, when he finally deserted Spanish service for the pay of England.[2]

Alonso de Chaves, who became pilot major in 1552, continued in that capacity till 1586, when he had reached the advanced age of ninety-four. And as Alonso was a pilot and cosmographer in the time of Cabot, and in fact one of those chosen to examine

[1] A pension of 10,000 maravedis was settled on the widow of Vespucci, deducted from the salary of his successors. *Viajes*, iii, pp. 305, 308.

[2] Harrisse says (*op. cit.*, p. 271), in part following Herrera, that when Cabot left Spain for the Moluccas in 1526, the Emperor continued him in his office, which in his absence was to be filled, at least so far as examining pilots was concerned, by Miguel Garcia and Juan Vespucci. In 1527 it was entrusted to Diego Ribero and Alonso de Chaves, and in 1528 the latter alone became pilot major ad interim. This 'Miguel Garcia,' however, was really Nuño Garcia Torreño, and Alonso de Chaves was not appointed pilot major till 1552, although late in 1528 he had received royal permission to read lectures on navigation in the house of Fernando Columbus. See Puente y Olea, *op. cit.*, pp. 256, 310, 313.

pilots in the latter's absence in America, he must have carried the tradition of the first American explorers almost to the threshold of the seventeenth century. Before the death of Charles V, the instruction of mariners was given over to a professor of cosmography, leaving to the pilot major only the task of final examination, with a general supervision over map and instrument making whether within the Casa or by individuals outside. The chair in cosmography was instituted by Prince Philip, then governing Spain for his absent father, in December, 1552, and the first incumbent was Jerónimo de Chaves, son of Alonso. In the seventeenth century, there were only two cosmographers attached to the Casa, the "catedrático" or professor, and the "fabricador" or map and instrument maker.[1]

In the early years of American exploration, a few foreigners of distinction, men generally combining with nautical training some scientific attainments which rendered their services particularly desirable to the Spanish Crown, were drawn into its pay with the title of naval captain, "capitan de mar," their salaries being settled upon the Casa de Contratación. Such a distinction was conferred on Sebastian Cabot in October, 1512, and on Magellan and his collaborator, Rui Falero, six years later. In each case the stipend from the Casa was 50,000 maravedis. Francisco, the brother of Rui Falero, for many years drew a pension from the same source, first of 35,000 maravedis and after 1532 of 50,000, probably to retain his services as a mathematician, for he published at Seville a *Tratado de la esfera y del arte de marear con el regimiento de las alturas*, in 1535.[2] It is interesting to note, in connection with the Spaniards' efforts to exclude foreigners, and especially Portuguese, from the American navigation, that so many of these early mariners were of foreign birth. Vespucci was

[1] Veitia Linaje, lib. ii, cap. 11, par. 15, 16.
There was also a "cosmógrapho-cronista" attached to the Council of the Indies, whose duty it was to record, not only the natural and political history of the Indies, but also geographical and astronomical data, as well as to make a collection of the accounts of voyages and sailing routes brought back to Spain by mariners from the New World. Later these duties were divided between two persons, a cosmographer major and a chronicler royal.
[2] Nicolás Antonio, *Bibliotheca Hispana Nova*, i, p. 423.

## THE CASA DE CONTRATACIÓN 39

of course a Florentine. Sebastian Cabot was born in Bristol or more likely in Venice. Ribero (or Ribeiro) was a Portuguese, as were Magellan, the Faleros (or Faleiros) and many others. Indeed Portugal seems still to have furnished the most cosmopolitan and competent mariners for distant enterprise, whether to the East or to the West. It also, in the sixteenth and seventeenth centuries, possessed a pilot major, and required examinations in nautical proficiency.

The nautical school at Seville was for a long time the object of admiration by visitors from the north of Europe. When the celebrated English navigator, Stephen Borough, was in Seville in 1558, the Spaniards, as he afterwards told Hakluyt, " tooke him into the cōtractation house at their admitting of masters and pilots, giving him great honour, and presented him with a payre of perfumed gloves worth five or six Ducates." And Borough, soon after his return, drew up a document setting forth:

Three especiall causes and consideracons amongst others whether the office of Pilott maior ys allowed and estemed in Spayne, Portugale, and other places where navigacon flourisheth.

Probably as a consequence, in January, 1563, Borough was appointed chief pilot and one of the four masters of the Queen's ships in the Medway. It hardly admits of doubt that the object in view in creating the office of chief pilot was emulation of the Spaniards — the instruction and examination of English mariners in the science and practice of navigation. But as there was no other machinery for carrying it into effect, such as existed in the Casa de Contratación, it was soon lost sight of, and the office of chief pilot allowed to lapse.[1]

So far the India House has been discussed in its aspects as a commercial and nautical bureau. It was something more, it was a court of law. In the original instructions of 1503 no mention is made of judicial powers, and no later decrees survive which confer such powers. Veitia Linaje himself is entirely in the dark as to their origin, although, being an interested party, he affirms that the Casa possessed them from the very beginning. An

[1] *Dictionary of National Biography*, art. " Stephen Borough."

ordinance issued in Joanna's name in 1508 refers to judicial authority (jurisdicción) as having been granted by her royal parents after the first discoveries to those in charge of Indian affairs, including later the members of the Casa de Contratación.[1] It is true that Columbus as admiral and viceroy possessed a judicial competence of a vague sort; but it was exercised chiefly in the appointment of colonial officials.[2] In the commissions issued to Fonseca nothing is said of a " jurisdicción " over the matters with which he was entrusted. It seems, however, from the general tenor of later decrees, that the members of the Casa very early sat as a court upon cases involving infractions of its regulations, or disputes between merchants and mariners engaged in the India trade. They constituted a civil tribunal similar to the " consulados " of Spanish merchants in Burgos, Barcelona and other cities. What means they had of enforcing their decisions does not appear. Nor is it likely that they possessed much, if any, criminal jurisdiction. They probably depended upon the municipal authorities to execute their mandates, and left criminal actions to the ordinary courts. It was not long before such a division of jurisdiction caused friction between the Casa and the city, as is evident from two letters of the summer of 1504. In one Ferdinand denies the request of the Casa for a judge to take charge of " las cosas de las armadas." In the other, of the same date, addressed to the Count of Cifuentes, Asistente or chief justice of Seville, he orders the count to see that in the future all law-suits touching the armadas and pending before him, his deputies or any other magistrates of the city, be disposed of as expeditiously as possible.[3]

Bickerings and vexation between the two sets of authorities continued for many years. Not only did the ordinary justices issue injunctions to restrain the Casa, but other officers of the city interfered with its activities, endeavoring to levy toll on wine and other articles brought there for outfitting the fleets or for transportation to America. Merchants importuned the king for relief, and even proctors from Hispaniola complained that because of

[1] *Colecc. de doc.*, 2d ser., v, p. 146.
[2] *Viajes*, ii, pp. 9, 57.
[3] *Colecc. de doc.*, 1st ser., xxxi, pp. 242, 248.

these impediments the islanders were often in want of supplies.[1] Apparently in the spring of 1508 Ferdinand had decided to remove the Casa from Seville altogether, when protests from the citizens caused him to suspend his decision until the two parties had time to compose their differences and report to him.[2] In the following July a decree issued over Joanna's name confirmed all former judicial powers of the Casa, and ordered the asistente and other judges in no manner or form to interfere with it.[3]

Yet through 1509 and 1510, as the business of the House increased, the disputes persisted, until finally in September, 1511, the Crown issued a general proclamation defining exactly certain categories of the new jurisdiction. It was extended to all lawsuits involving contracts or partnerships in American commerce, insurance or freights, procedure to be governed by the rules and customs of the consulado of Burgos. In all cases of barratry the Casa was to have complete authority, both civil and criminal, the criminal sentences to be executed by the king's ordinary justices of Seville or elsewhere. Persons arrested by order of the Casa were to be lodged in the public prison where the arrest was made, subject to the Casa's disposition. Finally, if necessary, officers of the Casa in their judicial capacity might impress carpenters, smiths, calkers, and other workmen to repair and fit vessels for the American navigation, paying them the wages justly due them.[4] Although not specified in this decree, it seems that appeals were taken to the royal justices of Seville. The Council of the Indies had not yet been created.

So, as the House justified its existence with the growth of the Indies, its jurisdiction was put on a more precise basis. Its three

[1] Complaints of interference against the municipal authorities are heard again in 1530, 1538 and 1557. A. de I., Patr. 2. 5. 1/6, ramos 26, 38; Veitia Linaje, lib. i, cap. 2, par. 8.
[2] *Colecc. de doc.*, 2d ser., v, pp. 161–164.
[3] *Ibid.*, p. 146; A. de I., Patr. 2. 5. 1/6, ramo 3.
[4] *Colecc. de doc.*, 2d ser., v, pp. 247, 299–303; A. de I., 139. 1. 4, lib. 3, fol. 165.

The Casa de Contratación in some of its judicial functions, especially later when its powers were more comprehensive, replaced the Admirals of Castile and their court of the Almirantazgo. This court, established in Seville in the thirteenth century, had till then entire jurisdiction in maritime matters. As we have seen, the Casa in 1503 was set up in the very quarters occupied by the Admiral's department.

members were thereafter referred to as "jueces oficiales." At about the same time we hear of a secretary for civil and criminal suits, and in the ordinances of June, 1510, read of one or more "letrados" of the Casa, lawyers employed to aid its officials in the capacity of legal counsellors.[1] Yet in after years, in 1518, in 1530, and as late as 1619, the Crown was compelled to intervene and warn the Seville judiciary not to meddle with the privileges of the Casa or its members.[2] Similar admonitions had to be sent to the royal judges in Cadiz after the establishment there of the Juzgado de Indias in 1535.[3]

It was left to the Emperor, however, by the definite formation of a Council of the Indies in August, 1524,[4] and by the further extension of the judicial competence of the Casa de Contratación, to make the political and juridical control of American affairs entirely independent of any authority in the state save the king. To the jurisdiction of the Casa he gave final shape in laws issued on the advice of his chief ministers, Francisco de los Cobos and the cardinal archbishops of Toledo and Seville, in the summer of 1539.[5] They were included in the collection of ordinances of the India House published in 1552, and remained the basis of all later enactments. All civil suits involving the royal exchequer or rules governing American trade and navigation, were to be heard by the Casa alone, without interference from any ordinary court, and with appeal (in cases involving 40,000 maravedis or over) directly to the Council of the Indies.[6] Other suits between private

---

[1] A. de I., 41. 6. 1/24, lib. i, fol. 69 v°; *Colecc. de doc.*, 2d ser., v, p. 220.
There seem to have been generally two *letrados* attached to the Casa.

[2] *Colecc. de doc.*, 2d ser., ix, p. 88; x, p. 11; Herrera, dec. ii, lib. 3, cap. 8; Veitia Linaje, lib. ii, cap. 7, par. 28.

[3] *Colecc. de doc.*, 2d ser., x, p. 370: cédula of June 2, 1537.

[4] Solórzano, *Política Indiana*, lib. v, cap. 15.

[5] *Colecc. de doc.*, 2d ser., x, p. 453; A. de I., Patr. 2. 5. 1/6, ramo 39.
D. Juan Tavera, archbishop of Toledo, was president of the Council of Castile; D. Francisco Garcia de Loaysa, archbishop of Seville, was president of the Council of the Indies.

[6] The transfer of appeals from the justices of Seville to the Council of the Indies was probably introduced much earlier, at the time of the creation of that Council.

There were four solicitors (procuradores), all royal nominees, attached to the Casa, to whom exclusively was given charge of civil suits brought before it. One of

parties relating to the Indies might be tried either by the Casa or by the ordinary justices, the choice lying with the plaintiff. In civil cases unconnected with the Indies the Casa was to have no part or jurisdiction whatsoever.

In criminal matters it was given an absolute competence over all infractions of its ordinances, and over crimes under the common law committed on the voyage to or from America. Its authority began the moment passengers and crews embarked and the cargo was put on board, and it ended only when the vessel returned and disembarkation was complete. If the sentence involved death or mutilation, however, the prisoner and his case after trial by the Casa, were to be delivered for review to the Council of the Indies. If the consequences of a misdeed appeared only after the voyage was finished and the passengers and cargo dispersed, it was left to the injured party to decide from which jurisdiction he would seek reparation.[1] By this decree, moreover, the execution of criminal judgments was left entirely in the hands of the Casa itself.[2]

A few years later the civil competence of the Casa was somewhat restricted by the erection in Seville of a consulado or gild of the merchants interested in the American trade. In August, 1543, in response to a petition from these merchants for an association similar to the gilds of Burgos, Valencia and other commercial cities, the Emperor published an ordinance directing them to gather in the Casa de Contratación on the second day of each year to elect from among their own number a Prior and two Consuls. These officials were to take charge of virtually all the civil pleas,

them also acted as proctor for the poor. *Ord. of the Casa*, 1552, no. 88; Veitia Linaje, lib. i, cap. 28, par. 22, 24.

[1] Except suits between owners of ships, masters, pilots, or sailors, which were under all circumstances reserved to the Casa.

[2] In January, 1526, a royal order was addressed to the archbishop of Seville to the effect that right of asylum in Spanish churches could not be respected when its protection was sought by those who had broken rules respecting American trade. There had been several cases of men who embezzled money sent from the Indies in their care, or smuggled gold and silver on which the Quinto had not been paid, and who had sought asylum in the churches and monasteries in and about Seville. Such fugitives were lodged in the prison of the Casa, though security was given that there would be no criminal proceedings. *Colecc. de doc.*, 2d ser., ix, p. 237.

including proceedings in bankruptcy, arising out of the India traffic, pleas which till then had gone to the Casa.[1] With the expansion of trade, such commercial lawsuits had naturally increased, the Casa was choked with business, and there were endless delays. The procedure of the prior and consuls was much simpler, shorter and more direct, and there were none of the distractions of lawyers and lawyers' fees. Legal briefs were forbidden under all circumstances. If the disputants disagreed with the decision, an officer selected annually by the king (known as the "juez de alzadas") and two merchants reviewed the case. If the judgment was upheld, there was no further appeal. If it was revoked, there was another hearing with two other merchants, and their decision was final. Execution was left to the constables of the Casa.

By virtue of this first decree, the prior and consuls might draw up a body of rules and ordinances, subject to the approval of the Council of the Indies. This was done in coöperation with Dr. Hernan Perez, member of the Council, and the ordinances published by Philip II in July, 1556.[2] They deal chiefly with the qualifications and election of officers. The prior and consuls were to be assisted by five deputies, and the retiring officials of one year were to act as advisers of those of the next. They were permitted to have a permanent legal counsel or " asesor," and to keep an agent and counsel at court to represent their interests before the Council of the Indies. From time to time numerous other officials were added to the Consulado, receivers of rents and tolls, auditors, a secretary, and an " alguacil " or constable to enforce mandates formerly left to the constable of the Casa.[3] There were unsuccessful attempts in the seventeenth century to make the Consulado more oligarchical, by lengthening the term of the prior and consuls, or by confining the choice to permanent electors consisting of former priors and consuls and the officers of the

---

[1] A. de I., 148. 2. 4, lib. 8, fol. 242. After 1588 the prior and only one consul were chosen each year, every consul serving two years in order to insure a continuity of policy. Veitia Linaje, lib. i, cap. 17, par. 4.

[2] A. de I., Patr. 2. 5. 1/6, ramo 52.

[3] Veitia Linaje, lib. i, cap. 17, par. 32.

## THE CASA DE CONTRATACIÓN 45

Casa.[1] But the institution retained essentially the character given it by Philip II. Consulados were also organized toward the end of the sixteenth century in America, in the metropolitan cities of Mexico and Lima.[2]

[1] Veitia Linaje, lib. i, cap. 17, par. 11, 12.
The prior and consuls were chosen by thirty electors nominated every two years by the whole body of merchants trading with America. Father and son, or two brothers, or members of the same firm, or priors and consuls of the two years preceding, were ineligible. Electors must be independent Spanish merchants (i. e., not foreigners, employees, notaries, or persons holding " oficios de tienda pública "), married or widowers, of twenty-five years of age or over. In 1623 it was ruled that sons and grandsons of foreigners be also denied the right to vote or become candidates for office. On the other hand, any eligible person refusing to accept office was fined 50,000 maravedis and still obliged to take it. Elections were held in the presence of prior and consuls and the " juez de alzadas," and the attendance of at least twenty electors was required to make them valid. In the seventeenth century elections were frequently suspended by the Council of the Indies, or prorogued for a year, because of important business pending which required the supervision and adjustment of officials already familiar with it.

To defray the expenses of the Consulado, a slight tax was levied on goods shipped to the Indies, and paid at the same time as the " almojarifazgo." Articles coming from the Indies were exempt. All traders were liable who had been engaged in the traffic more than a year, or whose first venture exceeded the value of 1,000 ducats. Accounts had to be rendered annually by the Consulado to the Council of the Indies.

The Consulado had the right to appoint persons in all the ports of the Indies to see to the enforcement of its ordinances and privileges. Its officers were provided with a room or " tribunal " in the Casa, and met for business three times a week, on Mondays, Wednesdays, and Fridays, from 9 to 11 in winter and 8 to 10 in summer.

A. de I., Patr. 2. 5. 1/6, ramo 52; Veitia Linaje, lib. i, cap. 17. See also Appendix I.

[2] Solórzano, *op. cit.*, lib. vi, cap. 14, par. 24. The Mexican consulado was erected about 1593-94, and its ordinances approved by the Crown in 1603. That of Lima was apparently organized in 1613. In 1618 Solórzano, with another judge Dr. Alberto de Acuña, was commissioned to draw up its ordinances, which received royal confirmation in 1627.

## CHAPTER III

### ORGANIZATION vs. EFFICIENCY

IT was in keeping with the general policy of the Spanish Crown, to increase the dignity and independence of the India House, that Philip II in October, 1557, created the office of President, the first post equal or superior in rank to that of the three original officials of 1503.[1] The first president was D. Juan Suarez de Carvajal, bishop of Lugo and commissary-general of the Santa Cruzada. He survived little more than a year, however, and then for some obscure reason the office was permitted to lapse for two decades, till 1579, when it was revived in the person of the licentiate Diego Gasca de Salazar.[2] Thereafter the presidential succession remained unbroken. Both Carvajal and Salazar had been members of the Council of the Indies, and in the warrant of 1579 it was expressly stated that presidents of the Casa must have had experience in that body. Although the rule was not invariably followed, it held for the great majority of cases, the president being sometimes taken from among the judicial members of the Council (letrados), sometimes from among the civilians (de capa y espada).[3]

The creation of this office was a natural step in the organization of the Casa. It helped to coördinate the activities of the treasurer, factor, and contador, gave their policy a cohesion which it may not have had before, and strengthened their relations with the Council of the Indies. For the first time the India House was subject to a single supreme executive head. The chief duties of the president were connected, of course, with matters of administration. But when a new chamber was established later to take charge of the judicial business of the Casa, it was equally under his supervision. Whether a "letrado" or not, he might attend its sessions in order to expedite proceedings; and if he belonged to that legal class, he

---

[1] Veitia Linaje, lib. i, cap. 3, par. 1.   [3] Ibid., lib. i, cap. 3, par. 4.
[2] Ibid., lib. i, cap. 37, par. 1, 2.

had a vote in the decision of all civil suits, and in criminal cases in the event of a tie. To him also belonged the right to preside over the tribunal of the Consulado, but he possessed no vote, and rarely exercised his privilege.[1] Although having a general oversight of all departments and activities of the Casa, it soon became his principal care, especially in the seventeenth century, to provide for the regular sailing of the " treasure fleets " to the Indies. That indeed was the purpose in which all the energies of the Casa culminated. And in the time of the Philips, owing to the decay of the Spanish marine and the bankruptcy of the treasury, it was a peculiarly arduous responsibility.

The administrative expansion of the India House after the time of Charles V followed along two fairly distinct lines of development. One had its origin in the treasurer's department, the other in that of the factor. One grew out of the increasingly large sums of money handled by the Casa on both public and private accounts. The other was related to the preparation and dispatch of the annual fleets.

By the first instructions of Ferdinand and Isabella, the treasurer was entrusted solely with the care of American gold, silver, pearls and precious stones credited to the royal exchequer.[2] But in 1555, when the rich silver mine of Guadalcanal was discovered on the borders of Estremadura, its revenues also were delivered over to him.[3] After 1560 he became receiver of the proceeds of

[1] Veitia Linaje, lib. i, cap. 3, par. 18, 20; *Recop.*, lib. ix, tit. 2, ley 2.
The president, with the approval of the jueces oficiales, made temporary appointments to all vacancies pending the action of the Crown, save in the superior chambers of administration and justice. Veitia Linaje, lib. i, cap. 21, par. 9.

[2] Strictly speaking, all gold and silver bullion, pearls, and precious stones from America were charged to the care of the three officials of the Casa conjointly; and when they were sold or otherwise disposed of, or the bullion converted at the mint into coin, then the proceeds in currency were charged to the treasurer alone. *Ord. of the Casa*, 1552, no. 44; Veitia Linaje, lib. i, cap. 5, par. 23; cap. 11, par. 1.

[3] This mine was worked for the Crown till 1576, and for a time vied in richness with the best in America. In 1558 it netted the king over 172 million maravedis, and in the twenty-one years, a total of nearly 900 millions (400,000 marcs). It was said that from its produce alone the Escorial was built. After 1573 its output began to dwindle, the cost of operating rapidly increased, and after several attempts of the Fuggers and others to work it, the mine was abandoned, and not reopened till the nineteenth century. A. de I., 39. 3. 6/4; Colmeiro, *Economía política*, ii, p. 436.

the Almojarifazgo de Indias, and in 1579, when the administration of all the almojarifazgos and alcabalas of Andalusia was vested in the Casa, of these moneys too.[1] The "bienes de difuntos" were in the beginning managed by all three officials together. This lasted till the end of the sixteenth century, when the king created and sold to Juan Castellanos de Espinosa for the sum of 133,000 ducats the office of trustee or depository-general of such property. But in 1601 Espinosa became bankrupt, owing on the account of his trusteeship $142\frac{1}{2}$ million maravedis, of which only $34\frac{1}{2}$ millions were eventually recovered. After this experiment, the bienes de difuntos were also handed over to the keeping of the treasurer of the Casa.[2] They remained from this time forward an added charge to his office; and although only 15,000 ducats additional security were demanded for their honest administration, they were managed with an efficiency unknown when the responsibility was divided, or when the office was sold to a banker who hoped by speculation to pick up a fortune for himself. There was a similar experience with the funds called in Spanish exchequer records, "ausentes y depósitos," i. e., money temporarily sequestered in the Casa by creditors or plaintiffs, or gold or silver come from the Indies the consignees of which could not immediately be found. In the modest beginnings of the Casa, such funds had been in the keeping of the three officials. Later, when the penury of the Crown became chronic, they were entrusted, for a consideration, to private individuals. And finally in 1624, after repeated bankruptcies, they were given over to the charge of the treasurer of the India House. These additional obligations of the treasury office naturally entailed an increase of staff. But they also concentrated financial responsibility, and discouraged money speculations in an atmosphere only too favorable to such adventure. If these funds were to be available for illegitimate purposes, thereafter it was the Crown which embezzled, and not private individuals.

The factor of the Casa de Contratación, after the Crown had renounced whatever mercantile ambitions it may originally have entertained, still performed many functions. If governors or other

[1] Veitia Linaje, lib. i, cap. 1, par. 9.   [2] *Ibid.*, par. 10–12.

officials in the Indies sent money or plate to Spain to purchase commodities for the royal service or for otherwise supplying the colonies, the business of buying and shipping belonged to the factor. Similar orders from the king or from the Council of the Indies were his particular concern. Anything remitted to the king from the Indies, except gold, silver or other treasure, was stored in the warehouse and charged to the factor's special account. Gold and silver were charged only to the treasurer.

To the factor, with the assistance of an "escribano de armadas," belonged also in the beginning the duty of provisioning and fitting ships or armadas for the India navigation. He was expected to purchase and keep on hand in the arsenal a supply of arms, artillery, munitions, ships' stores and tackle. The arsenal was his special domain (his deputy was required to live there), while the royal warehouse was more or less under the supervision of the treasurer and contador as well. In the second half of the sixteenth century, however, after the system of fleets and convoys became firmly established, these functions were gradually distributed among a large number of officials. In 1588 was appointed a Purveyor-General of the Armadas and Fleets of the Indies, in the person of Antonio de Guevara, member of the Council of the Hacienda.[1] He took over from the factor all the duties implied in his title. He not only supervised the purchase of provisions, but when vessels were careened and refitted, furnished the materials and supplies, and engaged the superintendent, carpenters, caulkers, timekeepers, etc., necessary for the operation.[2] Eventually his personal staff consisted of two deputies, four commissaries or buyers, two clerks and a constable. Though a royal nominee, he was subordinate to the president and jueces oficiales of the Casa, and in his absence one of the latter often filled his place. But in the seventeenth century the duties of the purveyor-general were in turn subdivided. A permanent superintendent was nominated by the Crown, the "capitán y superintendente de las maestranzas," a sort of commandant of the navy yard, who assumed entire management of the processes of careening and repairing.[3]

[1] Veitia Linaje, lib. i, cap. 22, par. 2. This office was created in imitation of a similar post in the Royal Navy (Armada del Mar Océano).
[2] *Ibid.*, par. 26–28.  [3] *Ibid.*, lib. i, cap. 23.

There was also a storekeeper, or "tenedor de bastimentos," an official who originally acted as receiver of the goods and munitions purchased by the factor, but who later was subordinate to the purveyor-general and handled only materials for the equipment of the fleets.

Supervision over arms, artillery and munitions intended for the Indies resided in the Casa de Contratación for over a hundred years, until 1607, when it was united with the general administration of such matters for the whole of Spain.[1] Thereafter the captain-general of artillery had control of this department. He appointed the captain of artillery who sailed with each armada to America, and also the gunners, both masters and ordinary. He nominated, with the approval of the Casa and the Council of War, a staff of officials which took charge of the business in Seville — a lieutenant-general, veedor, contador, pagador, mayordomo (storekeeper), and artillero-mayor. The first three held warrants directly of the king, the others were of inferior rank. All were creations of the seventeenth century except the artillero-mayor. His was an old office which had existed at least since 1575, when the factor was in charge of this service. He was an expert required to be present at the purchasing and testing of guns and powder. He inspected the armament of vessels about to sail to, or just returned from, America. He also conducted an artillery school, gave practical instruction in gunnery and the manufacture of powder, held examinations and issued certificates of proficiency.[2] At the recommendation of the Casa, a government foundry for the manufacture of brass artillery was established in Seville in 1611, in charge of Sebastian González de Leon.

There remained with the factor, however, as one of his principal duties, the receipt and packing of quicksilver exported by the Crown to America for use at the silver mines. Indeed, in the seventeenth century, the old arsenal of the Casa was chiefly em-

---

[1] Whether the supplying of artillery and munitions after 1588 still belonged to the factor, or was entrusted with his other duties to the purveyor-general, is not very clear.

[2] A. de I., 46. 6. 1/51, no. 2; Veitia Linaje, lib. ii, caps. 23, 24. The "veedor de artillería" had general supervision of the manufacture of the cannon used in the fleets.

ployed for the storage of this metal. After the introduction by a Mexican miner in 1556 of the process of amalgamating silver ores, the Spanish government shrewdly declared the export of quicksilver a monopoly of the Crown. The new method was found so profitable that it spread with extraordinary rapidity, and the sale of mercury in the New World grew to be a lucrative source of income. As the steady flow of silver from the mines of Mexico and Upper Peru became essential to the maintenance of a bankrupt government, so, conversely, an uninterrupted supply of mercury to these colonies was one of the government's most immediate concerns. In fact, as most European goods were paid for in bullion, the very continuance of Spanish-American trade seemed to depend upon it. And all the quicksilver sent to the Indies, whether from the mines of Almaden in Spain, or from more distant Hungary, passed through the Casa de Contratación.

The expense of maintaining armadas for the protection of the India fleets was met by a duty on exports and imports called the Avería. The administration of this tax devolved for a long time on the three jueces oficiales of the Casa. They were aided in its collection by a receiver (receptor de averías) and doubtless by other minor officials. But after the middle of the sixteenth century, when the income from the avería became greater, this business involved a heavy increase in administrative responsibility. Apparently to relieve this situation, in 1573 the general management of the avería was entrusted to a new official called the Deputy Auditor (diputado contador). He not only as auditor kept the accounts, but seems to have had charge of collection and expenditure as well.[1] There still existed the receptor de averías, and the two together were in all things responsible to the officials of the Casa. At about the same time there appeared a "pagador de averías," or paymaster, whose duties seem to have been more

[1] Veitia Linaje says that there was a deputy auditor from the very beginning, and that at first he had charge also of the purchase of provisions, artillery, and other supplies for the armadas. Both statements are doubtful. The "diputado general" of earlier years was probably that member of the Casa, generally the treasurer, to whom was deputed the cognizance of suits arising out of the collection of this tax. Cf. Veitia Linaje, lib. i, cap. 21, par. 2.

closely associated with those of the purveyor-general referred to above.

The deputy auditor's task, however, proved too great for a single individual. Overwhelmed with matters of administration, he let his accounts fall far behind. In response to an inspector's report to this effect, in 1580 the king appointed a Contador de Averías, whose sole duty was the keeping and adjustment of the books. In 1587, he added a second. But even these were unable to cope with the arrears, and four more contadores were appointed in 1596. The first two were " proprietarios," i. e., they held office for life. The four newcomers were employed for a limited time only. Together they formed the Tribunal de la Contaduría de Averías. In its final form the tribunal consisted of four permanent auditors and a superintendent (contador mayor superintendente) the latter place being first created in 1641. Elaborate instructions for the guidance of the tribunal were issued in 1588, in 1620, and in 1651, and are summarized in the Laws of the Indies.[1]

To this Court of Audits belonged the entire business of adjusting and correcting accounts arising out of the collection and expenditure of the avería. The existence of so thoroughly organized an office naturally suggested that other financial records be submitted to it. In 1597 the India Council decided that accounts connected with all departments and activities of the Casa pass before the Contaduría de Averías. The only exceptions made were the accounts of the royal exchequer and bienes de difuntos. These were still left to the contador of the India House.[2] In 1616, however, the records of the bienes de difuntos were also transferred. From this time forward the tribunal was the auditing office for the avería, reports of officers in the armadas and flotas, funds called " bienes de difuntos, ausentes y depósitos," factorial accounts, and those of the tenedor de bastimentos, correo mayor, mayordomo and pagador de artillería, and receptor de penas de

---

[1] A. de I., 46. 6. 1/51, no. 2; Veitia Linaje, lib. i, cap. 19, par. 2-5.
[2] On the second day of January the coffers of the India House were supposed to be examined, and immediately after the accounts of the treasurer, properly ordered and attested, were presented for audit.

camara.¹ It possessed its own notary and doorkeeper, and was under the general direction of the president and administrative chamber of the Casa. It was the president's particular duty to visit it frequently, to see that its members were at their posts and its rules properly enforced.

The offices of diputado contador and receptor continued through the seventeenth century, but their functions were confined to active administration of the avería. The diputado was the real manager of this branch of the royal service. It was his duty to adjust the schedules of the tax, making computation of the cost of each armada, and apportioning it among the goods and treasure carried on the voyage. This involved the examination of all the registers of outgoing and incoming cargoes. In addition, besides keeping record of the moneys received and paid out by the receptor, and of all official correspondence, he acted as sort of public prosecutor in judicial actions touching the avería. In 1650 this latter function was transferred to the fiscal of the Casa.²

The post of deputy auditor was one of the most important connected with the India House, and was always considered to require the highest degree of intelligence and assiduity. At a time, therefore, when most government places were knocked down to the highest bidder, it continued to be filled by direct royal appointment. In 1645 another deputy was added to share the onerous responsibilities of the office, and in 1651 a third was appointed for the port of Cadiz.³

For a hundred and twenty-two years the administrative division of the Casa de Contratación consisted only of the treasurer, contador and factor, the original three created in 1503. In the sixteenth century, they were usually men selected for their experience, or for talents which peculiarly fitted them to occupy these posts. An innovation was introduced in the seventeenth century, however, by Philip IV, one which was bound to affect the effi-

[1] Veitia Linaje, lib. i, cap. 19, par. 7, 8.
[2] Ibid., lib. i, cap. 7, par. 9; cap. 21, par. 3-5, 10.
[3] Ibid., lib. i, cap. 21, par. 6, 8, 11, 24. The office of receptor was at the disposal of the Casa, and in the seventeenth century its incumbent had to give bond to the amount of 30,000 ducats. His salary was a large one, 1,000 ducats in silver, doubtless to remove the temptation to peculate.

ciency and ésprit de corps of the Casa. In November, 1625, Philip created the Count-Duke of Olivares, his favorite and chief minister, "alguacil mayor" or high sheriff, and perpetual "juez oficial" of the India House. Olivares may already have felt some sentimental connection with the institution, for several years earlier, at his master's accession, he had been created Duke of San Lucar. As juez oficial, he was given precedence next to the president, and in the latter's absence might act in his stead. As alguacil mayor, an office created especially for him, he appointed the jailer and all the constables (alguaciles) employed in the service of the Casa or in the administration of the avería. The office was made hereditary, and as Olivares or his heirs were not likely to exercise its functions in person, they were empowered to appoint a deputy, with the approval of the Council of the Indies. The deputy, however, possessed no precedence over the older officials, and should the proprietor come to Seville, although he retained his seat in the Casa, could not vote. Olivares had also the privilege of selling or otherwise disposing of the office to any one approved by the India Council. His salary was the same as that of the other jueces oficiales.[1]

It was unfortunate that the highest administrative posts in so old and worthy an institution as the India House should suffer the blight which attacked all Spanish administration under the Philips, i. e., the sale and purchase of government offices. Men who had grown gray in the king's employ, and who owed their places to their own merits and services, found themselves outranked in the tribunal by royal favorites; or their deliberations vitiated by the voice and vote of deputies to whom these favorites entrusted duties which they themselves had neither the occasion nor the intention of fulfilling. And although the nomination of a deputy required the approval of the India Council, it was scarcely

[1] Veitia Linaje, lib. i, cap. 15, par. 1-3. At the same time there was created for Olivares the office of "escribano mayor," with the right to choose most of the scriveners or notaries attached to the Casa. In the seventeenth century there were six proprietary escribanos, four connected with the chambers of administration and justice, one with the contaduría de averías, and one appointed for the dispatch of the armadas and flotas. Each proprietor was aided by several clerks. Cf. *ibid.*, lib. i, caps. 26, 27.

to be expected that the Council would seriously question the proposals of the Count-Duke. There was introduced into the Casa an aristocratic element which it had been the aim of the Catholic kings and their immediate successors to eliminate from the government service. It was therefore a retrograde step, a falling away from the best traditions of the monarchy.

It was in keeping with this general tendency that Philip, twelve years after he had introduced Olivares into the India House, began the creation of supernumerary officials, "jueces oficiales supernumerarios" as they were called. These men were presumably appointed in recognition of services rendered to the Crown, probably in most cases for generosity to the royal purse. In nearly every instance they were given the reversion of one of the three original proprietary posts of the Casa on the death of the existing incumbent, but their functions as jueces oficiales began with the date of their patent. The first supernumerary was Andrés de Munibe, appointed in 1637, with the reversion of the treasurership, upon which he entered three years later. He had previously had experience as first assistant to the contador. Between 1637 and 1672, when Veitia Linaje wrote the *Norte de la Contratación*, there were six other such officials added to the pay rolls of the Casa.[1]

The most serious assault upon the constitution of the India House came in 1643, when Garcia de Avellaneda, Count of Castrillo,[2] was made "alcaide y guarda mayor" and perpetual "juez oficial," as well as "juez conservador" of the Lonja or Merchants' Exchange. His seat in the Casa was to be next that of Olivares, or in the latter's absence next to the president. He was paid a salary equal to the president's, and had the appointment of all the porters, the guards of the treasury, the first chaplain, and the officers stationed in the "aduana" or customhouse for the collection of the avería. The nomination to these places had previously belonged to the president of the Council of the Indies. Like the alguacil mayor, the alcaide might appoint a deputy, but

[1] Veitia Linaje, lib. i, cap. 37, par. 31.
[2] He was an uncle of D. Luis de Haro, who succeeded Olivares in the graces of the king as chief minister.

this deputy enjoyed all the honors and precedence of the proprietor.[1] It is significant that these lieutenants of the alguacil mayor and alcaide mayor were neither of them required to furnish sureties upon entrance into office, an exemption which was extended to no other members of the India House. It was not the least of their privileges, for not only were they relieved of the necessity of finding suitable bondsmen, but the proprietors need feel little responsibility for their nominations.

From the foregoing, one may suspect that in the latter part of the sixteenth century and after, the personnel of the Casa de Contratación was assuming proportions unwarranted by any corresponding increase in the volume of business transacted. The suspicion is further justified by the criticisms of some contemporary Spaniards.[2] Several reasons may be suggested for this course of development. It was in keeping with the tendency toward excessive bureaucratic organization credited to Philip II and his immediate successors. The Crown, in its anxiety to supervise and control every detail of commercial activity, added to the number of functionaries, and spun the "red tape" to an inordinate extent. At a time, moreover, when the government was virtually bankrupt, the more offices created the more there were to sell, and so meet the temporary exigencies of an empty treasury. It was a policy agreeable to a people somewhat disdainful of professional or commercial pursuits, tenacious of personal honor, and greedy of the distinction attaching to posts in the service of the Crown.

The Casa always suffered from an excess of solemnity and etiquette, and there is little evidence that administration improved with the increased staff of officials. The result was too often mere routine and procrastination. Alvarez Osorio, in his *Extensión Política*, published in 1687, says that the revenues from the India trade, amounting to about a million pesos, were mostly consumed in administrative expenses. The management of the ordnance department, a comparatively simple business, might have been as effective and more economical without the

---

[1] Veitia Linaje, lib. i, cap. 15, par. 6–13.
[2] A. de I., 46. 6. 1/51, no. 2; *Extensión Política*.

host of officers—veedor, contador, pagador, mayordomo, etc. — whose respective duties were slight enough, and whose chief function was probably the receipt of a salary out of the proceeds of the avería. Especially when the avería was farmed out to the Seville merchants as represented by their gild or Consulado, the elaborate machinery described must have been unnecessarily complex and expensive. And the critics doubtless had good reason for harking back to an earlier and simpler age.

The jurisdiction of the Casa de Contratación, as originally defined in 1539, suffered little alteration, except for the transfer of civil pleas, four years later, to the Consulado. What changes were made consisted chiefly in the addition of new officers to take care of the rising flood of litigation. In July, 1546, was created by royal warrant the office of "fiscal," or public prosecutor, the duties of which had till then been performed by nominees of the Casa.[1] The two letrados, appointed earlier in the century to aid the officials of the Casa in their judicial functions, were merely consulting lawyers, without the title or prerogatives of judge, although they assisted publicly at the pronouncement of sentence. In 1553 was added a "juez asesor," a more formidable official, who sat on the bench and took part in the proceedings.[2] And judicial business was disposed of in this fashion till well into the reign of Philip II. Then by a decree of September 25, 1583, was created a separate Court of Justice (sala de justicia de la casa de contratación). At first it consisted of only two Oidores, or " jueces letrados " (i. e., judges bred to the law, to distinguish them from the three original " jueces oficiales "); but in 1596 a third was added, and the court in form and procedure was made to approximate the chancel-

[1] Veitia Linaje, lib. i, cap. 7, par. 2. " El Abogado del fisco es la voz del Rey en sus causas, zelador de los que administran la Real Hazienda, inquiridor de los que la detentan, delator de los que la defraudan, Procurador de su mayor beneficio, y ultimamente la espada de dos filos, civil y criminal, que se esgrime en defensa del Patrimonio Real." *Ibid.*, par. 1. After 1595 the fiscal had the right to appoint an assistant attorney or " agente solicitador."
There was also from early times a reader or " relator," appointed at first by the Casa, later by the king.
[2] Veitia Linaje, lib. i, cap. 6, par. 1.

leries and other royal audiencias of the realm.[1] Thereafter the Casa consisted of two distinct chambers, one of administration, and one of justice, with the president as a connecting link between them. The new Sala was a final court for all cases involving less than 600,000 maravedis, and in all criminal trials save those involving confiscation, death, mutilation or other corporal punishment.[2] There were no territorial limits to its jurisdiction; it might withdraw suits affecting the ordinances of the Casa from any part of the realm, and its judges or their officers require aid or information in any province of the peninsula or the Indies.[3] There were endless conflicts in the following century between this tribunal and the multitude of other authorities in the kingdom, not only ordinary magistrates, but commissioners of the Cruzada, judges of the Hacienda, and the governors of Cadiz and San Lucar. The interests involved in Indian trade and finance were so extended that such officials were constantly tempted to interfere in business the governance of which belonged exclusively to the Casa. But usually the jurisdiction of the latter was steadfastly maintained by the Crown. The Casa had, of course, exclusive competence over all cases involving its own officials or subordinates.[4]

[1] By an earlier cédula, dated June 14, 1558, the Casa de Contratación was ordered to follow the procedure of the royal audiencias of Valladolid and Granada.
[2] Veitia Linaje, lib. i, cap. 6, par. 6, 7.
[3] Cédula of June 21, 1574 (*ibid.*, lib. i, cap. 2, par. 5 f.). A year and a half was allowed for securing necessary testimony from Spanish America, except from Peru, for which two years was the time limit. *Ord. of the Casa*, 1552, no. 24.
[4] Even after the establishment of the sala de justicia, it remained customary for criminal actions or civil suits to originate in the administrative chamber, and then be remitted to the judicial branch of the Casa. Veitia Linaje, lib. i, cap. 5, par. 5. The administrative chamber till 1604 also retained the cognizance of suits connected with the collection of the avería. Thereafter they, too, were transferred to the jueces letrados. *Ibid.*, lib. i, cap. 20, par. 10.

## CHAPTER IV

### REGISTERS AND CUSTOMS

THERE was no rule of the India House more ancient or longer maintained than that subjecting to government registry all cargoes and passengers crossing the Atlantic between Spain and America. It appears in the instructions to Columbus in 1493, is repeated in the first ordinances of the Casa ten years after, and its observance frequently enjoined in later decrees. Registration seemed an obvious and indispensable formality, and originated probably with the very beginnings of medieval maritime commerce. It not only made for clarity and precision in freight contracts between shipowners and merchants, but also facilitated the collection of customs and other royal dues. It provided the Crown with an easy means of keeping in touch with the course of trade, an important consideration for a government which pursued the paternal policy characteristic of the Spanish Hapsburgs.

At first, apparently, when private trade of the Crown was chiefly intended, there was merely a manifest made out by the ship's clerk, and countersigned by the captain, of the merchandise received on the vessel.[1] A copy was presumably deposited with the contador, or comptroller, of the Casa. But as the Casa became more and more a supervisory bureau for the trade of private merchants with the New World, all goods destined for America had to be declared before its officials, and included in a royal register of the ship upon which they were to be embarked. After the register was closed, no other articles might be put on board without special permission.[2] The captain or master had to give bond to the amount of 10,000 ducats that he would deliver the register and cargo unaltered to the treasury officials of the port of

[1] *Ord. of the Casa*, 1503, no. 8.
[2] Cédula of Nov. 9, 1526 (Antuñez y Acevedo, p. 148); *Ord. of the Casa*, 1552, nos. 157, 159.

destination, and bring back a receipt to the India House.[1] And it was strictly forbidden to any other authority, whether governors or judges in America, or admirals or other officers of the fleets, to open the registers or tamper with them in any way. Similar regulations were applied to vessels sailing between ports in the colonies.[2]

To the contador of the Casa de Contratación belonged the custody and preservation of these registers, and he was liable for the damages suffered by any individual through their loss or destruction, or because of errors of record or transcription. At a later time, the labor involved was left to a subordinate, approved by the India Council, who made out and corrected the papers, issued

---

[1] Ordinances, July, 1522, no. 5; *Ord. of the Casa, 1552*, no. 160. In 1525 Bartolomé Hernandez Franco, an inhabitant of Huelva, petitioned for permission to carry a shipload of fish from the coast of Guinea to the Indies without coming to register it in Seville. The petition was granted. A. de I., 139. 1. 5, lib. 10, fol. 19.

[2] Veitia Linaje, lib. ii, cap. 17, par. 34; cap. 27, par. 16.

The register of a vessel sailing from Seville seems in the sixteenth century to have been made up in the following manner. The merchant, or ship captain, who had goods to send to America, presented to the contador of the India House, a sufficient time before the fleet sailed, a signed memorial indicating the consignee, the nature and quantity of the shipment, and the vessel on which it was to be embarked. Only then was formal permission given to put the goods on board. (For a time after 1570, apparently, there had to be a sworn statement. *Recop.*, lib. ix, tit. 33, ley 4.) The whole number of such declarations for any particular vessel constituted the register of the vessel. They were sewed together, the necessary signatures added and attested, and the completed document entrusted to the captain for delivery to the royal officials in the Indies.

At a later time the procedure was slightly different. The registers were simple declarations attested by the ship's clerk after the goods were embarked, giving the consignor, consignee, vessel, fleet, destination, and in the margin the private marks identifying each shipment. To this were appended the receipts for the avería, almojarifazgo, and whatever other taxes were collected by the customs officers, with the appraised value of the articles; and only when these receipts had been secured was the declaration presented to the contador of the India House, to form part of the ship's papers. In the sixteenth century the registers were sealed, in the seventeenth generally not.

The registers of vessels coming from America consisted merely of attested copies of the bills of lading, made out before the proper authorities in the American port, in which were specified the nature, quantity, and quality of the articles shipped, the freight paid, and the names of the consignees.

*Ord. of the Casa*, 1552, nos. 54, 55; Veitia Linaje, lib. i, cap. 10, par. 11; lib. ii, cap. 17, par. 3, 9, 11; *Recop.*, lib. ix, tit. 33, leyes 1–9.

copies or certifications when called for, and was present at the inspection of ships preliminary to sailing.[1]

From the beginning, the penalty for shipping goods unregistered was confiscation. The ordinances of 1552 set aside one fifth of the value forfeited for the informer or the official who uncovered the fraud, and one fourth in case the discovery was made immediately after the register was closed and before the vessel sailed. But this rule in later practice applied only to disclosures by the jueces oficiales of the Casa. The laws on this score were numerous and conflicting, but in general one third of the forfeiture went to the informer and the judge before whom the denunciation was made (provided he was not a judge of the India House), to be divided equally between them. A decree of 1638 encouraged secret delation, offering the reward immediately upon apprehension of the delinquent.[2]

The interests of creditors and underwriters were carefully conserved. By a decree of July, 1511, any one who registered his own goods under another's name forfeited them on the first offense, and on the second suffered also the loss of half his property. One fourth of the confiscation went to the informer, one fourth to the judge who gave sentence, and the rest to the Crown. But the severity of the rule was soon mitigated. A law two years later (June 15, 1513) mulcted the offender, in addition to the goods confiscated, of four times their value; and eventually the fine was reduced to twice the value falsely registered. The law of 1513,

[1] *Ord. of the Casa*, 1552, no. 59.
[2] Veitia Linaje, lib. ii, cap. 17, par. 27–29; *Recop.*, lib. viii, tit. 17, leyes 7, 11; *Ord. of the Casa*, 1552, nos. 157, 159, 187.

A decree of August, 1577, stated that the claims of the avería and customs must be satisfied before the informer received his share; and a cédula of 1619 directed that when the forfeiture was a large one, or the informer did no more than report the offense (i. e., did not himself prosecute it), the court was to reduce the relative share of the reward. The decree of 1638 reduced the judge's portion to one third of the reward, and this seems to have been the rule in Veitia Linaje's time. Yet in the Recopilación of 1681 there was revived another law of 1657, allowing the judge one sixth of the entire forfeiture, and the informer one third of the rest.

Suits in American seaports involving offenses against the registry laws were in the second half of the sixteenth century made subject to the jurisdiction of the local treasury officials (after 1625 in conjunction with the governor or corregidor of the port), from whom appeal lay directly to the Council of the Indies.

however, continued to hold for any one who registered another's goods under his own name, or under any name but that of the owner.[1]

After import and export duties were imposed on trans-Atlantic commerce, and a tax for the maintenance of convoys to protect the merchant fleets, the inducements to smuggle became more attractive. Clandestine trade flourished on the Guadalquiver itself, and it was necessary to issue decrees time and time again, reiterating the penalties for any contravention of the rules. By a law of July, 1580, if a captain or other ship's officer carried secretly for another person unregistered money, bullion or merchandise, and the goods were confiscated, he had to refund their entire value to the person from whom they were received. Apparently thereafter the liability was to be incurred, not by the shipper, but by the carrier. Another decree, of the year 1593, provided that any ship's officer caught with unregistered articles in his possession, be punished with the loss of his place for four years; if the smuggler was a person of meaner condition, an ordinary seaman, he was sent to the galleys for a similar period.[2] In the same year severest penalties were decreed for the prior and consuls of the merchant gild, if bullion or other commodities were discovered to have been introduced into Spain at their orders without registration. They were to forfeit all of their property and go into perpetual banishment from the dominions of the Spanish Crown.[3] In the seventeenth century the punishments were made even harsher. The rule regarding the prior and consuls was extended to every owner of unregistered merchandise. If he was a member of the ship's company, officer or sailor, he was condemned to the galleys for ten years, and not permitted to have any connection again with the India navigation.[4]

The increasing rigor of these penalties is evidence enough of the wide extent of contraband trade. And in spite of laws and proclamations, this trade continued to increase, especially in the seventeenth century. Articles were hidden in the hold, away from

---

[1] *Colecc. de doc.*, 2d ser., v, pp. 94, 285; *Ord. of the Casa*, 1552, no. 205; *Recop.*, lib. ix, tit. 33, ley 34.
[2] *Recop.*, lib. ix, tit. 33, ley 57.    [3] *Ibid.*, ley 58.
[4] Veitia Linaje, lib. ii, cap. 17, par. 8 (cédula of March, 1634).

the inspectors' eyes, or taken on board after the ship had dropped down the river beyond San Lucar. Particularly the goods of foreign merchants, by law strictly excluded from the India trade, found their way to America by means of this fraud. And when, owing to the decay of Spanish industry, the manufactures supplied to the colonies were drawn more and more from France, England, and the Netherlands, the evil became ineradicable. Alvarez Osorio, writing in the second half of the seventeenth century, says that in his time contraband trade at Seville reached the value of ten million pesos a year.[1]

The Crown was even more solicitous about the registration of cargoes coming from America. For in the colonies supervision was apt to be more lax than under the eyes of the Casa's numerous officials; and the shipments themselves, consisting usually in large measure of gold and silver bullion, were of greater value and more easily concealed than those sent from Spain. American registers had to be signed by the treasury officials of the port from which the gold, silver or merchandise was originally shipped, and be sworn to before a notary, the "escribano de registros." Even wages and personal belongings of the master and crew were included, as well as letters of exchange calling for payment in Spain.[2] On arrival in the peninsula, nothing might be disembarked without permission, and all bullion, pearls or precious stones had to be deposited at the Casa de Contratación before delivery to their owners or consignees.

The law also provided that each ship bring to Seville, in addition to its own register, a copy of that of another vessel sailing from the same port.[3] This was intended to avert the confusion

---

[1] *Extensión Política*, punto iii, par. 1.

[2] *Colecc. de doc.*, 1st ser., xviii, p. 423; *Ord. of the Casa*, 1552, no. 158; *Recop.* lib. ix, tit. 33, ley 29; Veitia Linaje, lib. ii, cap. 17, par. 15, 16.

If, as in the smaller West Indian islands, the port was of too little consequence to require the presence of royal officials, the Cabildo appointed a notary to take charge of such business.

[3] *Ord. of the Casa*, 1552, no. 200. This rule dates back to 1493. The instructions to Bernal Diaz de Pisa, first royal contador in the New World, required that three copies of the registers of American cargoes be sent to Spain, one by the supercargo, one by the ship's clerk, and one by another vessel. *Colecc. de doc.*, 1st ser., xix, p. 222.

arising out of claims for damages, insurance, etc., should a ship be lost by storm, to pirates, or through some other mischance. But the rule, though so eminently reasonable, was rarely effective. If we are to believe Veitia Linaje, it was because of the haste with which fleets were got ready and dispatched, a haste which allowed no time for correcting the original registers, let alone drawing up duplicates. And although orders were issued requiring the observance of the law, they were never enforced.[1]

The greater the output of American mines, the more unavailing were the efforts of the government to secure a record of the precious metals coming from the Indies. It was forbidden to carry gold or silver out of the kingdom. Yet foreign-made goods imported into Spain or the colonies had to be paid for, and bullion from America was Spain's most valued and desirable commodity. So there was every inducement to break the law, and unregistered consignments were disembarked at the mouth of the Guadalquiver or in Cadiz harbor before the inspectors had time to come on board. All precious metals mined in the Indies, moreover, had to pay a certain percentage to the Crown, generally one-fifth, sometimes less. In many mining districts, a considerable amount of bullion was smuggled away without paying the royalty and receiving the government stamp; and as all bullion sent to Spain unstamped was confiscate, the only recourse was to hide it from the registry officers. This particular offense robbed the king twice of his revenues, and from earliest times (ordinances of 1510) incurred rigorous penalties.

In January, 1555, the flagship of the fleet commanded by Cosme Rodriguez Farfan was wrecked on the Zahara coast, between Cadiz and Gibraltar, and two hundred were drowned. In salving the treasure, it was found that more was being recovered than could be accounted for in the ship's papers. This increased the diligence of the treasure seekers, till it finally appeared that while 150,000 pesos had been legally registered, more than twice that amount was carried sub rosa.[2] In the seventeenth century, resort to smuggling seems to have become almost universal. In

---

[1] Veitia Linaje, lib. ii, cap. 17, par. 18.
[2] Fernandez Duro, *Armada Española*, i, p. 215.

1618, in the galleons commanded by the Marquis of Cadereyta, nearly 400,000 ducats of unregistered silver were seized. In 1649 the government, realizing that for some years not a single shipment of gold, in coin or bullion, had appeared in the registers from America, reduced the convoy tax on gold to 2 per cent. But no appreciable result ensued.[1] Not only merchants and foreigners, but governors, judges and other officials were often involved. After 1640, witnesses fourteen years of age were permitted to testify in such cases, and no " fueros " or privileges of caste might shield the offender from punishment. From 1662 onward, judges were allowed to convict on the testimony of government officers alone.[2] We are told by Veitia Linaje that in 1653 so much of the trade with America escaped registration, and therefore taxation, that over 90 per cent of the convoy tax was contributed by the Crown, on bullion brought back for the royal exchequer.[3] As early as 1643 it was suggested that this tax be abolished, and some other form of impost substituted. The question was discussed again in 1644, in 1648, and in 1659. Finally in 1660 the entire machinery of registration, customs and avería was abolished for cargoes from the Indies, and in its stead a fixed sum of 790,000 ducats was levied on each of the plate fleets, to be divided between the exporters in Andalusia, the royal exchequer, and the wholesale merchants of Peru, Mexico, and New Granada. And this practice continued to the end of the seventeenth century.[4]

There is evidence, however, that before 1660 the Crown was often very lenient in its treatment of offenders against the registry laws. Sometimes it suspended the rules, permitting merchants to escape the penalty of confiscation by declaring before the Casa de Contratación any goods or treasure which arrived from the Indies not properly registered. At other times, the property having been seized, the owners were let off with moderate fines, called " indultos."[5] It also came to be understood that if bullion got as far

[1] Veitia Linaje, lib. i, cap. 20, par. 27.
[2] *Ibid.*, lib. ii, cap. 17, par. 7.
[3] *Ibid.*, lib. i, cap. 20, par. 47.
[4] *Ibid.*, par. 46, 48.
[5] *Ibid.*, lib. ii, cap. 17, par. 19-24. Instances are cited in 1560, 1583, 1593, 1595, 1614, 1654, and 1663.

as the Seville mint, it was purged of any stain of illegality it might in anywise have incurred. A general pardon was issued in February, 1560, covering all unregistered goods imported in that or previous years, provided a declaration was made (manifestación) of the contraband articles, and the customs and other royal dues had been paid in America before embarkation. The concession was extended to include even goods carried directly to Portugal, France or any other foreign country, if the goods were brought back to Spain within four months — a naïve proposal which probably met with no enthusiastic response. The decree added, however, that thereafter failure to meet the required formalities would involve all the penalties prescribed by law, and any one who exported from America directly to foreign parts be liable to death and forfeiture of property.[1]

Nevertheless concessions continued to be made from time to time. In 1593, and again in 1595, a pardon was issued covering all persons, except royal officials, who made a declaration before the proper authorities of goods carried sub rosa on the fleets of those years. And although in 1618 "manifestaciones" were expressly prohibited, the prohibition was not observed. Indeed, clemency was much more frequently displayed in the seventeenth century, under the weaker Hapsburgs, than in the sixteenth. In the time of Charles V and Philip II, even admirals were punished with imprisonment or forfeiture for attempting to carry merchandise unregistered to the Indies for their own private profit, or for concealing a few bars of silver among their personal belongings. Veitia Linaje would lead us to believe that in his own time (1672) such rigor was uncommon. Manifestations and indults had become the rule.

There should be no illusions, however, as to the motives of the government in this matter of manifestations. The Crown did not intend to let goods actually denounced or apprehended escape. The concession applied only to articles which were effectively concealed, and might, if undeclared, have escaped the inspectors altogether. If the king seemed very lenient on occasion, there was always an ulterior reason. Either, owing to the mutilation or loss

[1] Antuñez y Acevedo, pp. 156 f.

of registers, it was necessary to know more exactly what a fleet or vessel carried; or, finding the registers suspiciously brief, he was solicitous for the collection of royal dues.

Clandestine trade always increases in proportion to the number and rigor of the prohibitions against it. And in Seville this could not fail to be so, when there were so many formalities to be observed, so many conditions to be met relating to the nature and origin of goods and the antecedents of their owners. On the other hand, this secret traffic could have assumed such enormous proportions only with the connivance of the officials appointed to prevent it. If the Casa, and the Council of the Indies behind the Casa, had insisted upon a rigid execution of the law, detection in most cases must have been inevitable. The India House probably compared favorably with analogous institutions in other countries. Accidental irregularities were difficult to avoid in an organization of such varied functions. But they cannot be made to account for the widespread disorders in the export and import trade with America. Abuses so widely prevalent, moreover, could certainly not have passed unperceived by the Crown. The likeliest explanation is that the king, being always in debt to the great merchant-bankers for large sums of money, and dependent on them for future favors, was in no position to act with the rigor which the situation demanded.

Registration was originally designed to make smuggling more difficult and dangerous. But it also facilitated the collection of royal imposts, and that soon became a principal consideration. Of such imposts there were chiefly two, the avería and the almojarifazgo. The first to be established at Seville was the avería.

The avería [1] was a contribution to defray the expenses of the convoys or other fleets maintained for the defense of the India navigation. From the beginning the need of such defense was patent, and after the first quarter of the sixteenth century it be-

[1] *Avería*, derived from an Arab word meaning damage or loss. Specifically applied to the damage suffered by merchandise or other articles on the sea. Solórzano defines the tax as the " pago de la seguridad que daban los galeones, al que se agregaba para su reparto el valor de los averías ó daños que en la navegación sufrieran las mercaderías."

came a matter of deep concern. Corsairing had been an institution among the seafaring peoples of western Europe centuries before the discovery of America. French, English, and Irish pirates not only infested the waters about Great Britain, but penetrated farther southward to the shores of Spain, Portugal, and the Azores. Sometimes they sailed under letters of marque from the authorities at home, but generally they pursued their primitive calling regardless of the circumstances of international politics. Indeed, in the time of the Renaissance, when national states were just emerging, and diplomacy was in its confused, unmoral beginnings, it was often impossible to define satisfactorily what the status of international relations might be. After the discovery of the western hemisphere, the field of activity of the corsairs was immensely widened. They tried to appropriate to themselves a share of the reputed riches of the New World by attack upon the Spanish argosies returning from those distant El Dorados. They hovered about the archipelagos of the Azores and the Canaries, where vessels from the west were accustomed to seek their first landfall. And when Spanish ships of war made their presence precarious, they transferred their operations to American waters. Spanish records of the first half of the sixteenth century are full of references to the capture of vessels in those regions, and to attacks on Havana, Santiago de Cuba, San Domingo, and other towns on the coasts of the Caribbean Sea.

Columbus met French corsairs near the Canary Islands on his voyage in 1492; and he declared on returning from his third that he had sailed for the island of Madeira by a new route to avoid a French fleet awaiting him near Cape St. Vincent.[1] As early as 1501 a royal ordinance prescribed the construction of carracks to pursue such privateers, and offered a premium to those whose measurements exceeded 150 tons.[2] In 1512 Ferdinand expressed surprise to the King of Portugal because he had received in his ports French boats cruising about in wait for ships from the Indies; and he ordered two armed ships to proceed to the Canaries to meet incoming vessels.[3] In 1513 a royal cédula to the

---

[1] Marcel, *Les corsaires français au xvi siècle dans les Antilles*, p. 7.
[2] *Ibid.*, p. 8.   [3] Fernandez Duro, *op. cit.*, i, p. 201, note 1.

officers of the Casa de Contratación directed that two caravels be sent to guard the coasts of Cuba and assure the India navigation against French pirates.[1] The danger greatly increased after 1520, with the beginning of the long wars between Charles V and Francis I; while the fame of the riches found by the "conquistadores" in Mexico excited the avarice not only of adventurous sailors and shipowners, but also of merchants and gentlemen of depleted fortune. The year 1521 seems to have witnessed the first serious disaster. Two caravels laden with treasure were captured by the French, to the dismay of the Seville merchants; and in response to their clamors, the government hastily sent a small squadron under D. Pedro Manrique to patrol the waters about Cape St. Vincent. This is the first recorded occasion for the collection of avería. The king ordered the expense of the armada to be met by a tax levied on all ships, merchandise, and bullion arriving in Spain from America or the Canary Islands, either on the account of the Crown or of private individuals, and levied also on any coast towns exposed to damage by the corsairs.[2]

In the following spring, as the French danger persisted, three caravels were fitted out under command of Domingo Alonso de Amilivia, which convoyed as far as the Canaries eleven vessels sailing to the Indies. At the same time, at the instance of the merchants, was proposed the establishment of a permanent armada to police the waters between Spain and the Azores. It was to be supported by a regular tax, similar to the contribution of the year previous, imposed on all trade with the Indies, Azores, Canaries, Madeira, and the coast of Barbary. The project was entrusted to the contador of the India House, Juan Lopez de Recalde, and to representatives of the Seville exporters. They were empowered to assess and collect the necessary funds, appoint captains and other officials, hire ships, fix wages, and provide artillery, munitions, and stores. The proceeds of all prizes were to be devoted to the armada's maintenance.[3] The rate of the tax is not stated, but was probably not much over one per cent.

[1] *Colecc. de doc.*, 2d ser., vi, p. 3.

[2] Herrera, dec. iii, lib. i, cap. 14; Fernandez Duro, *op. cit.*, i, pp. 202 ff.

[3] N.M.C., xxi, no. 3 (decree of June 13, 1522); Register of the Council of the Indies (Academia de la Historia, Madrid), fol. 4 v° (agreement with the Seville mer-

Meantime the squadron of Domingo Alonso had proved ineffectual for the protection of American shipping. In 1522 Cortes remitted to Spain in three caravels the king's share of the plunder of Mexico, besides gifts to his parents and to friends of influence. Two of the caravels fell into the hands of the French on reaching the Azores; the third escaped by coming to anchor without being seen in Santa Maria. In May, 1523, Captain Alonso's ships arrived there to escort the remaining treasure home. But near Cape St. Vincent, the " cape of surprises," six privateers led by Jean Florin of La Rochelle (by some identified with the explorer, Giovanni da Verrazano) captured two of the fleet, and secured all of the Mexican booty. Florin also seized at the same time, says the historian Gómara, another vessel from the West Indies laden with 62,000 ducats in gold, 600 marcs of pearls and 2000 quarters of sugar.[1]

How long the " armada de la carrera de Indias " established in 1522 was maintained is not very clear. There is some evidence that it was disbanded three years later.[2] If so, it was recreated in 1528, for in May of that year, owing to the return of the corsairs, a new contract was concluded with the merchants for the support of a fleet to protect the India navigation and guard the coasts of Andalusia.[3] The Casa de Contratación was put in charge of the business, and artillery was lent by the dukes of Medina Sidonia, Medinaceli, Arcos, and by other noblemen. Perhaps provision for such a squadron was remade every few years, for we find decrees and contracts for similar undertakings in 1533, in 1535, and again in 1536.[4] Generally four armed vessels are mentioned, and their radius of action confined to the waters of the Atlantic between Andalusia and the archipelagos.

chants, Sept. 11, 1522); A. de I., Patr. 2. 5. 1/24, **no.** 1 (reports to the Crown in 1523 and 1525 of the administration of the avería).

[1] Florin was captured off St. Vincent by a Spanish galleon in 1527, brought prisoner to Cadiz and hanged at Colmenar de Arenas. Fernandez Duro, *op. cit.*, i, p. 206.

[2] A. de I., 139. 1. 6, lib. 10, fol. 1 ff.; lib. ii, fol. 42.

[3] *Ibid.*, 139. 1.7, lib. 13, fol. 118 ff.; Reg. of C. of Indies, fol. 7 v°; Herrera, dec. iv, lib. v, cap. 4.

[4] A. de I., 139. 1. 8, lib. 16, fol. 160–169; lib. 17, fol. 108; Reg. of C. of Indies, fol. 8 v°, 60 v°, 61.

The system of little squadrons cruising about the capes and the Azores proved insufficient to cope with the increasing piracy, and the government was driven to other expedients. Ever since about 1526 merchant vessels had been forbidden to sail alone to or from America. They must go in flotillas for mutual aid and defense, armed according to rules already promulgated in 1522. In 1537, apparently for the first time, a royal armada sailed to the West Indies to insure the safe transport of gold and silver to Spain. It was the first of the great treasure fleets, consisted, with merchant vessels, of some twenty ships, besides smaller, lateen-rigged lighters, and was commanded by Blasco Nuñez Vela, the man who later went out as the first viceroy of Peru. In that year the Emperor and Francis I were again at war, French corsairs were unusually active in Caribbean waters, and it was reported that in Brittany a fleet of thirteen privateers was preparing to prey on Spanish shipping between Havana and Nombre de Dios.[1] Another armada was dispatched for treasure in the summer of 1542, under Martin Alonso de los Rios, which returned in May of the following year. And in August, 1543, at the solicitation of the commercial interests of Seville, decrees were issued making the sailing of vessels in yearly, protected fleets a permanent and obligatory rule. This further step again coincided with a war between Spain and France. Although the new orders were not in the beginning consistently observed, from 1550 onward the system of convoys between Spain and America was well established, and the avería a recognized and regular contribution.

The preparations and negotiations in 1552, in anticipation of the sailing of the fleet of Bartolomé Carreño, may be cited as a fair illustration of the situation toward the close of the reign of Charles V.[2] The convoy or armada was to consist of four ships ranging in size from 250 to 300 tons, and of two caravels of 80 to 100 tons, and was to carry 360 soldiers. It was expected to accompany the merchant fleet to the West Indies, and after the vessels had parted for their respective ports, make Havana its headquarters, whence it might scour the neighboring seas for corsairs. At the end of three months, the vessels gathered at

[1] A. de I., Patr. 2. 5. 5/13, no. 1, pt. 1, ramo 1.   [2] A. de I., 36. 4. 1/7, ramo 1.

Havana from New Spain, Honduras, Tierra Firme, and the islands were to be convoyed back to the Guadalquivir. The armada was to be fitted and provisioned for nine months, the time calculated as necessary for the entire voyage, and the cost defrayed by a contribution of $2\frac{1}{2}$ per cent, levied on the cargoes coming and going, and also on the value of any uninsured vessels in the fleet. The Crown was to pay on the same basis as the private merchant, and any surplus remitted after the voyage was completed.

To find the ready money needed for preparing the armada, loans were to be solicited from traders interested in the fleet, in proportion to the amount each had ventured, and from other merchants as the officers of the Casa and the Consulado saw fit. Any remaining deficiency could be met by advances from the royal treasurers, so that nothing might delay the sailing of the fleet.

These arrangements had been made in the middle of February. In April work on the convoy seems scarcely to have begun. Merchants waiting at San Lucar sent complaints to the Crown that they were losing valuable time and the cargoes spoiling. They begged for leave to sail alone, as their ships were strong, well armed and manned. The regent, Philip, to hasten the departure, ordered the Casa to choose six of the best merchantmen bound for Nombre de Dios, remove part of the cargo, and fit them out as men-of-war. The " armada " thus constituted was to sail directly to Tierra Firme, instead of waiting at Havana, and on the return voyage call at the latter place to pick up the rest of the fleet. All the gold and silver brought back was to be shipped for greater security on the six armed merchantmen.

It seems that, meanwhile, the officials of the Casa raised many objections as to the rate of the avería and the manner of collection. It was inconvenient to collect on outgoing vessels, for one could not know till the last moment which ships would sail. Those intending to go were sometimes unready at the last moment and compelled to wait over till the next fleet; while others, which had not planned to sail, found themselves unexpectedly in a position to depart at once. Moreover, it was impossible to estimate beforehand the actual cost of the armada, for expenditure was continuous and varied from day to day with the fluctuation in the cost of supplies. The same objection applied to assessments after the return voyage. If made only when the expense of the armada had been computed, it would cause great delays and hold up the goods and bullion of the merchants. Apparently the Casa offered an alternative scheme, although we know nothing of its details. A lower rate was also recommended, $1\frac{1}{2}$ per cent.

The regent, after consultation with the Consulado, decided that these objections were invalid. The suggested rate was too low, for outgoing cargoes were of great bulk and comparatively little value, while the character of incoming cargoes was unknown. A tax of $2\frac{1}{2}$ per cent must therefore be levied on all goods, whether the vessel actually succeeded in sailing with the armada in question or not. Later, however, the officials in Seville were authorized to alter the rate as they deemed most advisable; and in August, as the original fourteen or fifteen merchantmen had increased to more than thirty, the rate was lowered to 2 per cent. The fleet, apparently, did not sail till near the close of the year. It returned in the following October.

This episode is a sufficient indication that, in 1552 at least, the avería was not yet reduced to an established system. It was still a question how the money was to be collected, and whether both outgoing and incoming cargoes should pay. That merchantmen should be compelled to lie in the roadstead at San Lucar for almost a year awaiting the organization of a convoy, seems an intolerable state of affairs. Spanish administration was already choked by a procrastination which was inauspicious for the reasonable development of commercial traffic.

In March, 1573, the rules governing the collection and disbursement of the avería were codified in a series of forty-three ordinances addressed to the Casa de Contratación.[1] Every detail of administration was provided for with characteristic forethought and exactness. The general oversight of this royal service was entrusted jointly to the jueces oficiales and the prior and consuls of the merchant gild; the immediate control to a judge, a deputy

---

[1] Encinas, iii, p. 174: " De las averías que se repartan sobre las mercaderías que van y vienen de las Indias, para la costa que hacen las armadas para seguridad de las flotas, y otros gastos á ellas pertenecientes."

auditor and a collector (receptor) of the avería.[1] There was also a notary or scrivener appointed for each fleet who attested all official acts connected with the administration of the tax; and a "veedor" or overseer to accompany the fleet and see that the funds were honestly and economically expended.

The officials of the Casa, with the advice of the prior and consuls, estimated the minimum cost of providing the convoy for each fleet, and assessed the avería in time to have it collected when the merchandise was registered. After the return from the Indies, another estimate was made of all expenses incurred in maintaining the convoy or in any other way connected with the security of the fleet, and that amount levied on the gold, silver and raw materials brought back to Spain. The funds were kept in a coffer with three locks (arca de tres llaves) in the Casa, one key being entrusted to each of the officers immediately in charge.

No articles of whatever description shipped in the ordinary course of trade escaped payment of the avería, nor might privileges or exemptions, corporate or personal, be alleged against it.[2] Even royal bullion and remittances from colonial treasurers were subject to this tax. After 1564, it is true, an exception had been made in favor of goods from the Indies which represented the wages of sailors, or the profits of ship captains accruing from their freights. But the exemption did not extend to merchants who purchased ships and loaded them with their own goods, unless the merchant himself went aboard to act as bona-fide master or pilot. In the latter case, the proportion of the return cargo representing the normal freight charges had to be sworn to before the Casa, and was entered free. Every shipowner who sent out vessels under command of another person had to pay avería on the freights collected. The exemption applied only to those personally

[1] See Chapter III, pp. 51–53.

The judge of the avería, almost invariably an officer of the Casa, had primary jurisdiction over all cases arising out of the administration of the tax. Cadiz, always jealous of Seville's ascendency, protested against the transference of suits to the neighboring city, but without success. A. de I., 144. 1. 14, informaciones.

[2] Sometimes remittances for a pious object, as the canonization of a saint, or the redemption of captives in Barbary, or lamps, monstrances, etc., for Spanish churches, were exempted by special decree. Quicksilver exported by the Crown was also free.

engaged in the sea-faring profession.[1] Apparently the practice had arisen of defrauding the government under cover of this rule. India merchants exported goods in their own vessels, and brought back their value in gold and silver, registering everything as freight returns. In the seventeenth century, generals, admirals and captains of the armadas were also allowed to bring in free a certain amount of coin supposed to represent their legitimate perquisites during the voyage.

The oath and sureties of the receptor upon entry into office; the rules to be observed by the contador to insure completeness and accuracy in his accounts; the obligations of the scrivener; the signing and countersigning of warrants and drafts; the final audit of all accounts connected with the administration of the tax, from those of the contador, through the receptor, factor and admiral, to the captains of the ships comprising the armada; all was provided for in the ordinances of 1573 with admirable clearness and order, but with a prolixity associated with Spanish administrative documents in the sixteenth century. Every entry in the ledgers of receipt and expenditure had to be signed by the three "llaveros," and attested by the scrivener. All purchases must be made by the factor of the Casa (later by the purveyor-general) or his representative, with the aid of the veedor and the scrivener, and a report, certified by these three, with detailed prices, presented at the India House. No money might be withdrawn from the coffers without an order signed by the jueces oficiales. It was the special care of the latter, moreover, to see that the armada sailed with an adequate supply of wine, vinegar, fish, powder, lead and other articles necessary for its provisioning and defense. For such things were scarce in the colonies, and unless a sufficiency for the entire voyage was carried from Spain, could be had only at excessive prices. Finally, within two months of the return of a fleet to Seville, the completed accounts had to be forwarded for examination to the Council of the Indies. Otherwise a commissioner was sent by the Council at the contador's expense to conclude the accounts and render the report.

[1] *Recop.*, lib. ix, tit. 9, leyes 20–22. According to Veitia Linaje, after 1613 all freights, whatever the circumstances, were exempted.

In the seventeenth century, a contribution to the avería was required from persons who sailed as passengers in ships of war composing the armadas. There is no law to this effect in the *Recopilación* of 1681, but Veitia Linaje assures us that it was the rule in his day, and had been from time immemorial.[1] Every passenger on the galleons paid twenty ducats to the avería, not only for himself, but for each of his servants, dependents or slaves. The rule included bishops and government officials, and even viceroys and their families.

As the avería was reckoned upon the cost of convoying each individual fleet to and from America, the rate was not fixed or constant. Veitia Linaje says that until 1587 it was usually between 4 and 5 per cent.[2] There is evidence, however, that it fluctuated considerably. According to Herrera, in 1525 Pedro Xuarez de Castillo, treasurer of the Casa and at that time in general charge of the avería, received orders that the tax must not exceed 1 per cent. But in 1528, when the armada for the protection of the India navigation was reëstablished, it was raised to 5 per cent.[3] In August, 1542, after the departure of the fleet of Alonso de los Rios, and because of the ubiquity of French privateers, there were orders to the Casa to equip another armada of six ships and six caravels, to guard the coasts and await Rios' return. The avería was to be 6 per cent, levied presumably on the cargoes expected from America. The merchants objected, and the rate was probably reduced. At all events, in the next year the avería is referred to as a tax of $2\frac{1}{2}$ per cent.[4] From other data found in what remain of the papers of the early receptores de avería, the following figures were obtained:[5]

The rate in 1552–53 was about 2 per cent.
" 1554–55 " 5 "
" 1557–58 " 4 "
" 1559–60 " $2\frac{1}{2}$ "
" 1563–64 " 1 "

[1] Veitia Linaje, lib. i, cap. 20, par. 14.
[2] *Ibid.*, par. 11.
[3] Herrera, dec. iv, lib. 5, cap. 4.
[4] N.M.C., vol. xxi, no. 11; Veitia Linaje, lib. i, cap. 20, par. 11.
[5] See Appendix III.

The total expenditures for the convoys in certain years of this period were:

| | | |
|---|---|---|
| 1537–38—(fleet of Blasco Nuñez Vela)......... | 12,712,600 | maravedis |
| 1552–53—( " " Bartolomé Carreño)......... | 21,296,610 | " |
| 1555–56—( " " Pedro Menéndez de Avilés).. | 37,613,525 | " |
| 1557–58—( " " Pedro de las Roelas) ........ | 30,639,576 | " |
| 1559–60—( " " " " " ) ........ | 10,922,179 | " |

After the peace of Cateau Cambresis, the danger from French corsairs became less. Catherine de Medici, finding herself by the sudden death of her husband, Henry II, virtually arbitress of France, determined thereafter to keep in her own hands the balance of power. Beset by rival parties intriguing for the control of the kingdom, she married her fourteen year old daughter, Elizabeth, to Philip II, and hoped by this dynastic union to make her own interests secure. Her policy was not a complete success. Neither Philip nor Catherine would be a tool for the designs and ambitions of the other. Yet, as neither dared brave the open hostility of the other, for many years there was comparative peace and friendship between the two Crowns. And French privateering, so constant during the reign of the Emperor, ceased to be a nightmare in the countinghouses of Seville.

Meanwhile, a new danger was arising from another quarter. In 1563 John Hawkins appeared in the West Indies with his first cargo of Guinea blacks. Three years later he sailed with his friend and pupil, Francis Drake, again on a slaving voyage, but also prepared to indulge in piracy if opportunity offered. They stormed Rio de la Hacha on tierra firme, but encountered a Spanish fleet in the harbor of Vera Cruz and were badly worsted. The pace had been set, however, and Philip was soon to see these freebooters with their compeers, Clifford, Grenville and the rest, rifling Spanish ships and sacking towns on the Main with a vigor and pertinacity that outrivalled the French.

The avería tended, therefore, to increase rather than to diminish. In 1587 it was 4 per cent; in 1596, owing to the exigencies of the naval war with England, it was 7 per cent; and a like figure in 1627. In the seventeenth century, with the growth of contraband trade, as the registered cargoes decreased in bulk and value the rate of the avería became correspondingly higher. In effect, those who obeyed the law were penalized, and the result was to drive merchants to seek new means of fraud, new avenues of escape from an intolerable situation. All the efforts of the Council of the Indies and its officers were insufficient to cope with the problem. Affairs moved in a vicious circle, the increase of one irregularity merely serving to accentuate the other. Finally, in June, 1644, Philip IV issued a cédula promising that thenceforth the avería on registered commodities from the Indies would never exceed 12 per cent, and that for any deficit the royal exchequer would be responsible. But even 12 per cent was double the rate of former times, and this display of royal clemency did not induce merchants to conform to the law. As fraud continued unabated, the Crown was constrained in 1660 to make the radical change in the system of collection already referred to.

At various times before the middle of the seventeenth century, the mode of administration established by the laws of 1573 was suspended, and the collection of the avería, with the organization of convoys, let out by contract (asiento). The date of the first asiento is uncertain. According to Veitia Linaje, a bargain of this nature was concluded in 1598 with the Consulado acting for the merchants of Seville. Of its conditions he had no knowledge. There is evidence, however, that there were agreements earlier than 1598. Probably the first was in 1591, when the prior and consuls offered for the privilege to contribute 80,000 ducats to the maintenance of ten galleons and four " pataches " or dispatch boats. In 1602 and in 1608 other asientos were made with the Consulado, of which more information survives. That of 1608 was to endure for six years, during which time the " asentistas " were again to furnish annually eight or ten armed galleons and four smaller vessels, with a combined burden of 5200 tons and carrying 2500 mariners and soldiers. From 1614 to 1617 the older form of administration was revived, but agreements with the Consulado and other participants were renewed in 1618 (three years), 1621 (six years), 1627 (six years), 1633 (three years) and 1640 (three years). The partners in the asiento of 1640 advanced various sums, and the king lent 257,000 ducats to the enterprise. But following the dispatch of their first armada, the contractors became bankrupt; and thereafter it was not found possible to continue this system.[1]

Veitia Linaje reproduces in detail the terms of the asiento of December, 1627.[2] The individuals interested undertook to dispatch in six years six armadas to Tierra Firme, six flotas to New Spain, and two armed ships to Honduras; and they deposited with the Crown by way of security 300,000 ducats in silver. It was agreed that, with the approval of the officers of the Casa, they should select four of their number to act as managers, with the title of Purveyors. The merchant gild was to have a fifth vote and precedency in all their deliberations.

The armadas sent with the fleet to Tierra Firme were to consist of eight galleons of at least 600 tons each, and three dispatch boats, one of 100 tons to secure the pearls at Margarita, and two of 80 tons to follow the fleet. They were to carry about 900 soldiers and 1100 seamen and gunners.[3] The fleet of New Spain was to be protected by a "capitana" (flagship) and "almiranta" (rear-admiral's ship), each of 600 tons, with two dispatch boats of 80 tons, carrying in all 520 men. The capitana and almiranta might each take on board 200 tons of cargo. If no fleet sailed to New Spain, three of the Tierra Firme galleons were to proceed to Vera Cruz to secure the royal treasure. The two ships for Honduras were to be of 500 tons burden each and carry a crew of 100 men. The asentistas were also obliged to dispatch each year four advice boats, two to Vera Cruz and two to Porto Bello, in accordance with the directions of the Casa. The arms and artillery for all the vessels were at the charge of the government, the contractors supplying only the ships, powder, munitions and stores. All provisions purchased for the fleets were free of taxes, as if requisitioned for the Crown.

The vessels chosen for this service had to be acceptable to the administrative chamber of the Casa, and the galleons ready to

---

[1] Antuñez y Acevedo, p. 199.
[2] Veitia Linaje, lib. i, cap. 20, par. 36 ff.
[3] When this asiento was renewed in 1633, the number of galleons for the Tierra Firme fleet was raised from eight to fourteen, and the rate of the avería from 6 to 12 per cent.

sail on the 20th of March of each year. On the return voyage all ships had to come to San Lucar on pain of 6000 ducats fine, and any vessel returning alone, not under convoy of the galleons, suffered the forfeiture of its cargo.

The asentistas were empowered to maintain in American ports factors and purveyors who, if they needed funds, might requisition from the treasure registered for shipment, to the extent of 60,000 ducats in Tierra Firme and 20,000 ducats at Vera Cruz, to be repaid from the avería at Seville. If the fleets were detained over the winter in America, the expense was to be covered by an extra assessment on the merchantmen awaiting convoy. In such a contingency, as new galleons would have to be sent out in the following spring, the king promised to advance 200,000 ducats to help meet the extraordinary expenditure. On the other hand, the contractors guaranteed each year 60,000 ducats to pay certain fixed charges on the proceeds of the convoy tax.[1]

The final clause (there were sixty-three in all) is interesting as a reminder of the aristocratic prejudices of those days. It stipulated that this asiento was not to be called an "arrendamiento" (i. e., a lease, renting or "farm"), an ignoble term implying rather the status of tradesman. It concerned merely the administration of a branch of the royal service, which the signatories engaged to manage with the aid of their private fortunes, and as such it must in no way detract from their claims to "nobleza."[2]

As already related, after the financial crash of 1641 the farming of the avería was discontinued, and in 1643, owing to the extensive frauds in connection with registration, it was proposed that the India merchants, instead of paying an ad valorem tax, pledge a fixed sum each year for the upkeep of the armadas and flotas. Not till the spring of 1660, however, was the suggestion acted

[1] This was called the "avería vieja." When the government turned over to private hands the administration of the avería, it was debtor for large sums of money owing on account of provisions and other supplies furnished the fleets, sums which it was unable to pay. These debts were eventually converted (1612) into 5 per cent annuities; and it was for the payment of these annuities, and also for salaries of the president and other officers of the Casa funded in the avería that the asentistas had to set aside 60,000 ducats before incurring any other liability.

[2] Antuñez y Acevedo, p. 198.

upon. By a royal decree of March 31, it was provided that gold and silver might be shipped from America without registration or even a declaration at the Casa de Contratación, and that all products of the Indies were exempt from avería, customs or any other impost previously levied at their entry into Spain. In return, the mercantile houses engaged in this trade, and the royal exchequer, should contribute in the following amounts:

| | |
|---|---|
| Merchants of the provinces of Peru.......................... | 350,000 ducats |
| "        "    "        "    " New Spain.................... | 200,000   " |
| "        "    "        "    " New Granada................. | 50,000    " |
| "        "    "        "    " Cartagena.................... | 40,000    " |
| The royal exchequer........................................ | 150,000   " |
| | 790,000   " |

The new law involved a radical alteration in an ancient and venerable system, and was promulgated, moreover, rather hurriedly, without giving time for the Seville merchants to be heard. The situation was fully grasped by the Crown, and provision made in the decree for future amendment. It seems that the quota of the colonial merchants of New Spain, New Granada and Cartagena was levied indirectly, by an additional impost on goods sent out from Spain. To this the exporters in Seville objected. Consequently in June of 1667, after a report from a joint committee of merchants and officials, the scheme was somewhat changed. Of the 200,000 ducats apportioned to New Spain, the merchants of that region were to pay directly about 90,000, the remainder to be levied on the commodities imported at Vera Cruz. So, too, in the case of the 90,000 ducats contributed by New Granada and Cartagena, about 29,000 were thereafter paid directly, the rest collected in the form of a tax at the port of entry in America. The revised schedule, therefore, stood as follows:

| | |
|---|---|
| Merchants of the provinces of Peru.......................... | 350,000 ducats |
| "        "    "        "    " New Spain.................... | 90,000    " |
| "        "    "        "    " New Granada and Cartagena...... | 29,000    " |
| "        " Andalusia...................................... | 171,000   " |
| The royal exchequer........................................ | 150,000   " |
| | 790,000   " [1] |

[1] Veitia Linaje, lib. i, cap. 20, par. 47–51.

Such was the form of this tax when the laws of the Indies were published in codified form in 1681.

The above figures are in some ways rather significant. The Peruvian merchants paid a composition of 350,000 ducats, while those of New Spain paid only one fourth of that amount, or 90,000, the rest being secured by an impost on goods registered from Seville. One would gather, therefore, that Peru still produced much more bullion than Mexico, while Mexico, with its agricultural interests and larger population, consumed greater quantities of European manufactures, which could be made to bear an increased taxation. It is also noteworthy that from this time forward, with the rule regarding the registration of bullion abrogated, it was the more necessary to confine trade strictly to Seville — unless the government was surrendering altogether its ancient pretense of forbidding the export of precious metals to foreign countries.

Armadas fitted out at the expense of the merchants were sometimes used for purposes other than the escort of the India fleets. During the stress of a foreign war, the Crown was apt to requisition a squadron, or to require the asentistas to contribute to enterprises only remotely connected with the defense of the India navigation. Vessels intended for convoy were sent to cruise for hostile fleets, and funds were diverted to furnish fortresses in America with munitions and other supplies. In the decade from 1592 to 1602 the extraordinary charges so incurred amounted to more than a million ducats, charges which legitimately belonged to the royal exchequer.[1] It was the decade which saw Essex and Howard burn the shipping in the Bay of Cadiz, Hawkins and Drake make their last, fatal, privateering voyage to the West Indies, and Cumberland plunder the island of Porto Rico. But, although the Seville merchants were hard hit, bankers and others failing, the asentistas apparently weathered the crisis without serious embarrassment. It was a tribute to the wealth and resources of the mercantile princes of the Andalusian metropolis.[2]

---

[1] *Colecc. de España*, lii, pp. 555–565.

[2] In the seventeenth century, we hear of a special form of this tax, the "avería gruesa." It was a second assessment on the same goods, and according to Veitia

Customs duties, or almojarifazgo, were not exacted from the American trade at Seville till toward the end of the reign of Charles V. Entire exemption had been conceded by Ferdinand and Isabella in 1497, and confirmed at frequent intervals not only by the Catholic kings but by their grandson. In the case of commodities introduced into Spain from the Indies, it comprehended indefinitely " todas las cosas "; in the case of exports, only " cosas para proveimiento y sostentimiento." But in the beginning the European settlements in the West Indies were so poor and limited in extent that obviously few articles of luxury would be sent out by way of trade. The exemption, therefore, was practically complete both ways.

This situation was terminated by a decree of February 28, 1543, as regards both almojarifazgo and other payments to the Crown customary in Andalusian ports. Charles V ordered that " todas y qualesquier personas que traxesen á estos reynos, de las Indias, qualesquier mercaderías y mantenimientos y otras cosas, ó las cargaren en estos dichos reynos para las llevar á las dichas Indias, paguen de entrada por tierra, y cargo, y descargo, y venta de ellas los derechos de almojarifazgo y alcabala, y otros derechos que de ellas nos debieren, conforme á las leyes y condiciones del quaderno del almojarifazgo del arzobispado de Sevilla y obispado de Cadiz."[1] Only the personal and household property of passengers was excepted, articles declared on oath to be not intended for sale or trade. No duty was paid, of course, on anything connected with the royal service; and this came to include provisions and other

Linaje might be levied for two reasons: (1) if some addition to the convoy or other expense was necessary for the better security of the treasure; (2) when part of the cargo was jettisoned in a storm, or accidentally damaged through no fault of the ship captain, the loss being distributed among all the shippers. The avería gruesa was analogous to the custom in English trade called the "general average," and in fact may be traced back through the Digest of Justinian to the law of ancient Rhodes. See Marsden, *Select Pleas in the Court of Admiralty*, ii.

There was also an avería levied in Peru, for the maintenance of an Armada of the South Sea, to carry the bullion from Callao to Panama. At first the rate was ½ per cent, to cover the expense of a single vessel. But after Francis Drake, in his cruise around the world, had captured this treasure ship near Panama, the number of vessels was increased to two, and the rate doubled. Later the rate was raised again, to 2 per cent. Antuñez y Acevedo, pp. 190–192.

[1] Antuñez y Acevedo, p. 211.

supplies purchased for the convoys of the India flotas. At first affecting only ships of war, the privilege was in 1613 extended also to merchant vessels. In 1548 books not on the Index were likewise declared free.[1]

The duty upon exports at Seville and Cadiz was $2\frac{1}{2}$ per cent ad valorem; that upon imports 5 per cent. But imported goods also paid immediately an alcabala of 10 per cent on the first sale, whether actually sold or not.[2] The rule of 1543, therefore, involved a considerable burden upon colonial products shipped to Spain. For the time being it added nothing to goods exported to the Indies. From the very outset, almojarifazgo of $7\frac{1}{2}$ per cent had been collected on commodities entering American ports, a duty which represented in fact the usual 5 per cent plus the export tax of $2\frac{1}{2}$ per cent which had been remitted at home. As this impost contributed to the support of the government in the Indies, it was an arrangement calculated to strengthen the resources of the new and struggling colonies. In 1543, however, after the $2\frac{1}{2}$ per cent had been imposed at Seville, it was specifically stated that the import duty in America should thereafter be only 5 per cent. Thus the whole tax upon goods sent to the colonies remained $7\frac{1}{2}$ per cent, just one half that exacted from trade the other way.

The necessities of the royal exchequer soon gave excuse for reducing this inequality. A cédula of May 29, 1566, doubled the almojarifazgo on the outbound traffic. Thereafter 5 per cent was collected at Seville, and 10 per cent in the Indies, the total customs being 15 per cent.[3] In the same year, apparently, an export duty of $2\frac{1}{2}$ per cent was imposed in American ports, raising the total on the eastbound trade to $17\frac{1}{2}$. And almojarifazgo continued to be collected on this basis until the new form of impost was established in 1660. As this affected only duties on goods entering the peninsula from the colonies,

[1] Veitia Linaje, lib. i, cap. 22, par. 21, 22; Recop., lib. viii, tit. 15, ley 27.
[2] Antuñez y Acevedo, p. 213.
[3] The tariff on wines was put even higher, 10 per cent being levied at each end of the voyage. In the following year, however, the export duty on Sevillan wines was reduced to $7\frac{1}{2}$ per cent, making $17\frac{1}{2}$ per cent in all.

those on outbound traffic remained unchanged till the early years of the eighteenth century.¹

The duties exacted in the Indies were based, not upon the schedule of values employed in the customhouse in Spain, but upon prices in the American market at the time of payment. These were in almost every case very much higher, sometimes by several hundred per cent. On the other hand, the merchant was protected in case of deterioration or breakage in his goods. Merchandise shipped from Spain to Peru paid almojarifazgo first on the appraised value at Nombre de Dios, and on arrival at Callao 5 per cent of the increase in value which had accrued in transit from the isthmus. And this rule held good for all the Indies, with respect to European commodities reshipped from one colonial port to another, even though they lay within the same province, and no change of ownership was involved. But it applied only to bona fide reshipments; in other cases the regular 10 per cent of the increase in value was exacted. Customs were also levied upon intercolonial maritime trade in local products, at the ancient Sevillan rate of 5 per cent on imports and 2½ per cent on exports. Only wheat, flour, and vegetables between ports in the same province were exempt. And in the event of reshipment to a third port, full duty was again charged at both ends, unless province and ownership remained unchanged, when the same rule was enforced as for Spanish goods. After 1591 an additional duty of four reals was imposed on every " botija " of South American wine transported to market by sea, or two reals if carried by land. There was no export duty in America on European articles shipped from one port to another.²

¹ In 1561 Philip II granted a reduction of one-half on products of the island of Hispaniola for a period of twelve years, and renewed the privilege in 1573. The ostensible plea was the services rendered by the inhabitants, and the fact that the city of San Domingo was the " llave, puerto y escala de todas las Indias." But the real reason was without doubt the poverty stricken condition of the colony in contrast with the more flourishing communities on the mainland. The privilege was later extended to the other West Indian islands, and to Venezuela, Cumaná, and Rio de la Hacha. In the seventeenth century the import duty on commodities from Hispaniola was further reduced to two per cent.

² *Recop.*, lib. vliii, tit. 15, *passim*.

It was a favorite device of exporters to transfer registered goods from one vessel to another en route, and on reaching the Indies escape payment of the import duties by declaring that the merchandise had never been shipped, owing to the hurry in dispatching the fleet. Should the concealed goods be discovered on the other vessel, the merchant resisted forfeiture on the plea that they had been properly registered, although not as on the ship where they were found. It was this subterfuge which prompted the decrees of 1540 and later years ordering officials in the colonies to collect almojarifazgo on all articles noted in the register, whether they were in the ship or not, unless sufficient evidence was presented that the goods had been lost at sea, or certification was brought from the Casa, or its representatives at Cadiz or San Lucar, that they had not been embarked. Another scheme was to secure the receipt for the duties at Seville, but neglect to have the goods included in the ship's register, hoping thereby to evade the colonial customs; and if the articles were found and denounced, to present the Spanish receipt as proof that no fraud was intended. This artifice was countered by a royal order of June, 1582, requiring the " almojarifes," or customs collectors of Andalusia, to send with each ship or fleet a separate statement of all the merchandise on which duty had been paid.[1]

At the opening of the reign of Philip II, the revenues from the almojarifazgo at Seville amounted to 65,000 or 70,000 ducats a year. A century later they were probably little more than 700,000 ducats. And most of that income was consumed in expenses of administration.

In the seventeenth century, American commerce was subjected to several minor imposts which had no counterpart in earlier times. In 1608 a tonnage duty (derecho de toneladas) of one and one-half reals of silver on every ton burden was levied on all vessels sailing to the colonies from Seville, Cadiz, or the Canary Islands. Its proceeds went to the support of the university or gild of mariners sailing in the India navigation. This gild had been formed early in the reign of Philip II by shipowners, masters and pilots, and had its headquarters in the suburb of Triana, across

---

[1] Antuñez y Acevedo, p. 216; *Recop.*, lib. viii, tit. 15, leyes 4, 8.

the river from Seville. One of the original statutes of this fraternity provided that on trans-Atlantic vessels a sum equal to the fourth part of a seaman's wages should be reserved to the use of the gild, and it was this ancient custom which Philip III converted into a tonnage tax. The impost continued to be collected probably to the end of the seventeenth century.[1]

In 1642, perhaps as a measure of imitation, a second tonnage duty was levied, in favor of the Crown. In that year the privilege was conceded to any Spanish vessel to depart for ports in America other than the regular emporia of Cartagena, Porto Bello, and Vera Cruz, without special license as theretofore from the Council of the Indies, provided several sailed together or in convoy of the treasure fleets, and a tonnage tax was paid to the government. This new contribution was fixed at 2 ducats silver per ton for vessels going to Havana, Campeche, Honduras, Gibraltar (on Lake Maracaibo), and La Guayra; a ducat and a half for those bound to Margarita, Cumaná, Nueva Córdoba, Rio de la Hacha and Santa Marta; and a ducat for those sailing to Hispaniola and Porto Rico. Ships desiring registers for some of the poorer, more backward, settlements (Trinidad, Orinoco, etc.) were allowed to go free.[2] Vessels subject to this new regulation, i. e., those trading outside the customary, stereotyped track of the great fleets, were called "navios de registro suelto," or simply "registros sueltos."

To this tonnage duty was added a surtax of 2½ per cent of the full amount of the impost, charged to the revenue known as the "media anata." The media anata, or semi-annate, established in 1632, was theoretically the half of the first year's income from any office, civil or military, secured from the Crown, or a payment in acknowledgment of some special privilege or dispensation. As

[1] Veitia Linaje, lib. ii, cap. 7, par. 13.

[2] *Ibid.*, par. 35. Forty years later, in 1681, although Spanish vessels were rapidly disappearing from the seas, the rate vastly increased. The schedule was then fixed as follows: for Buenos Aires, 20 ducats; for Carácas (La Guayra), 12 ducats; for Campeche, 11 ducats; for Havana or Honduras, 10 ducats; for Tabasco, 8 ducats; for Cumaná, Maracaibo, or Cuba, 7 ducats; for Santa Marta or Trinidad, 6 ducats; for San Domingo or Porto Rico, 3 ducats. It is possible that the admission of foreign bottoms under Spanish title was responsible for this increase.

applied to the privilege of carrying cargoes to these particular colonial ports, it took the form noted above.

Another addition to the tonnage duty was the " derecho de extrangería," first exacted in 1681. It was a charge of three ducats for every ton burden of any foreign ship admitted to the India navigation, since by law all but Spanish-built ships had always been excluded. On this also was paid the media anata of $2\frac{1}{2}$ per cent.

In the same year, the mariners' gild, in return for various concessions, agreed to still another contribution, of ninety-six reals *vellón* (about four and one-third ducats) on every ton freighted in the merchant ships included in the flotas, and thirty-two reals in the case of the " registros sueltos." This last tax was intended for the foundation and maintenance of a school of navigation in Seville, known as the Seminario de San Telmo, an institution which persisted down to the nineteenth century.

All of these imposts together comprised the " derechos de toneladas," as they were known at the close of the Hapsburg era.

The almojarifazgo and tonnage duties were gathered at Seville and Cadiz by the ordinary custom officers of the port, representing either the Crown or the farmers of the tax. In the Indies, where only almojarifazgo was collected, its supervision was one of the particular duties of the officers of the royal exchequer. As already related, there were three in each of the principal cities, a treasurer, contador, and factor, corresponding in their origin and some of their functions to the three original officials of the Casa de Contratación, and known specifically as the Royal Officials, the " oficiales reales." [1]

Their most onerous task in this connection was that of appraisal; and numerous decrees and instructions survive prescribing the manner of performing this always thankless business. The valuations had to be made by all three officials together, and embodied in a formal instrument indicating the day, month and year, and the nature and ownership of the goods. All diligence must be used in seeking information on which to base a judgment, from the ship's register, and from trustworthy witnesses as to the

[1] See Chapter II, pp. 26 f.

conditions current in the local market. And the order is frequently repeated that the appraisal be just and moderate, so as to prejudice neither the royal revenues nor the interests of the merchants.[1] Later instructions, issued to the oficiales reales in 1554, after the system of annual fleets was under way, provided that when such a fleet arrived at its American destination, the president and judges of the local audiencia should assist the treasury officers in this matter. But it happened that in some regions the principal seaport was situated a considerable distance from the residence of the audiencia. Such was the case of Vera Cruz, the objective of the rich Mexican flotas. The oficiales reales of Vera Cruz, therefore, were ordered to make the appraisals alone, and send them before publication to the viceroy in Mexico City. The latter then called a financial session (acuerdo de hacienda) of the members of the audiencia, the attorney-general and the treasury officials of the capital, to approve or revise the schedules submitted, before returning them to the coast. And when the schedules were put into effect, no appeal was permitted from the merchants, because of the delays attending any further negotiations with the viceregal government. Considering the distance between Vera Cruz and Mexico City, and the methods of communication in those days, the procedure seems a peculiarly clumsy and dilatory one.[2]

A later decree, of December, 1579, ordered goods to be valued at the average wholesale price current within the first thirty days after the arrival of the fleet. But by the opening of the following century it had apparently become the general practice to add to the valuation stated in the ship's register at a uniform rate of 45 or 50 per cent, according to the state of the market.[3] In any case, the appraisal was made without unpacking or opening the goods for detailed examination, the officials trusting to a formal oath by

[1] Encinas, iii, pp. 472-475.
[2] Ibid., p. 470 (decree of Jan. 17, 1593). If a single vessel entered an American port, however, the oficiales reales might take turns in officiating at the appraisal and discharge of the cargo.
Goods passing over the isthmus were appraised by the oficiales reales assisted by a judge of the audiencia of Panama delegated for that purpose by its president.
[3] *Recop.*, lib. viii, tit. 16, leyes 8, 15.

the merchant that they were as represented in the register. This seems to have been the rule at Seville since 1543, when the almojarifazgo de Indias was first collected there. The officers at the aduana never examined the boxes and bales shipped, or demanded invoices of the shippers, unless there was direct evidence of fraud and an order from a competent judicial court. Only a general statement was required under oath of the nature and quality of the goods. In 1586, as several times in the following century, the administrators of the customs endeavored to change this practice. But each time they met with determined opposition from the Casa de Contratación and the merchants; an opposition, curiously enough, which received the approval and support of the Crown. If we may judge from a letter of Philip II to the Casa in August, 1586, the Crown put promptness and dispatch in the sailing of the fleets before the increase of revenue which might result from a stricter collection of the almojarifazgo. The possible dishonesty of a few merchants was held to be of far less consideration than the delay and prejudice to American trade in general, if customs officers were permitted to inspect goods or require a detailed statement of their character.[1] This view of the situation is especially interesting when we remember the financial straits of Philip's government at the time, two years before the sailing of the great Armada. And from what we know of the Seville trade in the sixteenth century, frauds against the customs must have been very extensive.

Why Spanish merchants should not have been able to meet all the formalities encountered in a modern customhouse, and still ship their goods with sufficient alacrity to insure the punctual sailing of the fleets, is hard to say. The situation is stranger if we consider that there were only two fleets at most each year, that they departed at fairly uniform times in the year, and that their going was heralded and prepared for six months in advance. Yet it is clear that there were endless and seemingly inexcusable delays; and the Crown was justified in its anxiety that embarkation and departure be prompt. Perhaps the entire difficulty may be ascribed to an incurable procrastination and want of what an

[1] Veitia Linaje, lib. i, cap. 18, par. 4–7.

Anglo-Saxon would call business efficiency, limitations which would be as formidable in the countinghouse of the merchant as in the customhouse of the king.

There is also a suspicion that there may have been another reason, unexpressed, for the opposition to a more exact appraisal of goods passing through the customs; another reason for the Crown's willingness to trust to the good faith of the shipper. It was inconvenient to the Seville monopolists that exact knowledge of the cargoes sent to the great fairs at Porto Bello and Vera Cruz should become public. For, as the colonies were chronically undersupplied, the general level of prices at these fairs was governed by the comparatively simple procedure of balancing the whole value of the goods brought out with the whole amount of raw materials and bullion offered by the creole merchants for exchange. And the Castilian exporters, by manipulating each year the nature and quantity of the merchandise to be shipped to the Indies, raised prices at will and reaped enormous profits, said to have amounted sometimes to 300 or 400 per cent. It was a matter of some concern, therefore, that the character of the shipments should not be known till the fleets reached their destination. And as the king was usually under obligation to the wealthy monopolists for gifts and loans to the exchequer, he was the more apt to connive at practices of this sort.

Repeated conflicts with the administrators or farmers of the almojarifazgo resulted in a radical change in the methods of appraisal in 1624. After that date no statement at all was required of the shipper. Instead, articles for export were divided into a few comprehensive classes, and a uniform valuation for each class imposed on boxes and bales according to weight, and on rougher cases according to bulk. Veitia Linaje says [1] that the usual custom thereafter was to value each quarter (arroba = twenty-eight pounds) embarked for Porto Bello at 5100 maravedis, and each quarter for Mexico at 3600 maravedis, and on that basis to assess the almojarifazgo and other duties. The new method seems to have been more remunerative than the old, and was continued almost to the close of the century. The schedule for exports at

[1] Veitia Linaje, lib. i, cap. 18, par. 6.

Seville was never changed. In the case of raw materials imported from the colonies, alterations were made in years when certain articles suffered violent fluctuations in price, but only with the consent of the president of the Casa.[1]

At the very end of the century, in 1695, another innovation appeared, all commodities being assessed according to cubic measurement. This lasted for three years, till 1698, after which the appraisal was based on the number of pieces, regardless of measurement or value. Finally, in 1707, the method of cubic measurement was reëstablished, and remained in force till 1778.[2]

The Crown was always very solicitous that a strict and regular accounting be kept of those who represented its financial interests in the New World. In 1510 Ferdinand Columbus and other officials in Hispaniola were instructed to transmit thereafter detailed reports of receipts and expenditures to the Casa de Contratación; and the Casa was directed to keep a copy of such reports in a separate book, as well as similar records for any other islands or provinces which might be colonized in the future. Spaniards appointed to treasury posts in the Indies took oath of office prior to sailing before the officials of the Casa, and at the same time gave bond or surety for the proper performance of their duties.[3] But after 1608, oficiales reales might reserve half the security until arrival at their destination; and by Veitia Linaje's time it had become customary for the whole bond to be presented before the governor or other authorities in the colonies.

Among the so-called "New Laws" promulgated by Charles V in 1542–43 was one providing more specifically for the care and transmission of colonial exchequer records:

. . . porque nos tengamos entera noticia de nuestra hazienda, mandamos que los nuestros oficiales de todas las nuestras Indias, Islas y tierra firme del mar Oceano, nos embien en fin de cada un año un tiento de cuenta de su cargo, de todo lo que ovieren recibido y cobrado aquel año; ansi de nuestros quintos y rentas de almoxarifadgo como de los tributos que recibieren de los Indios que estuvieren en nuestra cabeça, y de las penas de cámara, y otras

---

[1] Veitia Linaje, lib. i, cap. 18, par. 6.     [3] *Ord. of the Casa*, 1552, no. 23.
[2] Antuñez y Acevedo, p. 247.

## REGISTERS AND CUSTOMS 93

qualesquier rentas y derechos nuestros, poniendo muy clara, y especificamente, lo que de cada cosa ay, y que da en nuestra arca de las tres llaves; y que tengan especial cuydado que todo lo que ansi recibieren y cobraren lo pongan y tengan en la dicha arca de las tres llaves; . . . y que de tres en tres años embien á la casa de la contratación á Sevilla la cuenta por entero y particular de todo lo que fuere á su cargo de aquellos tres años, poniendo en ellos el cargo y data y resolución della; porque de lo contrario nos ternemos (sic) por deservidos; y lo mandaremos castigar con todo rigor; y encargamos y mandamos á los nuestros Presidentes y oydores de las dichas nuestras audiencias que tengan muy particular cuydado de que los dichos nuestros oficiales que residieren en las Islas y provincias de sus districtos hagan y cumplan todo lo de suso contenido, y de nos avisar de los que no lo hizieren.[1]

The rule was repeated in a cédula of October, 1548, and in the code of instructions issued for the colonial treasuries on May 10, 1554.[2] The accounts were received by one or two specially deputed judges of the audiencia, within two months after the New Year, and remitted by the audiencia to Seville. And although copies were filed by the Casa, their destination was the Council of the Indies, where they were audited and given their final quittance.

In spite of the reiteration of orders and instructions, the transmission of colonial ledgers was often very irregular. The newly-appointed viceroy of Peru, Francisco de Toledo, on his arrival at Panama in June, 1569, found that the accounts of the oficiales reales there had not been properly audited since 1552; and he directed the books to be brought down to date and closed, under supervision of the audiencia, so that they might be sent to Spain. The sums involved were a matter of about 7,000,000 pesos.[3] In 1591, again, orders were sent to the audiencia of La Plata (Upper Peru) to remit immediately to the king the exchequer accounts for the years 1573, 1576, 1577, and 1578; and in 1596 a royal letter enjoined greater strictness in this matter, on threat of heavy penalties.[4]

There were often disputes and misunderstandings, moreover, between the treasury officials and the viceroys or governors. These may have been due in part to mutual jealousies, arising out

[1] *Leyes y ordenanzas . . . para la gobernacion de las Indias.* Madrid, 1585.
[2] *Colecc. de doc.*, 1st ser., xii, p. 143.    [3] *Colecc. de España*, xciv, pp. 232 f.
[4] *Colecc. de doc.*, 1st ser., xviii, pp. 440, 449.

of the circumstance that exchequer officers held their posts directly of the Crown, and were therefore outside the charmed circle of viceregal influence. But they also resulted from nepotism and corrupt practices in high places. From the second half of the sixteenth century, most offices in the Spanish Indies were purchased. The viceroys of New Spain and Peru, who usually were grandees, obtained their appointments through favor at court. But the governors of the ports, and the presidents of the audiencias, bought their posts in Castile; while minor offices in the colonies were in the gift of the viceroy or sold to the highest bidder. The consequences were not far to seek. Each official expected to recover his initial outlay, and amass a competence as well. The viceroys themselves, great nobles as they were, too often accepted the distinction for the opportunity it seemed to offer of repleting a diminished family fortune. And, with an expensive establishment to maintain, and a host of clamoring dependents to satisfy, they had every temptation to use their authority and influence in ways which prejudiced the king's revenues. If the viceroy and treasury officials were on friendly terms, irregularities were connived at, and no complaints reached Madrid. They might even discover some interests in common. But if there was friction or jealousy, accusations from both quarters were sure to flow to Spain. Viceroys, it was said, gave offices, pensions, and "repartimientos" of Indians to their relatives and servants, and to others whose services to the Crown did not warrant such favors. They drew money from the treasury for purposes not provided for in the royal instructions, and against the protests of the exchequer officials. Governors of the ports winked at the shipment of unregistered merchandise by their friends, and if the culprits were caught, or made defendants in fiscal suits, they compounded with them for less than they owed the king.[1] Viceroys, on the other hand, complained of the restrictions and impediments offered by the oficiales reales to the proper exercise of their functions, and begged for greater freedom in the control of government expenditure. They were helpless, they said, if treasurers would pay out nothing except fixed charges on any but royal

[1] *Colecc. de España,* xiii, p. 549; lii, p. 484; cxiv, pp. 132, 153.

warrant. They urged that the oficiales throughout their provinces be made to observe viceregal provisions for the good administration of the exchequer, and sought power to hold them responsible for arrears, in spite of any cédulas they might possess excusing discrepancies in their ledgers. Such recriminations were inevitable when the centre of authority was four thousand miles away, and when the policy of the government, consistently that of " divide et impera," allowed little or no initiative to its colonial servants.

It was probably the very distance from Spain, the difficulty of securing a regular remission of accounts to the India Council, and the consequent delays in bringing guilty officials to justice, that prompted the innovations of 1605. In that year, three Tribunals of Accounts were set up in the Indies, in Mexico City, in Lima, and in Santa Fé de Bogotá. Acting in the name of the king of Spain, and fortified by the possession of the royal seal, they audited all public accounts in the Indies, and from their decisions there was no appeal.[1] They were the counterpart, in many ways, of the Tribunal de la Contaduría of the Casa de Contratación.

When royal moneys from the Indies arrived in Seville, they were deposited with the jueces oficiales of the Casa, and a courier sent posthaste to the king with word of the amounts of gold, silver and precious stones received, and the probable value of the bullion after coinage. The latter was immediately sold or turned over to the mint in Seville, so as to avoid any delay in meeting drafts upon it. No money might be paid out by the treasurer without an order from the Councils of the Indies and the Hacienda, except for the salaries of the Casa's officers. The rule was that the Council of the Indies, after conference with the Council of the Hacienda, released certain sums of money as subject to draft, whereupon the latter Council issued warrants to the creditors of the Crown. These warrants were carried to the administrative chamber of the Casa in Seville, where the jueces oficiales signed an order upon the treasurer for payment.[2]

---

[1] *Recop.*, lib. viii, tit. 1.
[2] Veitia Linaje, lib. i, cap. 2, par. 15, 16; cap. 11, par. 18, 19; *Ord. of the Casa*, 1552, no. 44.

## CHAPTER V

### EMIGRATION AND THE FOREIGN INTERLOPER

BEFORE the nineteenth century, it was accepted as more or less axiomatic by European states that colonial commerce should be the exclusive privilege of merchants of the home country. As the new community owed its existence to the mother country, receiving from it constant succor in the way of immigrants and capital, it was regarded as only natural and just that the metropolis have the enjoyment of its surplus products, and of all its external trade. The maritime nations, it is true, were always ready to encroach upon the colonial domains of other peoples, but they were equally determined to maintain their own preserves inviolate. This principle of colonial exclusivism was the dominating idea in the rigid and complicated commercial system evolved by Hapsburg Spain. From the discovery of America trade with the New World, and even the right to reside there, was reserved, except for a very short interval, to subjects of the Spanish Crown. In theory, no foreigners were tolerated.

The historian and chronicler, Oviedo, tells us that till the death of Isabella emigration to the Indies was closely restricted to inhabitants of Castile and Leon, except by special grace to a servant or favorite of the sovereign. But after her death, Ferdinand allowed Aragonese and other Spaniards to cross the seas in either private or public capacity. And finally Charles V accorded similar privileges to his non-Spanish subjects, so that in Oviedo's time men from all kingdoms and lordships under the imperial monarch passed freely to the New World.[1]

This seems to be an accurate résumé of the situation in the first half of the sixteenth century. True, Veitia Linaje asserts, and Antuñez y Acevedo repeats after him, that from the beginning the Aragonese enjoyed equal rights with the natives of Castile,[2] but

---

[1] *Historia general de las Indias*, lib. iii, cap. 7.
[2] Veitia Linaje, lib. i, cap. 31, par. 3; Antuñez y Acevedo, pp. 268–269.

the evidence they adduce is faulty. It is probable that before Isabella's death Aragonese were not permitted to participate without special license in trade with the West. A royal letter of November 17, 1504, concedes to Juan Sanchez de la Tesorería, resident in Seville but native of Saragossa, in return for certain services to the crown, permission to carry to Hispaniola "las mercaderías é otras cosas que puedan llevar los vecinos é moradores naturales de estos nuestros reinos . . . no embargante que no seais natural dellos."[1] In this instance, "estos nuestros reinos" can have no application except to Castile and Leon. Nine years earlier, in 1495, Ferdinand and Isabella had granted the right to emigrate and trade to natives "de nuestros reinos é señorios"; and the instructions to Governor Ovando in September, 1501, had provided that no one not "natural destos reinos" be allowed to live in the Indies.[2] But in view of Oviedo's testimony and of Ferdinand's letter to Juan Sanchez, it is reasonable to conclude that "estos reinos," in 1495 and 1501 as in 1504, refer only to Castile and Leon, not to Aragon. There are also the petitions which two proctors from Hispaniola presented to Ferdinand in 1508. Among other things, the colonists requested that trade with the island be thrown open to all Spaniards, whether Castilians or Aragonese, and to all seaports in the peninsula.[3] Finally, there is the testimony of the queen herself. In her last testament she speaks only once of the Indies, and then as follows:

> Por quanto las Islas é Tierra ferme del Mar Oceano, é Islas de Canaria, fueron descubiertas, é conquistadas á costo de estos mis Reynos, é con los naturales dellos, y por esto es razon que el trato é provecho dellas se aya, é trate, é negocie destos mis Reynos de Castilla y de Leon, y en ellos, y á ellos venga todo lo que dellas se traxere: por ende ordeno, é mando que assi se cumple assi en las que fasta aqui sea descubiertas, como en las que se descubrirán de aqui adelante en otra parte alguna.

The undertaking of the Indies, therefore, belonged exclusively to the kingdom of Castile. Isabella's own subjects alone were permitted to trade in the newly-discovered lands, as it was by them

[1] *Viajes*, iii, p. 525.
[2] *Ibid.*, ii, p. 165; *Colecc. de doc.*, 1st ser., xxx, p. 13. The prohibition was repeated in the ordinances of the Casa of 1505 (no. 5), and of 1510 (no. 20).
[3] *Colecc. de doc.*, 2d ser., v, p. 125.

and at the cost of the Castilian Crown that these regions had been found and subdued. It is natural, however, that when Ferdinand alone ruled Castile, in the name of his daughter, Joanna the Mad, the New World should have been made accessible to the subjects of his own kingdom. This, Oviedo says, was the case, although apparently no decree survives which formally registers the change. After Ferdinand's death, the inheritance of the Spanish crowns by a Fleming, and his evident intention to distribute among his Flemish friends and courtiers the offices and emoluments of the Spanish kingdoms, made Castilians apprehensive lest the American trade might also become a perquisite of non-Spaniards, or perhaps be transferred from Andalusia altogether to some foreign port. In the Cortes which assembled at Santiago and Coruña in 1520, just prior to the king's return to the north, the deputies petitioned that under no circumstances should the Casa de Contratación be removed from Seville, or its officers be any but native Castilians. Charles replied that he had made no innovation in this regard, and intended none; and in this instance he kept his word.[1] But he had made no promise to respect the commercial monopoly enjoyed by Castilians, and the edict referred to by Oviedo, embracing all his subjects within the Hapsburg dominions, was issued in 1526.[2]

Two transactions before that year were indicative of the policy the new sovereign was to pursue. In 1522 Jacob Fugger secured the admission of German merchants to a share in the projected spice trade with the Moluccas by way of the Strait of Magellan. And in 1525 the Welsers of Augsburg were put on equal footing

[1] *Actas de las Cortes de Castilla y Leon*, iv, p. 322. The petition also appeared in the memorial to the King drawn up later in the year by the Santa Junta, during the insurrection of the Comuneros.

[2] Herrera, dec. iii, lib. 10, cap. 11. Antuñez y Acevedo (pt. v, art. 1) discredits the testimony of Herrera, on no ground except that he has failed to find a copy of the original decree. Throughout the article, the eighteenth century writer is very evidently pleading a special case.

At least as early as 1520, families of emigrants were sent to the Indies from the Canary Islands. A. de I., Patr. 2. 5. 1/6, ramo 12. Navarrese were declared naturalized for emigration or trade with America by a decree of April 28, 1553. Encinas, i, pp. 174 f.; Solórzano, *Pol. Ind.*, lib. iv, cap. 19. A law of 1596 also mentions as included the inhabitants of Majorca and Minorca. *Recop.*, lib. ix, tit. 27, ley 28.

with Spanish traders in America; on the basis of which they immediately established factories in Seville and at San Domingo on Hispaniola, and embarked on a vigorous program of colonial activity.[1] Three years later, in the spring of 1528, in alliance with another German house, the Ehinger of Constance, they concluded a whole series of agreements with the Emperor: in January, to carry over fifty German miners for the instruction of the Spanish colonists; in February, to supply four thousand negro slaves to the Indies within four years; and in March, the more celebrated treaty for the conquest and colonization of the province of Venezuela.[2] A royal order of April 4 also conceded to them the extraordinary accommodation of storage room in the atarazanas, or warehouse of the Casa de Contratación. This stood on the river bank, and assured them a place in the often overcrowded harbor where they could always lade and unlade their merchandise and ship's stores. In the same year, Ambrosius Ehinger, who had been factor at San Domingo, passed over to Venezuela as the first German governor.

In contrast to the enterprise of the Welsers was the prudent restraint of the other great banking house of Germany, the Fuggers. To them, even more than to the Welsers, the Crown was beholden for various financial services, and to them also the new regime of Charles offered opportunity for colonial exploitation. But only once, doubtless under the influence of the Venezuela compact, did they contemplate any similar adventure. In 1530 they made proposals for taking over the coast of Chile, and a formal agreement was drawn up in the following year. They were to have the government of all they conquered and discovered within eight years, from the Strait of Magellan to the limits of Peru, comprising the mainland for two hundred leagues from the coast, and all islands not included in any earlier grant. They were to bear the titles of Governor and Captain-General for three lives, beginning with Anton Fugger, with a salary of 4 per cent of the net royal revenues, and the title of Adelantado in perpetuity. They were to build four forts, though none in a seaport, command

---

[1] Haebler, *Die überseeischen Unternehmungen der Welser*, pp. 48–51.
[2] *Ibid.*, pp. 53–56.

of which was reserved to them and their heirs. They might nominate judicial, municipal and other officials to the king, have the proprietorship of one fifth of the soil (though nowhere more than thirty leagues square or including a seaport or a capital of a province), and within that area exercise the right of ecclesiastical patronage, save in the case of a bishopric. The contract was to run from the first day of 1532, within twelve months of which their factor must have a fleet of three or four vessels fully equipped and ready to sail. Five hundred colonists must be sent over on the first three expeditions; but the second need not depart till news arrived from the first of the nature of the country. And within four months thereafter they had permission to repudiate their agreement.[1]

For some unknown reason, this project was never carried out, although we hear of representatives of the Fugger house in other provinces of Spanish America in following years. The conquest of Chile was left to Almagro and his more fortunate successors from Peru.

These concessions to foreign merchants and bankers, which distinguish the policy of Charles V from that of other Spanish sovereigns, may have been the expression of broader, less provincial ideas in the mind of the Emperor. They may also have been the consequence of pressure brought to bear by these same bankers on a prince already dependent upon the tender mercies of his creditors. Whatever the explanation, the privileges thus secured were not long retained. The Welsers, although from Hispaniola they had pushed on to New Spain, exploiting silver mines in the neighborhood of Zultepeque, gradually withdrew from all their American undertakings.[2] Their colonial venture had proved to be a signal failure. In Venezuela no German settlements were created; after about ten years, trade and planting were aban-

[1] Rich Collection (Mss. Dept., N. Y. Public Library): *Papeles varios — Sta. Fé, Venezuela, Amagua*, etc.
[2] Ulrich Schmidt accompanied a vessel belonging to the Welsers in the fleet of Pedro de Mendoza to the Rio de la Plata in 1534, and has left us a celebrated account of his experiences. See the " Voyage of Ulrich Schmidt to the rivers La Plata and Paraguai," in *The Conquest of the River Plate*, publ. by the Hakluyt Society in 1891.

doned for the gold hunt, culminating in unsuccessful efforts to find the fabled El Dorado; the regime at Coro went to pieces, necessitating the intervention of the Spanish authorities; and at the end of over a decade of litigation, the Welsers were compelled to retire, leaving not a trace of German occupation in the land.

Meanwhile the custom was insensibly renewed, especially in Charles' later years, when he became more and more immersed in imperial affairs and left the regency of the peninsula to his Spanish son, Philip, of excluding strangers, even religious, from America. A letter of the Emperor to the Council of the Indies, dated June 30, 1549, in response to proposals by the Council that foreigners be entirely forbidden to trade in the colonies, is illuminating. Charles finds it inconvenient publicly to revoke the privilege. But he reiterates the order that all intending to cross to the Indies must come in person to the Casa de Contratación to be examined and obtain a license; and he secretly instructs the Casa to find excuses for granting no licenses to any but Spaniards.[1] Thus the Emperor was compelled to choose between his solicitude for his German and Flemish subjects and the jealous demands of the Castilians. The enlightened principles of 1526 were virtually abrogated, though the statute book remained unchanged. After the accession of Philip to full sovereignty in 1556, practice and theory were reconciled. In April of that year the province of Venezuela was escheated to the Crown, and in June the colonists in America stringently forbidden to have any relations with strangers of any nation whatsoever.[2] Thereafter, overseas trade and immigration remained the monopoly of the Spanish people. The maxim might have been a profitable one, had they been able to supply and to populate so vast a country. But the task was beyond their strength, and the consequences in many ways disastrous.

The early rule was that every passenger for America, native or foreigner, no matter what his profession or purpose, must have a

---

[1] Rich Collection, iv.
[2] Haebler, *op. cit.*, pp. 389-391; *Recop.*, lib. iii, tit. 13, ley 8.

permit from the Crown or, in some cases, from the Casa de Contratación.[1] Whatever the letter of the law, therefore, the king sometimes granted dispensations, and even in the very beginning the appearance of foreigners in the Spanish settlements was not unusual. A letter from the Catholic Kings to Ovando in March, 1503, makes it clear that there were already fifteen residing on Hispaniola. The governor was authorized to permit them to remain, in view of their past services, but to receive no others into the colony.[2] Every emigrant had to be registered in a book kept by the contador of the Casa, in which were set down his name,

[1] *Viajes*, ii, p. 257 (cédula of Sept. 3, 1501); *Colecc. de doc.*, 1st ser., xxxi, p. 212 (cédula of Jan. 8, 1504); *Ord. of the Casa*, 1505, no. 7.

The Casa was permitted to issue licenses to Spanish or colonial merchants, to their factors, and to wives of men already in the Indies. If a merchant left his wife at home, he had to have her written consent, and give security of at least 1000 ducats that he would return within three years or bring her out to America. Commercial factors had to return within three years, whether married or unmarried (decree of Dec. 1554). Mestizos, and colonists with wives in the Indies, might be compelled by the Casa to return.

Unmarried women were absolutely forbidden to go to the colonies, unless they were the daughters or servants of migrating families. And no emigrant, even if a royal official, might sail without his wife, except by express dispensation from the Crown. Officials had to have a permit to embark, in addition to their royal commissions, and pass through the same formalities at the Casa as ordinary passengers. Licenses indicated the number of servants and dependents taken along, and were invalid if not used within two years of the date of issue. Passengers were forbidden to sail in the guise of sailors or soldiers, though it sometimes happened that the admirals, for lack of soldiers, were permitted to enlist passengers in that service during the voyage.

Residents in the Indies, if they wished to come to Spain, had likewise to secure formal permission from the viceroy, president or governor of the province, declare their reasons for the voyage and the intended length of absence. They were supposed also to obtain a certification that they owed nothing to the royal exchequer.

There seemed to be particular difficulty in compelling married merchants sojourning in the colonies to obey the law. In October, 1544, strict orders were sent to Peru and Mexico that such persons remaining there without their wives be shipped immediately to Spain, unless they gave sufficient security that their wives would come out within two years; and similar instructions were frequently repeated to governors and viceroys in later years. Presumably the offenders sometimes compounded with the government, for in the ledgers of the colonial treasurers we find " penas de casados " itemized as a fairly regular, though inconsiderable, source of income.

Encinas, i, pp. 415–422, 424, 426; iv, pp. 286 f.; *Recop.*, lib. ix, tit. 26, leyes 25, 29; Veitia Linaje, lib. i, cap. 29.

[2] *Colecc. de doc.*, 1st ser., xxxi, p. 156.

parentage, birthplace, whether married or single, the ship in which he was sailing, and the port to which he was bound.[1] It was a useful provision, for if a colonist died in the Indies, there would be less difficulty in tracing his heirs at home. Registers of trans-Atlantic vessels were also expected to include a personal description, with age and place of origin, of each person who embarked.[2]

The penalty for crossing without a license was 100,000 maravedis' fine and ten years' banishment from Spain, if the offender was of gentle blood; or 100 lashes instead of the fine, if a person of meaner condition. Judicial authorities in the colonies were instructed to apprehend unlicensed new-comers, and ship them back to Spain on the first available vessel. As time went on, the penalties became progressively more severe, a sure indication that fraud was common. In 1560, they included forfeiture of all property, real or personal, acquired in the Indies. In 1604, the 100 stripes were altered to four years in the galleys, and in 1622, to eight years; while banishment for persons of quality was narrowed to ten years in the penal colony of Oran. After 1604, ship captains had to give bond for 1000 ducats silver, in addition to the ordinary sureties, that they would carry no unlicensed persons, and if caught *in delicto*, not only forfeited the bond, but suffered the same punishment as the offending passengers. By a decree of November, 1607, captains, pilots, boatswains, etc., were threatened with the death penalty, and generals and admirals of the fleets with loss of rank and other dignities.[3] Veitia Linaje, however, complained that in his time (circa 1670) the punishment had been reduced to a pecuniary fine, to the grave injury of the colonies, and especially of the Seville merchants. For, he adds, this mildness filled the New World with vagabonds, and the fleets with small traders who ruined the American fairs for the great exporting houses.[4] If these small traders helped to decrease the exorbitant profits of the monopolists, their presence was no doubt welcome to the colonists. In the eighteenth century there was a

[1] *Ord. of the Casa*, 1552, no. 65; Encinas, i, p. 444.
[2] Encinas, i, pp. 398, 404 ff.
[3] *Ord. of the Casa*, 1552, nos. 121-124; Veitia Linaje, lib. i, cap. 29, par. 7, 32.
[4] Veitia Linaje, lib. i, cap. 29, par. 7.

return to the earlier strictness; but the repeated edicts (1739, 1758, 1778, 1785) are proof that the practice of smuggling passengers did not abate.[1]

The supervision maintained by the India House over emigration to America was the more necessary, as the government endeavored to confine the privilege to persons of unquestioned orthodoxy. As far back as 1501, Ovando, on preparing to go to Hispaniola, was instructed that no Jews, Moors, reconciled heretics, or recent converts from Mohammedanism be allowed in the colony.[2] In 1508 the colonists showed themselves to be equally solicitous, for the two proctors from Hispaniola petitioned that the descendants of infidels and heretics, down to the fourth generation, be forbidden to enter the island. Ferdinand complied by sending orders to Ovando and to the officers in Seville, debarring the sons and grandsons of Jews, Moors and "conversos," and the sons of those who had come into the hands of the Inquisition.[3] In 1518 and many times thereafter these prohibitions were reënacted, and extended to include also the grandsons of heretics[4]; but they were evidently difficult or impossible to enforce, especially as the conversos or New Christians comprised the very class most apt to possess the capital required to develop the colonial trade. Relief from these restrictions, moreover, was a tempting financial expedient to the chronically empty Spanish treasury, and as early as 1509 reconciled New Christians were permitted, in return for a heavy composition, to go to the Indies and trade there for the space of two years on each voyage.[5] Indeed, commercial attractions proved so powerful that in the later sixteenth and in the seventeenth century conversos were found in America in ever increasing numbers; especially Portuguese, for after the annexation of Portugal by Philip II in 1580, subjects of that kingdom seem to have experienced little difficulty,

---

[1] Antuñez y Acevedo, pp. 322–326.   [3] *Ibid.*, 2d ser., v, pp. 133 f.
[2] *Colecc. de doc.*, 1st ser., xxx, p. 13.
[4] *Ibid.*, 1st ser., xviii, pp. 9, 138; xlii, p. 476; Encinas, i, pp. 452, 454; *Recop.*, lib. ix, tit. 26, leyes 15, 16.

Gipsies were also excluded from the American colonies, and frequent orders were sent out to expel them.

[5] Lea, *Inquisition in the Spanish Dependencies*, pp. 193 f.

with or without license, in reaching the Spanish colonies. The vigorous measures taken between 1625 and 1640 to exterminate the Portuguese judaizers in Spain was soon reflected in the terrible activity of the Lima inquisition in the years 1634-39, and in that of the Mexican tribunal in the following decade.[1]

One might gather from these measures that emigration to the New World was from the beginning rapid and easily maintained. It has often been asserted that the depopulation of Spain under the Hapsburgs was due to the superior attractions of the American continent. The case has never been established. And in the first three decades at least, before the occupation of the richer regions on the mainland, the transplanting of colonists was slow and discouraging. It is even probable that Columbus had difficulty in securing companions for his third voyage; for a decree of June 22, 1497, authorized the justices of the kingdom to deliver men and women condemned to death or transportation to the admiral's agents for banishment to Hispaniola.[2] In 1499, the Spanish sovereigns exempted for twenty years such as would go and settle in the Indies from every form of local taxation to which their other subjects were liable.[3] But emigration apparently failed to pick up, for the prospects for the planter or miner were still meagre, and the perils to life and health very great. The elaborate preliminaries of inquiry and examination by the Casa must have been expensive for the poor artisan or farmer. Their searching character, too, doubtless deterred many who might otherwise have tried their fortunes overseas. In September, 1511, therefore, the bars were temporarily dropped, any Spaniard was allowed to emigrate without formalities beyond the registration of his name and residence, and inducements were again offered of lesser taxation on the other side. Sons and grandsons of infidels and heretics, however, were forbidden to hold any repartimiento of Indians, or office of a public character in the Indies.[4]

---
[1] Lea, *Inquisition in the Spanish Dependencies*, pp. 229, 419.
[2] *Viajes*, ii, pp. 207, 209, 212; iii, p. 507.
[3] *Colecc. de doc.*, 2d ser., ix, p. 109.
[4] Encinas, i, p. 396; *Colecc. de doc.*, 2d ser., v, pp. 307, 331. See also the privileges and exemptions conceded to those who would accompany Pedrarias Dávila for the colonization of Tierra Firme in 1513, *ibid.*, ix, pp. 4-21.

One of the chief obstacles to permanent and effective colonization was the Spaniards' greed for gold. When the gold-washings on the islands were exhausted, the inhabitants drifted on to Darien and Central America, and later to the provinces of New Spain. On the mainland this same passion blinded them to the rich agricultural possibilities at their very feet. As a result, the population was in a condition of economic instability, both in the Antilles and on the continent. As early as 1517 and 1518, the Hieronymite fathers and others complained to the cardinal-regent Ximenes and to the king of the growing depopulation of Hispaniola, and of the increasing unrest of those who were left behind. Word, too, came from Tierra Firme that the region remained unpeopled because of the Spaniards' single devotion to the search for treasure. And both in 1518 and 1520 the citizens of San Domingo urged that foreigners, especially Genoese and French, be permitted to emigrate and settle.[1]

This situation impelled the Crown to offer still greater attractions to the prospective colonial farmer. Those who would go to Tierra Firme or Hispaniola were promised free passage and maintenance from the day they arrived in Seville till they disembarked in America. They were to be furnished with lands, implements, plants, and live stock, and their living for a year, until they were settled and cultivation was under way. For twenty years they would be relieved of the alcabala and all other payments except the ecclesiastical tithe. Lands would be given them in as large quantity as each desired to cultivate, and would remain theirs and their heirs' forever. The king would order the best locations to be sought out for their villages, the communal rights attaching to which would descend to their children. Physicians and apothecaries would be sent them, and the first son of any immigrant to marry in the colony would receive lands, live stock, etc., on the same terms as the father. Finally, premiums were offered for the best husbandry: 30,000 maravedis to the first who produced twelve pounds of silk; 20,000 maravedis to the one who first gathered ten pounds of cloves, ginger, cinnamon or other spices; 15,000 maravedis for the first 1500 pounds of woad; and 10,000

---

[1] *Colecc. de doc.*, 1st ser., i, pp. 281, 293, 298, 362, 389, 428; xl, p. 565.

for the first hundred weight of hulled rice or olive oil.¹ This particular edict appeared in response to the representations of the bishop, Las Casas, and the worthy priest was instructed to travel through the towns and villages of Castile, exhorting the laborers to emigrate, and explaining to them the excellences of these newly discovered lands. The same terms were repeated in a decree of the following May, and were renewed by Charles V in 1531.

Meantime, in November, 1526, the Crown had to adopt the extreme measure of forbidding migration from the Antilles to the continent, on pain of death and confiscation of property.² But such a rule could not be enforced, and its terms were gradually modified. An order of 1534 made the permission of the governor necessary for any one to pass from one province or island in the Indies to another. And by 1548, apparently, Spanish subjects in the colonies had the right to go and live wherever they pleased.³ The Crown, however, in spite of its desire to foster emigration, continued its policy against infidels and heretics, and applied it with ever-increasing thoroughness. Purity of faith and of Spanish blood — " limpieza de sangre " — remained the ideal.⁴

To turn from emigration to the matter of trade in particular: from the time of Philip II, a merchant, to engage in transAtlantic commerce or navigation, had to be a native Spaniard. That was interpreted to mean that he must be the son of a Spanish father, or of a Catholic foreigner who had acquired a domicile in Spain of at least ten years' standing. Such seems to have been the accepted practice till the end of the seventeenth

¹ *Colecc. de doc.*, 2d ser., ix, pp. 77–83 (cédula of Sept. 10, 1518). These premiums represented 110, 73½, 55 and 37 dollars in silver respectively, not the figures given by Bourne (*Spain in America*, p. 217).
² Lowery, *The Spanish Settlements within the Present Limits of the United States*, i, p. 173.
³ Herrera, dec. iii, lib. 10, cap. 2; Encinas, i, pp. 411, 433.
⁴ Velasco (*Geografía . . . de las Indias*) says that San Domingo, which formerly had a thousand householders, in 1574 possessed no more than 500. Santiago de Cuba, at one time as populous as San Domingo, and provided with one of the best harbors in the Indies, was reduced to 30 householders. At the same time, there were 3000 in Mexico City, 2000 in Lima, 500 in Puebla de los Ángeles, 400 in Panama, and 250 in Cartagena.

century. Early in the eighteenth, the right of Spanish-born sons of foreign residents to a share in the trade was disputed by the Consulado, but in the end the Council of the Indies sustained the older practice.[1] Neither the sons nor the grandsons of foreign residents, however, might vote or be candidates for office in the Consulado. The law, as published in the *Recopilación* of 1681, forbade strangers to trade with the colonies from Spain, or with Spain from the colonies, either on their own account or through the intermediary of a Spaniard or company of Spaniards. The penalty for infraction of the rule was forfeiture of the goods involved, and of all other property of the culprits, not only of the foreigner who attempted to trade, but also of the native who shielded him behind a Spanish name.[2] Colonists who had anything to do with them were ordered to be sent prisoner to Spain (decree of March, 1557), and in the seventeenth century were put in jeopardy of their lives.[3]

It was policy, however, to concede a sort of naturalization to strangers who, though born outside the peninsula, gave proof of their desire to make Spain their permanent home, and established themselves there with family and property. Absolute exclusion, moreover, was difficult or impossible even for the doctrinaire Philip II, when foreign merchant-bankers made themselves indispensable to the smooth working of the Spanish exchequer, and when the products of the peninsula fell far short of supplying the needs of the American colonists. Very early, therefore, certain foreign-born residents secured the right of admission to the India traffic.

In February, 1505, Ferdinand the Catholic, in reply to a doubt expressed by the officers of the Casa as to the definition of the term "foreigner," gave the opinion that strangers resident in Seville, Cadiz, or Jeréz, who possessed real estate and a family, and had lived in the country for the space of fifteen or twenty years, might be considered as naturalized for purposes of trade

---

[1] Antuñez y Acevedo, pt. v, art. 2, 3; *Colecc. de doc.*, 2d ser., v, p. 74.
[2] *Recop.*, lib. ix, tit. 27, ley 1.
[3] *Ibid.*, lib. iii, tit. 13, ley 8; lib. ix, tit. 27, ley 7; Veitia Linaje, lib. i, cap. 31, par. 10.

with the New World.[1] And in the following month he embodied the substance of this opinion in a decree which included all foreign residents of Castile, provided, however, they acted not as principals, but in association with Spanish merchants, and used Spaniards as their factors abroad. The rule was put on a broader basis in an edict of July 14, 1561. Any merchant who had lived in Spain or America for ten years, with a house and other real property, and married a Spanish woman, was to be regarded as a subject of the king.[2] Bachelors were specifically barred. After 1608, twenty years continuous residence were required, and the applicant had to go to the Council of the Indies for a decree of naturalization expressly habilitating him for the India traffic. But even such a decree did not empower him to vote in the Consulado, or to own or command ships in the American navigation. He might trade, moreover, only with his own capital, or forfeit his license and all of his estate.[3]

Licenses for a single voyage, or for a limited time, were occasionally issued to persons otherwise excluded from this commerce. Sometimes they were given in recompense for particular services rendered the Crown, especially if of a pecuniary nature. More often they were for the transport of cargoes of negroes, the supplying of which was generally in the hands of foreigners — Portuguese, Germans, Dutch, or Genoese. An order of May, 1557, directed that such visitors to the colonies must not enter into the country with their negroes or other merchandise, but make their trade in the port to which their license assigned them.[4]

These elaborate rules governing the right of trade, as in so many other instances of overregulation, seemed made only to be evaded. In spite of the law, great numbers of unlicensed persons found their way to the Indies. The preparation of forged certificates became a profession at Seville; and when punish-

[1] *Colecc. de doc.*, 2d ser., v, pp. 74, 78.
[2] Encinas, i, p. 449.
[3] Veitia Linaje, lib. i, cap. 31, par. 9; *Recop.*, lib. ix, tit. 27, ley 31. Within thirty days of the issue of the license, a sworn statement of the merchant's property had to be filed with the judicial authorities of the town in which he resided, or the license was invalid. In 1618 the minimum amount of property necessary to secure such a decree was fixed at 4000 ducats in silver.
[4] *Recop.*, lib. ix, tit. 27, ley 4.

ments were made more severe, the principal effect was to increase the price of these desirable papers, and develop the ingenuity of brokers and buyers. A letter to the Casa de Contratación, in November, 1546, explains that persons pretending to go only to the Canaries were, in collusion with the ship's captain, carried to America, or were taken on board at San Lucar after the inspectors had left the vessel. Another letter to the Casa in September, 1560, was directed against foreigners and other forbidden persons who went over secretly, as sailors, soldiers or would-be merchants or factors, or who landed from foreign vessels professing to be driven by tempest into Indian ports. The officials were charged to keep closer watch, and to see that the legal penalties were carried out.[1] Admonitions of this character were frequently sent out to the various provinces of the Indies: in 1551, to the governor and officials of Tierra Firme; in 1564, to the governor of Guatemala; in 1568 to the audiencia at Lima, mentioning especially Portuguese and gipsies; in 1571, to the governor of Cartagena and the audiencia of Panama; in 1587, to the viceroy of Peru, complaining that the host of foreigners at Potosí added to the number of idlers, increased public disorder, and raised the price of foodstuffs.[2]

As foreigners continued, nevertheless, to appear in the colonies, the government, at some time near the close of the sixteenth century, began to temporize with what was evidently an irretrievable situation. If strangers could not be kept out, they might at least be made to compound the illegality of their presence, and incidentally help meet the exigencies of an impoverished Crown. A certain Miguel Sanchez de la Parra presented a memorial to the king in 1584, presumably from Peru, in which he suggested that every foreigner or Spaniard in the viceroyalty without a license be fined 50 pesos, or if he was rich, more according to his means. It would not only create a new source of revenue, but would protect these unauthorized residents from the blackmail of colonial officials; for, he continued, "viven estos con gran temor porque cada vez que quiere un alguacil ó ministro de justicia destruir alguno por algun enojo que con el tenga, le piden la licencia con

[1] Encinas, i, pp. 398, 443.   [2] *Ibid.*, pp. 446, 451, 461.

que pasó de España, y como no la tiene, le prenden, y le cuesta mucho dinero y desasosiego, y al cabo le hacen gastar lo que tiene, y no le vuelven á España, fuera de que dan muchas dadivas porque les dejen."[1] This or a similar proposal was acted upon, for in the early nineties a scheme of pecuniary compositions was in effect. We have a letter of Philip, dated January 13, 1596, in reply to a communication from one of the judges of the Lima audiencia, advising greater leniency in the matter, especially toward poor foreigners, and toward those who were naturalized or were vassals of the Spanish Crown (i. e., Flemings, Italians, etc.). Those who had lived in the Indies many years, had shared in the discoveries or served the community in other capacities, were married and had sons and grandsons in the colony, or who held encomiendas of Indians, were to be passed over, even though technically liable. This mode of relief, however, was to apply only to those already living in America, and under no circumstances to foreign clergy or unmarried women. In the future, unlicensed persons must not be permitted to disembark, but be sent back immediately to Spain. The fines were not a regular tax, but a payment which, once made, permanently legitimatized one's residence in the colonies. From time to time, apparently, general orders (cédulas generales de composiciones) were issued by the Crown to mulct foreigners whose presence was not in one way or another accounted for; and no viceroy, president or governor might act without such authorization. Those who had paid their fines could engage in trade, except with the metropolis, or between Peru and Mexico, or with the Philippine Islands. They must live in the interior, therefore, away from the maritime ports, as far as seemed best to the local magistrates, so as to have no connection or correspondence with over-seas traffic.[2]

As pointed out in an earlier chapter, there was a vast amount of clandestine trade between Spain and America. Much of it was an effort to shield those whom the law so rigorously excluded. At Cadiz and at San Lucar, foreign merchants laded goods upon the

[1] *Colecc. de España*, civ, p. 283.
[2] *Colecc. de doc.*, 1st ser., xix, p. 47; *Recop.*, lib. ix, tit. 27, leyes 12–17, 20, 21.

flotas directly from their own vessels in the harbor, without registry at the Casa de Contratación, and on the return of the fleet, received their value in ingots of gold and silver by the same device.[1] Or, to elude the law, they traded under the name of Spanish merchants established in Seville, who became little more than factors of foreign commercial houses. In 1670, M. Lemonnet wrote to Colbert concerning this traffic:

> . . . toutes les marchandises qu'on leur donne à porter aux Indes sont chargées sous le nom d'Espagnols, qui bien souvent n'en ont pas connaissance, ne jugeant pas à propos de leur en parler, afin de tenir les affaires plus secrètes et qu'il n'y ait que le commissionaire à le savoir, lequel en rend compte à son retour des Indes, directemente à celui qui en a donné la cargaison en confiance sans avoir nul egard pour ceux au nom desquels le chargement à été fait, et lorsque ces commissionaires reviennent des Indes soit sur les flottes galions ou navires particuliers, ils apportent leur argent dans leurs coffres, la pluspart entre pont et sans connoissement.[2]

Although written in the second half of the seventeenth century, Lemonnet's letter applied as much to conditions in the sixteenth, as to later times. The king, in October, 1569, warned the officials of the Casa to beware, when dispatching the fleets, lest foreigners embarked merchandise in the name of a third party; and a cédula four years later, addressed to officers in the Indies, ordered them to keep a sharp lookout for such shipments, and send advice to Seville of the persons by whom they had been consigned, so that

[1] "Les étrangers pour le compte desquels les effets sont venus, se servent de jeunes gentilshommes espagnols qu'on appelle 'metedores.' Ce sont des cadets des meilleures maisons du pays qui n'ont pas de biens. Les marchands leur donnent 1 % de toutes les marchandises qu'ils leur sauvent, et moyennant ce profit ils vont prendre les barres d'or et d'argent qui sont entrées á Cadix et les jettent de dessus les remparts sur le bord de la mer, où d'autres metedores, qui se tiennent là exprès, les reprennent, et selon le chiffre qui est marqué sur le ballot, ils le portent dans la chaloupe de celui à qui il appartient. On gagne pour cela le gouverneur, le major et l'alcade de Cadix, aussi bien que les sentinelles qui sont sur les remparts et qui voient tout cela sans en rien dire. Ces metedores remportent d'ordinaire à chaque retour des flottes 2,000 ou 3,000 pistoles, qu'ils vont depenser à Madrid, où ils sont connus de tout le monde pour faire ce métier-lù."

Quoted by E. W. Dahlgren from a "Mémoire touchant le commerce des Indes Occidentales par Cadix, 1691," among the Spanish papers in the French Foreign Archives. *Les relations commerciales*, etc., p. 42.

[2] Margry, *Relations et mémoires inédits pour servir à l'histoire de la France dans les pays d'outremer*, p. 185.

proceedings might be instituted against them in Spain.[1] After 1592 the law forbade a foreigner to dispose of goods to a Spanish subject to be paid for in the Indies, as it occasioned the withdrawal of American bullion to other countries, often without touching Spanish shores. Payments must be made at the place where the sale was concluded, or at least somewhere within the Spanish peninsula.[2] In effect, therefore, no gold, silver or other commodities might be withdrawn from the colonies in the name of, or consigned to, any but a Spaniard.

We learn from a royal *provisión* of June, 1540, that Portuguese vessels were in the habit of sailing from Spain presumably for the Canary Islands, but going to the West Indies instead, there making their trade, and lading a return cargo which they carried directly to Portugal. Or the Portuguese captain touched at the Canaries, made a fictitious sale of the vessel to one of the islanders, and continued the voyage as master of a pretended Spanish ship. And because of the lower rates offered by these foreign captains, Andalusian vessels in the Indies were deprived of their freights. Reiterated orders were issued by the Crown to the authorities at Seville and in the colonies for the suppression of this practice.[3]

Under the later Hapsburgs, with the increasing demands of the colonies on the one hand, and the utter ruin of Spanish industry on the other, the dependence of the Seville export commerce upon foreign manufactures was complete. They supplied five sixths of the cargoes of the outbound fleets. It was a time, therefore, of almost universal contraband trade; and as the government seemed powerless to stop it without threatening the very continuance of communications with its American empire, it recompensed itself by imposing heavy fines or " indultos." It was also furnished, incidentally, with a convenient instrument of retaliation upon unfriendly nations. Veitia Linaje, as treasurer of the India House, took part in proceedings of this nature in 1667, on the occasion of the outbreak of war with France. As a measure

[1] Encinas, i, p. 447.
[2] Veitia Linaje, lib. i, cap. 18, par. 23; cap. 31, par. 9; *Recop.*, lib. ix, tit. 27, ley 3.
[3] *Colecc. de doc.*, 2d ser., x, p. 516; Encinas, i, pp. 442, 447.

of reprisal, all goods consigned to Frenchmen on the galleons arriving in that year were to be seized; and to make sure of their quarry, the Council decided to place immediately on each of the vessels a person of high rank to take the business in hand. For the purpose were chosen seven of the ranking members of the Casa and four from the Audiencia of Seville, and the president was empowered to add as many subordinate officers as he deemed advisable. When the merchants realized what preparations were being made for the reception of the galleons, they came forward with a composition or indult of 200,000 pesos. And in addition, says Veitia Linaje, this unwonted zeal resulted in the declaration or " manifestación " of more unregistered silver than ever before in the history of the Casa.[1]

On the other hand, in that age when all Europe was dominated by the aggressive spirit of Louis XIV, French squadrons sometimes appeared off Cadiz at the time the American fleets were expected to sail or arrive, to suggest circumspection on the part of the Spanish government. Under the protection of French cannon — for it amounted to that — Frenchmen were free to transgress the law of the country, either embarking their merchandise on the galleons or abstracting from them bullion for export abroad. And sometimes the French king even threatened to let loose upon the Spaniards in the West Indies the buccaneers and pirates of that region, if their government put any obstacle in the way of this clandestine commerce. In the instructions to the Marquis of Villars, appointed ambassador to Madrid in 1679, we read:

> Et, comme, sur l'exécution de tous les points contenus en la présente instruction, Sa Majesté est persuadée qu'il faut toujours qu'outre les raisons de justice, d'équité et l'exécution des traités, les Espagnols connaissent qu'elle est toujours en état de se faire faire raison par sa puissance, lorsqu'ils ne la veulent pas faire. Sa Majesté veut que ledit marquis de Villars soit informé qu'elle tiendra toujours en mer de fortes escadres de vaisseaux, sur les côtes de son royaume et d'Espagne, et même dans les îles de l'Amérique et dans le golfe du Mexique, lesquelles paraîtront souvent, soit aux rades de

---

[1] Veitia Linaje, lib. ii, cap. 18, par. 11. According to a French memoir, the galleons arriving at Cadiz in 1682 brought from America 22,809,000 pesos. Of this sum, $2\frac{1}{2}$ millions went to France, $2\frac{1}{2}$ to England, $3\frac{1}{2}$ to Holland, and $4\frac{1}{2}$ to Genoa, altogether 13 millions. Dahlgren, *Les relations commerciales*, etc., i, p. 77, note 3.

Cadix, lors du départ ou du retour des galions, soit sur leur route, lorsqu'ils partiront des ports de l'Amérique, afin que Sa Majesté puisse prendre les résolutions qu'elle estimera necessaires au bien de son service.[1]

The most serious and widespread development of contraband trade, however, was in merchandise introduced into the colonies directly from foreign markets. Portuguese, French, Dutch and other interlopers smuggled their cargoes into the West Indies, through the closed port of Buenos Aires, or even to the Pacific shores of Spanish America. The illicit trader was eagerly welcomed by the colonists, for he supplied their needs at reasonable prices, gave them an opportunity of enriching themselves and of adding to the comforts and luxuries of living. Two circumstances combined to make this commerce easy. One was the great length of sparsely settled coast on both the Atlantic and the Pacific sides of the continent, effective surveillance over which was beyond the resources of any nation in that era. The other was the venality of Spanish governors in the ports themselves. Apparently they often tolerated or even encouraged the traffic, on the plea that the necessities of the colonists demanded it. They not only accepted bribes, but engaged in the buying and selling of contraband articles.

This interlopers' trade had its inception very early, almost as soon as the Spaniards were well established in the New World. The exploitation of a virgin continent appealed from the first to adventurous spirits outside the Iberian kingdoms. Not only were French and English mariners exploring the more northern shores of the American continent, but merchants sailed westward to brave Spanish arrogance, and perhaps to compel a trade with the white settlers. As early as 1527, an English vessel appeared in the

[1] Dahlgren, *op. cit.*, pp. 83 f. See also the instructions of Louis XIV to the Comte d'Estrees, April 1, 1680, printed by Margry. The French admiral was to visit all the Spanish ports in the West Indies, especially Cartagena and San Domingo; and to be always informed of the situation and advantages of these ports, and of the facilities and difficulties to be met in case of attack upon them; so that the Spaniards might realize that if they failed to do justice to the French merchants on the return of the galleons, His Majesty was always ready to force them to do so, either by attacking these galleons, or by capturing one of their West Indian ports.

neighborhood of Hispaniola and Porto Rico, and three years later William Hawkins, father of the more famous John Hawkins, sailed to Brazil from the coast of Guinea to traffic with the natives. These were rather isolated English voyages, for not till the second half of the century did John Hawkins, Drake, Winter, Knollys, Clifford, and the rest make a practice of resorting to the Spanish Indies; and then they came rather as privateers than as peaceful traders. But French, and especially Portuguese, interlopers were already busy in the time of Charles V.

The greater strictness toward foreigners initiated by Philip II was soon reflected in threats and in legislation directed against these intruders. A cédula of November, 1560, informed royal officials in Cuba that several vessels had set out from France with cloths to be sold in America, and that the Crown had information of ships sailing from other regions on a similar errand.[1] In 1563 the king complained to the audiencia of San Domingo because cargoes from Portugal and other foreign countries were received in Hispaniola and elsewhere in the West Indies, and permitted by the judges to be exchanged for gold, silver, and other colonial products. The vessels sometimes pretended that they were bound for Brazil, and driven by storm into the Caribbean. The changed attitude of the Spanish government John Hawkins discovered to his cost on his first slaver's voyage in 1562-63. He disposed of two thirds of his shipload of 300 blacks to the colonists at San Domingo, and as neither they nor Hawkins anticipated any serious displeasure on the part of the Crown, the remaining 100 slaves were left as a deposit with the authorities of the island. Hawkins invested the proceeds in hides, half of which he sent in Spanish bottoms to Cadiz in the care of his partner, Thomas Hampton, while he returned with the rest to England. Philip, however, did not for a moment tolerate this intrusion of the English upon his preserves. On Hampton's arrival in Spain, his cargo was confiscated, and he himself narrowly escaped the Inquisition. The slaves left in Hispaniola were forfeited, and Hawkins, though he "cursed, threatened and implored," could not obtain a farthing for his lost hides and negroes.

[1] Encinas, i, p. 446.

The region of the Rio de la Plata, far from the beaten paths of trans-Atlantic commerce, became one of the favorite haunts of the interloper. The governor of Buenos Aires, in a letter to the king in 1599, gives an illuminating account of the appearance in the river of what was apparently a Dutch merchantman from Amsterdam armed with twenty guns. The governor thought that the vessel was bound for Peru, and had put in for provisions. It was in fact one of a fleet of five which had sailed in June, 1598, from Holland for the Pacific coast of South America. Its captain sought leave to exchange some merchandise for products of the country. But the Spaniard, in view of the scarcity in the colony, and in spite of royal orders that no ship be admitted except from Seville, urged that the entire cargo be put ashore at once, after which, and the payment of customs, traffic might begin. As the Dutchman insisted that the operation be carried out gradually, he was taken prisoner with eight of his crew. After a month and a half of negotiation with those still on board the ship, and of vain strategems on the part of the colonists to take it by assault, the vessel sailed away with all of its cargo, abandoning the captain and his companions to the Spaniards.[1]

It is said that at the beginning of the seventeenth century, as many as 200 ships sailed each year from Portugal with cargoes of silks, cloths, and woolens intended for the Pacific provinces of Spanish America. The Portuguese secured these articles from English, Flemish or French looms, laded them at Oporto or Lisbon, ran the vessels to Brazil and up the Rio de la Plata as far as navigation permitted, and then transported the goods overland through what are now the Argentine and Bolivia into Chile, Peru, and even as far as Lima.[2] Spanish merchants in Peru kept agents in Brazil as well as at Seville, and so many Portuguese, most of them converted Jews, found their way to Lima that in 1636 they were said to control the retail trade of the city.[3] As a natural corollary, the route through Buenos Aires and Brazil became one of the principal channels for the fraudulent export of the precious

[1] Madero, *Historia del puerto de Buenos Aires*, i, pp. 298 f.
[2] Weiss, *L'Espagne depuis Philippe II jusqu'aux Bourbons*, ii, p. 226.
[3] Medina, *Inquisición en Chile*, ii, pp. 96 ff.; Lea, *Inquisition in the Spanish Dependencies*, pp. 425 ff.

metals. Repeatedly in the course of the seventeenth century, the Suprema urged the creation of a tribunal of the Inquisition at Buenos Aires, to keep out the heretic trader; and in 1663 a royal audiencia was established on the Rio de la Plata, in the hope of restraining this illicit traffic, but with no visible success, for it was abolished a decade later.

The possession of asientos by foreigners for the supply of negroes to the Spanish colonies also facilitated contraband trade. For, given the privilege of entering American ports with shiploads of blacks from Africa, the asentistas often found opportunity for introducing merchandise as well, and generally without the least obstacle. It was a precedent which the English were not slow to follow when they secured the privilege of the Asiento at Utrecht in 1713.

The second quarter of the seventeenth century opened a new era, moreover, in the history of the West Indies. Before that time, French, English, and Dutch had resorted to tropical America as corsairs or as merchant interlopers from Europe. They often combined the two callings. From 1625 onward, they came as permanent colonizers. They established themselves on most of the smaller islands, which had been wholly neglected by the Spaniards — Barbadoes, St. Kitts, Martinique, Curaçoa, etc. — forming centres of trade and population in the very heart of the Spanish seas. These islands, "easy to settle, easy to depopulate and to repeople, attractive not only on account of their own wealth, but also as a starting-point for the vast and rich continent off which they lie," were indeed to become the pawns in a game of trade and diplomacy which continued for one hundred and fifty years. And from them the foreigner prepared to capture the commerce of the Caribbean.

In this region, the ubiquitous Dutch trader was especially in evidence. With headquarters on the tiny, desert island of Curaçoa, close to the South American coast, he trafficked with impunity with all the Venezuela region, and played the rôle of carrier between the Spanish colonies and English and French settlements in the Lesser Antilles. In 1600 the governor of Cumaná had suggested to the king, as a means of keeping Dutch vessels from the neighboring salt pans of Araya, the ingenious scheme of poisoning the salt. The advice, it seems, was not followed, but a few years later, in 1605, a Spanish armada of fourteen galleons surprised and burnt nineteen Dutch ships found loading salt, and murdered most of the prisoners. To Rio de la Hacha, Maracaibo and La Guayra the Hollanders brought cloth and negroes, in exchange for silver reals, gold dust, emeralds, and pearls. They even had a settlement, with a Protestant church, on Spanish ground near Puerto Cabello. They virtually monopolized the trade in cocoa and tobacco, so that, until the erection of the Carácas Company in the eighteenth century, nearly all the cocoa consumed in Spain passed through their hands, though grown in Spanish possessions. And the Spaniards paid from 50 to 60 per cent more for this commodity than if it had been imported in their own vessels.[1] Alvarez Osorio declared that all the foreign nations together by this clandestine trade in the West Indies secured six times as much of the products of Spanish America as returned on the Seville fleets.

For a few years after the settlement of the Lesser Antilles, the Spaniards, who were then at war with most of their neighbors, made scattered and ineffectual efforts to dislodge the intruders. Usually the armed galleons were detailed, between the arrival and departure of the flotas in the West Indies, to attack one or other of the islands. Thus on September 17, 1629, just before the conclusion of peace with Charles I, D. Fadrique de Toledo, accompanying the combined fleets of that year with an unusually powerful convoy, appeared suddenly at the English island of Nevis, seized eight small vessels in the roadstead, destroyed the fort, burnt the tobacco warehouses, and drove the few defenders into the woods. On the following day he dropped anchor before St. Kitts, and captured or scattered the English and French inhabitants there. The French temporarily evacuated the island and sailed for Antigua; but of the English some 550 were carried to Cartagena and Havana and thence shipped to England, and all the rest fled to the mountains and woods.[2] Within three months,

[1] B. M., Add. Mss. 13,987, fol. 205.
[2] *Calendar of State Papers*, colonial series, i, pp. 102–119; Fernandez Duro, *Armada Española*, iv, p. 109; B. M., Add. Mss. 13,964, fol. 296.

however, the settlers had returned and reëstablished the colony. A similar raid was undertaken in the summer of 1633 by the New Spain fleet, which after a week's siege and bombardment captured the Dutch stronghold on St. Martin, and left in charge a Spanish garrison of 250 men. According to the naval historian, Fernandez Duro, there were seventeen galleons in Toledo's armament and twenty-four in that of 1633; which would seem to indicate a healthy respect for the puny settlements against which they were directed.

Old Providence and the adjacent Henrietta, situated close to the Mosquito coast, were peculiarly exposed to Spanish attack; while near the north shore of Hispaniola the island of Tortuga, colonized by the same English company, suffered repeatedly from the assaults of its hostile neighbor. In consequence of an unsuccessful attack upon Providence in July, 1635, the Company obtained from the English king the liberty " to right themselves " by making reprisals, and thereafter Philip IV was all the more intent upon destroying the plantation. In the early summer of 1641, the general of the galleons, D. Francisco Diaz Pimienta, with twelve sail and 2000 men, fell upon the colony, razed the forts and carried off all the English, about 770 in number, together with forty cannon and half a million of plunder.[1] It was just ten years later that a force of 800 men from Porto Rico invaded Santa Cruz, killed the English governor and more than 100 settlers, seized two ships in the harbor and pillaged and burnt most of the plantations. The rest of the inhabitants escaped to the woods, and after the departure of the Spaniards deserted the colony for St. Kitts and other islands.[2]

In the second half of the century, after the English were established upon Jamaica, although schemes of aggression were occasionally discussed in the India Council, the Spanish power was too weak, and its foes too firmly rooted in the Caribbean, to make such efforts practicable. The Council, without doubt, so far as it was able, saw jealously to the enforcement of the laws. The president of San Domingo, D. Felix de Cunega, the governors of

---

[1] B. M., Add. Mss. 36,323, no. 10; Fernandez Duro, *op. cit.*, iv, p. 339.
[2] Rawlinson Mss. (Bodleian Library, Oxford), A31, fol. 121; A32, fol. 297.

Buenos Aires, Cartagena, and Cuba, were removed for admitting Dutch and other traders from the northern nations into their ports. Yet contraband trade was more flourishing than ever, and in 1662 the galleons, after an interruption of two years, still found their market so well provided with merchandise that they were forced to return without disposing of a great part of their cargoes.[1]

The French Jesuit, Labat, who visited the West Indies at the close of the seventeenth century, has left us an account of the methods adopted by the interloper in his day, methods doubtless in vogue for one hundred and fifty years earlier. When a vessel wished to enter an American port to trade, the captain sent a polite note to the governor accompanied by a considerable gift, alleging that provisions had run low, or that the ship had sprung a leak or lost a mast. He usually obtained permission to come in, unload and put the ship in a seaworthy condition. All the formalities were minutely observed. The cargo was shut up in a storehouse, and the doors sealed. But there was always found another door unsealed, and through this goods were abstracted during the night, and coin, hides, cocoa, or bars of gold or silver substituted. When the vessel was repaired to the captain's satisfaction, it was reloaded and sailed away.

There was also along the shores of the Caribbean a less elaborate commerce called " sloop-trade "; for it was generally managed by smaller boats, which were able to negotiate the reefs and shoals and ran up the rivers and creeks. They hovered near some secluded spot, and informed the inhabitants of their presence by firing a shot from a cannon. Often a larger ship was concealed outside, behind a headland, and made its trade by means of the smaller craft. The inhabitants, usually in disguise, came off in canoes by night. The interlopers, however, were always on their guard against these visitors, and admitted only a few at a time; for if the Spaniards found that they outnumbered the crew, and a favorable opportunity presented, they were quite ready to attempt the vessel.[2]

[1] A. de I., 153. 6. 19.
[2] Haring, *The Buccaneers in the West Indies in the Seventeenth Century*, pp. 26 f.

A flood of restrictions, a jealous monopoly, on the one hand — on the other, a flourishing contraband trade of outsiders, aliens, either by way of Seville and Cadiz, or directly with ports in the colonies — such is the story of Spanish-American commerce in the sixteenth and the seventeenth centuries. The Crown of Castile sought to extend Spanish power, and monopolize all the treasure of the Indies, by means of a rigid and complicated commercial system. Yet in the end, it saw the trade of the New World pass into the hands of its rivals, its marine reduced to a shadow of its former strength, crews and vessels supplied by merchants from foreign lands, and its riches diverted at their very source.

## CHAPTER VI

### THE SPANISH MONOPOLY

ALTHOUGH the tendency to an exclusive and restrictive organization of colonial trade appeared so early and continued so persistently in Spain, there was little systematic interference with American industry such as happened in the dependencies of most European peoples in the mercantilist era. Foreigners were barred with fair consistency, and for what were in great measure economic reasons. To reserve what grew to be the magnificent profits of this traffic to the king or to his subjects, and above all to prevent the leakage of American gold and silver into foreign countries, were clearly among the principal motives of the Crown. But the metropolis, while maintaining its privilege of alone supplying European commodities, did not insist that the colonists take these commodities in preference to products of their own manufacture. We find some prohibitions, but we also find the sovereigns ready to encourage and protect industrial and agricultural activities.

The attitude of the government was, to be sure, excessively paternalistic. It gave, and it took away, what seem today the most obvious rights of the subject. Humboldt somewhere observes that the Spanish rulers, in assuming the title of Kings of the Indies, regarded these distant possessions as the private appanage of the Crown of Castile, rather than as colonies in the sense attached to that word by other nations. This observation is confirmed by all the American legislation of Ferdinand and Isabella. The royal absolutism which they did so much to create in the Spanish peninsula found in the western hemisphere a field for complete and logical self-expression, unhampered by any of the traditions and customs of older communities. The fixing of prices, the ferry charge on the river at San Domingo, the right to own fishing boats, the farming of monopolies, the providing of ornaments for the churches, these and countless similar matters remained with the Crown in Spain for decision. In the instructions to the governor of Hispaniola, dated March 20, 1503, the colonists are given permission to import from Spain cattle and foodstuffs necessary for their subsistence, but not for purposes of trade; and they are specifically forbidden to introduce wine, clothing, shoes and hardware, a monopoly of which is reserved to the Crown. A decree of 1511 conferred upon the settlers of Porto Rico the right to trade with their immediate neighbor, Hispaniola, and with the home-country; and another two years later conceded to Hispaniola a similar privilege with the new settlements on the isthmus of Darién. In 1516 the Hieronymite fathers, entrusted for the moment with the government of the Indies, received orders to allow the inhabitants of Cuba to build and own vessels for trade with other islands. An edict of Charles V, in 1545, directed colonial governors to encourage the natives to raise hemp and flax. But later their cultivation was in certain provinces forbidden, while the manufacture of silk, cotton, and woolen textiles was permitted in Peru and New Spain. These are a few of many instances of paternal interference and control; but they furnish no evidence of the systematic application of mercantilist ideas.

The interest of Isabella and her immediate successors in the agricultural development of the new lands has often been dwelt upon. They introduced from Europe and the Canaries the domestic animals, cereals, vegetables, and fruits which flourished in the temperate regions of the upper plateaus; and also tropical and sub-tropical plants belonging to the moister and hotter lowlands, such as the orange, sugar cane (and later), coffee and rice. All these added vastly to the agricultural possibilities of the young colonies, while the imported animals — cattle, swine, horses, and sheep — increased with extraordinary rapidity, and often ran wild over what were formerly grassy wastes. A considerable number of plants cultivated by the indigenes — cocoa, cotton, paprika, maize — were also taken over by the Spaniards, and produced in such quantities as to become, next to sugar, leather, and woods, the most important articles of export.

The government of Charles V was deeply concerned about the welfare of the larger West Indian Islands, Cuba, Hispaniola,

Jamaica and Porto Rico; for, as already related, with the destruction of native labor and the lure of richer regions subdued on the continent, they were declining rapidly in population and wealth. The growing of sugar cane was especially fostered, and workmen were sent over from the Canaries skilled in the construction of machinery for grinding the cane.[1] Repeated attempts were made early in the century to acclimatize wheat, though without success. In 1520 materials needed in the construction of sugar works were excused from the payment of import duty; nine years later, such works on Hispaniola were exempted from seizure for debt; and in 1531 the whole of the royal income from Cuba was devoted to the purchase of negroes to be distributed among the cultivators of the island on long-term payments.[2] Frequently in later years, the rate of the almojarifazgo or of the avería was reduced on commodities exported by the islanders to Spain.

The Spanish Crown, moreover, did more than foster the production of raw materials not competing with metropolitan industries, or primarily necessary for the well-being of the colonies. It also, at least in the time of Charles V, permitted the growth of industries which ranked among the most important of the home country. Ferdinand in 1503, while contemplating a royal monopoly of American trade, had forbidden the production of wine on Hispaniola. But in 1519 the Casa de Contratación was instructed to send with every ship sailing for the island a number of vines to be planted there.[3] And in Peru, after the imposition of

[1] Sugar cane, perhaps the most valuable agricultural product of Spanish America in the sixteenth and seventeenth centuries, was carried from the Canaries to the New World by Columbus on his second voyage. According to Las Casas, the first attempt at making sugar on Hispaniola was in 1505 or 1506, while the historian Oviedo claims to have taken the first sample to Spain some ten years later. The planting of cane was begun on a large scale in Hispaniola about 1520, and within fifteen years more than thirty sugar works were set up. From Hispaniola it was carried to Cuba and the mainland, but the industry in Cuba was not on its feet for another hundred years, and Hispaniola remained for some time the principal source of the West Indian supply. Gómara, writing in the middle of the sixteenth century, says that Mexico was already producing so much sugar that it was exported from Vera Cruz and Acapulco to Spain and Peru.

[2] *Colecc. de doc.*, 2d ser., iv, p. 196; A. de I., Patr. 2. 6. 1, ramo 8; *American Historical Review*, xxi, p. 755.

[3] A. de I., 139. 1. 6, lib. 8, fol. 138.

almojarifazgo at Seville, and the consequent increase in prices, the cultivation of the grape and olive was taken up by the colonists, for many years without governmental hindrance. By Philip II the viceroy, D. Francisco de Toledo, who went out in 1569, was secretly instructed to prevent the further planting of vines, but he did little or nothing to that end. Near the close of the sixteenth century, and in after years, it was proposed that the production of Peruvian wine be forbidden altogether, in order to eliminate competition with that brought on the fleets from Europe. The vineyards, however, had been planted with the tacit consent of the king, and to destroy them would have entailed infinite hardship and injustice. Various alternatives were suggested: that the Indians be permitted to use wine instead of chicha, and so consume the local product; that all Peruvian wine put up for sale be bought by the royal exchequer; that any extension of the industry be prohibited under severe penalties.[1] This last was always the remedy adopted. In 1614 and 1615 it was forbidden to export oil or wine to Panama or Guatemala, regions which could be supplied from Spain. A tax of 2 per cent was also imposed after 1595 on wine produced and bottled in the viceroyalty, and by ordinances of 1601 and 1609 the use of forced native labor was forbidden. Yet vineyards and olive plantations continued in Peru, and in spite of reiterated decrees, increased in area and importance.

The manufacture of textiles — so attentively nurtured in Spain by Ferdinand and Isabella, and showing such promise till destroyed by the epileptic policy of their successors — was more widely developed in the New World than any other industry. In October, 1537, Martin Cortes, son of the Conquistador, entered into an agreement with the viceroy of New Spain, in consideration of certain privileges, to plant within fifteen years 100,000 mulberry trees in the districts of Guajocingo, Cholula, and Tlascala, for the production of silk.[2] The licentiate Laisa, deputy from the city of Mexico, reported to the Council of the Indies in 1543 that there were already in Mexico more than forty establishments for

---

[1] B. M., Add. Mss. 13,975, fol. 219; *Colecc. de España*, lii, p. 565; Solórzano, *Polit. Ind.*, lib. ii, cap. 9.

[2] *Colecc. de doc.*, 1st ser., xii, p. 563.

the manufacture of velvets, and that the city, hoping to foster so useful an industry, had issued ordinances to insure the quality and regularity of their product.[1] And in 1548 a royal cédula specifically authorized the inhabitants of Puebla de los Ángeles to set up factories for the making of silks, without restriction or impediment of any sort.[2] Henry Hawks, an Englishman who lived five years in New Spain, says in 1572 that the country not only manufactured all sorts of silks — taffetas, satins and velvets — as good in quality as those of Spain, except that the colors were less perfect; but it was well supplied with wool, and produced enough cloth to clothe all the common people and export to Peru. Hats also were made in the colony, better and cheaper than in Spain, and exported to the southern viceroyalty.[3] The cloth industry was officially recognized in Peru by a decree of September, 1565, which provided that " en la fábrica de los paños se guarden en las Indias las leyes y pragmáticas de estos reinos de Castilla."[4] And the present-day republics of Peru and Ecuador still dispute the distinction of having had within their territories the first cloth manufactory of South America. The textiles of the southern viceroyalty were mostly woolens.

Till 1569 the Spanish government apparently left this nascent industry altogether alone. But again with the coming to Peru of Francisco de Toledo, there was a change. Manufactures in the peninsula were palpably decaying, and petitions for assistance were presented by the deputies in the Cortes. Philip II undertook to remedy the situation by what he doubtless considered the most efficacious means at his disposal. Among the secret instructions to Toledo was one to close the textile factories.[5] The new governor, however, on arrival in Peru, testified that he found the demand of the country for such goods far greater than the supply from Spain, since no fleet had been dispatched from Europe for three years; and he disregarded his orders. He published a code of

[1] Cappa, *Estudios críticos acerca de la dominación española en América*, vii, p. 39.
[2] *Recop.*, lib. iv, tit. 26, ley 5.
[3] Hakluyt, *Navigations* (ed. of 1904), ix, p. 378.
[4] *Recop.*, lib. iv, tit. 26, ley 3.
[5] Cappa, *op. cit.*, vii, p. 44.

ordinances to stop the exploitation of Indian workmen, rules which required that they be treated more nearly like free subjects of the Crown, and the wisdom and moderation of which are perhaps his chief title to remembrance. But the entrepreneurs remained free to manufacture cloths in any quantity and quality they desired. This action of Philip would have affected only the production of finer cloths; for it did not apply to establishments run by Indian caciques in the native pueblos. The exception was consistent with Spanish interests, as only the better qualities were produced in Spain, and the Indian factories supplied to the pueblos the means of paying the royal tribute. But it seemed to favor the natives over and above the Spanish and creole manufacturers.

The prohibition was renewed in the instructions to the viceroy, D. Luis de Velasco, in 1595, though in somewhat milder form. Existing factories were to be allowed to continue, even if erected in defiance of previous orders. But no new ones might be created, or old ones enlarged or repaired, without first consulting the Crown.[1] Nevertheless, so many private interests were bound up with the welfare of this industry, and its extension seemed so vital to the prosperity of the Peruvians, that still the viceroys dared not interfere. And the number of establishments continued to increase till toward the middle of the seventeenth century.

In 1601 a decree was promulgated forbidding Spaniards in Peru to employ Indians in any capacity whatsoever in their workshops.[2] But its purpose was to protect the native rather than to hamper the manufacturer. Many stories had come to the ears of the Council of flagrant violations of Toledo's ordinances, and the viceroys themselves complained that it was impossible rigorously to enforce them, or prevent the exploitation of the aborigines by the Peruvian factory owner. The latter, by the new law, were restricted to the use of negroes and half-breeds. Mulattoes and mestizos, however, regarded themselves as of superior race to the indigenes, and their connection with an occupation formerly confined to the latter as a personal degradation. The manufacturers raised a storm of complaint over the higher wages they were forced to pay, and in 1609 the cédula was revoked. Twenty-five

[1] Cappa, *op. cit.*, vii, p. 66.   [2] *Ibid.*, p. 68.

years earlier, in 1584, a memorial to the king had asserted that the fleets, owing to the growth of the wine and woolen industries in Peru, had already lost trade representing an annual return of 200,000 ducats to the royal exchequer.[1]

As an extreme instance of eccentric legislation, may be mentioned the case of Carácas tobacco. In June of 1607 the cultivation of tobacco on the coast of Venezuela was interdicted for ten years; not because it was an article grown in Spain, or not to be encouraged in America, but because the Dutch were accustomed to rendezvous there and engross the entire crop. At that time the use of tobacco was much more general in the northern countries, England, the Lowlands, and Germany, than in Spain; and in 1613 the Spanish governors of Flanders, the Archdukes Albert and Isabel, sought the concession of the Venezuela trade, offering to send three ships each year and supplant the intruders.[2] But the Castilian Crown, rather than permit its exclusivist pretensions to be called into question, preferred to destroy altogether an industry on which the prosperity of the colony chiefly depended. In this particular case, the result was disastrous. The Spaniard was merely cutting off his nose to spite his face. The white planters, having no other means of subsistence left to them, deserted the region, while the wild Indians left behind still cultivated tobacco to sell to the ubiquitous Dutchmen.[3] In 1614 the decree apparently was repealed.

From the foregoing, it is evident that Spanish policy toward colonial industries lacked the clearly defined outlines one associates with the mercantilist ideas of that age. Indeed it is difficult to discover any characteristic " policy " at all, unless it be one of blind opportunism. Sometimes the government put obstacles in the way of American industries, presumably to favor those of the metropolis, but the measures were variable and arbitrary, and often of little effect. Frequently the reasons for restriction were local or transitory, to shield the natives from their conscienceless masters, or to destroy the profits of the foreign interloper.

[1] *Colecc. de España*, civ, p. 278.
[2] A. de I., 140. 3. 9.
[3] B. M., Add. Mss. 13,975, no. 47; 36,319, nos. 20, 23; 36,320, nos. 3, 5.

Cappa cites a petition of the Cortes of Valladolid in 1548 as indication that among Spanish manufacturers at that time there was no opposition to the rise of competing industries in the Indies. The petition urged that it would be to the interest of the consumer in Spain that the colonies supply themselves with their own manufactured goods.[1] The deputies were attempting to handle a situation arising out of the increase in prices during the previous decade. They not only suggested prohibiting the export of manufactures to America, but petitioned the Emperor to permit the introduction into Spain of cheap cloths from abroad. Certainly such action revealed little appreciation of mercantilist theories. The government, however, acceded to these naïve proposals, and in the following year, to remedy further the scarcity, also forbade the production of the finer qualities in Spain, a blow to one of the most important industries in the kingdom.[2]

The same idiosyncrasies crop up in the time of the Philips. In a vain effort to check the rising cost of living, Spanish export trade was hampered, and the manufactures from other countries allowed free play. The articles unlawful for export included gold and silver, it is true, but they also comprised cereals, cattle, copper, and textiles. In the eighteenth century, under the more enlightened regime of the Bourbons, mercantile theories doubtless had more weight in the councils of the government; in the sixteenth and seventeenth, it is difficult to see the application of any intelligent system.

The Spanish Crown may be said to have kept the colonies, in an indirect way, peculiarly in a state of dependence upon the home country. It transferred to these frontier regions the aristocratic and ecclesiastical organization of a much older and more sophisticated community. The land was divided into great estates granted to the families of conquistadores, to favorites at court, or to the cathedrals and monasteries. There grew up, therefore, on the one hand, a numerous and privileged nobility, which congregated mostly in the larger towns, and set the rest of the inhabi-

---

[1] Cappa, *op. cit.*, vii, p. 19.
[2] Bernays, "Zur inneren Entwicklung Castiliens unter Karl V." (*Deutsche Zeitschrift für Geschichtswissenschaft*, 1889), p. 412.

tants a pernicious example of luxury and idleness; on the other, a powerfully endowed church, which, while it did some splendid service in converting the Indians, engrossed much of the land in mortmain, and filled the New World with thousands of parasitic, and often licentious, friars. As early as 1509, a pragmatic had to be issued to the colonists on Hispaniola, prohibiting expenditure for silks, and other extravagances in dress. The sumptuary decree was extended in 1513 to Castilla del Oro, the first region on the mainland permanently settled by white men, and to other provinces as they were added to Spain's ultramarine empire.

The Church from an economic point of view was especially oppressive. From the year 1501 the payment of tithes was required in all the colonies, and the mode of collection regulated by law.[1] All products of the soil, as well as cattle and sheep, came within the scope of this tax, and its effect must have been very prejudicial to the development of a struggling agricultural society. The estates of the Church, too, soon expanded to an incredible degree. In a pioneer country, where lands are to be cleared and reduced to cultivation, comparatively small holdings and the stimulus of private ownership are generally needed to secure the most profitable and economical use of the soil. If estates are large, the proprietor can obtain ample returns from a careful tillage of a relatively small part, or from the primitive cultivation of larger areas. There is little incentive to improvements in agriculture. Such were the conditions in Spanish America, not only on the ecclesiastical estates, but also on those of the great landed families; though on the former the outlook was more hopeless because of the " dead hand " of the Church. Land was tilled with servile or semiservile labor, and by primitive methods, and great areas were entirely neglected. In 1535 the Crown had declared that estates in New Spain might be bestowed on conquistadores and other early settlers only with the proviso that they were never sold to a church or monastery. And another decree of the same year forbade the establishment of monasteries except with the express permission of the king, or of the viceroy in his name.[2]

[1] *Colecc. de doc.*, 1st ser., xxxiv, p. 22; 2d ser., v, p. 23; Encinas, i, pp. 179 f.
[2] *Colecc. de doc.*, 2d ser., x, pp. 298, 302.

But while the Crown took these early precautions, in the long run it showed little disposition to restrain the clergy's growing wealth and influence. Philip III, in a letter to the viceroy of Peru in 1620, remarked that the convents in Lima covered more ground than all the rest of the city. And Humboldt, when he visited Mexico at the beginning of the nineteenth century, found in some of the provinces as much as 80 per cent of the landed property in the control of the Church.[1]

Furthermore, the men who came to subdue and colonize the new continent were frequently of a type little suited to such an endeavor. Sober, but not very industrious, distracted for generations by national and religious conflict from work in the fields, the Spaniards of that day sought in the Indies occupations more lucrative or less laborious than farming and trade. Although displaying qualities of resistance and heroism, they too often expected to pursue beyond the seas a life free from exertion, using native labor or blacks from Africa to cultivate the ground and work the mines of gold and silver. Velasco wrote, about 1574:

> Los españoles en aquellas provincias serian muchos más de los que son, si se diese licencia para pasar á todos los que la quisiesen; pero comunamente se han inclinado parar destos reynos á aquellos los hombres enemigos del trabajo, y de animos y espíritus levantados, y con codicia mas de enriquecerse brevemente que de perpetuarse en la tierra, no contentos con tener en ella segura la comida y el vestido, que á ninguno en aquellas partes les puede faltar con una mediana diligencia en llegando á ellas, siquiera sean oficiales ó labradores, siquiera no lo sean, olvidados de si se alzan á mayores, y se andan ociosos y vagamundos por la tierra, hechos pretensores de oficios y repartimientos. . . .[2]

The Indians of many regions, consequently, instead of being protected and civilized, were reduced to virtual serfdom, and confined to a laborious routine for which they had neither the aptitude nor the strength. The government at home, as we have seen, sometimes showed interest in their welfare, but it was too distant to interfere effectively in their behalf. It is, in fact, very doubtful if the mass of the natives were much better off after, than before, the conquest. They lived in their own villages, separated from

---

[1] P. P. Leroy Beaulieu, *De la colonisation chez les peuples modernes*, p. 22.
[2] Lopez de Velasco, *Geografía y descripción universal de las Indias*, p. 36.

the whites, and in deepest ignorance. Of the blessings of European civilization they had scarcely any noteworthy share. Their lot had perhaps been slightly ameliorated by the introduction of domestic animals, plants, and vegetables from the east; but they also received many diseases. And almost all of their ancient culture was gradually lost. Christianity they had accepted, but many of them retained, as they do to-day, heathen beliefs and practices mingled with the higher religion. In the rural districts, therefore, native modes of building, and often of agriculture too, prevailed. Only houses in the towns, and the chief buildings of the plantations and cloisters, were in the customary south-European style. The cities were those of Spain, the country retained an Indian guise.

Spaniards and creoles remained the real supporters of industry and commerce. Yet toward them the government exhibited a chronic fear and distrust of individual initiative. Self-reliance, independence of thought and action, in the colonists was discouraged, and divisions and factions fostered among them. Progress in scientific knowledge was effectually blocked by the Church, and American presses confined their attention mostly to the production of catechisms, martyrologies and books of pious verse. Virtually all public matters, great or small, had to be referred to Spain for decision, and the higher administrative posts, under the Hapsburgs at least, were universally reserved for Spaniards of European birth.

The general policy of the Crown in Spanish America, therefore, and the character of the colonists themselves, were not calculated to the conditions of a new and unexploited world. The white inhabitants were concentrated in cities, and as emigration was restricted to keep the colonies free from the contamination of heresy and foreigners, the growth of population was slow. The Indians were either serfs on the great estates, or if free, lived by the most primitive agriculture mingled with hunting and fishing. Creole agriculture, in spite of favorable natural conditions and valuable articles of production, reached no very high stage of development. The ancient Indian crafts declined, and while in the cities of the Spaniards some large establishments of a European type arose, most of the manufactures required by the colonists came from Spain.

Certain classes of articles were from the first forbidden to be carried to the Indies. Among the ordinances drawn up for the Casa in 1504, just before Isabella's death, there is one: " Que ninguno pase á las Indias oro ni plata, ni monedas, ni caballos, ni yeguas, ni esclavos, ni armas, ni guanines . . ." without a special license.[1] The rule also appears in a set of instructions delivered in the same year to Nicolás de Ovando.[2] The interdiction of the export of precious metals from Spain, whether as plate, coin or bullion, was a constant maxim of state from the sixteenth century to the eighteenth, just as we find it in England under the Yorkists and Tudors; and it would probably have been enforced against the colonies even if the latter had not discovered so abundant a supply in their own mines. Obedience to the law was evidently difficult to enforce. Merchants and emigrants smuggled jewelry and plate out of the country, in spite of royal pragmatics, and in the summer of 1519 and later, proclamations reiterated the pains and penalties so incurred.

The introduction of slaves into America was doubtless restricted for reasons at first largely of a religious character. While a few bondmen existed in Spain — Guinea negroes acquired from the Portuguese, and Moorish captives from Africa — the institution of slavery was not yet regarded with favor by the Church; and the Catholic Kings, zealous allies of the Spanish clergy, saw no good reason for extending it to their new provinces, especially as it might complicate the supreme task of converting and civilizing the American aborigines. Even after such considerations were thrown by the board, the export of blacks remained a privilege reserved to favorites of the Crown, or to private individuals or companies which paid a handsome royalty on every negro carried over. The government continued to be heedful, however, that slaves of Moorish extraction, or " de levante," were excluded, for fear of perverting the religion of the Christianized Indians. " Esclavos de levante " were those bought in Sardinia or the

---

[1] *Colecc. de doc.*, 2d ser., v, p. 94.  [2] *Ibid.*, 1st ser., xxxi, p. 233.

Balearics, most of whom were either Moorish or Jewish half-breeds, or converted to the Mohammedan faith.[1] The revenues from the negro trade became a large and regular source of income. In the middle of the seventeenth century, 30 ducats per head were paid to the Crown, besides a tax of twenty reals called the Aduanilla. If this obligation could not be discharged at Seville, the rate was 40 ducats and thirty reals after sale in the colonies.[2] In 1665, the annuities to creditors of the exchequer charged upon this revenue amounted to 50,000,000 maravedis.

The early rule against the export of horses and asses is difficult to understand, unless we regard it, with that touching firearms, as a precaution against the possible disorders of unruly spirits in the raw and untamed American communities. There is no mention of horses or arms in the codified ordinances of the Casa printed in 1552, although in Veitia Linaje's time arms, and especially pistols, were again included among the prohibited articles.[3]

A decree of September, 1543, forbade the introduction into the colonies of "libros de romance que traten de materias profanas y fabulosas, y historias fingidas." It left little room for anything except books of a moralistic or religious complexion — "libros tocantes á la religión Cristiana y de virtud," to quote from the ordinances of 1552 — and augured ill for the literary future of Spanish America. No work relating to the New World might be printed in Spain, or sent out to the colonists, without preliminary examination and approval by the Council of the Indies. If unauthorized books were printed in the colonies, they must be collected and shipped to Spain. All writings, of course, had to have the license of the Holy Inquisition. A cédula of January, 1585, required that the stewards (provisores) of bishops or archbishops of

---

[1] Antuñez y Acevedo, pp. 132 f. By a decree of 1563, shipmasters were forbidden to have slaves serving in any capacity on board. After 1572, they might carry two or three Guinea blacks, on giving 50,000 maravedis security per head that they would be brought back to Spain. Veitia Linaje, lib. i, cap. 35, par. 22.

[2] Veitia Linaje, lib. i, cap. 35, par. 8.

[3] *Ibid.*, lib. ii, cap. 16, par. 10. In the seventeenth century, iron from Flanders or Germany, whether manufactured or in bars, was forbidden in the colonies, in order to favor the iron industry of the Biscayan provinces.

maritime cities in America be present with the royal officials at the inspection of ships, to see that they brought no works of a heretical tendency. And any mariner who carried prohibited articles in his vessel without royal license incurred a fine of 50,000 maravedis.[1]

As already explained, a merchant, to engage in the India trade, had to be of Spanish birth, or naturalized and domiciled in the peninsula. As a matter of fact, the lines were drawn much more narrowly. Traffic with America became, to all intents and purposes, the monopoly of a comparatively few commercial houses of Seville. Not only was export confined to this city, and to its subsidiary, Cadiz, but it was made difficult or inconvenient for the small trader to have a direct part in it. From the middle of the sixteenth century, no one might cross the Atlantic to trade, either on his own account or as factor or supercargo, unless he had laded for the voyage merchandise of considerable value. At first probably left to the discretion of the officers of the Casa, by the early years of the seventeenth century the minimum had been definitely fixed at 300,000 maravedis in silver, as appraised for the payment of customs. After 1668 it was reduced to 200,000. But the change was only in appearance, for members of the Consulado, presumably in return for some service to the Crown, had secured the privilege of declaring only two thirds of the value of their goods at the aduana; and it was assumed that if a " register " of 200,000 was presented, the shipment was worth at least 300,000.[2] The original object of such a rule was doubtless to prevent the emigration of persons who represented themselves fraudulently as exporting merchants. The consequence of putting it on a basis of capital invested was practically to confine trade to the wealthier Andalusian firms. In America, too, the importing business was controlled by a few influential houses, which kept their factors at Vera Cruz and Panama, and in their Consulados at Lima and Mexico City enjoyed the same favored treatment as their correspondents in Seville.

[1] Encinas, iv, p. 135; Veitia Linaje, lib. ii, cap. 16, par. 14, 15.
[2] Veitia Linaje, lib. i, cap. 29, par. 10.

It was obviously to the interest of these firms to act in concert, a step which was made easier by the creation of the Consulado. Through the Consulado they could control the character and size of outbound cargoes, and dictate prices at will. In practice, if not in theory, they resembled the exclusive trading companies of the same period in England and Holland. They constituted a perpetual coalition for the exploitation of the public, and in restraint of trade. The effect was to diminish the supply of European goods in America, and of American products in Europe. The colonies especially suffered, for they looked to Europe not only for articles of immediate consumption, but also for the means of production such as iron and steel. They were kept chronically understocked, and the exorbitant prices they had to pay for all foreign commodities, even in the eighteenth and early nineteenth centuries, was one of the most serious obstacles to growth in manufactures, in population and in general well-being.

The decisions of the government during the Hapsburg regime generally tended to the strengthening of this monopoly, and to the maintenance of a close alliance between the Crown and the merchant. In June, 1530, Charles V issued an order allowing Spanish merchants in New Spain to sell goods they imported at any price the market would permit, and forbidding the colonial authorities to impose a fixed schedule or rate.[1] Some twenty-five years later, the Mexican audiencia urged that the prohibition be removed, especially as affecting foodstuffs, the manipulation of which was very grievous to the inhabitants. But Philip II, replying in 1559, sustained his father's ruling.[2] And the Crown continued to support the cause of the merchants, especially after 1574, when the alcabala was collected in Spanish America. Thereafter any check upon monopoly prices decreased the revenues from this tax on sales. As the almojarifazgo was an ad valorem duty, its proceeds were similarly affected. The lawyer, Solórzano, remarks that this protection might be invoked only if the merchant acted honorably, and did not attempt to corner goods or control prices in disservice of the public.[3] But there can be no doubt as to the advantage that accrued to the Seville monopolists.

---

[1] Encinas, i, p. 429; A. de I., Patr. 2. 2. 1/1, no. 36.
[2] Encinas, i, p. 430.   [3] *Polit. Ind.*, lib. vi, cap. 16.

Not until the eighteenth century was an exclusive company, in the more usual form of a single joint-stock organization, given a trial in Spanish-American trade. A project of this sort, to which even foreigners were to be admitted, had been drawn up for Charles II in or about 1672. It was suggested by Manuel de Lira, one of the Council of the Indies, as the only means of restoring Spanish commerce, the decay of which was then complete; but the idea was too radical to find approval among his associates. Similar proposals were made by Alvarez Osorio in his *Extensión Política* in 1687, and in 1705–06, during the War of the Spanish Succession.[1] Eventually in 1714, when the new dynasty was firmly seated on the throne, the Company of Honduras was created to take over the trade with Central America, and in 1728 the Guipuzcoana Company to develop the resources of Venezuela, a region till then almost completely ignored by the Spaniards. Their activity was restricted to comparatively small areas, but perhaps for that very reason, though endowed with a monopoly, their influence was more beneficent than that of the irresponsible firms combined in the Consulado of Seville or Cadiz.

To maintain more readily this restrictive system, legitimate ports of entry for the greater portion of Spanish America were made few and far apart. For New Spain there was the single city of Vera Cruz, while all of South America, except the Caribbean coast, was supplied via the isthmus of Panama and the Pacific. Direct trade through the Strait of Magellan was entirely forbidden. After commerce was confined to the annual fleets, the lesser Caribbean ports and the principal West Indian islands were supplied by small vessels sailing each year in their company. Merchandise allotted to these inferior regions was permitted, except for a short time between 1589 and 1591, to be distributed from one port or island to another. But it had first of all to be disembarked at its original destination, and under no circumstances might it be carried to the major ports of Cartagena, Porto Bello, or Vera Cruz, which were stocked by the galleons or by the Mexican flota.[2]

[1] Bibl. Nat., Mss. Espagne, vol. 152, fol. 81; Antuñez y Acevedo, p. 276.
[2] Veitia Linaje, lib. i, cap. 18, par. 14, 15.

The number and tonnage of these supplementary ships was fixed by law, and the choice of vessels and cargo generally left to the discretion of a proctor or attorney kept in Spain by most American towns and provinces to represent their interests. To San Domingo were usually assigned from two to six ships, and perhaps as many to Havana. Two small vessels sailed to Porto Rico, and as many to Yucatan, to Honduras, to Florida (for a few years early in the seventeenth century), and to the island of Margarita as long as the pearl fisheries endured; one to Trinidad (after 1616), two to Rio de la Hacha (one in the seventeenth century), and after 1607 one small ship to meet the combined needs of Jamaica and Santiago de Cuba.[1] Cumaná, La Guayra and other settlements on tierra firme were similarly provided for. Vessels intended for the Greater Antilles, Honduras and Yucatan sailed with the New Spain fleet; those which supplied Margarita, Trinidad and the South American mainland, with the galleons bound for the isthmus of Panama. All ships going out under convoy of the former, except those for Porto Rico, were expected to rejoin the fleet at Havana for the homeward voyage. Those sailing with the galleons reassembled at Cartagena, to meet them on their return from the isthmus. Porto Rican vessels, being so far to the windward of Havana, were not required to call there. If there were five or six returning from Hispaniola, they were sometimes permitted to form a separate squadron with those of Porto Rico, and sail to Spain alone. From time to time an isolated ship received license to depart for one of these secondary ports in the Indies, but only with the condition that it return under convoy.

Veitia Linaje tells us that one of the most flagrant sources of harm to the India commerce was the practice of "arribadas maliciosas," i. e., trading vessels entering ports not indicated in their licenses with the plea that they were driven in by foul weather or other misfortune, or appearing in America without any license at all on the pretense of sailing under letters of marque. In 1591 the penalty for such deceits was made the same as for sailing apart from the fleets — forfeiture of ship and cargo,

[1] Veitia Linaje, lib. ii, cap. 13.

and ten years in the galleys for the master and pilot. If a ship was really in distress, it could require every reasonable aid and comfort; but it was not permitted to land any of the cargo unless unfit to proceed farther, when the goods were unloaded and put in bond till other freights could be secured to the port of registry. Persons who purchased goods of such vessels were also liable to loss of property and condemnation to the galleys. Unlicensed slave-ships with their cargoes had to be remitted to Spain for judgment by the Council of the Indies.

The " question of Buenos Aires " is one of the most striking examples of the eccentricities of Spanish policy. The La Plata region, to-day the commercial metropolis of South America, and rivalling New York in the variety and volume of its shipping and other mercantile activities, was till near the end of the eighteenth century almost completely closed to the rest of the world.

Buenos Aires as a permanent settlement dates from 1580. Its location, far from the centre of Spanish power in the West Indies, and next door to the Portuguese in Brazil, made an adequate control of trade there extremely difficult. And as it became the object of the Sevillan merchants to prevent European goods from reaching the Pacific coast through any channel save that of the galleons and the Porto Bello fair, from the beginning direct trade with this region without special license seems to have been forbidden, though the actual decrees are wanting. Under the circumstances, the proximity of Brazil was an irresistible temptation to the settlers to secure by illicit trading what was denied them in Spain. And the fact that Portugal was then a dependency of the Spanish Crown did not make such traffic any less unlawful. Fray Francisco de Vitoria, bishop of the interior province of Tucuman, was apparently the first to send a vessel to his Brazilian neighbors. With silver from Potosí he purchased from them a second, and laded the two with sugar, conserves, and merchandise to be disposed of in Tucuman and Upper Peru. The expedition had an unfortunate ending, for on its return to the Rio de la Plata in February, 1587, it fell in with three English ships commanded by Thomas Cavendish on their way to the Pacific. The Spaniards were robbed of all their cargo, and to preclude their giving an alarm, compelled to sail away with the corsairs for a space of twenty-nine days, after which they returned to Buenos Aires.[1] In the following year, the colonists exported to Brazil flour to the value of about 3500 ducats, and imported over 6000 ducats worth of merchandise. And in spite of royal commands, the governors tolerated the introduction of slaves and other commodities, in exchange for the products of the country, wheat, hides, wool, and tallow.

This region could not hope to prosper, however, so long as it was dependent solely upon an irregular commerce of this sort. A new governor, Diego Rodriguez de Valdes y de la Banda, who arrived at Buenos Aires in January, 1599, reported the conditions there as very miserable. He wrote to the king that for years past not a single vessel had come from Spain, and that the settlers, while they had an abundance of beef and a few vegetables, lacked all the other necessaries of civilized life. Many went about covered with skins, like the Indians. European articles imported via Panama and Peru cost from 800 to 1000 per cent more than in the peninsula, and there was no money with which to buy them. The treasury did not contain a real. He urged the need of opening the port to Brazilian trade, and represented that the province could easily consume 60,000 ducats worth of goods a year.[2]

As a result of this and other appeals, in August, 1602, Philip III accorded to the inhabitants of La Plata for six years the privilege of exporting annually in their own vessels, to Brazil, Guinea " y otras yslas circunvecinas de vassallos Mios," 2000 bushels of grain, 500 quarters of tallow and 25 tons of jerked beef. They might bring back any commodities they required, provided the goods were not reëxported to another part of the Spanish Indies. But immigration and the introduction of slaves was stringently forbidden, as well as direct trade with Spain.[3] Already in 1600 and 1601 the king, and his viceroy at Lima, had published orders repeating the ban on trade of Peruvian merchants through

---

[1] Madero, *Historia del puerto de Buenos Aires*, i, p. 259 (Letters of Rodrigo de Zárate and the treasurer Montalvo, 1587).
[2] *Ibid.*, pp. 295 f.     [3] *Colecc. de doc.*, 1st ser., xviii, p. 323.

Buenos Aires and Brazil, and forbidding persons to go to Spain by that route.[1] Indeed the privilege of Buenos Aires was interpreted in so narrow a sense that not even the contiguous region of Tucuman was allowed to share in it, as becomes clear in a later decree of 1606.[2]

Whether the concession was renewed at the end of the six years is uncertain. We only know that the settlers petitioned to have it made perpetual, and unlimited as to the character of ships and exports. To this the Consulado of Seville steadfastly opposed its objections. An open port at Buenos Aires would create a wider door for the fraudulent extraction of Peruvian gold and silver. It would decrease the tonnage of the galleons, already greatly diminished, and make the annual sailing of the fleets impossible. For the monopolists naïvely admitted that freights and other charges would be cheaper by way of the Rio de la Plata.

In September, 1618, therefore, the older policy was renewed, and the inhabitants of Buenos Aires restricted to the miserable allowance of two vessels a year, of not over one hundred tons each. Of the scant importations thus possible, a part might be carried overland to Peru, on payment at Córdoba on the frontiers of a customs duty of 50 per cent, over and above the regular almojarifazgo and avería already imposed at Seville and Buenos Aires.[3] It was a bounty not likely to be appreciated by the La Plata settlers.

Time and time again in the seventeenth century, the colonists begged for an outlet for their products, and as often the vested interests of the merchants of Seville and Lima proved too strong. The latter, indeed, demanded the retrocession of what little liberty had already been granted. The provinces of La Plata, they maintained, were of slight importance, possessed all that was necessary to human life, and could exist without maritime connections. If they suffered any prejudice, it was as nothing compared with the possible damage to the ancient and noble commerce of the galleons. Moreover, after 1681 the island of San Gabriel, a Portuguese settlement on the Rio de la Plata, was

---

[1] *Colecc. de doc.*, 1st ser., xviii, p. 298; xix, p. 185.
[2] Antuñez y Acevedo, p. 122.   [3] *Recop.*, lib. ix, tit. 14, ley 1.

maintained as a base for clandestine trade, and under cover of the right of importation through the aduana of Córdoba introduced contraband goods into the interior of the continent.

It was, in fact, never found possible to reconcile the prosperity of this region with the existence of that lucrative monopoly, to the comfort and extension of which Spanish legislation was mainly directed. In spite of an abundant and fertile soil, the province remained unpeopled. In 1677, a century after the foundation of Buenos Aires, the Marquis of Barinas pointed out to a junta of the Council of the Indies that there were not 3000 Spaniards in a country which could easily support 100,000 or more.[1] Even after the abolition of the galleons in 1740, when the principal motive for this policy disappeared, the trade of Buenos Aires was left subject to the old limitations. The port remained closed till 1778, when Charles III, among other reforms, placed the Rio de la Plata on an equality with the rest of the Spanish Indies. Meanwhile, except for the trade of the interloper, goods from Europe had to go first to Porto Bello on the isthmus, be carried across to the city of Panama, be reshipped down the Pacific to Callao, and finally transported overland through the mountains of Peru and present-day Bolivia, to Paraguay and the Argentine — an incredibly expensive and burdensome process.

One suspects at times that the Andalusian merchants were not altogether honest in their concern for the suppression of the port of Buenos Aires. The few ships permitted to sail there were laded at Seville by these same commercial houses; and under cover of the permission to send over a limited quantity of goods, perhaps 100,000 pesos a year, on which they paid the customary duties to the king, they embarked several millions on which they paid no duty at all. It was to their interest, therefore, to keep the concession as small as possible. The less that was legally permissible, the wider were their opportunities for illegitimate gain.

Another avenue through which vanished potential profits of the Sevillan merchants was the trade across the Pacific with the Philippine Islands and China. The Philippines had been visited

[1] *Colecc. de doc.*, 1st ser., xix, pp. 239 ff.

first by Magellan in 1521, and formally claimed in the name of the Spanish Crown. Although by the treaty of Saragossa in 1529 Charles V had impliedly relinquished his rights over the archipelago, the fact was later ignored by the Spaniards, and in 1542–43 an unsuccessful attempt made from New Spain by Rui Lopez de Villalobos to take possession of the islands. Permanent settlement by white men, however, dates from the time of Philip II, the achievement of another expedition fitted out on the Mexican coast and commanded by the distinguished conquistador, Miguel Lopez de Legaspi. In 1565 was founded San Miguel on the island of Cebú, to-day the town of Cebú, and in 1571 the city of Manila, which became the Spanish capital. By the time of his death in the following year, Legaspi, although he encountered enormous obstacles, not the least of which was the neglect of the government at home, had explored and pacified a large part of the island territory, and established the colony on a practicable basis.

Legaspi's expedition was also the occasion for another discovery important for the navigation of the Pacific. Until then no one had succeeded in crossing the sea from Asia to America, for all had sailed within the tropics, where the equatorial current and the prevailing east winds, while rendering the voyage from Mexico comparatively easy, paralyzed any attempt to return. One of Legaspi's ships, however, the *San Pedro*, guided by his chief navigator, Andrés de Urdaneta, by taking a northeast course from the Philippines entered a region of variable winds, and was thus enabled to reach the vicinity of the Californian coast, at about the fortieth parallel of latitude, whence the prevailing northwesters carried it easily back to Mexico. The most prominent points on the North American littoral were soon tolerably well known, and so became established the route which the Acapulco galleons were to follow for the next two centuries.

For a score of years after the conquest, the islands were apparently allowed free trade with Spanish possessions, and several fleets sailed directly from the peninsula through the Strait of Magellan. But the storms, the cold, and the ocean currents in that region were too formidable for navigators of the sixteenth century, and communication was soon restricted to the shorter,

## THE SPANISH MONOPOLY 145

safer route across the north Pacific from the shores of New Spain. The Philippines, however, lay close to China, Japan and the Moluccas, with their rich possibilities in the way of trade; and it was soon realized that an opening was afforded for the introduction into Spanish America of oriental fruits, silks, cottons, porcelains and other commodities, to the great advantage of the colonial consumer. The trade began with the establishment of the Spaniards at Manila, where Chinese junks were already accustomed to resort to traffic with the natives, and China fabrics at once undersold those of Europe in Mexico and Peru. As tropical America produced little of which the Orient stood in need, the returns had to be made in silver coin or bullion; and the more silver sent to the East, the less remained for Spain. It was a situation which Spanish merchants could only view with the greatest misgivings. And so there followed the familiar restrictions, limiting commerce, as at Buenos Aires, to a fixed amount annually, and hindering the natural economic development both of the islands and of America.

At first ships had sailed to the East from Callao, Panama and other southern ports, as well as from the shores of New Spain. A Spanish merchant wrote from Panama on August 28, 1590:

> Here I have remained these twenty days, till the shippes goe for the Philipinas. My meaning is to carie my commodities thither; for it is constantly reported, that for every hundred ducats a man shall get six hundred ducats cleerely. We must stay here till it be Christmasse. For in August, September, October and November is it winter here and extreme foule weather upon this coast of Peru, and not navigable to goe to the Philipinas nor any place else in the South Sea. So that at Christmasse the shipes begin to set on their voyage for those places.[1]

Two months earlier, on June 20, Sebastian Biscaino was writing to his father from Mexico City:

> ... foure moneths past, I came from China, and landed in Acapulco, seventy leagues from Mexico, which is the harbor where the ships that goe downe to China lye: and all the marchants of Mexico bring all their Spanish commodities downe to this harbour, to ship them for that country ... here are foure great ships of Mexico of 600 and 800 tunnes a piece, which onely serve to cary our commodities to China and so to returne backe againe. The order is thus ... from hence their two first ships depart at one

[1] Hakluyt, *Navigations* (ed. of 1904), x, p. 176.

time to China: and are thirteen or fourteen moneths returning backe againe. And when these two ships are returned, then the other twaine two moneths after depart from hence . . . I can certifie you of one thing; That 200 ducates in Spanish commodities, and some Flemish wares which I caryed with me thither, I made worth 1400 ducates there in the countrey. So I make account that with those silkes and other commodities which I brought with me from thence to Mexico, I got 2500 ducates by the voyage.[1]

It was this extraordinarily lucrative commerce which the Spanish government undertook to curtail for the benefit of the Seville monopolists. The shipment of Chinese cloths from Mexico to Peru or Tierra Firme was forbidden in 1587, and at about the same time, it seems, direct trade between South America and the Philippines or China was also prohibited. In 1591 Peru was again allowed to import from New Spain, by special license of the viceroy, such oriental goods as were not there required; but the ban upon direct trade with the East was reiterated, and in 1593 and 1595 it was extended to Panama and Guatemala.[2] In 1593 Mexican commerce with the Philippines was confined to two ships a year, neither to exceed 300 tons burden. The two vessels sailed under charter of the royal exchequer, might bring 250,000 pesos in China goods to New Spain, and carry 500,000 in silver back to the islands. This limited commerce, moreover, was declared a monopoly of the Spanish settlers in the archipelago, those in America being debarred from any share, direct or indirect, under severest penalties.[3] Navidad, from which Legaspi sailed in 1564, had remained for some years the principal Mexican port for the Philippine connection. But it was quickly superseded by Acapulco, which had a larger, deeper harbor and better overland communications with Mexico City. And to this port the Eastern trade was confined until the end of the eighteenth century, a town of negroes, Chinese, and mulattoes, which owed its distinction entirely to the annual Philippine fair. Ships usually departed from Manila in the month of June, and by a law of 1633 were required to set sail from Acapulco no later than the end of

---

[1] Hakluyt, *Navigations* (ed. of 1904), x, p. 164.
[2] *Recop.*, lib. ix, tit. 45, ley 5; *Extracto Historial*, p. 247b; Encinas, i, pp. 283 ff.
[3] *Colecc. de España*, lii, p. 565; N.M.C., xviii, no. 55; *Colecc. de doc.*, 1st ser., xix, p. 124; *Recop.*, lib. ix, tit. 45, leyes 1, 6, 9, 10, 12, 15, 44, 68.

the following December. The eastward trip consumed from five to six months, the return no more than three.

The temptation to circumvent such restrictions was, of course, irresistible. Within a decade, the silver withdrawn each year from New Spain to pay for Chinese imports rose to over two million pesos, and the clause forbidding reëxport to Peru remained a dead letter. The effect upon the trade of the Atlantic fleets, and on the king's revenues therefrom, was instantaneous; and this oriental commerce must have been one of the principal causes for the relative decline of that between Spain and America in the seventeenth century. In a code of ordinances published in December, 1604, the king renewed the embargo in a more rigorous form. No oriental goods might be sent to Peru even as a gift, charitable endowment, or for use in divine worship.[1] In 1619 he was petitioned to stop the Acapulco trade altogether, and permit ships to sail only from Spain.[2] And in 1621 it was suggested that the traffic be transferred to Panama, where mercantile interests would be less inclined to its abuse, and supervision by the resident audiencia more strict. The archbishop of Seville, in a letter to the king several years before, had expressed the fear that political independence might grow out of the economic independence stimulated by this commerce; and later in the century the idea was ventured that the Philippines be exchanged for Brazil, in order to forestall such dangerous tendencies.[3] On the other hand, in 1637, 1640 and later years the citizens of Manila petitioned for an increase of the " permiso " conceded to the Philippine trade. The population, and therefore the needs, of the islands had doubled since the beginning of the century, yet the appeals met with no response. And the system established in 1593 continued without change till the time of the Bourbons.[4]

In the East, no Spanish subject was permitted to trade with China directly. That commerce was in the hands of Chinese mer-

[1] *Recop.*, lib. ix, tit. 45, ley 69.
[2] Veitia Linaje, lib. ii, cap. 13, par. 11.
[3] *Colecc. de España*, lii, p. 565; B. M., Add. Mss. 13,975, fol. 219.
[4] After a long controversy between the peninsular authorities and those of Manila, from about 1697 to 1734, in the latter year the " permiso " was raised to 500,000 pesos, with a return value of 1,000,000 pesos.

chants, who formed the major part of Manila's population, and engrossed the local, retail business.[1] It may have been because the Flowery Kingdom was regarded as within the Portuguese sphere defined in the treaty of Tordesillas. But the risks from pirates and typhoons were also confined to the heathen foreigner, while government regulation obviated the danger of monopoly prices. The Spanish inhabitants were officials, priests, landowners, or speculators in the Acapulco trade. The latter, circumscribed as it was, yielded enormous profits. It was managed like a huge government lottery, but a lottery in which each ticket drew a prize.[2] The nature and quantity of goods required were generally arranged beforehand between the Chinese importers and the authorities at Manila; and the right to ship was apportioned among the Spaniards according to their capital or their standing in the community. The capacity of the two vessels (later there was a single galleon of larger dimensions) was measured by taking as a unit a bale of a certain size, and the value which might be shipped in each bale reckoned by dividing the whole number into the total value of the cargo permitted by law. The bales were represented by tickets or "boletas," and their distribution determined at the town hall by a joint board of officials and citizens. Small holders who did not care to take a venture in the voyage disposed of their tickets to merchants, who were often affiliated with importing houses in Mexico City, or to speculators who borrowed money from the religious corporations at 25 or 30 per cent per annum, and frequently purchased as many as two or three hundred. The command of the Acapulco ships was the most coveted office in the gift of the governor. At the end of the seventeenth century it was worth 40,000 pesos, gleaned from commissions, the sale of tickets, and gifts from the merchants, although by law all ship's officers were forbidden to have any share in the trade. The pilot cleared 20,000 pesos, the mates 9000 each. The adventurers expected to realize from 150 to 200 per cent.[3]

[1] *Recop.*, lib. ix, tit. 45, ley 34.
[2] Bourne, introduction to *The Philippine Islands, 1493–1898*, ed. by Robertson and Blair, i.
[3] Martinez de Zuñiga, *Estadismo de las islas Filipinas*, i, pp. 266 ff.

It was an absurd system, which discouraged industrial enterprise among a naturally indolent people. The gains from the Acapulco trade were so easy and considerable that the Spanish inhabitants had little incentive to apply themselves to anything else. Agriculture, mining, and other native industries remained for a long time in a very backward state, and the increase and prosperity of the islands' population were retarded.

There was an import duty at Manila of 3 per cent (after 1606, 6 per cent) on articles from China, and a 2 per cent export duty to New Spain. At Acapulco was collected the usual 10 per cent almojarifazgo. At the beginning of the seventeenth century freights on the royal ships were 40 ducats a ton.

There had been a maritime trade between New Spain and Peru from the early days of the conquest. Peruvian merchants were permitted to carry silver and gold in bars or coin to Guatemalan ports or to Acapulco, and exchange them there for the agricultural products of the northern viceroyalty. With the development of Peruvian plantations, however, the export of wine and oil to the north was forbidden, and after 1587, as we have seen, the importation of China goods was likewise restricted or prohibited. In 1604, and again in 1620, this intercolonial traffic was further limited by the Crown, finally to an annual exchange of the value of 200,000 ducats.[1] But here, too, fraud was the rule. One ship sailed each year from Callao to Acapulco, and it often brought, not 200,000 ducats, but over a million. If there was not sufficient trade at Acapulco, the money was carried to Mexico City, whence the goods purchased were smuggled down to the coast and embarked on the ships by night. For form's sake a few articles, on which the customs were lowest, appeared in the registers. On the return voyage, the vessel called first at Payta or some other harbor, and under cover of darkness discharged the excess cargo, meanwhile sending a messenger overland to Lima to announce their approach. Or the goods were taken off in barks, landed near

---

[1] *Extracto Historial*, pp. 15, 249. It is said to have ruined the cocoa trade of Guayaquil, the price suddenly dropping from 36 pesos to 3 pesos per quarter. González Suárez, *Historia general del Ecuador*, iv, p. 102.

Callao and carried on mules into the capital city. Sometimes they were put into a vessel loaded with lumber from Guayaquil, and entered Callao hidden under the wood from the eyes of the king's officers. The risks were great, but so also were the profits. And it was estimated that in one way or another the Crown lost through this secret trade 200,000 ducats a year in revenue.[1] As the regulations continued to be evaded, in 1634 all trade between New Spain and Peru was interdicted for the space of five years;[2] but although the law remained on the statute books, and was printed in the *Recopilación* of 1681, it was apparently not enforced.

Wine, too, in spite of the pragmatics, was introduced into the provinces of Mexico and Central America. In 1669 the Seville Consulado complained to the king that the Honduras trade was declining, Spanish ships with wine from Europe often finding their market gone, and returning with a loss to their owners. Under such circumstances, with contraband trade flourishing, both in Oriental commodities to Peru and in wine to New Spain, it is not to be wondered at that when the inhabitants of Guatemala or Mexico begged the king for greater freedom of commercial intercourse, as frequently happened in the seventeenth century, the India Council was adamant.

It must be admitted, however, that some of the restrictions upon intercolonial trade were proposed by the colonists themselves. The decree forbidding the importation of Peruvian wines into Guatemala was first suggested, it seems, by the cabildo of Guatemala City, because such wines were stronger than the Spanish, readily distilled into brandy, and very injurious to the natives. And while this same cabildo clamored for free trade with the southern provinces, it was just as insistent that cocoa from Guayaquil should not be introduced to compete with the home product.

The principal reason for the persistence of these irregularities is fairly obvious. Illicit trade between the colonies was possible because colonial officials were easily corrupted, and officials were corruptible because of the pernicious system, already alluded to,

---

[1] B. M., Add. Mss. 13,975, fol. 229.
[2] *Recop.*, lib. ix, tit. 45, ley 78; *Extracto Historial*, p. 15.

of buying and selling government functions. Spaniards, proud as a race, and covetous of public distinctions, displayed these admirable, but perhaps uneconomic, qualities most intensely in the American colonies. Large sums were paid for the proprietorship or life tenure of a post whose salary was comparatively meagre, but the possession of which lent social dignity to the incumbent. Under such a regime, especially when the centre of control lay beyond the seas, slackness and inefficiency in the performance of public duties was almost universal.

The narrative written by Francisco de Toledo of his journey to Lima in 1569 to assume the post of viceroy furnishes interesting testimony to the lax enforcement of the law in the colonies.[1] At Cartagena, where he called with the fleet on his way to Nombre de Dios, he found articles in the customhouse schedule appraised at one third less than their real value in the city. He also discovered Frenchmen sojourning there, who by law were excluded from the Indies, and ordered them to be expelled. At Nombre de Dios, there was a similar discrepancy in the collection of customs; and thirteen or fourteen Spanish merchants were unearthed who had left their wives in Spain, and had neglected to send for them as the statutes required. Being men of wealth, they had made it unprofitable for the local authorities to enforce the king's decrees. Toledo had them arrested and delivered to Nicolás de Cardona, general of the fleet. From the city of Panama, too, unlicensed Spaniards without their wives were apprehended and shipped to Spain.

Public morals in Panama he found in a very bad way. Of two criminal clerics at large, one had concealed several murderers and aided them to escape from the province. The other Toledo had arrested in the house of his mistress. And the viceroy had to give formal warning to the bishop to attend more closely to such matters, and to see that services were regularly held in the cathedral. Because of the great number of mistresses in the city, he ordered the apprehension, so he told the king, of all unmarried men and women, and the banishment of such as the audiencia designated. He also issued regulations for the dress of negroes,

[1] *Colecc. de España*, xciv, p. 225.

Indians, and half-breeds in public places. The laws respecting prohibited books had never been observed, and those found in the hands of booksellers or private individuals he ordered brought before the audiencia. Finally, the judges themselves of this high court were bidden to keep copies of all royal letters and decrees in a separate book apart — something which till then they had consistently neglected to do.

A memorial to Philip III in 1603, from Francisco de la Guerra y de Cespedes, royal factor in Lima, complains of the irregularities in the trade between Peru and Tierra Firme. The armada which carried the king's treasure to Panama, he charged, brought back, concealed between decks, unregistered merchandise for the admiral and his friends. Not only was the Crown defrauded in the way of freights and customs, but because of this traffic the fleet took six months instead of three for the voyage, at the king's expense. The ship captains, formerly chosen by the treasury officers from among practical, experienced men, were now creatures of the viceroy, and connived with the admiral, also a viceregal appointee, to rob the Crown and waste its ships. The captain of the port at Callao, too, under protection of the viceroy's favor, visited merchant vessels leaving or entering the harbor, and manipulated the registers to his own satisfaction; while in the customhouse, goods from Panama or New Spain were appraised below their proper value.[1]

The program suggested by the Marquis of Barinas in the second half of the century for the better protection of the Spanish Indies makes repeated reference to the wide extent of illicit trade between colonial ports. The committee to which his proposals were referred, composed of the Duke of Medinaceli, president of the Council of the Indies, the Marquis of Mancera, formerly viceroy of New Spain, and one or two others conversant with Indian affairs, displayed a remarkable tolerance of the situation. Regardless of the law, they advised that the exchange of provincial products be acquiesced in, and even the trade in China goods, rather than entirely prohibit commercial intercourse.[2] It was a

[1] *Colecc. de España*, lii, p. 484.
[2] *Colecc. de doc.*, 1st ser., xix, p. 239. For the life and character of the Marquis of Barinas, see Fernandez Duro's introduction to vol. xii of the *Colecc. de doc.*, 2d ser.

tolerance probably born of the consciousness that Spain was commercially and politically impotent. For nearly two centuries, she had persisted in an economic policy fatally inconsistent with her powers and resources. Although struggling under tremendous disabilities in Europe, she was still attempting, upon the slender pleas of prior discovery and papal investiture, to reserve half the world to herself. That Seville should try to supply Spanish-American markets with all the foreign merchandise they required, that Castile should undertake to absorb all the metallic riches of the western hemisphere, were stupendous blunders. One city was sufficient to conduct the early trade with Hispaniola and neighboring islands; but its success was no justification for permitting what might have been a temporary provision to become a perpetual right. As it was, restrictions and prohibitions proved to be little avail, and the system of great annual fleets and single ports of call in the end a failure. The galleon trade grew every year weaker, and seemed destined to disappear altogether.

Spain did not invent the colonial system. It had been applied earlier by the Portuguese in the East Indies. It was imitated later by the Dutch, English, and French. It was the policy then current, and believed to be best for the welfare and independence of the state. Nor did Spain's exclusivism greatly exceed that maintained by the other colonial powers. Her distinction rests upon the fact that she had the opportunity to employ it in a vaster theatre than was given to any other nation before the nineteenth century. And when, in the nineteenth century, the British Empire surpassed in extent and resources the former domains of the Hapsburgs, the older, mercantilist regime was already discredited. Spain was no less judicious or disinterested than her neighbors. But, industrially bankrupt at home by reason of mistaken economic ideas, the colonial system in her case was peculiarly disastrous.

Outside Seville, the state of decomposition of the Spanish monarchy was clearly manifest. Not only were the Andalusian merchants losing their grip upon the trade with the colonies, but the inhabitants of the north, in the Biscay provinces, were forced to fall back upon methods of the Middle Ages, in order to save from total ruin the industries by which they had always lived. Failing of support and protection from the central government, they negotiated on their own account with foreign states; with France for the continuation of fishing rights on the Newfoundland banks; with England, to attract merchants to their ports by offering special privileges and exemptions.[1] It was only the advent of a new dynasty which postponed for a hundred years the final dissolution of the Spanish Empire.

[1] Fernandez Duro, *Armada Española*, v, p. 338.

## CHAPTER VII

### THE PRECIOUS METALS

OF all that Spain drew from her vast colonial empire, the most remarkable commodities, in value, in volume, and in influence upon the destinies of the nation, were gold and silver. The New World abounded in other metals, copper, iron, lead, and mercury, but it was to gold and silver, and to mercury because it was useful for the extraction of silver, that the Spaniards devoted all their attention. Iron they imported from Spain, as well as much of the copper required in the colonies. The Indians, who had used gold and silver only for ornament, employed copper in the working of tools and weapons. But with the introduction of iron and steel by the white man, the copper mines were neglected. A few were operated in Chile, in the eastern part of Cuba near Santiago, in Hispaniola in the sixteenth century, and in Venezuela (the mines of Corcorote). Ore from Hungary was preferred, however, as being easier to reduce and in the end less expensive. And in Seville most of the copper used in the casting of artillery came from the German possessions of the Hapsburgs.[1]

Under the Spanish monarchy, as in all medieval countries, mines were included among the regalia of the Crown. In 1501 Ferdinand and Isabella forbade any one to seek or operate mines in the New World without their express permission.[2] By the early part of 1504, this permission had been extended generally to all Spaniards, provided they first registered their claims before the governor and oficiales reales, and swore to bring all the produce of the mines or gold washings to the royal smeltery (casa de fundición) to be assayed, taxed, and stamped. The ordinance was reissued in December, 1526, and its benefits applied also to the

---

[1] In 1655 the Crown paid 25 ducats silver per cwt. for Hungarian copper. At about the same time it cost 29 pesos per cwt. to secure copper from Chile, the source of the best American ore.

[2] *Viajes*, iii, p. 518.

Indians. Only public officers, such as corregidores, governors, alcaldes, their deputies, etc., were specifically excepted.[1] Not till 1584 did Philip II decree that in the future mines were to be the permanent possession of those who discovered them, rather than a concession from the Crown, and as such might be freely sold or otherwise disposed of.

It was never a practice of the Crown to exploit American mines on its own account. The quicksilver mines at Huancavélica in Peru appear to have been the only important exception. Apparently in Porto Rico and in Veragua, immediately after the conquest, there were a few gold deposits worked for the king. But as a rule the interest of the Crown in mines discovered on royal lands was sold, leased, or given away, and Humboldt, when he visited America at the opening of the last century, was able to say that "all the metallic wealth of the Spanish colonies is found in the hands of private individuals."

The king, however, having the ultimate title to all mines within his dominions, from the earliest times required large royalties from his subjects for the privilege of their development. In Spain the Crown's share, at least since the reign of John II, had been two thirds.[2] And this proportion was exacted, at the very first, in the New World.[3] But to hasten the discovery and exploitation of the mineral resources of the colonies, it was quickly reduced. Between 1500 and 1504, in consequence of petitions from the island of Hispaniola, then the sole Spanish settlement in America, the king's portion became successively one half, one third and one fifth.[4] The "quinto" was established for ten years by a cédula of February, 1504, continued in Hispaniola till 1520, and remained till the eighteenth century the general law for all of Spanish America.

[1] *Recop.*, lib. iv, tit. 19, ley 1. Decrees were repeatedly issued in later times to protect the natives in their rights, doubtless without appreciable effect. Cf. *ibid.*, ley 14.

[2] Gallardo Fernandez, *Origen, progresos y estado de las rentas de la Corona de España*, vi, pp. 1–19.

[3] *Viajes*, ii, p. 165 (Instructions of April 10, 1495).

[4] *Colecc. de doc.*, 1st ser., xxxi, pp. 13, 216; 2d ser., v, p. 43. In the case of rich mines in Hispaniola, a surtax of 1/9 or 1/10 was added to the quinto. *Ibid.*, 2d ser., v, pp. 269, 334.

Further reductions were made from time to time on bullion from regions where the operating costs were high or the ores of a low grade. In 1520, with the gradual exhaustion of the gold-washings on the islands, and the extinction of the Indian laborer, the tax there on placer gold was fixed at one tenth, and later, in 1552, at one twelfth.[1] The "diezmo" was extended in 1530 to Nicaragua and Castilla del Oro, and in 1537 to the province of Honduras.[2] It appears from the papers of the colonial treasurers that in New Spain between 1523 and 1529 various percentages were charged upon the precious metals. In some cases one fifth was paid, in others one eighth, one ninth or one tenth. From 1530 to 1539 the quinto seems to have been universal, but after 1539 an eighth, and later a tenth, was collected on silver from particular districts.[3] One fifth was the royalty on gold bullion till 1572, when it too was reduced to a tenth; and the diezmo became general for all mines in Mexico in 1716. In Peru the quinto prevailed without exception till 1735.[4] As decreed in 1504, no miner might dispose of bullion, or have it wrought into plate or jewels, until it was presented at the casa de fundición, where it was smelted if necessary, assayed, and after the subtraction of the quinto impressed with the royal stamp. By laws of 1537 and 1550, treasury officials were required to be present three hours on Monday and Thursday mornings for the transaction of business, keep a detailed account of all gold and silver which passed through the assay office, and send a statement each year to the king.[5]

It is related in an earlier chapter that the supplying of quicksilver to the colonies became, after the middle of the sixteenth century, one of the important functions of the Casa de Contratación. There were shipments to America, apparently, before that time. A curious decree survives of April 19, 1495, less than three years after Columbus' discovery, directing a certain Alonso

---

[1] *Colecc. de doc.*, 2d ser., ix, p. 460; A. de I., 6. 3. 2/14, ramo 5.
[2] A. de I., Patr. 2. 2. 1/14, no. 15; Patr. 2. 6. 1, ramos 15, 29.
[3] A. de I., 4. 1. 1/19; 4. 1. 4/22; 4. 1. 5/23; 4. 2. 10/1.
[4] Gallardo Fernandez, *op. cit.*, vi, pp. 1–19; Duport, *De la production des métaux précieux au Mexique*, p. 161; *Colecc. de España*, v, pp. 170 ff.
[5] *Recop.*, lib. iv, tit. 22, leyes 11, 12.

de Badajoz to send to the bishop of Badajoz in Seville fifteen hundredweight of mercury for transmission to the Indies.[1] That such a shipment was actually made is extremely doubtful; yet, if we accept the testimony of the historian, Muñoz, as early as 1525 a miner named Paolo Belvio was sent to Hispaniola with a supply of quicksilver to expedite the gold washings by means of amalgamation.[2] As 1525 is also the year in which the Welsers secured equal commercial rights in the New World with Spanish subjects, it is possible that the incident may be connected with that concession. The ancients knew of the amalgamating properties of mercury, and it seems certain that German miners, even before the discovery of America, used that element in extracting gold from auriferous earths and ores.

It was the invention of a process of amalgamating silver ores, however, which created the demand for quicksilver in the Spanish colonies. The credit for this invention is generally given to Bartolomé de Medina, a native of Seville who had gone out as a miner to Pachuca in Mexico. From a letter of the audiencia of Mexico to Charles V in December, 1554, it appears that Medina did not discover the method, but learned it from a German companion in Europe. This German, whose name remains unknown, Medina wished to bring with him to New Spain, but was forbidden by the Casa de Contratación. The audiencia requested the king to let down the bars, and permit the foreigner to cross.[3] The process, introduced by Medina in the beginning of 1556, was soon used throughout the colonies wherever silver mines were found, and was largely responsible for the great influx of the precious metals into Europe.

The two sources of quicksilver in Europe were the mines of Almaden in southern Castile, and those of Idria in the Austrian Alps. The latter had not been operated till 1497, but the Spanish mines were of a distant antiquity. They had been extensively worked by both the Romans and the Moors, and under Christian rule were included in the territory given to the medieval knightly

---

[1] *Colecc. de doc.*, 1st ser., xxx, p. 348.
[2] Humboldt, *The Fluctuations of Gold*, p. 26.
[3] Haebler, *Die Geschichte der Fugger'schen Handlung in Spanien*, p. 138.

order of Calatrava. In 1524 they were leased by Charles V to the German banking house of the Fuggers, and operated by them till 1550. The interior fabric being destroyed by fire in that year, the Fuggers claimed, by virtue of a clause in their lease, that the Crown should pay the cost of reconstruction; and as the Crown refused, the mines were abandoned.[1]

The finding in 1555, however, of the rich silver deposits of Guadalcanal in the Sierra Morena, and experiments with the process of amalgamation in Mexico a year later, gave the government a new interest in quicksilver. The export of this metal to the New World was made a royal monopoly, and in 1557 commissioners were sent down to Almaden to attempt a restoration. But as the Crown possessed neither the means nor the experience needed to accomplish the work, in 1562 the mines were leased again to the Fuggers. They were evidently to be set in order at the Fuggers' expense, for the latter paid no rent for their privilege. They were only obliged to sell all the product to the Crown at a stipulated price.[2]

The lessees in 1562 agreed to deliver 1000 quintals annually. In 1567 the amount was raised to 1200 quintals, and two years later to 1500. But Almaden at best, in the sixteenth and seventeenth centuries, probably never produced more than 3000 quintals a year. And as this was insufficient to meet the requirements of New Spain alone, recourse was had for a time to Germany. German quicksilver was supplied to the colonies by a system of contracts or asientos with private individuals. Thus, in February, 1561, a certain Rodrigo Vaco entered into agreement with the Crown to import 1000 quintals from abroad, and send them to the Indies for sale there within sixteen months. He might bring the quicksilver to any port of Spain, and carry it to any port in America, provided he registered it with the officials of the Casa de Contratación. For the privilege he paid into the treasury of the Casa 20,000 ducats, or twenty ducats per quintal; and the king agreed during the period to issue no

---

[1] Haebler, *Die Geschichte der Fugger'schen Handlung in Spanien*, pp. 94, 103 f.
[2] *Ibid.*, pp. 138–142. The Almaden mines are still among the richest in the world, producing from 800 to 1000 tons a year.

general license, although he reserved the right to make asientos with other individuals.¹ Another contract was made with Andrés de la Rea in the following July, for 2000 quintals to be delivered and sold within three years. But Rea had to pay the Crown twenty-five ducats per quintal, instead of twenty, and deposit 15,000 in advance. He evidently encountered some difficulty in fulfilling his agreement, for his time of grace was extended to five, and later to six, years.²

In 1564 was discovered the famous quicksilver mine of Huancavélica in Peru, which proved so rich that Philip II, after preliminary investigation in 1568, instituted suit for its possession. According to Solórzano, eventually it was sold to the government by Amador de Cabrera (whose Indian had found it) for 250,000 ducats.³ Other pits in the vicinity were taken over by the Crown in the same way, to the disgust of their owners. As they were to be operated by contract, however, like that of Almaden, it was agreed that in giving leases the discoverers and their descendants should be preferred before any others. The lessees were assured a reasonable price for the mercury they extracted, but must dispose of all of it to the government. The amalgamation process was not imported from New Spain to Peru till 1573, when it began to be used at Potosí. But the deposits at Huancavélica were so productive that they supplied both Peru and part of New Spain. A decree of 1591 ordered the shipment of 1500 quintals a year to the northern viceroyalty.

Almaden and Huancavélica between them were thereafter able to meet all the requirements of the New World. For a few years in the second quarter of the seventeenth century, an accident to the works at the Peruvian mine stopped the supply from that source, necessitating the use again of German quicksilver. But after 1642 Germany was no longer tapped, and the shipments from

---

[1] A. de I., 41. 2. 1/11.   [2] *Ibid.*
[3] A. de I., 109. 7. 14, lib. 2, fol. 123 v°; Solórzano, *Política Indiana*, lib. vi, cap. 2, par. 13, 14. Cabrera, after he had sold his holdings, became convinced that he had been cheated, said that the mine was worth at least 500,000 ducats, and entered suit against the Crown. He carried his plea to Spain, and died there shortly after. In the *Colecc. de doc.*, 1st ser., viii, pp. 422 ff. there is a somewhat different account of the transaction.

# THE PRECIOUS METALS 161

Europe generally seem to have decreased toward the end of the Hapsburg regime. Occasionally, quicksilver was sent to New Granada and to Guatemala. An order of July, 1619, directed that 100 quintals be shipped annually to Guatemala, and another of February, 1626, set aside 200 quintals for the Grenadine provinces. Neither was regularly observed.[1]

Veitia Linaje declares that the Crown always sold quicksilver at cost.[2] An examination of the evidence makes it difficult to understand what he meant by the statement. In 1562 the Fuggers agreed to deliver the produce of the Almaden mine to the government for twenty-five ducats a quintal. By the new contract of 1567 the price was raised to twenty-six ducats, and in 1569 to twenty-nine ducats. In Mexico at the same time, prices ranged from 80 to 110 pesos, an increase of 250 per cent.[3] It is scarcely possible that the costs of transportation alone were responsible for this difference. Acosta, in 1590, reckoned the annual yield of Huancavélica at 8000 quintals, and the royal revenue therefrom at 400,000 pesos, which presupposes a profit of fifty pesos per quintal.[4] In 1601, a memorial of Felipe Fernandez de Santillan to Philip III concerning the mines at Potosí, states that mercury was sold there at seventy-five pesos; while Solórzano, writing a few years later, says that the Crown in his day paid only forty pesos at the Huancavélica mine.[5] A royal cédula of October, 1617, fixed the price in New Spain at sixty ducats, or eighty-two and three-fourths pesos; and from that time there was no marked decrease till the second half of the eighteenth century. According to Humboldt, between 1767 and 1776 quicksilver was distributed to the miners in Mexico at sixty-two pesos per quintal. In 1777, under the administration of

[1] Veitia Linaje, lib. i, cap. 14, par. 10.
[2] *Ibid.*, par. 5.
[3] Haebler, *op. cit.*, p. 143. Humboldt says (*Essai Politique*, ed. of 1811, iv, p. 89) that in 1590, under the viceroy, D. Luis de Velasco, a quintal of mercury sold in Mexico for 187 pesos. But this was without doubt an extraordinary figure, due to the temporary derangement of the India trade and the shutting off of the quicksilver supply after the destruction of the great Armada. See the letter of Bartolomé Cano from Mexico, May 30, 1590, in Hakluyt (ed. of 1904), x, p. 166.
[4] Acosta, *Historia de las Indias*, lib. iv, cap. 11.
[5] *Colecc. de España*, lii, p. 447; Solórzano, *op. cit.*, lib. vi, cap. 2, par. 25.

the enlightened Gálvez, the price of Spanish quicksilver was fixed at forty-one and one-fourth pesos, that from Germany at sixty-three pesos.[1]

The packing and shipping of this commodity from Seville was subject to elaborate precautions. Each half quintal was bottled in a soft, well-sewn skin, and placed in a watertight, reënforced cask. If intended for New Spain, three casks, i. e., one and a half quintals, were enclosed in a wooden box, nailed, bound with cord, and wrapped about with matting on which were painted the royal arms. Packages for Tierra Firme contained only two casks. Eighteen quintals were reckoned as one ton freight; and with each shipment went an agent accountable for its safe transmission to the oficiales reales of the port of destination. In the seventeenth century, he was paid twelve ducats for every ton delivered.[2]

In years when the fleets did not sail, two small galleons were dispatched to Vera Cruz with the mercury requisite for the mines. If necessary, it was divided between New Spain and Peru by the viceroy in Mexico City, who forwarded via the Pacific the portion intended for the south. These vessels, called the mercury ships or "azogues," carried from 2000 to 2500 quintals, and sometimes convoyed a few merchantmen. The practice was especially common after the middle of the seventeenth century, when New Spain was no longer able to support the trade of annual flotas.[3] Those whose interest it was to advocate direct trade with the Rio de la Plata, urged that it was cheaper to send mercury to Potosí from Europe via Buenos Aires, than to transport it over the mountains from Peru. But as always happened when the opening of the Rio de la Plata was involved, their solicitations were denied.

In view of the rôle played in European politics by the Spanish Hapsburgs, it is interesting to know exactly the extent of the revenues drawn by the Spaniards from their ultramarine possessions. Precise figures are the more important because of the vague ideas of contemporary and later historians. The extraor-

---

[1] *Essai Politique*, iv, p. 89.  [3] *Ibid.*, par. 11.
[2] Veitia Linaje, lib. i, cap. 14, par. 15, 18.

dinary character of the remittances from America gave an exaggerated image of their volume and value, and to many minds, apparently, they were the very foundation of Spain's political greatness. Early observers were as a rule comparatively modest in their assertions, but in the seventeenth and eighteenth centuries Castilian fancy knew no bounds. Peter Martyr wrote in the second decade of the sixteenth century, before the conquests had extended to the mainland: " Solo de la Española se trae á España todos los años la suma de 400,000, y á veces de 500,000, ducados, se entiende que eso es, del quinto que viene para el Real Fisco, 80,000, 90,000 y 100,000 castellaños de oro, y á veces mas. . . ."[1] The Venetian ambassador, Gasparo Contarini, in a letter of November, 1525, estimates the income of the Crown from the Indies at about 100,000 ducats a year.[2] Another Venetian, Niccolò Tiepolo, in 1533 remarked that the treasure from America in one year amounted to 150,000 ducats, in another to not more than 50,000. In 1548 Mocenigo gives the entire returns for the Crown as about 350,000 ducats,[3] and three years later Marino Cavalli raises the figure to 400,000. In 1558 Michel Soriano, ambassador to Philip II at his accession, remembers that people spoke of " millions " of pesos; but in fact the king was receiving only between 400,000 and 500,000 ducats a year. Even in 1561 Andrea Badoero reckons the income from America at not more than half a million. Finally, the Spanish historian Gómara wrote in 1552 that in the sixty years the Spaniards took to discover, conquer and explore the American continent, the gold and silver they won thereby was not to be reckoned. It passed sixty million ducats.

Among seventeenth century writers, we find estimates less restrained and judicial. It is true that in 1618 Luis Valle de la Cerda (*Desempeño del Patrimonio Real*, etc., cap. xv) calculates in round figures the amount of gold and silver received from

[1] Decade iii, lib. 8, cap. 3. Decade iii was finished in October, 1516, and this chapter was probably written in that year.
[2] Ranke, *Die Osmanen und die spanische Monarchie* (ed. of 1857), p. 399. The actual income was very likely nearer 75,000 ducats.
[3] *Ibid.* The receipts of the Casa de Contratación in that year were little over 108,000 ducats. The annual average for the decade was 148,000 ducats.

America during the first hundred years at more than 500 millions for the king and private individuals;[1] an estimate which was probably not far from the reality. In 1626, however, Pedro Fernandez de Navarrete (*Conservación de Monarquías*, etc., Disc. xxi) computed the returns up to his time at 1536 millions;[2] while the worthy Dr. Sancho de Moncada (*Restoración Política*, etc., 1619, Disc. iii, cap. i), in deploring the scarcity of money already noticeable in the peninsula, accepts the statement that the registered income from America for the sixteenth century alone had been two billion pesos.[3]

It would be fruitless to quote the figures of other and later Spanish publicists. Their estimates for the sixteenth century were generally based upon the word of writers who preceded them, men who possessed little real information, and whose methods were as uncritical as their own.

The bullion from the New World which each year entered the Guadalquivir or the Bay of Cadiz, while scarcely sufficient to " pave the streets of Seville with blocks of gold and silver,"[4] was remarkable enough to a country where poverty has always been rather a virtue than an offense. The receipts of the treasurers of the Casa de Contratación show a steady increase from 1503 until well into the reign of Philip II, though they fluctuate widely from year to year. Much depended upon the security of the seas about Europe, and also upon the vicissitudes of colonial expansion in America. The royal income from the Indies, only about 3,000,000 maravedis when the Casa was organized, rose suddenly to over 22,000,000 in 1505, to 34,000,000 in 1512, to 46,000,000 in 1518, and in 1535 to 119,000,000. In the intervening years the remittances sometimes dropped very low. In 1516, and again in 1520, they were only about 13,000,000, and in 1521 a little over 2,000,000. But this was also the time when the wars between Haps-

---

[1] Colmeiro, *Economía Política*, ii, p. 431, note 2. The unit referred to is probably the ducat.

[2] *Ibid.* Navarrete was copied by Gil Gonzalez Davila (*Teatro de las grandezas de la Villa de Madrid*, 1623, pp. 471 f.); and later in the century probably by Solórzano (*De Indiarum Jure*, 1629–39, lib. v, cap. 1), and by Nuñez de Castro (*Solo Madrid es Corte*, 2d ed., 1669, lib. i, cap. 13).

[3] *Ibid.*    [4] Alonso Morgado, in his history of Seville published in 1587.

burg and Valois began to oppress Europe, and French corsairs were swarming about the Azores. In the Indies, too, while the gold washings on the islands were failing, Spanish energies were directed toward the reduction of the Aztec provinces of Mexico. It was not till later that the wealth of New Spain compensated for the decline of insular gold production.[1]

After 1535, when it became the practice to accumulate American treasure on occasional armadas, the receipts of the Casa in certain years were unusually heavy. Thus, with the arrival of the squadron of Blasco Nuñez Vela in 1538, there were over 371,-000,000 maravedis credited to its treasurer. The gold and silver for the king on this fleet amounted to 280,000,000 maravedis, or about 750,000 ducats,[2] most of it from Peru. Of the Peruvian treasure, about 268,750 ducats were in gold, and 335,000 in silver. There were also nearly 80,000 ducats from Cartagena, 208 ducats worth of pearls, and a gold nugget weighing over fourteen pounds and worth 1630 ducats. The rest of the treasure came from Central America and the West Indian islands.[3] The fleet of Martin Alonso, which entered San Lucar in June of 1543, carried 573,000 ducats in bullion, about equally divided between Peru and Mexico, and over 9000 ducats value in pearls.[4] The Peruvian bullion was sent home by the licentiate Vaca de Castro, who had gone out in 1540 to compose the differences among the Spanish conquistadores. It is probable that up to this time the Crown had received something over a million ducats from the former Inca dominions.[5]

[1] See Appendix IV.

[2] The ducat in Spain was worth 375 maravedis, the escudo, 350. The silver peso of the colonies was valued at 272 maravedis, and the gold peso or "peso de oro" at 450.

[3] See Appendix VII.

[4] The largest pearls came from the Pacific islands near Panama. Those on the Caribbean coasts were smaller, weighing at most from 2 to 5 carats, but were found in greater quantities. Oviedo, in his History published in 1547, declares that the royal quinto from the pearl fisheries amounted to 15,000 ducats and more a year. He says that he himself possessed a round pearl weighing 26 carats, and secured another in 1529, pear-shaped, which he sold to a representative of the Welsers in San Domingo for 450 pesos de oro. Pedrarias Dávila paid over 1200 pesos for a pear-shaped pearl of very fine color in Santa Maria del Darién in 1515. It weighed 31 carats, and later found its way into the possession of the Empress. *Historia de las Indias,* lib. xix, caps. 2, 8.

[5] A. de I., Patr. 2. 2. 1/6, no. 37; 10. 3. 1/25, ramo 1.

The most celebrated of the treasure fleets of Charles' reign, one which profoundly impressed men of the time, was that which carried Pedro de la Gasca to Spain after he had finally restored the king's authority in the South American viceroyalty. When this wily Jesuit arrived in the Indies in 1548, he is said to have had with him no more than 400 ducats. He borrowed what was needed to buy arms, artillery and horses for the war against Gonzalo Pizarro, and during the two years he was in Peru spent altogether about 900,000 pesos de oro.[1] Before leaving, he scraped together all the funds he could lay hands on, and the gold and silver forfeited by the rebels, and after repaying the 900,000 pesos de oro, was able to bring back to his king a store of bullion worth 567,000,000 maravedis, or a million and a half ducats! One of the eight vessels comprising the squadron, which carried a quarter million more, was cast away about twenty-five leagues east of Nombre de Dios, but the treasure was saved, and sent to Spain in the following year.

In the reign of Philip II, the bullion remitted on the Indian flotas increased steadily in volume, from between six and eight hundred thousand ducats in the beginning to two or three million toward the close.[2] It was partly owing to the development of the gold deposits of New Granada and the rich silver mines of Mexico and Potosí; partly the result of the concentration after 1560 of almost the entire trade with the Indies, and all the traffic in bullion, upon yearly fleets to Vera Cruz and Nombre de Dios. In an accounting made in Madrid in October, 1608, of the probable receipts and expenditures of the royal exchequer during the following twelve months, the revenue from the Indies was reckoned at 2,000,000 ducats.[3] The fleet which arrived in the autumn of 1626 under command of Tomás de la Raspuru, with the bullion from both Vera Cruz and Panama, carried on the king's account 3,504,000 pesos (about 2,540,000 ducats) in gold, silver and

[1] Lopez de Gómara, *Historia de las Indias*, lib. v, cap. 81.

[2] In 1587, the Mexican treasurer forwarded to Spain 1,343,000 ducats, the largest remittance in the sixteenth century.

[3] *Colecc. de España*, xxxvi, p. 549. At this time, the drain of the Low Countries alone upon the Spanish monarchy averaged over 3½ million ducats. *Ibid.*, p. 509.

reals, although some of the ships had been lost by storm and from attacks of corsairs.[1] Nuñez de Castro, in his panegyric of Spain, *Solo Madrid es Corte*, written at the close of the reign of Philip IV, when fleets no longer sailed every year, declared the average returns of the galleons and flota to be three and a half million ducats. And that was perhaps as much as the Crown received at any one time in the seventeenth century.[2]

In the beginning the government endeavored to limit the amount of gold and silver which might be transmitted on a single vessel, doubtless to reduce the risks from pirates and shipwreck. In Ferdinand's time, when vessels were very small, the maximum was 5000 pesos de oro. Under Charles it was soon raised to 10,000, and later to 15,000 (12,000 and 18,000 ducats). A decree of July, 1552, fixed it at 25,000 pesos. But the rule was not strictly observed. In a ship from Cartagena in June, 1545, there came on the royal account about 44,000 pesos de oro.[3] Another vessel from Vera Cruz in July, 1551, brought 39,000 pesos.[4] The law, moreover, was not applied to the large fleets which sailed under convoy. The armada of Pedro de la Gasca carried an average of 180,000 pesos in each ship. In the Mexican fleet of Diego

[1] B. M., Add. Mss. 13,976, fol. 16.

[2] The remittances from New Spain under Hapsburg rule reached their maximum at the close of the sixteenth century, about a million and a half pesos. From that time the annual average gradually declined to about 400,000 in the middle of the following century; rising to over 700,000 during the government of the archbishop-viceroy Fray P. Henriques de Ribera (1672–79); and then slowly dropping again, till in the last decade it was less than 200,000. The decline is to be accounted for less by the decreasing productivity of the mines than by the heavier charges upon the treasury in Mexico City. On individual flotas in the last decade the returns were as follows:

```
1689  .........................  137,343 pesos.
1690  .........................  389,052    "
1693  .........................  400,819    "
1696  .........................  426,922    "
1697–1700  .....................  609,182   "  (three fleets).
```

The whole sum remitted to the king between 1663 and 1700, during the government of six viceroys, was 13½ million pesos. B. M., Add. Mss. 13,964, fol. 196; N. Y. Public Library, Mss. Dept., Ford Collection: *Mexico. Real Hacienda . . . 1688–1696*, etc.

[3] A. de I., 2. 3. 6/7, ramo 1.

[4] A. de I., 2. 3. 7/8, ramo 2.

Felipe in 1555, the average was 80,000, and in the fleet of the same year from Nombre de Dios it was 40,000. But most single vessels which tapped the main sources of bullion supply conformed with the regulations. Finally, in July, 1556, the Crown, in its need for money, ordered the colonial authorities thereafter to remit all royal funds at their disposal on the first ships departing for Castile. And from the nature of later shipments it is clear that any amount was embarked as opportunity and vessels offered.[1]

These remittances, of course, do not comprise the total importation of coin and bullion from the New World. Other sums, doubtless much more considerable, came over to pay for the European goods sent to the colonies, or on the account of mine proprietors residing in Spain, or of other individuals who after making their fortune in America returned to spend it in the old country. All this mass of bullion, whatever its destination, had first to be deposited with the Casa de Contratación, and only after long and minute formalities was it finally distributed to its rightful owners. The government, as already explained, had two motives for insisting upon this procedure. It wished to be assured that all the imposts owing to the Crown had been paid, and that the treasure was really destined to Spanish subjects. Unfortunately, we have no records of these private remittances approaching in completeness those for the receipts of the king. No permanent account of them was kept by the Casa, and almost all the ships' registers have disappeared, the few surviving in the Archivo de Indias being of too desultory a character to make any generalizations from them possible.

The scattered notices in other contemporary documents do not materially assist us. We are told that the value of the cargoes on eight barks from America in May, 1525, was 58,000,000 maravedis, or over 150,000 ducats. But how much belonged to the king and how much to his subjects, is not stated.[2] In February, 1534, Hernando Pizarro returned to Spain with the first instalment of the booty from Peru. Two hundred thousand pesos de oro were registered in the names of private persons, and it was

---
[1] A. de I., 4. 2. 10/1, ramo 1.
[2] Fernandez Duro, *Armada Española*, i, p. 423.

said that the actual sum was nearer three hundred thousand. In March, 1535, when Charles V was preparing at Barcelona a naval and military expedition against Barbarossa, there arrived at Seville from Nombre de Dios four ships carrying about 2,500,000 ducats of Peruvian gold and silver; and to help defray the expenses of his African campaign, the Emperor seized 800,000 ducats out of the bullion consigned to private individuals.[1] A fleet returned from New Spain in 1562, under command of Bartolomé Carreño, with 5,000,000 pesos de oro, at least four fifths of which must have been private treasure.[2] The French ambassador at Madrid, M. Fourquevaux, who kept his king fully informed of the coming and going of the India fleets, reported in September, 1566, a flota of thirty-seven ships carrying 4,047,000 escudos de oro; in August, 1567, a fleet from New Spain bringing 2,000,000; in June, 1568, a Peruvian fleet with 3,500,000 of which about a million belonged to the Crown; and 2,500,000 on another armada of the same year from Vera Cruz.[3] The historian, José de Acosta, says that when he returned from America (1587), the bullion on the two fleets of Mexico and Tierra Firme totalled 11,000,000, the royal share of which was less than half.[4] In 1621 the consulado exchanged with the Crown for *billon* money one eighth of the registered silver in the armadas of the previous autumn, or 800,000 ducats; from which we gather that the remittances by private hands amounted to nearly 6,500,000.[5] Finally, the fleet of La Raspuru, mentioned above, which brought home 2,540,000 ducats on the king's account, carried over 8,000,000 in addition for passengers and merchants.

We may gain some idea of the extent of private importations from another source. The Crown early fell into the habit, whenever it was in straits for money, of appropriating all or most of the bullion transmitted from America. The dispossessed persons were generally recompensed with perpetual annuities paying from 3 to

---

[1] A. de I., 2. 3. 2/3; *Colecc. de doc.*, 1st ser., xlii, p. 492; Oviedo, *op. cit.*, lib. vi, cap. 8.
[2] N.M.C., xxi.
[3] Lowery, *Spanish Settlements*, ii, appendix 1.
[4] *Historia de las Indias*, lib. iv, cap. 7.
[5] Veitia Linaje, lib. i, cap. 17, par. 53.

6 per cent on the capital seized.¹ All treasure so embargoed was noted as part of the receipts of the Casa de Contratación. The first important confiscation of this sort I have found was in 1523. It amounted to 300,000 ducats, and represented all the gold and silver that came in five vessels from the Indies. The money was required for the war between the young Emperor and his rival Francis I.² In 1535, as already related, 800,000 ducats were seized out of the treasure from Peru, most of it doubtless the remittances of Pizarro's soldiers to relatives at home. Only sums of 400 pesos or over were taken, and their owners were given annuities bearing $3\frac{1}{3}$ per cent, which if not redeemed by the Crown within six years were to become perpetual. For the African war 60,000 ducats from the bullion on other vessels were appropriated in the same year.³ In 1538 all the private moneys, or over 230,000 ducats, were confiscated from the armada of Blasco Nuñez Vela, and the sequestrations amounted to a like figure in 1545.⁴ Six hundred thousand ducats were taken from the fleet of which Bartolomé Carreño was admiral in 1553; and two years later 425,000, about 375,000 from the fleets and the rest from funds in the chests of the Casa's treasurer.⁵ The most considerable embargo of that time was in the winter of 1556–57, at the very outset of Philip's reign, comprising all the bullion on two fleets which returned from Vera Cruz and Nombre de Dios in the previous autumn. It reached a total of 1,600,390 ducats, and was two and one-fourth times the sum brought on the account of the king. Altogether, the money so secured in the time of Charles V alone was about 5,000,000 ducats.⁶

¹ Annuities (juros) settled upon certain royal revenues, and granted in discharge of loans to the exchequer, were not frequent till the time of the Catholic kings. They were of two sorts, perpetual and redeemable (perpetuos y alquitar). They received a wide extension under Charles V, and continued to be a favorite resource of Hapsburg rulers. At the death of Ferdinand, they amounted to scarcely 350,000 ducats a year. At the accession of Philip II, they consumed about a million.
² A. de I., 139. 1. 6, lib. 9, fol. 186.
³ *Ibid.*, 2. 3. 2/3; Patr. 2. 5. 1/6, ramo 32.
⁴ *Ibid.*, 2. 3. 4/5; 2. 3. 6/7, ramo 1; 39. 3. 3/1.
⁵ *Ibid.*, 2. 3. 9/10, ramos 2, 3; 39. 3. 5/3. The annuities issued in 1553 paid, those given to merchants $6\frac{1}{4}$ per cent, those to other persons $4\frac{1}{6}$ per cent.
⁶ *Ibid.*, 2. 3. 9/10, ramos 4, 5. Yet Charles V wrote to Philip from Yuste that

In the seventeenth century, such forced loans continued to be frequent. Philip III, just before his death in 1621, embargoed one eighth of the registered treasure on the fleets which had arrived near the close of the year previous, amounting to over 800,000 ducats. It was returned within the year, however, as his son and successor hastened to inform the frightened colonists. In 1629 Philip IV took a million ducats of the eight million registered in the fleet of La Raspuru. In 1630, 500,000 were sequestered from the silver brought back in the armada of Fadrique de Toledo, and 200,000 in 1632 from another fleet of La Raspuru. Five hundred thousand ducats were confiscated in 1638, and in 1649 another million from the Mexican and Porto Bello fleets together.[1] In each case, annuities, settled upon the proceeds of certain taxes, were issued by the king in exchange.

The Crown did not confine its solicitude to the bullion on the fleets. It repeatedly required aids or subsidies from the Sevillan merchants through the gild or consulado, either as a free gift to succor the king in his dire necessities, or in return for what was often the pretense of a royal favor. Thus in 1625, when one per cent was added to the avería to defray the cost of an armada to rid the Pacific of Dutch privateers, the consulado paid the king 400,000 ducats in silver to secure that the tax should not become permanent. Incidentally, Philip needed the 400,000 for the siege of Breda in the Low Countries. In 1628, in spite of the destruction of the Mexican flota off the Cuban coast by the Dutch admiral, Piet Heyn, the merchants lent the king 200,000 ducats for the entertainment of his sister, the Queen of Hungary. For half of the loan they were reimbursed with $6\frac{1}{4}$ per cent annuities settled on the millones tax. A hundred and forty thousand pesos were paid by the consulado in 1651, by way of composition in criminal suits directed against certain merchants for exporting they were robbing him in Seville, and that the sequestrations were not made with the rigor desired.

American products other than gold and silver were generally exempt from these seizures; on the ground, says Veitia Linaje, that, being less easily concealed, they were more likely to pay the full quota of taxes to the king. A more plausible reason was the greater difficulty in converting them immediately into money.

[1] Veitia Linaje, lib. i, cap. 17, par. 53; *Colecc. de doc.*, 1st ser., xvii, p. 215.

silver contrary to law and embarking contraband goods for the Indies. And in 1662 it compounded for another 120,000, for disregarding the registry laws.[1] Under the peculiar conditions then prevalent in the India trade, the Seville merchants must have been constantly exposed to royal mulctings of this sort.

These benevolences to the Crown are sufficient testimony of the wealth and prosperity of the merchant princes of Andalusia. On the other hand, the American traffic was often hampered, and its very continuance endangered, by such wholesale confiscations from the plate fleets, and by the demands for loans and subsidies. The discharge of the debts thus incurred by means of pensions or annuities, instead of ready money, deprived the merchant of the capital required to maintain his business; and if, as sometimes happened, the government was in no position to honor them, the results were disastrous. The process, long continued, meant an ever greater resort to credit based upon the good faith of a king whose solvency was daily more suspected. And but for the extraordinary profits of the India trade in favorable years, it would have ended in the speedy decay of that mercantile aristocracy of which Seville was so proud.

An appreciation of the danger of such practices manifested itself early in Spain, and found expression in protests of the Cortes to Charles V and to his son. The Cortes at Valladolid in 1537 petitioned the Emperor to desist from taking the gold of those trading with or returning from the Indies; for if such seizures continued, there would be no one to carry on American commerce, and men in the colonies would not dare to come to Spain.[2] Charles replied that the taking of private treasure had been confined to times of great necessity, and would be so limited in the future — poor satisfaction in a matter which touched so closely the reputation of the government and the healthy development of mercantile and industrial activities. And he almost immediately increased popular irritation by confiscating all the wealth on the fleet of Blasco Nuñez. It is true that in a cédula of September, 1538, he gave his royal word not to repeat the per-

---

[1] Veitia Linaje, lib. i, cap. 17, par. 53.
[2] Colmeiro, *Economía Política*, ii, pp. 410 f.

formance.¹ But five years later, in December, 1543, Philip was writing to the Casa in his father's name, relaying a command to sequester all the gold and silver that arrived from the Indies. The officials were to act with all dissimulation, "con toda disimulación," and give no hint that such an order had emanated from the Crown.²

At Valladolid in 1555, the deputies remonstrated with greater emphasis, explaining that " de tomar el dinero en Sevilla á los mercaderes y pasajeros que vienen de las Indias, y darles juro por ello, se recrecen muchos daños, así á aquellos á quien los toman, porque no pueden hacer sus tratos y negociaciones y poco á poco se iría disminuyendo la contratación, como á aquellos á quienes ellos daban, porque no pudiéndoles pagar, se vienen á alzar con sus haciendas, y tambien las rentas reales vienen en disminución por causa de cesar el dicho trato." ³ As before, the response of the Crown included a vague promise of redress, which it did not display the least intention of fulfilling; for in 1556–57 occurred the gigantic confiscation of 1,600,000 ducats. In 1558 the Cortes returned to the charge, but received no more satisfaction from Philip II than from his imperial father.

Sooner or later the consequences foretold by the deputies made themselves felt. Spaniards in the colonies hesitated to send their gold and silver on the fleets, or found another reason for concealing and shipping unregistered even that which in the ordinary course of trade was carried to Seville or Cadiz. Philip in the end felt impelled to move more circumspectly, and with greater regard for the interests of his subjects. A letter of the king to the audiencia of Las Charcas in April, 1590, reveals a chastened spirit vividly contrasting with that shown three decades earlier. He writes:

> . . . haviendose offrecido de presente nescessidad . . . de socorrerme de alguna buena cantidad para proseguir algunos yntentos muy ymportantes . . . accorde de ymbiar a Joan de Ybarra, Mi Secretario, a la Ciudad de Sevilla, con orden de que sin hacer daño al trato y comercio, ni al abiamiento de las flotas, y particularmente a los mercaderes, procurase que los pasaxeros

---

[1] A. de I., Patr. 2. 5. 1/6, ramo 37.
[2] *Ibid.*, ramo 43.
[3] Quoted by Colmeiro, *op. cit.*, ii, p. 410.

y personas que truxesen hacienda para emplear en renta, en las flotas que ultimamente llegaron, comprassen juros y officios segun la publicidad e yntentos que cada uno truxese, tratandolo con las mismas personas o con sus agentes, de manera que fuesse con su voluntad y contentamiento; y que si por este camino no se pudiese juntar la cantidad nescesaria, se pidiere lo demas prestado a los pasajeros, mercaderes que vinieren en la flota de Tierra-firme a emplear sus haciendas, dandoles a entender, que pues la flota de Tierra-firme en que ellos an de volver con sus empleos no a de salir hasta Otubre deste año, y para entonces seran venidas las (haciendas) que se esperan, se les pagara de alli muy a satisfaccion . . . y hentendido que desta . . . deligencia a resultado mucho sentimiento en mercaderes y pasajeros . . . y haviendo Yo mirado en que, si con esta Mi falta de discurso llegare alla la voz, podria ser de mucho yncombiniente, Me a parecido avisaros de la verdad de lo que en esto passa, para que la hagais alli entender . . . la satisfacion que en esto se da, para que teniendola de lo que se hace, prosigan en sus contrataciones, y cada qual ymbie su hacienda con entera seguridad de que Yo no mandare tocar en ella por ninguna caussa.[1]

Sequestrations did not cease in the following reigns, but they seem never again to have reached the proportions, compared with the whole volume of trans-Atlantic trade, which they assumed in the middle of the sixteenth century.

The Crown, and private individuals, in order to expedite the conversion of bullion into coin of the realm, sold it to bullion merchants who, after reducing the gold and silver to legal fineness, presented it at the mint; for Spanish mints in those days did not undertake the operation of refining. In Seville there were usually several private companies devoted to this occupation, and known as the " Compradores de Oro y Plata." Eight in number at the opening of the seventeenth century, they were later reduced to four. For the business was a very speculative one, profits depending on the chance of buying at a reasonable figure bullion which, if not poorer than indicated by the American assayers, was at least not very much richer. Earnings, apparently, were rarely more than four maravedis on a marc of silver, or one maravedi on a peso of gold.[2] Veitia Linaje says that of the bullion merchants in earlier times many went bankrupt and few left a fortune behind. On the other hand, if leagued with a dishonest minter, they might be tempted to reduce bullion below the standard

---

[1] *Colecc. de doc.*, 1st ser., xviii, p. 424.
[2] Veitia Linaje, lib. i, cap. 33, *passim.*

which the law required. In 1590 suit was brought against the brothers Castellanos for this very offense, a firm which had conducted their business on a vast scale, and by the boldness of their operations had made themselves masters of the bullion market. In the years 1584 and 1585 they had bought up all the lingots offered by the royal exchequer, at thirty-four maravedis above the current market price; and their prosecutors maintained that they could have emerged without loss from such a transaction only by converting the gold and silver into coin defective in weight or fineness. They were accused, indeed, of having realized in this way, between 1570 and 1588, as much as 244,000,000 maravedis, at the expense of the king and of the public. The figures were doubtless grossly exaggerated, but they serve to illustrate the dangers of such a system.[1] Perhaps to insure a closer regulation, the Crown in 1615 tried to make the business a monopoly, but the Sevillans protested that it was too precarious to support the additional burden of a purchase price to the government.

The Compradores de Oro y Plata seem also to have engaged in banking. They received deposits of coin or bullion, and after 1608, at least, gave 40,000 ducats security to the consulado to protect such operations. In the purchase of gold and silver from the Crown, however, or from funds like the "bienes de difuntos," special surety was in each case required by the Casa.[2]

It had originally been customary for the Casa to publish the number of marcs to be sold, and receive bids without a preliminary trial of the fineness of the bars, leaving that to the uncertainties of speculation. A marc of Mexican silver generally brought from 2172 to 2190 maravedis, after deducting the seigniorage tax, which in Philip II's time was calculated at fifty maravedis per marc. Lingots from Peru were presumed to have been more carefully assayed, and sold for 2300 maravedis or more. Sometimes, however, a contract was made by the Crown

---

[1] Gounon-Loubens, *Essais sur l'administration de la Castille au xvi$^e$ siècle*, pp. 262-265.

[2] A charter, setting forth the duties and liabilities of the partners, had to be approved first by the prior and consuls, and then by the president and officials of the Casa, and a copy deposited with the Contaduría of the latter.

with one or more compradores in advance of the arrival of the fleets to take all the bullion, the buyer engaging to deliver its value in reals at the court in Madrid, or deposit them immediately in Seville. Or the Casa tried the experiment of refining the bullion itself, under the direction of the factor. But in the latter case, the result was usually delay and eventual loss to the Crown.

In Veitia Linaje's time, the treasurer of the mint at once credited the Casa de Contratación with the number of escudos or reals equivalent to the bullion purchased by the compradores, the latter being obliged to bring the refined metal to the mint within a specified time. Silver was then sold at six and one-half maravedis per marc above the value indicated by the assayers in the Indies. But sometimes, owing to the dishonesty, carelessness or ignorance of these officials, their figures could not be trusted. Such a case had occurred as early as 1563, when silver bars were found to contain from 60 to 100 maravedis less than pretended; whereupon the bullion merchants refused to buy any more till they had been reassayed by the Casa.[1] There was the same possibility of deception in connection with gold, and as the greater value of that metal made it the more redoubtable, after 1603 gold was sold only after it had been assayed in Seville.

It was generally understood that if American bullion got as far as the mint, it was purged of any guilt it may have incurred for nonregistration. The same held true of that which had come into the hands of the compradores. Sometimes the Council of the Indies attempted to contest this, but without permanent success, for all the weight and influence of the mercantile interests of the city were against it. The houses of the compradores enjoyed the privilege of freedom from visitation by any judicial authority under any pretext. A decree of August, 1647, exempted American treasure in their possession from sequestration without the approval of the president of the Casa; and their books and accounts from examination except on the president's order.[2] These rulings were intended, as much as anything, to protect the merchants who had dealings with the compradores, so that their

---

[1] Veitia Linaje, lib. i, cap. 33, par. 15.    [2] *Ibid.*, par. 20.

resources might not be made public except for such purposes as they desired.

The report that one of the plate fleets had been sighted off the Azores was news of supremest interest, not only to the Seville merchants, but at the court of Madrid, in Flanders, and in Germany. On the safe arrival of the galleons before San Lucar at the mouth of the Guadalquivir, or in Cadiz harbor, often depended, even in the time of Charles V, the momentary solvency of the government.

Not only the American trade, but the industrial and financial insufficiency of Spain herself attracted hosts of foreign merchants to the country. Germans and Genoese in the sixteenth century,[1] and in the seventeenth the French, gathered into their hands not only a virtual monopoly of the Spanish fairs, but all the financial business as well. As early as 1515, the Cortes tried to limit their activities. In the Emperor's reign they were already a serious menace. As neither the revenues in the peninsula nor the treasure from the Indies was sufficient to cope with the expense of the wars, Charles and his successors were forced into greater and greater dependence upon these foreign capitalists. The returns of gold and silver from America were mortgaged in advance, and the Fuggers, the Haros and the Grimaldi were as much concerned with the safety of the Indian fleets as was the Crown itself. In 1520–21 the Fuggers had 33,000 ducats hazarded upon the remittances from the New World; and of the 800,000 ducats embargoed by the Crown in 1535–37, over 100,000 went to this same German house.

Increasing production of gold and silver was the most important cause of the price revolution of the sixteenth and seventeenth centuries. As by far the greater part of this metallic wealth came from America, the function of Spain in the movement was a very significant one. She became the distributor of the precious metals to the rest of Europe. And since she "produced little and manufactured less," she performed this function with an efficiency

[1] In the earlier part of the century also a few Spanish houses established at Antwerp, like the Haros and the Vaglios. The ledgers of the India House frequently mention the payment of interest to foreign bankers.

which startled even the Spaniard. The balance of trade in Spain was always unfavorable. In time of greatest prosperity and in spite of all laws, money passed out of the country. But with the injury to agriculture which must have resulted from the revolt of the Comuneros, and with the naïve efforts of the Cortes to stem the rise of prices, the situation of Spain toward the middle of the sixteenth century was already becoming intolerable. Her manufactures, even her grain, came to her from France, England and the Netherlands, and thither went her gold and silver in exchange.[1]

Another circumstance contributed to the export of the precious metals: Hapsburg imperialism, — the wide distances separating their dominions, the universality of their interests, the expense of their endless wars. While troops in Italy or in the Netherlands were starving or without pay, the Spanish Cortes was inveigled into doubling the servicio,[2] or into an increase of the alcabala; or the cargoes of the plate fleets were requisitioned for the needs of the Crown. Spanish funds were used to maintain an alien empire.

On such occasions the help of the ubiquitous foreign merchant princes was again indispensable. The arrival of a rich Indian fleet in the Guadalquivir did not in itself mean the instant satisfaction

---

[1] Bernays, "Zur inneren Entwicklung Castiliens unter Karl V." (*Deutsche Zeitschrift für Geschichtswissenschaft, 1889*), pp. 404 ff.

"The second [cause for the decay of Spanish trade] is the residence of many Genoa merchants amongst them, who are found in good numbers to abide in every good city, especially on the sea coasts, whose skill and acuteness in trade far surpassing the native Spaniard and Portuguese, and who, by means of their wealth and continual practice of exchanges, are found to devour that bread which the inhabitants might otherwise be sufficiently fed with; and by reason that the King of Spain is ever engaged to their commonwealth for great and vast sums at interest, he is their debtor, not only for their moneys, but also for their favor, which by many immunities throughout his kingdom he is found continually to requite them, and amongst the rest it is observed that there is no Genoa merchant resident in Spain, or any part, but has a particular license to transport the rials and plate of this kingdom to a certain round sum yearly, which they seldom use really to do, but sell the same to other nations that are constrained to make their returns in plate for want of other more beneficial commodities, which for the certain profit it is found ever to yield in other countries, is often preferred before all the other commodities of the Kingdom." Roberts, *The Merchants' Mappe of Commerce*, p. 165.

[2] Bernays, *op. cit.*, p. 391. In Ferdinand's later years the servicio was 50 millions annually. After 1539 it was 150 millions.

of the needs of the moment. Even if remittances were sufficient in quantity, they could not forthwith be transported as bullion to Italy or Flanders. They had first to be coined into escudos and reals. The Spanish kings moreover rarely possessed the marine necessary to convoy the treasure in safety to their distant provinces. The government, therefore, called in the aid of the great commercial houses with international connections. Through them it was possible to make payments abroad with certainty and dispatch, the bankers being recompensed with cash in Spain, or with assignments upon future revenues.[1]

Spain, in the sixteenth century, perhaps felt no immediate harm from this depletion of her coinage. A nonindustrial country could not well absorb all the produce of the American mines. Moreover her stock of precious metals was continually being replenished from an apparently inexhaustible source. On the other hand, this American wealth did serve " to feed an unpractical vanity and further unfit the nation for manufacturing and commercial life." Everything could be purchased with gold and silver, not only cloths and grain, but armies, heretics, and the hegemony of Europe. The opportunity for conquest was offered by the Hapsburg connection. And Spain, by the loss of her industry and the plundering of her fleets, paid the cost of Hapsburg imperalism.

[1] Ehrenberg, *Das Zeitalter der Fugger*, pt. iii, cap. 3.

## CHAPTER VIII

### THE ISTHMUS OF PANAMA

IN September, 1513, Vasco Nuñez de Balboa, looking southward from the heights of Darién, beheld the waters of the Pacific Ocean, and revealed for the first time the existence of a new continent. Six years later, Balboa's executioner, Pedrarias Dávila, founded in the same neighborhood the city of Panama, the oldest surviving European settlement on the American mainland. And from Panama as a base, the exploring expeditions crept northward and southward along the shores of the Pacific in search of gold and adventure. Especially after the conquest of Peru by Francisco Pizarro, the city grew rapidly in importance. The shortest and easiest route to this southern kingdom lay over the isthmus, and Panama became the entrepôt for the exchange of commodities with the Old World.

The portage between the two oceans was from the beginning a matter of great interest to the Spanish Crown. The instructions to Pedrarias, when he came out to America in 1514, provided, not only for a settlement on the Pacific, but also for a practicable road across the isthmus from Santa Maria del Darién to the Gulf of San Miguel.[1] And later letters to Pedrarias and to his successors emphasized the necessity of facilitating communication between the North and South Seas. Before the discovery of Peru, the objective was trade with the Spice Islands in the Far East. In 1522, a "casa de contratación" had been set up at Coruña for the organization of this commerce; and the difficulty of the voyage through the newly-found Magellan strait soon turned the Emperor's attention to the possibility of securing spices via the isthmus and the Caribbean. The idea is outlined in the instructions issued in May, 1526, to Pedro de los Rios, recently appointed governor of Castilla del Oro. Paragraph 5 reads as follows:

---

[1] *Colecc. de doc.*, 1st ser., xxxix, p. 325.

Ansi mismo porque ... uno delos mas principales medios por donde parece que puede conseguirse el trato y comercio de la especeria que cae dentro de los limites de nuestra demarcacion es trayendolo y navegandolo por la mar del sur por ser tan breve navegacion para las n̄ras islas de Maluco y las otras partes donde lo ay, y para ello a parecido que entre tanto que se alla estrecho, que combernia mucho hazerse dos cassas una en la ciudad de Panama en la costa del sur, y otra en la costa del norte en la parte mas aproposito y ser respondiente y cercana a ella para que las armadas que nos embiamos y embiaremos a las dichas islas de maluco y a otras partes dela speceria veniesen a descargar en la dha ciudad de Panama y alli descargase y se truxese la speceria en carros o en bestias a la casa que estuviese para ello fecha en la dicha costa del norte y de la misma manera se podrian passar dela costa del norte a la dicha Panama, las mercaderias y rescate que se ovieren de enbiar de aca para contratar la dicha speceria y que las armadas que se despachasen para la dicha Panama, y todos son de parescer que desta manera se podria mejor y con mas seguridad y a menos costa hazer, y porque esto esta importante cossa como vecis para nuestro servicio y para el acrecientamiento y noblescimiento destos reynos yo vos mando y encargo que luego como llegareis vos y el lic. Salmeron y n̄ros oficiales con mucho cuidado y diligencia como la grandeza del negocio lo requiere ... .[1]

The coveted trade with the Moluccas was never realized, and in 1529 Charles sold his claim to the islands for ready cash to the Portuguese. The isthmian highway, however, after the opening of the silver mines at Potosí in 1545, and the concentration of South American trade in the annual galleons, became the most vital link in the transportation system between Spain and Peru, and the goal of West Indian pirates and buccaneers.

This highway long remained nothing but a primitive mule path, largely because of the physical obstacles attending any more ambitious design. To build and maintain forty miles of road over mountains covered with tropical forest and through swamps and jungles, in one of the deadliest climates of the world, was a large order to demand of a struggling community scarcely two decades old. In 1528 the project was still in the stage of discussion. The inhabitants of Panama represented it as too costly for purposes of trade. They suggested that goods might better be carried to the upper reaches of the Chagres River, and floated down in boats to the Caribbean; and urged that Nombre de Dios be moved farther westward, near to the river's mouth. A force of fifty

[1] A. de I., 139. 1. 1, lib. 1.

negroes they deemed desirable to keep the stream free from floating timbers and other obstructions. The Chagres had been explored for the first time in the spring of 1527, at the direction of Pedro de los Rios, doubtless in response to the instructions quoted above. The expedition, entrusted to captain Fernando de la Serna, a mariner Pedro Corzo, and a notary Miguel de la Cuesta, returned with glowing reports of the possibilities of the stream. Further investigations were made at the instance of the Crown in 1531 and 1533; and in February, 1534, an order was sent to a new governor, Francisco de Barrionuevo, for the expenditure of a thousand pesos de oro in clearing the river and constructing a warehouse where it joined the sea. One third of the expense was to be borne by the king, the rest met with the proceeds of a tax on merchandise.[1] Whether the warehouse was built or not is uncertain, but two years later, in December, 1536, a royal decree empowered the municipality of Panama to erect one at Venta Cruz, or Cruces, at the head of navigation on the Chagres; and Venta Cruz continued until the nineteenth century to be the principal station in the journey across the isthmus. Storage rooms were rented to the merchants, in Philip II's time at one-half peso a day, and the income of the city from these rentals was nine or ten thousand pesos a year. In the seventeeth century, with the decline of the galleon trade, it sank to a third of that figure.[2] It was this warehouse at Cruces which Sir Francis Drake destroyed by fire in 1572, with, it was said, 200,000 ducats worth of merchandise.

Efforts were also made from time to time to repair and improve the overland route; as, for instance, in 1535, when the king, in a contract with Bernardino Gaona and Diego de Enciso, allowed these two Spaniards to export for ten years an unlimited amount of wool from Peru to Spain, on condition that they contributed to

---

[1] A. de I., 140. 3. 9; *ibid.*, Patr. 2. 2. 1/14, no. 18.
[2] *Ibid.*, Patr. 2. 2. 1/14, no. 31; Peralta, *Costa-Rica, Nicaragua y Panamá en el siglo xvi*, p. 527; *Relaciones históricas y geográficas de América Central* (Madrid, 1908), p. 163.

No customhouse was ever set up at the mouth of the river. All goods transported across the isthmus had to pass the customs at Nombre de Dios and Panama. Veitia Linaje, lib. ii, cap. 17, par. 40.

the maintenance of the transisthmian highway.[1] Yet when Francisco de Toledo passed through that region in 1569, he found the old highway still so bad and unsafe as to occasion considerable loss each year in life and goods. The negroes kept at Nombre de Dios and Panama for its repair were of little use. The governors and magnates of the two towns were concerned each with their own selfish interests, while robberies and other excesses of the wild, cimaroon Indians were a constant menace both to travellers and to the settlements. Toledo made provision for the surveying and building of a new road passing through Venta Cruz, at such cost as the king should determine; and in conformity with his instructions, imposed a duty on exports to the amount of 10,000 pesos, for the support of a military colony on the highway of 200 Spaniards, to subdue the savages.[2] This may have been the origin of a tax called the " avería del camino," which in the early years of the seventeenth century produced an annual income of several thousand pesos. In 1640 an ecclesiastic residing in Tierra Firme still referred to the route as a " malíssimo camino, peor que jamás yo he visto en todo lo que he andado."[3] And not until the eighteenth century was a permanent, paved road finally constructed across the isthmus.

There were, therefore, before the age of steam, two ways of transferring goods between the Pacific and the Caribbean Sea. The overland route, eighteen leagues in length (twelve as the crow flies), was used only in summer, the dry season; the other, by way of the Chagres River, in winter, when roads were rendered impassable by the great rains and floods. The river route was

[1] A. de I., Patr. 2.2.1/14, no. 24. That interesting Sevillan scapegrace, D. Alonso Enriquez de Guzman, in his autobiography describes the road in this same year as follows: "I travelled across the land to Panama, a distance of 18 leagues. For the first seven the road passes between two high ranges of hills, densely covered with forest, along the banks of a river which was nearly dry . . . and to those who travel on foot, it is a very weary journey. For the last eleven leagues the road is better, though there are several rivers to pass. There are three inns on the road, one called Capira, the second La Junta, and the third La Venta de Chagres, because here they disembark from another deep river called Chagres." *Life and Acts, 1518–1543* (tr. by Sir C. R. Markham), p. 88.

[2] *Colecc. de España*, xciv, pp. 225 ff.

[3] *Relaciones hist. y geog. de América Central*, p. 78.

longer, but also less difficult and expensive. From Panama to the Chagres at Venta Cruz the distance was five leagues, and from Venta Cruz to the river's mouth about eighteen leagues more. When the Chagres was high, the transit could be accomplished in three or four days, but at other times from eight to twelve were required. To transfer goods from the mouth of the river to Nombre de Dios was a matter of only eight or ten hours.

The Tierra Firme fleets, till near the close of the sixteenth century, carried their cargoes to Nombre de Dios. But this port, situated to the eastward of the present Colon, was never more than a makeshift. The bay was shallow, full of reefs and open to the sea. The town, an unwalled settlement of about 150 houses built of wood, with the usual plaza and streets at right angles, had a stretch of sandy beach before it, the jungle behind. Fever raged the year round, and women were sent to Venta Cruz to bear their children and rear them to the age of five or six. Most of the buildings belonged to citizens and merchants of Panama, and remained vacant except so long as the fleet tarried in the harbor. Between fleets, the population was reduced to about fifty households.

As early as 1536, Francisco de Montejo, governor of Honduras, proposed that the Darien route to Peru be abandoned for another through his province. Atlantic ships should be directed to Puerto de Caballos, goods transferred overland to the port of Fonseca on the Pacific, and thence carried by sea to Callao or Guayaquil. Merchandise intended for Vera Cruz, Panuco, etc., had also better be shipped to Caballos, thence to Istapa in Guatemala, and by water up to Acapulco. This Honduras route was recommended as safer, and the port of Caballos as healthier than Nombre de Dios. The idea was revived some twenty years later by a certain Juan Garcia de Hermosilla, who interested the cabildo of Guatemala City in the project, and was sent to Spain as its proctor or commissioner to push the matter with the authorities there. It was opposed, not only by the interests at Panama, but also by the province of Nicaragua, which foresaw the extinction of its own trade, and suggested that the route pass by way of the San Juan River. The bundle of memorials preserved in Seville[1] is only another monument to the Spaniards' gross ignorance of the geography of these regions. To carry goods to New Galicia via Honduras and the Pacific was about as practicable as by way of the St. Lawrence and the Great Lakes. And the physical difficulties attending the isthmian route bore no relation to those involved in the passage through Honduras and Guatemala. Yet it appears that the scheme was reconsidered in later years, notably in 1587 and 1606.

There was another port, however, destined eventually to supersede Nombre de Dios. In the same year that Hermosilla presented his petition, the king had sought information from the Casa de Contratación regarding the situation and general advantages of Porto Bello, lying some five leagues farther west.[2] And in 1584 he ordered the older settlement to be abandoned in its favor. Porto Bello stood on the southeast side of what was perhaps the best natural harbor on the Atlantic side of the isthmus, deep and easy to fortify; but it proved to be just as unhealthy as its predecessor. The removal from Nombre de Dios was not accomplished till about ten years later, owing to the necessity of remapping the road from Venta Cruz to the coast. A century afterward, Dampier described the older site as a tropical waste. " Nombre de Dios," he says, " is now nothing but a name. I have lain ashore in the place where that City stood, but it is all overgrown with Wood, so as to have no sign that any Town hath been there."[3]

The city of Panama, as the emporium for the trade of colonial South America, enjoyed a vast reputation in those early days. And by modern writers it has been exuberantly described as comparable in wealth and splendor with the capitals of the Orient. Such is scarcely the testimony of contemporary visitors. In 1575 the city contained some 350 or 400 buildings, many of them mere huts and all constructed of wood, even the churches. There were about 500 Spanish householders, the greater number of Andalusian origin, and 400 negroes. The town was the seat of a bishop-

---

[1] A. de I., Patr. 2. 5. 1/14, ramo 24; 2. 5. 2/15, ramo 15; Milla and Gomez Carillo, *Historia de la América Central*, ii, p. 234.
[2] A. de I., Patr. 2. 5. 1/6, ramo 57.   [3] *Voyages* (ed. of 1906), i, p. 81.

ric (1521), and of a supreme court or audiencia (1538); but the cathedral, besides a dean and a precentor, had only one canon, and the three monasteries together possessed but eighteen inmates. Virtually all the citizens were merchants or transportation agents, the few exceptions being engaged in agriculture and ranching in the surrounding country, or in the pearl fisheries among the neighboring islands. It was the carrying of goods and bullion across the isthmus which provided much of the income of the city. Some maintained stables of pack animals for use on the highway to Cruces and Nombre de Dios, while others had large flatboats on the Chagres, navigated by negro and mulatto slaves. The merchants were reputed to be wealthy, but prices were high, the mode of living extravagant, and the standard of comfort not very great.[1]

In an elaborate report of the audiencia to the king in 1607, the wealth of Panama, including only estates of a thousand pesos or more, was computed at over two and a half millions. One citizen was worth 250,000, another 200,000, and a third 50,000. The rest were all men of lesser means. Cattle ranches in the country were not included in the estimate.[2]

At that time there were only four streets running east and west, and seven running north and south. The extent of the city was 487 by 1412 paces. There were now five monasteries and a hospital, with forty-five monks and twenty-four nuns; and 372 dwellings large and small, besides a hundred or more thatched huts occupied by negroes. The number of European householders was about 550, of whom fifty-three were foreigners (mostly Portuguese and Italians), and only sixty-three of creole birth. Of the 3700 negro slaves, nearly a thousand were employed in the trans-

[1] Fish, fruit, and vegetables were more plentiful than flesh, but all were dear except beef and cocoa. In 1590, twenty pounds of beef could be bought for one real, while a pound of bread cost two reals and a quart of wine four. Letter of Hieronymo de Naberes (Panama, August 24, 1590), in Hakluyt, x, p. 176. Mutton and pork were very scarce. Flour came from Peru and Nicaragua, cocoa from Guayaquil. Most of the wine, too, was brought from Peru, although its importation in competition with Spanish wines was forbidden, and it was reported to be deleterious to the health. There was no good drinking water, what was used being carried for a mile or two by negro water carriers or by the slaves of the citizens.

[2] *Relaciones hist. y geog. de América Central*, p. 177.

port service. As yet there were only eight buildings constructed of stone, the halls of the audiencia and the town council, and six private dwellings. Twenty-nine citizens were wholesale merchants, twenty-one retail, and thirty-five owned droves of mules. There were about 850 of these pack animals, the largest stable possessing seventy-five.

It is clear that in thirty-five years the city had grown little. It was still a rather small, mean, frontier town. The judges who drew up the survey of 1607, moreover, complained that the place was declining in wealth and prosperity, because of the falling off of the galleon trade. The fleets were smaller in size, and came only every two or three years instead of annually as before. Brokerage licenses sold by the city in 1580 for 6550 pesos, in 1607 brought only 4200 pesos. The office of town crier, farmed out in 1575 for 2200 pesos, in 1607 was worth only 150. And the rents of the municipal meat market had dropped from 700 pesos to 200 pesos a year. Formerly Panama had been able to muster a militia of 800 foot and fifty horse, all well-armed. In 1607 scarcely a third of that number were available. The reasons given for the decline of the galleons were the new commerce with the Philippine Islands and China, and the increased trade between Peru and New Spain, European goods finding their way to Peru via Mexico in order to pay for the colonial wines exported to the north.

The harbor or roadstead of Panama was very shallow and exposed to the sea, and the tides so great that all larger ships resorted to the neighboring harbor of Perico, two leagues to the west, the cargoes being transshipped on small sloops to the city. The roadstead, moreover, was rapidly silting up. In 1575 vessels of sixty tons could still approach at high tide. In 1607 even small boats often encountered difficulties. Perico was partly enclosed by three rugged islands laying about two miles from shore in the general form of a half-moon; and it was to this neighborhood that Panama was removed after the destruction of the old city by Henry Morgan in 1671. In the sixteenth century, from forty to fifty vessels called there annually from Peru and Nicaragua. Both harbors were unfortified.

Panama did not change greatly in appearance in the course of the seventeenth century. Thomas Gage, who was there in 1637, says that it then contained some 5000 inhabitants; but the houses, he continues, " are of the least strength of any place that I had entered in; for lime and stone is hard to come by, and therefore for that reason, and for the great heat there, most of the houses are built of timber and bords; the President's house, nay the best church walls are but bords, which serve for stone and bricke, and for tiles to cover the roof." Wooden construction was probably retained also because experience had proved it to be the most successful in withstanding earthquake shocks.

It is tolerably clear that the city never gave the appearance of a great commercial metropolis. Buildings both public and private must have been of modest dimensions, and as is the rule in southern Spanish towns, packed closely together. We are specifically told that there were no gardens in the city. And there could never have been the streets, large, beautiful and regular, such as the Frenchman, François Coreal, who probably never saw the city, described them to be in the second half of the seventeenth century. In modern Panama most of the streets are narrow and crooked.

The approach of one of the great fleets to the coast of Tierra Firme was the sign for an outburst of unwonted activity among officials and merchants in that region. The first port of call was Cartagena, the door to New Granada, and one of the richest and best-fortified cities in the Indies.[1] On arrival, their commander or " general " forwarded the news to Porto Bello, together with the packets destined for the viceroy at Lima. From Porto Bello a courier hastened across the isthmus to the president of Panama, who spread the advice among the merchants in his jurisdiction, and sent a dispatch boat to Payta in Peru. The general, meanwhile, was also sending a courier overland to Lima, and another to Santa Fé de Bogotá, whence runners carried the news to Popayan, Antioquia, Mariquita, and adjacent provinces. The galleons were instructed to remain at Cartagena generally

---

[1] The following description is taken largely from *The Buccaneers in the West Indies in the Seventeenth Century* (London, 1910), pp. 16-19.

for a week, but bribes from the merchants often made it their interest to linger far beyond that time. To Cartagena came the gold and emeralds of New Granada, the pearls of Margarita and Rancherias, and the indigo, tobacco, cocoa and other products of the Venezuelan coast. The merchants of Guatemala, likewise, sometimes shipped their commodities to Cartegena by way of Lake Nicaragua and the San Juan River, when it was dangerous to cross the Gulf of Honduras to Havana because of French or English corsairs hanging about Cape San Antonio.

Meantime the viceroy at Lima, on receipt of his letters, ordered the Armada of the South Sea to prepare to sail, and sent word down to Chile and throughout the provinces of Peru from Las Charcas to Quito, to forward the king's revenues for shipment to Panama. Within a fortnight all was in readiness.[1] The armada carried the royal treasure from Callao, and touching at Truxillo and Payta, was joined by the Navio del Oro with the gold from Quito and neighboring districts. While the galleons were approaching Porto Bello the South Sea fleet arrived before Panama, and the colonial merchants began to transfer their goods on mules across the high back of the isthmus.

Then began the famous fair of Porto Bello. The town, whose permanent population was composed mostly of negroes and mulattoes, was suddenly called upon to accommodate an enormous crowd of traders, soldiers, and seamen. Food and shelter were to be had only at extraordinary prices. When Thomas Gage was in Porto Bello in 1637, he was compelled to pay 120 pesos for a very small, meanly-furnished room for a fortnight. Merchants gave as much as 1000 pesos for a moderate-sized shop in which to store their commodities. Owing to overcrowding, bad sanitation, and the extremely unhealthy climate, the place became an open grave, ready to swallow all who resorted there. In 1637, during the fifteen days the fleet remained there, 500 men died of sickness. Meantime, day by day the mule trains from Panama were wind-

[1] To transport the silver from Potosí down to Arica on the coast often required as much as a fortnight. The voyage from Arica to Callao generally consumed about eight days, and from Callao to Panama another three weeks. But the shipments of bullion from Upper Peru to Lima were probably fairly regular, and did not wait upon the arrival of the galleons from Spain.

ing their way into the town. And while the king's treasure was being transferred to the armed ships in the harbor, the merchants made their trade. Gage in one day counted 200 mules laden with bars of silver, which were unloaded in the market place and permitted to lie about like heaps of stones in the street, without causing any fear or suspicion of loss.[1] The fair was supposed to be open for forty or fifty days, but in later times was often completed in ten or twelve.

On the return voyage from Porto Bello, the galleons first sailed eastward to call again at Cartagena, and thence worked their way north through the Yucatan Channel to Havana, and back to Spain.

The project of a waterway joining the two oceans, realized by American engineers in the twentieth century, is not a very modern idea. In the sixteenth and seventeenth centuries, it was frequently proposed to the councils in Spain, though, as so often happened in Spanish councils, it rarely passed the stage of discussion. The discovery of the Pacific by Balboa stimulated exploration among Spanish navigators, who during the following decade scoured the coast of America from Labrador to Patagonia in the hope of finding a strait to the waters beyond. Ferdinand Magellan was successful in 1520, but the passage which bears his name was too remote for those seeking a short cut to the Orient; and thenceforth the search was mainly confined to the isthmian region, where it was now generally recognized that the oceans lay least widely apart.

In 1521 Hernando Cortes sent one of his officers, Diego de Ordas, to explore what is now called the Coatzacoalcos River in the isthmus of Tehuantepec, the narrowest part of the present republic of Mexico. Ordas reported that from the size and depth of the stream he suspected the existence of a waterway to the other sea. No such passage existed, but the Coatzacoalcos River was later utilized as part of an overland route for heavy goods, and has been more than once suggested as the location for a canal. Two years later, Cortes was directed by Charles V to take up the

---

[1] Gage, *A New Survey of the West Indies* (ed. of 1655), pp. 196 ff.

quest for a strait, and the conquistador entered upon the business with his customary energy. Expeditions were equipped to explore both the eastern and western shores of Central America. " Como yo sea informado," he wrote to the Emperor, " del deseo que V.M. tiene de saber el secreto deste estrecho, y el gran servicio que en le descubrir su real corona recibiría, dejo atrás todos los otros provechos y intereses que por acá me estaban muy notorios, para seguir este otro camino."[1]

At about the same time, Gil Gonzalez Dávila, a kinsman of Pedrarias, in searching along the Pacific for the elusive strait, discovered a great inland sea, which was called Nicaragua after the principal native chieftain of that country. Lake Nicaragua, however, had no outlet into the Pacific, and although joined to the Atlantic by the San Juan River, the course of this stream was not definitely ascertained till 1539, by Alonso Calero.[2] Calero's voyage first gave the civilized world a clear notion of the canal route which has been the most serious rival to that finally adopted by the United States government. It is said that legends survive to this day among the Indians of Central America of a waterway which once existed across this region but was closed up by volcanic action.

It was probably the opening of navigation on the Chagres River which suggested the possibility of a ship canal through the isthmus. Alvaro de Saavedra Ceron, a relative and lieutenant of Cortes, seems to have led the way in this ambitious design. He had been with Balboa in Darien, and recalling the narrowness and comparatively low elevation of the isthmus, is said to have proposed a scheme for a canal at that place. His death, however, on the celebrated expedition to the Moluccas in 1528–29, prevented his bringing it to the attention of the Crown. How daring the project was can better be understood to-day than by the men who originally conceived it. In fact, until the nineteenth century, few of those who in turn urged the construction of a canal had any true appreciation of the difficulties in the way of its consummation.

[1] Cortes, *Letters* (ed. Gayangos), fourth letter, Oct. 15, 1524.
[2] Peralta, *op. cit.*, pp. 94, 728.

Charles V, who had directed Cortes to find a strait in 1523, and had impressed upon the governors of Castilla del Oro the need of a practicable highway across the isthmus, now adopted the idea of an artificial channel. In a cédula of February, 1534, he ordered the local governor, "tomando personas expertas," to go and examine the territory between the head of navigation on the Chagres and the South Sea, and ascertain the most feasible means of cutting through from river to ocean. He was to estimate the amount of money, time and labor necessary for the undertaking, and the proportion of the expense which the American provinces could bear. In October of the same year, the report, drawn up by Pascual de Andagoya, the lieutenant governor, was forwarded from Nombre de Dios. The obstacles, Andagoya declared, were insurmountable. With a knowledge of the conditions realized by few of his contemporaries, he expressed the opinion that it would be virtually impossible to construct a waterway through the isthmus at that or any other point, and that the undertaking would exhaust the richest treasury in Christendom.

We hear of no further efforts in this direction during the Emperor's reign. In 1550 the Portuguese navigator, Antonio Galvao, published a book to demonstrate that a canal could be cut at Tehuantepec, Nicaragua, Panama or the Gulf of Darién, and a year later Gómara, in his History of the Indies, suggesting the same four routes, forcibly urged that the work be undertaken without delay. "Sierras son, pero manos ay. Dadme quien lo quiera hazer, que hazer se puede. No falte animo que no faltara dinero, y las Indias, donde se ha de hazer lo dan. Para la contratacion de la especeria, para la riqueza de las Indias, y para un Rey de Castilla poco es lo posible."[1] Means, however, *were* lacking, even to a king of Castile, and Charles V needed everything for his interminable wars against France, the Protestants and the Turks.

The finances of his son, Philip II, were no easier; yet in the first decade of the new reign there seems to have been some consideration given to schemes of this sort. In 1555, and again in 1556, a certain Ruy Lopez de Valdenebro offered to make navi-

---

[1] Ed. Antwerp, 1554, cap. 104.

gable the Desaguadero de Nicaragua, as the San Juan River was then called. The project was referred by the Council to the Casa de Contratación, but apparently was never accepted. Nine years later, in July, 1565, a definite agreement was drawn up between the Crown and Jorge Quintanilla, a Spaniard who had formerly held a judicial post in Cartagena de Indias. He was to "discover" at his own expense the waterway (paso por agua) in Tierra Firme from the North to the South Seas, and within three years to establish one or more towns on the shores of the latter. As recompense, he was designated governor of these towns, and given a monopoly of the new route. After a long illness in Seville, Quintanilla embarked for Cartagena in the spring of 1567. In Cartagena he fell into other difficulties, and the contract was never executed. No mention is made of the particular region he intended to explore, but there is reason to believe that it was again the route through Nicaragua. If this be true, it is evident that even in 1565 the Spanish Crown was unconvinced of the barriers lying between Lake Nicaragua and the Pacific Ocean.

About this time, the policy of Philip seems suddenly to have altered. Whether owing to an empty treasury, or because the power of the French and English at sea — and especially the depredations of corsairs in the West Indies — made him fear that he would be unable to control a canal should one be constructed, he decided to leave well-enough alone. He not only gave up all projects for a waterway, but forbade the discussion of them, and imposed the penalty of death on any one who should disclose, or attempt to find, a better route across the isthmus than the overland road between Panama and Nombre de Dios. Monopoly of communications with Peru was now more important than a shorter sea passage to the Pacific. It was then that the headwaters of the Atrato River, in the extreme south of the isthmus, were discovered to be comparatively near the Pacific shores, and speculation was rife over the possibility of cutting a channel through this region. Philip ordered the navigation of the river to be abandoned on pain of death. He may also have concluded, like the pious Jesuit, José de Acosta, that even if it were within human power to break through the barrier separating the two oceans, to attempt to correct the works which Providence had ordained and disposed for the framing of the world would surely invite disaster.

For a generation the plan of an isthmian ship canal slumbered. It was revived in 1616, when Philip III ordered Diego Ferdinand de Velasco, governor of Castilla del Oro, to make surveys for one by way of the Gulf of Darién and the Atrato River, the very route whose use his predecessor had so strenuously forbidden. Velasco's report, if ever made, has been lost, and nothing came of the matter. Four years later, a Fleming named Diego de Mercado, one of the settlers of Santiago de Guatemala, wrote a " relación y descripción " of the Nicaragua region, and a plea for a Nicaragua canal. Between the lake and the port of Papagayo on the Pacific, he says, " hay cinco leguas, quatro por una quebrada ó barranca honda, en que en invierno entra el agua de la laguna, y una legua de piedra á manera de pared. Rompiéndola y limpiando la quebrada," he continues, " podrán juntar las mares de Norte y Sur, porque entrará la mar del Sur en la laguna de Nicaragua, y bajará por el Desaguadero al puerto de San Juan de la mar del Norte, y podrán subir y bajar navios de poca porte." He believed that the intervening league of rock might easily be dislodged with gunpowder, and offered to provide that the labor required to clean out the Desaguadero should cost no more than the food and drink of maintenance.[1] Apparently not till the end of the eighteenth century was it understood in Spain that Lake Nicaragua lies 134 feet above the Pacific.

From about 1630 onward, apprehensions were again aroused by the activities of a new kind of sea rover, the West Indian buccaneer. In 1655, moreover, a formidable expedition sent out by Oliver Cromwell seized the island of Jamaica, in the very heart of Spain's West Indian possessions. Jamaica became the buccaneers' principal headquarters, and served as a base for a series of piratical inroads upon the provinces of the Spanish Main, culminating in the celebrated capture and sack of Panama by Henry Morgan. In April, 1680, a party of 300 buccaneers led by Bartholomew Sharpe, after plundering Porto Bello, burst across

[1] A. de I., 145. 7. 7.

the isthmus into the South Sea. For eighteen months they cruised up and down the Pacific coasts of America, burning and plundering Spanish towns, keeping the provinces of Quito, Peru and Chile in a fever of anxiety, finally sailing the difficult course round Cape Horn and returning to the West Indies in January of 1682. They had forced the door which the Spaniards supposed was fastest shut,[1] and their exploit was imitated by numerous other bands which followed after.

The magnificent project of the Scotchman, William Paterson, in 1698, to plant a colony on the isthmus of Darién and establish a free trade route to the Pacific — a scheme which should, in his own words, secure for Great Britain " the keys of the Universe, enabling their possessors to give laws to both oceans and to become the arbiters of the commercial world " — ended in failure in 1700. But Paterson, in a pamphlet published a year later urging a new Darién expedition, recorded his conviction of the practicability of a canal. If interoceanic communication were established, he wrote, through its ports would flow at least two thirds of the commerce of the East Indies, aggregating no less than thirty millions sterling, while the time and expense of a voyage to the East would be cut by one half.

The idea continued to be broached at intervals throughout the eighteenth century, but no real progress was made, and few systematic surveys were undertaken. Discussion was vague and academic, and the plans prepared were generally quite impossible. They often served only to perpetuate the grossest misconceptions regarding actual conditions in America. In 1735 the French astronomer, Charles-Marie de la Condamine, accompanied by several other scientists French and Spanish, measured an arc of the meridian on the plains of Quito, and after his return addressed a plea to the French Academy of Sciences for an isthmian canal. But the expedition had made only a superficial examination of the ground. The viceroy of Mexico in 1771 directed two engineers, Agustín Cramer and Miguel del Corral, to survey the Tehuantepec route. They found a place where they thought two rivers might be joined by a channel to form a continuous waterway

---

[1] Dampier, *Voyages* (ed. of 1906), i, pp. 200 f.

across the continent. But Charles III was not satisfied with their report, and in 1779 had the Nicaragua route surveyed more thoroughly than had been done before. The government was informed that it would be impossible to build a canal from the Lake to the Pacific, and this conclusion was echoed by Manuel Galisteo who examined the same region two years later.

When Spain declared war on Great Britain in 1779, the latter dispatched an invading force from Jamaica to San Juan de Nicaragua. Horatio Nelson, then a post captain, had charge of the naval operations, and in a letter from the West Indies betrayed what were probably the aims of his superiors, the control of the canal route: " In order to give facility to the great object of the government, I intend to possess the Lake of Nicaragua, which for the present may be looked upon as the inland Gibraltar of Spanish America. As it commands the only water pass between the two oceans, its situation must ever render it a principal post to insure passage to the South Ocean, and by our possession of it Spanish America is divided in two." The plan was frustrated by the deadly climate, and Nelson did little more than permanently impair his health.

The Panama route, meanwhile, was not entirely forgotten. A Frenchman, M. de la Nauerre, presented a memoir before the Academy of Sciences in Paris in 1785, recommending a ship canal via the Chagres River. He estimated the cost at one million francs (!). But he had never been to America, and prudently suggested going there to study conditions on the spot. Nauerre brought his scheme to the attention of the Spanish ambassador, the Conde de Aranda, who forwarded it in April, 1786, to Floridablanca. Of the author Aranda said, that he was " un torrente de verbosidad y de presunción de inteligencia, pero instruido en la teoría del ramo." He did not think much of the scheme. The Council of the Indies gave the matter some consideration, and requested several of its members, including the historian Muñoz, to investigate the outcome of such projects in the past. And it was finally decided to hand on the papers to the viceroy in New Granada, where engineers could draw up exact plans. In April, 1787, however, the king ordered the proceedings to be indefinitely postponed. An analogous scheme was being discussed at the same time in the Sociedad de los Amigos de Madrid, by a certain D. Manuel Gijón y Leon, a native of Quito. And Muñoz declared that he had proposed a canal through the isthmus at Panama seven years before. With the death of Charles III in 1788, and the coming of the Godoy regime, all thoughts of a canal were banished from the official mind.

Alexander von Humboldt, when he visited Mexico and Central America at the beginning of the nineteenth century, expressed surprise that after three centuries of Spanish occupation there was so little scientific knowledge of the physical features of the country. The elevation of not a single mountain, plain or city from Mexico to New Granada had been accurately measured. Indeed, it was largely the publication of Humboldt's stupendous work, the *Essai Politique sur la Royaume de la Nouvelle Espagne*, which roused a new interest in such matters in Europe and in America. The Spanish government itself was stirred to definite action. In 1814 the Cortes passed an act providing for a transisthmian canal capable of accommodating the largest vessels, and authorizing the formation of a company to execute the work. But Ferdinand the Well-beloved and his camarilla were already on their way back from France, and in America Spain's colonies were busy securing their independence. Spain's last chance to seize the honor and advantage which such an undertaking would have brought her was rapidly slipping from her. And in the nineteenth century, she was almost the only nation of western Europe to have no part in the negotiations so frequently entertained for the construction of an interoceanic waterway.

# PART II
# NAVIGATION

## CHAPTER IX

### GALLEONS AND FLOTAS

THE circumstances which attended the origin of the system of convoyed merchant fleets sailing between Spain and America have been described in an earlier chapter. Squadrons were first sent out in 1537 under Blasco Nuñez Vela, in 1540 under Cosme Rodriguez Farfan (carrying Vaca de Castro to Peru), and under Martin Alonso de los Rios in 1542. All made Nombre de Dios their objective, to collect the gold and silver of Peru, and picked up the treasure from Mexico and other provinces at Havana or San Domingo on the homeward voyage.

Apparently the rule establishing the periodical sailing of fleets was promulgated in August, 1543, on the occasion of the renewal of war with France. It was published by the licentiate Gregorio Lopez, member of the Council of the Indies, deputed in that year to make an official "visitación" or inspection of the Casa. Thereafter only ships of 100 tons or more might carry cargoes to the Indies, in fleets of at least ten vessels. Two sailings a year were provided for, one in March, the other in September, each fleet to be protected by a man-of-war equipped and maintained from the proceeds of the convoy tax or avería. The armed ship was to accompany the merchantmen until they separated for their respective destinations in the Caribbean, and then from Havana as a base sail after pirates among the neighboring islands. Such merchantmen as intended to return immediately were to reassemble at Havana, and after three months depart with the convoy to Spain. Ships from San Domingo, still one of the more important colonial ports and lying far to the windward of Havana, were permitted to return as a separate squadron, choosing one of their number as flagship, which was to carry less cargo and be more heavily armed than the rest.[1]

[1] N.M.C., vol. xxi, no. 13.

The next fleet which sailed from the Guadalquivir, in November of 1543, conformed, except in the date of departure, with these instructions. Its commander was Blasco Nuñez Vela, who this time went out to America as the first viceroy of Peru, and with him was the licentiate Sandoval of the Council of the Indies, on a mission as " juez de residencia " to New Spain. The real business of both was to impose the " New Laws " of Charles V upon his refractory colonial subjects. Soon after Blasco Nuñez' departure, the Seville exporters realized that a single armed vessel furnished rather inadequate protection; and the newly-created Consulado dispatched three other ships together with material for the arming of two in the Indies, to reënforce the fleet on the voyage back to Spain. And thereafter when convoys were provided they were generally of greater strength than the ordinances of 1543 required. In 1552, as we saw in another connection, the same regulations were operative, but the armada consisted of six ships instead of one, four ranging from 250 to 350 tons, and two from 80 to 100 tons.

The armada of 1552 was at the time designed to be the last of its sort; for in the beginning of that year, probably on the advice of Captain Diego Lopez de Roelas, it had been momentarily decided to abolish convoys and the convoy tax altogether, and compel each merchantman to be sufficiently armed to withstand attacks of the average corsair. Two naval squadrons were to be maintained by the Crown, one at Seville to guard the Andalusian coast and the seas between Cape St. Vincent and the Azores, the other at San Domingo to protect the islands and ports of the West Indies. Shipowners and masters were given nine months in which to comply with the king's decree, unarmed vessels which sailed before the expiration of that time having to accompany the armada then preparing. After the nine months, any ship properly equipped might depart for America alone.[1] The Seville squadron, in charge of Juan Tello de Guzman, saw active service in the next few years, pursuing corsairs and escorting treasure from the Azores to San Lucar. The flotilla for the defense of American waters was kept busy on various missions in Europe (among

[1] N.M.C., vol. xxi, no. 31.

others, accompanying Prince Philip to England), and did not sail for San Domingo till 1555, then under command of the same Tello de Guzman.

The intention to do away with fleets and convoys, however, was not long persisted in. At the prayer of the Consulado, the Emperor in 1553 issued a cédula restoring during the period of the war the semiannual flotas. They were now to leave in January and September respectively, each accompanied by four armed vessels maintained by the avería. The idea was that when the convoy reached the Caribbean it should disperse, one of the ships sailing with the merchantmen bound for San Domingo and the islands, another with the Tierra Firme ships to Nombre de Dios, and the remaining two with the Mexican flotilla as far as Cape San Antonio, whence they turned eastward to Havana. As before, Havana was the port of reunion for all homeward-bound vessels, except those from San Domingo and the other windward isles. Indeed, Havana was becoming so important in the scheme of the India navigation, that in February of the same year the audiencia of San Domingo ordered the residence of the Cuban governor to be removed there from Santiago, " por ser la Habana lugar de confluencia de navios de todas las Indias y la llave de ellas."[1] And as Cuba till the close of the sixteenth century remained very poor, its agricultural possibilities unknown or untried, for many years Havana drew its life and prosperity almost entirely from the sojourn of fleets and single vessels on their way to Europe, supplying fruits, salt meats and other provisions for the crews, and providing accommodations in the town for the passengers at exorbitant rates.

The prior and consuls of 1554, while approving the new measure as promising greater security, and therefore incentive, to trade, objected to the size of the armadas, chiefly on the score of expense. Each armed ship, they calculated, would cost 20,000 ducats, making 160,000 in all, without counting interest on money borrowed. Such a sum they pretended to be at a loss to know where to find. The avería alone could not furnish it, and since the Emperor had sequestered so much of the bullion remitted to

[1] *Colecc. de doc.*, 2d ser., vi, pp. 339, 347.

Spanish merchants, the latter were unable or unwilling to lend. The Consulado suggested instead a modification of the plan of 1552: that two squadrons be maintained by the king to cruise for pirates about the coasts of Spain and the West Indies, and that only two ships of war and a small, armed dispatch boat or patache accompany the fleets to America, one convoying the merchantmen to Tierra Firme, and the other with the patache the ships for Vera Cruz.[1] Vessels for Hispaniola or Honduras should follow the Mexican contingent till in the vicinity of their respective ports, trade with these regions being too slight to warrant a separate convoy. The armed ship and patache at Vera Cruz would be instructed to lade the treasure in all haste, within fifty days at the outside, and sail for Havana to join the vessels from Nombre de Dios and elsewhere for the voyage to Spain. Merchant ships at Vera Cruz, because of the time required for making their trade, could not be expected to depart so promptly, and must wait in the Indies for the next armada. The cost of such an enterprise might be met by a tax of $2\frac{1}{2}$ per cent on ex-

[1] La Villarica de la Vera Cruz, at the western extremity of the Gulf of Campeche, the sole port of entry for European commodities into the Mexican provinces, was founded by Cortes on Good Friday of 1519, before his march into the Aztec empire. Removed three years later to another site near by, it was transferred again to its present location, opposite the small, rocky island of San Juan de Ulua, in 1599. Old Vera Cruz, six leagues away, had too dangerous a roadstead for ships by reason of its complete exposure to the violent north winds prevalent in that region; and long before 1599 the narrow channel between San Juan de Ulua and the coast had served as a harbor, goods being transported in small barks to the city. The Spaniards began to build a fort on the island after Hawkins' visit in 1567, which was later elaborated into one of the strongest in the West Indies. The harbor, from a quarter to a half mile wide, was sheltered only by the island and a line of small reefs. As the water on the land side drops away suddenly to a considerable depth, vessels to withstand the winds were made fast to a wall by iron chains, bow end on, with anchors thrown from the stern to landwards, being moored so close to the island that one might step from the prow to the wall. The city itself stood on a flat, sandy, barren beach only a few feet above the sea level, surrounded by marshes and sand dunes, and so extremely unhealthy that many sailors unused to the country were stricken there. The better part of the population, given entirely to trade and maritime interests, remained there only while the fleets were in the harbor, living the rest of the time in the healthier town of Jalapa, higher up in the interior. And at Jalapa, after the unlading of each fleet, was held the great fair, to which flocked the merchants of the country to purchase at exorbitant prices the commodities from abroad.

ported goods, and on commodities brought back whatever was necessary to make up the required sum.[1]

Whether these proposals were adopted or not is uncertain. According to Veitia Linaje, a royal cédula of the following month (July 20) prescribed that whenever eight or ten vessels were ready to leave for the Indies, and armed according to the king's ordinances, they should be given license to depart. Another decree of August 11 apparently reduced the required number to six.[2] Such a ruling, however, is not inconsistent with the consulado's scheme, for, as often happened in later years, two of the merchantmen might be but partially laden, and armed as ships of war.

So was slowly evolved, toward the end of Charles' reign, the organization of the treasure fleets. Alternate schemes were offered by the Crown and by the merchants. About fundamentals there was general agreement; the differences affected the execution of details. No rule was very rigidly observed. Although to the close of the century the order was reiterated that no vessels sail except under convoy, exceptions were frequently made; and single ships, doubtless well armed, continued to cross the Atlantic. In 1554 there were at least three, in 1555 at least six. Sometimes one, sometimes two large, convoyed fleets sailed in the year. But in 1556, when a five years' truce was concluded with France, there seems to have been no convoy at all. Usually each flota consisted of vessels bound for every American destination, only dividing into two squadrons on entering the Caribbean, one turning southwest toward Venezuela, New Granada and Darién, the other supplying the major islands, Honduras and New Spain. These squadrons, moreover, after 1554 did not always return together from Havana. More often than not, the Mexican ships were delayed, and arrived at Seville later than those from Nombre de Dios; while other vessels returned without convoy in groups of from three to a dozen, and at any time of the year. Thus in 1551, among the ships carrying royal treasure, three arrived from New Spain in June, and one in July; eleven came

---

[1] *Colecc. de doc.*, 1st ser., iii, pp. 513–520.
[2] Veitia Linaje, lib. ii, cap. 6, par. 2.

together from the isthmus of Darién in September, and one alone in the same month; in October arrived two from Honduras, and two from San Domingo in November. In the following year, there was one from Tierra Firme and one from New Spain in February, another from the latter place in June, seven from Tierra Firme in July, three from San Domingo in September and one in December.[1] And such a record was characteristic of that time.

The convoys, too, varied considerably in size. In 1557 there were only two armed ships, the capitana and almiranta; in 1558 there were six, and on several occasions as many as eight. But for some years after the French war, two was the usual number. And they were not always employed solely as ships of war. As already intimated, they frequently carried merchandise like the other vessels. But they were the largest and stoutest ships, and they were supposed not to be loaded to capacity, reserving part of their tonnage for the accommodation of artillery and soldiers. By an ordinance of June 16, 1561, the capitana and almiranta comprising the convoy were to lade 100 tons less than their full burden, and carry at least thirty soldiers.[2] And it was the freight charge for this space, the cost of arms and munitions, and the pay and rations of the soldiers, which were defrayed out of the proceeds of the convoy tax. As was customary in most countries in the sixteenth century, even royal men-of-war were private ships hired by the Crown for a single voyage or for a stipulated term. But under no circumstances, according to the decree of 1561, might the general or rear admiral of the flotas be the proprietor of the ship in which he sailed. This same ordinance again declared it obligatory to depart in convoyed fleets on pain of forfeiture of vessel and cargo.

The royal revenues, and often bullion belonging to private persons, were carried on the armada, and on the largest merchantmen.[3] Before 1554 it was unusual for any of the armed

---

[1] A. de I., 2. 3. 7/8, ramo 2.
[2] Fernandez Duro, *Armada Española*, ii, p. 464; Veitia Linaje, lib. ii, cap. 6, par. 2.
[3] Whether this was the wisest practice or not was sometimes questioned. J. Andrea Doria in 1594 urged upon Philip II that bullion should always be shipped

ships to proceed as far as Vera Cruz. Some made for Nombre de Dios, the rest sailed round Cape San Antonio to Havana. Mexican gold and silver were shipped on small boats to Havana (earlier to San Domingo), and there transferred to the Seville fleet. From 1554 onwards, however, one or two ships of the convoy always accompanied the merchant vessels to Vera Cruz to receive the king's treasure. The change is strongest evidence of the increasing mineral output of the northern viceroyalty.[1]

It was in the years 1564–66 that the India navigation was given the organization it retained with little variation throughout the Hapsburg era. On October 18, 1564, appeared a new set of ordinances, providing for a separate fleet each year to New Spain and the isthmus of Panama, one to sail in the beginning of April (in 1582 advanced to May) for the Gulf of Mexico, taking with it the ships for Honduras and the Greater Antilles, the other departing for Nombre de Dios in August, and convoying vessels to Cartagena, Santa Marta and other ports on the northern coast of South America. Both, according to these regulations, were to winter in the Indies, the Panama ships leaving in January, those at Vera Cruz in February, so that each might make Havana in March. But to secure favorable weather conditions, they were not to depart thence for Europe before the tenth of that month. It was the first time that a sharp distinction was made between the flotas for New Spain and Tierra Firme; and although occasional circumstances made it necessary for the two fleets to sail together, thereafter they always retained their separate character and organization. Each was conducted by its own convoy, each had its own general, and almirante or rear admiral.

on lighter, swifter vessels which could outsail the English and Dutch. Bullion on the galleons of the convoy, he maintained, ran the greatest risk; for it was the business of the latter to fight, and even if the issue favored the Spaniards, there could be no assurance that every galleon would survive the encounter. *Colecc. de España*, ii, p. 171.

[1] Toward the close of the century, two armed ships were sent with the Mexican fleet each year to Honduras, to convey the king's treasure in the dangerous passage from Puerto de Caballos to Havana. At Havana it was usually transferred to the galleons. These "naos de Honduras" are sometimes referred to as a separate fleet, though they can scarcely be regarded as such. In 1633 they were suppressed, and the revenues from Central America thereafter sent to Spain via Vera Cruz. Veitia Linaje, lib. ii, cap. 5, par. 24 ff.; Milla and Gomez Carillo, ii, p. 272.

The times of sailing did not remain so constant as the above ordinances might imply. Sometimes the Mexican flota alone wintered in the colonies, that for Tierra Firme leaving San Lucar in the beginning of the year, often as early as January, and returning in July, or in September at the latest. Or, if the Panama fleet got away late, and the Crown was in immediate need of its American revenues, the general, with his flagship and one or two of his best vessels, was directed to return at once with the royal treasure, leaving the almirante to come with the rest of the fleet in the following spring. Such an arrangement was made in 1579, in 1582, and frequently toward the end of Philip II's reign. The August sailing was the more usual, and had the approval of the cosmographers and pilots associated with the India House. It allowed the fleet to arrive at the isthmus in the healthiest season of the year, and at a time when transport across to Panama was easiest and cheapest. It gave merchants at Nombre de Dios sufficient time to make their exchanges, and enabled the ships to sail in the spring months, regarded as safest for the navigation back to Spain. As for the Vera Cruz fleet, its departure from Seville remained fixed in April or May, because of the hurricane season later in the year, and the dangerous "northers" in the Mexican Gulf.

Annual sailings, too, were not the invariable rule, although they were the the ideal striven after, and sometimes achieved. From about 1580 onward a year was frequently skipped, and toward the middle of the seventeenth century, as the monarchy declined, the sailings became more and more irregular.

The incurable dilatoriness of the Spaniard also contributed to confuse the schedule of the American fleets. The Mexican flota sometimes did not get away till the end of June or even August and that for Panama till October or November. There was always a plausible excuse for the delay. At times it was the contrariness of the winds in the difficult port of San Lucar. Again, because of heavy rains the roads were impassable, and carts unable to bring the fruits of the country to Seville for shipment; there was a lack of efficient mariners or gunners; or, owing to the late return of the convoy with the fleet of the previous year, it could not be got ready in time to conduct the next fleet on the published date. But generally, we may believe, the underlying difficulty was the absence of any adequate system for compelling merchants and mariners to conform to schedule. Or if the system existed — for of laws and rules there was no end — the officers of the Casa were unwilling, or found it unprofitable, to make its operation effective. Indeed, in a cédula of 1582, precise dates were set when the capitana and almiranta should have been selected, the merchantmen careened and inspected, the fleet laded at San Lucar, the artillery and other equipment received on board; but these dispositions were rarely observed. And when in 1607 the Council suggested renewing them, the oficiales of the Casa interposed many objections.

The final touches to this maritime organization were added in 1565 and 1566. Till then, as already stated, the "armada" was usually composed of a few merchantmen more heavily equipped than the rest with artillery, gunners and soldiers. But the avarice of their proprietors and captains so encumbered them with goods, above decks and below, that they were of little or no use when occasion appeared for attacking corsairs or defending the fleet. In January, 1565, therefore, the decree went forth that thereafter the flagship or capitana must be a galleon of at least 300 tons, armed with eight large brass guns, four of iron, and twenty-four smaller pieces, and carrying 200 men in crew and soldiers. And under no circumstances was it to carry merchandise, unless it be the cargo rescued from vessels lost at sea. In October of the following year, the same rule was applied to the ship which bore the flag of the almirante.

In addition to these convoys, there still existed the Armadas de la Guardia de la Carrera de las Indias, naval squadrons which policed the waters between Cape St. Vincent, the Canaries and the Azores, and which occasionally accompanied the merchant fleets to the West Indies. These squadrons, it will be remembered, originated about the year 1521, when the danger from French pirates first became ominous, and it was for their maintenance that the tax called avería was originally established. When in the later years of Charles' reign large convoys of six or eight men-of-war are mentioned as sailing with the American fleets, we may feel certain that they were this Armada de la Carrera de las Indias, for the moment drawn upon for service in more distant regions. In Philip II's time it became more or less customary to send the armada with the fleet that went to Nombre de Dios, in order to give adequate protection to the enormous quantities of silver bullion exported from Peru when the yield of the Potosí mines was at its zenith. In the seventeenth century this was the invariable practice, so that the Tierra Firme fleet came to be known collectively in popular speech as the Galleons, from the type of war vessel composing its convoy. In contradistinction, the Mexican fleet became specifically the Flota, being defended only by the capitana and almiranta provided for in the decrees of 1564 and 1566.

In the asientos for the administration of the avería, concluded with the Consulado in the first half of the seventeenth century, it was usually stipulated that the armada de la carrera consist of six or eight galleons and several pataches or dispatch boats. But the accidents of war sometimes necessitated an increase, while occasionally in times of peace, when the comparative safety of the seas made large convoys seem an unwarranted burden upon commerce, the number of galleons was allowed to drop. In 1595, for instance, an armada of twenty ships sailed to the West Indies in pursuit of Drake and Hawkins, and to convoy the merchant fleets back to Spain. In December, 1630, again, the India Council decreed that the total of twelve galleons provided for in the contract of 1627 should in the following year be raised to twenty. And as the wars with Richelieu showed no signs of abatement, the new asiento with the merchants in 1633 required the regular maintenance of fourteen galleons in the India navigation, a number which in the following year was increased to sixteen.[1] On the other hand, in 1655 the armada commanded by the Marquis of Montealegre consisted of only four ships of war and two pataches, although the treacherous diplomacy of Cromwell made such reductions a dangerous economy, as was proved by the event. In times of great peril, extra squadrons were frequently

---

[1] Veitia Linaje, lib. ii, cap. 4, par. 13.

mustered in Andalusia or on the coasts of Cantabria, to reënforce the galleons when they arrived at the Azores.

The number of merchantmen comprising the India fleets varied considerably, depending on the state of American trade, the size of the ships employed, and the security of the seas. In Biedma's fleet of 1550 there were eleven or twelve trading vessels, convoyed by an armada of eight. Two years later, Bartolomé Carreño took out forty ships, twenty-four for Tierra Firme and sixteen for New Spain. Most of them were in so wretched a condition that only seven of the former and five of the latter returned with him to Europe. Four or five remained in America to engage in local, coastwise traffic, but at least twenty had to be careened and repaired before they could attempt the voyage back across the Atlantic.[1] In general, it may be said, squadrons returning from the Indies were smaller than when they set out from the Guadalquivir. The cargoes from America, consisting in the beginning principally of bullion, with some cotton, sugar and dyewoods, were less bulky than those sent to supply the needs of the new settlements. The Seville "armadores," therefore, frequently bought old ships which could be trusted to make one more voyage and might be scrapped on the other side. Farfan's fleet in 1554 included at least fifteen merchantmen. Of these, eight returned with him from Tierra Firme in the following year, and four from New Spain under his almirante, Diego Felipe. In 1556 the same numbers comprised the fleets from Nombre de Dios and Vera Cruz respectively. In 1557 fourteen merchant vessels accompanied the armada of Juan Tello de Guzman, and in the next year Pedro de las Roelas came from the Indies with nineteen. In 1562 Pedro Menéndez de Avilés went out with the extraordinary number of forty-nine ships, thirty-five from Seville and fourteen from Cadiz, and Roelas took twenty-eight from Seville in 1563. Toward the close of the century, the size of the fleets varied from thirty to ninety vessels. The following is a table of those sailing from Nombre de Dios:

[1] N.M.C., vol. xxi, no. 37.

| Year | General | Ships |
|---|---|---|
| 1585 | Antonio Osorio | 71 |
| 1587 | Miguel de Eraso | 85 |
| 1589 | Diego de Ribera | 94 |
| 1592 | Francisco Martinez de Leiva | 72 |
| 1594 | Sancho Pardo | 56 |
| 1596 | Francisco de Eraso | 69 |
| 1599 | Sancho Pardo | 56 |
| 1601 | Francisco del Corral | 32 |
| 1603 | Gerónimo de Torres y Portugal | 34[1] |

Throughout the greater part of the sixteenth century, the fleets dispatched to Tierra Firme and the Caribbean seem to have been larger than those sent to Vera Cruz. In the seventeenth, the reverse was more apt to be the case. In the northern viceroyalty increase of population, and therefore of the demand for European goods, if slow, was constant. There was also a considerable development of agriculture; and the inhospitable shores of New Spain offered few openings to the foreign interloper. In Peru society seems to have remained much more stationary, while on the Caribbean coasts Dutch and English traders were beginning to monopolize the commerce formerly confined to the Seville flotas.

In the seventeenth century, moreover, the whole number of vessels in the American fleets, whether bound for Vera Cruz or for Porto Bello, was as a rule less than earlier. This was a consequence of the increase in size of Atlantic ships, while trade, if it was not falling off, at least showed few signs of normal growth. In the time of the later Philips, the combined tonnage of the Panama and Mexican fleets was usually about 10,000 tons, of which 7000 were assigned to New Spain and 3000 to Tierra Firme.[2] It is difficult to believe that under Philip II, when ships rarely exceeded 200 or 300 tons burden, American flotas, even if composed of 40 or 50 vessels, could have surpassed this aggregate tonnage. If there were fewer ships, it was because the caravels of the sixteenth century were being superseded in

---

[1] *Relaciones hist. y geog. de América Central*, p. 174.
[2] This assignment was not invariable. Sometimes the tonnage was more equally divided, as in 1624, when 5500 were set apart for New Spain and 4500 for Tierra Firme. Veitia Linaje, lib. i, cap. 25, par. 23.

trade by the more capacious, and often clumsier, galleons and "urcas." Indeed the tendency to build larger ocean-going carriers outstripped the capacity of Spanish harbors to receive them. To obviate the delays incident to crossing the bar at San Lucar, a decree of June, 1618, excluded from the American navigation any vessel with a beam exceeding eighteen cubits and a maximum depth of more than eight and a half. And a later cédula, of December, 1628, decreed that no ships should be constructed for the India fleets, either merchantmen or men-of-war, of more than 550 tons.[1]

If, however, there was no actual decline in the tonnage of the fleets, it was not increasing in proportion to the growth and development of the colonies. Not only was the influence of the contrabandist and of the Philippine trade already severely felt, but the gradual extension of colonial industry probably helped to abate the demand for goods from Spain; while the Crown, in its straits for money, with increasing frequency granted permission to single vessels, "naos de registro," to sail to America, to the detriment of the regular fleets. Already in 1582 the Casa had exercised the right to limit the number of merchantmen in the flotas in accordance with the demand for European merchandise in America. This may or may not mean that trade was then beginning to fall off. It was just as likely a part of the monopolists' policy of keeping up prices by understocking the colonial market. In the early years of the following century, however, the lamentations of pessimistic observers began to arrest the attention of the king and his councillors. In 1603 the archbishop of Seville wrote to Philip III that the galleon trade was so weak and failing, that if the Crown did not speedily do something to remedy it, in a few years it was likely to disappear altogether.[2] So strong a statement may not have been unjustified, for only two years later, in September, 1606, it was questioned whether any merchantmen should be dispatched with the armada to Tierra Firme, as that region and Peru were understood to be abundantly supplied. And in 1612 the Marquis of

[1] Veitia Linaje, lib. i, cap. 25, par. 21, 31.
[2] *Colecc. de España*, lii, p. 565.

Salinas, president of the Council of the Indies, admitted to the king that the decay of trade was responsible for the limitation in the tonnage of the fleets. Apparently the Mexican trade was more flourishing, since Veitia Linaje tells us that in 1608 it was proposed to send two fleets in one year to Vera Cruz, to accommodate the demands of the exporters for shipping facilities.[1] Yet in 1620, while the New Spain ships were preparing, on news that the market in the colony was very poor, two of those elected for the voyage were excluded, the loss to the owners being distributed by means of an assessment among their more fortunate fellows.[2] A similar situation occurred in 1622, and in 1627. As in theory the vast region of New Spain was stocked with European commodities entirely by the Seville flotas, only two explanations are likely. Either prices had been raised by the monopolists to the point of diminishing returns, or the market was supplied from non-Spanish sources. In 1636 the Consulado petitioned the India Council that no merchantmen at all be sent to Vera Cruz in that year, for Mexico was glutted with wine, oil and manufactures, and the mere report of another fleet would still further embarrass the importing houses in the colony. And on other occasions in the following decades, the Consulado made similar proposals, either that the Tierra Firme fleet be omitted, or that intended for New Spain. Sometimes the council in Madrid heeded these pleas, sometimes for good reasons of its own it ordered a small flota to sail anyway.

This growing disinclination of the mariners and traders of Seville to join in the dispatch of flotas to the New World may be ascribed in part to the circumstances of the great European war, in which Spain under the guidance of Olivares was endeavoring to play too conspicuous a part. The Thirty Years War was a disastrous piece of business for the already decrepit Spanish monarchy. The State was utterly exhausted, the fountains of industry dried up, the treasury in bankruptcy. And the maritime interests of Andalusia especially suffered. The owners or lessors of ships which were taken over by the government, unable to

[1] Veitia Linaje, lib. ii, cap. 4, par. 29.
[2] *Ibid.*, par. 34; cap. 8, par. 3.

collect from an empty exchequer, faced entire ruin; while the sequestrations of American bullion threw the calculations of the merchants into confusion. Novoa, the historian of Philip IV, writes:

> No querían cargar si no los aseguraban el no tomarlos el dinero, las barras del oro y de la plata, y que les habían de dar y pagar lo que les debían y les habían tomado en las otras flotas pasadas, afianzado tantas veces y derogado otras tantas promesas y palabras, cédulas y firmas reales; porque si con lo que habían de cargar se lo habían tomado, ¿con qué caudal habian de prosiguir?[1]

In the second half of the seventeenth century, the decay of the galleon trade was complete, and the proud commercial aristocracy of Seville declined rapidly in numbers and wealth. Veitia Linaje says that after 1651 Mexico was no longer able to support an annual flota; and that whereas formerly the fleets attained to a size of eight or nine thousand tons, in his own day if one of three thousand could be dispatched every two years, it was considered a miracle.[2]

It was a matter frequently argued in the seventeenth century, by the Casa and the merchants, and in the Council of the Indies, whether the galleons of the armada de la carrera might be permitted to carry a limited amount of merchandise, or should be reserved solely for offense and defense and the transport of the king's treasure. The capitana and almiranta of the New Spain fleet, in spite of the decrees of 1565 and 1566, were frequently given such license. One of the principal motives urged was that of economy, the Casa either hiring vessels outright and then making what it could from the freights, or securing the ships at a reduced rate with the understanding that the owners might lade a stated amount of goods. But it was also admitted that the galleons carried cargoes *sub rosa* anyway, whatever the letter of the law, and that the government might as well gain some benefit by legalizing the practice. In the sixteenth century the concession was never made. In the seventeenth, the policy of the Crown fluctuated. Thus in the year 1613 the five galleons comprising

[1] *Colecc. de España*, lxxx, p. 239.
[2] Veitia Linaje, lib. i, cap. 14, par. 11; lib. ii, cap. 4, par. 29.

the armada, of an average capacity of 600 tons, were each permitted to carry 200 tons of cargo " de registro." And this continued till December, 1619, when in response to a petition of the mariners' gild, the privilege was apparently withdrawn.[1] The gildsmen declared that the galleons were often so overloaded as to be compelled to transfer part of their cargo at sea to vessels of the flota; and that the competition in freights deterred private enterprise from building merchantmen for the India trade. It was the latter circumstance, we may believe, which weighed most in the minds of the complainants. Whether or not as a consequence of such representations, in 1625 the capitana and almiranta of the Mexican fleets were again forbidden to ship any merchandise whatsoever. Yet in the spring of 1632 the practice was renewed, at least for a year or two, one-fourth of the capacity of the galleons being reserved for freight, and the factor of the Casa instructed to take charge of the business. In 1636, when the India Council proposed adding a surtax of $1\frac{1}{2}$ per cent to the 12 per cent of the avería, to defray the cost of new galleons, the Casa countered with the suggestion that the money be secured by selling to the highest bidder space equivalent to one-third of the available tonnage of the armada. Its officers explained that the concealment of merchandise defrauded the Crown of its customs, subjected honest traders to unfair competition by lowering prices in American ports, and opened the way for the introduction into Spain of unregistered silver, the proceeds of such traffic. The objection that the carrying of cargoes rendered the galleons unfit for fighting purposes, and destroyed public confidence in their efficacy, they met by the assertion that so long as the gun decks were free, a cargo in the hold made vessels steadier and more amenable to the helm, and in nowise detracted from their powers of defense. The Consulado and the mariners' gild, however, seem again to have opposed the scheme, and in that year the permission sought was not granted.[2] The curious feature of the situation was that both parties to the argument freely admitted, not only that the galleons carried goods when forbidden to do so, but that they carried them above decks where they were readily

[1] Veitia Linaje, lib. ii, cap. 4, par. 15. [2] *Ibid.*, par. 16.

detected and interfered with the ship's armament. Yet no effective measures were taken by the officials of the Casa to stop the practice. They pretended that, with the necessity of dispatching the fleet promptly, even if they had suspicion or knowledge of fraud, they dared not detain it for the time required to make a thorough examination. Captains sometimes made as much as 100,000 or 150,000 pesos in a single voyage from these clandestine freights, and from the sale of posts on the ship to merchants or their factors. There is no doubt that throughout the seventeenth century this was a crying abuse. Alvarez Osorio wrote, in the reign of Charles II, that the convoys were often so heavily laden that the greater part of the artillery was below the water line!

In the summer of 1638, the idea of freighting the men-of-war was broached again, this time by the India Council itself, the plan, apparently, being to send the galleons to Porto Bello alone, without any merchantmen at all. And in 1643 the rapidly diminishing returns of the avería, owing to the extension of clandestine trade, caused a recurrence to the project. But in each instance the old objections were renewed, and the matter allowed to drop.[1]

The captain general and almirante of the armada de la carrera were considered of superior rank to the flag officers of the flotas, for from the beginning they received their appointment directly of the king, whereas the others were for many years chosen by the jueces oficiales of the Casa. From about 1554 there were frequent disputes over this latter point, the opponents of the Casa maintaining that its nominees were incapable and little respected by captains, pilots and passengers, as a result of which many ships were lost by wreck or to corsairs. The Casa, on the other hand, clung tenaciously to its privilege, and found many means of persecuting, in a petty way, officers whose warrants issued from the Council at Madrid. So Pedro Menéndez de Avilés, who

[1] By a cédula of June, 1644, however, sailors and soldiers serving in the armadas were conceded the privilege of embarking free a certain number of jars of wine for sale in America, ranging from 250 jars for the pilot to 10 jars apiece for the "grumetes" or apprentices. The proceeds in silver were exempt from the payment of avería. Veitia Linaje, lib. ii, cap. 12, par. 20.

was probably the first so appointed, found to his cost.[1] The controversy seems to have been frequently between Andalusian seamen and those from other provinces of the kingdom. By the seventeenth century, however, all generals and almirantes were nominees of the Crown. The Junta de Guerra of the Council of the Indies presented lists of eligible persons to the king, from which the latter made his choice.[2]

There were two sorts of captains general, " proprietarios " or those appointed to the title and dignity for life, and those selected for a single voyage. It appears that like all other Spanish officials they usually bought their posts, or, in the later decay of the monarchy, advanced to the Crown a sum of money, 100,000 or 150,000 pesos, to be repaid in the Indies, generally at 8 per cent interest. After it became customary for the armada de la carrera to accompany the Tierra Firme flota to the isthmus of Panama, there were four flag officers in the fleet, two for the armada and two for the merchantmen, a superfluity which was not corrected till 1647, when appointments to the flota were discontinued. In 1583 was introduced the practice of sending with each fleet two "entretenidos," or aspirants to the command, one with the general and another with the almirante, to gain experience of their future duties.[3]

The generals and admirals took oath of homage and fidelity before the Council of the Indies, if they happened to be in Madrid, otherwise before the president and jueces of the Casa. In any case, they had to present themselves at once in Seville with their warrants and instructions, where they unfurled their standards in the harbor, and entered upon the multifarious duties connected with the outfitting of the fleets. Recruiting stands, with piper and drummer, were set up for the enlistment of mariners and soldiers, men between the ages of twenty and fifty and unrelated

---

[1] Ruidíaz y Caravia, *La Florida; su conquista y colonización por Pedro Menéndez de Avilés*, ii, pp. 34-59.

[2] B. M., Egerton Mss. 320. From 1625, at the suggestion of the Junta, commanders who had served in the India navigation, and were awaiting another appointment, were detailed to serve as supernumeraries with the captain general of the royal navy (Armada del Mar Océano), until otherwise provided for.

[3] When a viceroy of New Spain or Peru sailed on the fleet, the king usually gave him the rank of captain general for the voyage, but the office was purely an honorary one.

in any way to the officers of the Casa. The general saw to it that the gunners were of nautical experience, and examined by the captain of artillery; that passengers were inscribed on the registers, carried the requisite arms, and conformed to all the regulations governing their passage;[1] that each ship sailed with sufficient provisions for the voyage, and carried a chaplain to hear confession and comfort the sick; that charts, astrolabes, etc., were inspected and sealed; in short, that all obligations touching the preparation and armament of the galleons under his command were strictly observed. In conference with the almirante and the pilot major of the fleet, he also drew up sailing instructions, to be distributed to the captains and pilots on the day of departure. Just before setting out, word was sent to Cadiz that ships laded there should be ready to join the fleet as it dropped down the Andalusian coast. And in the sixteenth century, when Canary boats were compelled to sail in company of the Seville flotas, a small vessel was dispatched to the islands to warn merchants to be prepared at the fleet's approach.[2]

A number of appointments in the armada were within the gift of the general: the chaplain of each galleon, the master carpenter and the master calker, the physician (a post first created, apparently, in 1593), the barber-surgeons, the commanders of pataches or dispatch boats (in earlier times often those of merchant ships as well), and the quartermasters and other petty officials of the flagship. Petty officers of the other galleons were nominated by the respective captains.

The armada also carried a regiment of infantry, called the " tercio de galeones," commanded by a " gobernador " appointed by the king, and distributed by companies among the fleet. In the seventeenth century, its officers often secured their posts in return for loans of money to the Crown, to be repaid in the Indies.

[1] Passengers on the armadas had to take along their own rations for the voyage, captains and other officers being forbidden to maintain them at their table. It is very doubtful whether the rule was enforced.

[2] Veitia Linaje, lib. ii, cap. 1, par. 9–11, 14, 15, 19, 20; Fernandez Duro, *Armada Española*, ii, pp. 206 f.

The general of the galleons exercised complete authority in his fleet from the moment of induction into office; the general of a flota only after departure from San Lucar or Cadiz, the authority meanwhile lying with the Casa de Contratación.

The gobernador had the next choice of galleon after the general and the almirante, his vessel being usually called the "gobierno." Veitia Linaje says that this regiment was for many years one of the most distinguished in the royal service, until the government in 1634 ordered the special quarters and pay of the soldiers to be discontinued, and the regiment joined to the garrison at Cadiz. It lost, consequently, its distinctive character and corporate tradition, and when the muster was called for the next voyage, many of the former members had scattered and were not to be found.[1] Two companies of infantry were generally assigned to the Mexican fleet, sometimes recruited for the occasion, sometimes drawn from the Cadiz garrison. No passengers might be enrolled as soldiers, on pain of a heavy fine. But occasionally, owing to lack of men, the rule was suspended, especially for the voyage back from America. Persons so enlisted received rations, but no pay.

Each fleet carried a veedor (on the galleons called the veedor general), a sort of king's attorney, whose business it was to see that all laws and ordinances respecting the management and governance of the fleet were observed, and that each man performed his duties, from the captain general down to the least of the commissioned officers. Every detail of the daily life of the ships, whether at sea or in port, was supposed to come under his eye. He was at the general's side during the inspections and musters, a sort of royal watchdog for all occasions. He was appointed by the king on the nomination of the Consulado, was immune from arrest or judicial process, and like the general provided with elaborate instructions from the council or the Casa de Contratación.

Other officers were a contador, or comptroller general, on each armada (not on the flotas); an alguacil mayor or chief constable for each ship; gunners and a captain of artillery; maestres de plata, entrusted with the coin, bullion and precious stones both of the king and of private persons;[2] stewards, or maestres de

[1] Veitia Linaje, lib. ii, cap. 2, par. 2, 3.
[2] Maestres de plata were apparently first appointed near the close of the sixteenth century, when it was no longer customary to 'ship bullion on merchant vessels. Before that time gold and silver had been entrusted with other registered articles

raciones, who had charge of the provisions, powder and munitions, together with their assistants, the clerk of rations, water bailiff, and dispenser; quartermasters and their assistants; a clerk or notary for each vessel, and a notary general for the entire fleet; apothecaries, carpenters, calkers, and coopers; a diver on the flagship and on the almiranta; four trumpeters for the general; and eight gentlemen-in-waiting, at the discretion of the general, distributed among the ships of the armada.[1]

After 1605 the final authority in all matters pertaining to the preparation and dispatch of the American fleets was vested in the Junta de Guerra y Armadas de Indias, a committee of the Council, and the nominations to the principal posts either originated in it, or were made to it by the president and judges of the Casa. All commissioned officers, before admission to their places, had to give security to the Casa for the faithful performance of their duties. Apparently till the middle of the seventeenth century, this was fixed at double the year's salary. In 1647 a schedule was drawn up as follows:

|  | ducats silver |
|---|---|
| General de galeones | 8,000 |
| Almirante de galeones | 4,000 |
| General de flota | 4,000 |
| Almirante de flota | 3,000 |
| Capitán, veedor, contador, gobernador del tercio, maestre de plata | 2,000 |
| Sargento mayor (military engineer) | 1,500 |
| Piloto mayor, contramaestre, alguacil mayor, escribano | 1,000 |
| Piloto, alférez, escribano de raciones, dispensero | 500 |
| Alguacil de agua | 400 |
| Médico, cirujano | 300 [2] |

to private ship captains. The maestres were usually men of considerable means and reputation. In the beginning chosen by the general of the fleet, after 1592 their selection devolved upon the Casa, and after 1615 upon the Council of the Indies. They gave a special bond of 25,000 ducats on entering upon their duties.

At first these officials received 1% of the treasure given over to their care. In the seventeenth century, the schedule was: 1% for coin; ¾% for bullion from New Spain; 1 peso de ocho of every 100 pesos de minas of Peruvian bullion; ¼% of all royal treasure from New Spain; and 90 maravedis for every bar of 50 marcs weight sent to the king from the southern viceroyalty.

[1] Veitia Linaje, lib. i, cap. 27; lib. ii, caps. 2, 3, 9, 10, 23, 24. The notaries and notaries-general were all nominated by the Consulado and approved by the Casa.
[2] *Ibid.*, lib. ii, cap. 1, par. 8.

As the fleet sailed out from Cadiz or San Lucar, the flagship led the van, the other vessels keeping its standard in sight by day, and following its great ship's lantern by night. Instructions of 1573 ordered the merchantmen to sail in battle formation (orden de batalla), probably meaning in several ranks arranged in the general shape of a half-moon. The almiranta brought up the rear, while the rest of the armed convoy kept to the windward, so as to be able to come to the assistance of any in danger or distress. The almiranta was instructed to speak with the flagship twice each day, and both were to take daily count of the ships, awaiting those which had dropped behind, and seeking the intentions of any stranger in their midst.[1] Captains or pilots who deliberately permitted their vessels to fall out of sight or drift from the course, were threatened with death, later mitigated to a fine of 50,000 maravedis, immediate loss of rank, and two years exclusion from the India navigation.

Beyond Cape St. Vincent, the general or almirante visited each ship of the fleet, to see that the artillery was properly mounted and served, to punish offenders against public order and decency, to discover and seize unregistered or prohibited merchandise, or goods stored in places forbidden by the ordinances, and to arrest unlicensed passengers, so that they might be landed in the Canaries and sent back to Spain. The same formality was observed before leaving Havana for the homeward voyage. And at regular intervals, usually once a fortnight, whether at sea or in port, the general was expected to hold a muster of all persons under his jurisdiction. From the very first there were strict instructions that no blasphemy be permitted in the fleet, and that no single women be allowed on board except a few laundresses. Till the middle of the seventeenth century, commanders of armadas exercised during the voyage an exclusive judicial authority over the mariners and soldiers of the men-of-war, but not over those of the flota, the latter being reserved for the Casa de Contratación. After 1651, however, a special judge or auditor

[1] A fifth of the proceeds of prizes taken at sea was reserved to the Crown, and usually conceded by the king to the captain general. The rest was divided among officers and crew, including the general, according to rank. Spanish vessels recaptured from the enemy were restored entire to their owners.

was designated to accompany each armada for the cognizance of civil and criminal suits.[1]

The route from the Andalusian coast was southwest to the shores of Africa, and thence to the Canaries, considered a run of seven or eight days. In early times it was customary to stop at these islands, complete there the provisioning of the fleet, and pick up Canary boats sailing to the west. In the seventeenth century the practice apparently was discontinued. But in any case, if the general found it necessary to call, he was strictly enjoined to allow no one to land except for food and water, permit no changes in cargo or equipment, and to make another general inspection of the ships upon resuming the voyage. Usually dispatches for the king were dropped there, and sometime a patache sailed ahead to Cartagena and Porto Bello, carrying letters from the court and announcing the fleet's approach. The general had orders to put into no port not designated in his instructions, and in case he was driven in by storm or other accident, to remain only twenty-four hours. For any loss or damage resulting from a longer delay, he would be held to account and rigorously punished.

From the Canaries the fleet sailed west by southwest to about 16 degrees, and then catching the trade winds continued due west, rarely changing a sail until Deseada, Guadaloupe or one of the other West Indian islands was sighted. Occasionally the Tierra Firme fleet pointed farther south, and entered the Caribbean by the channel between Tobago and Trinidad, afterwards named the Galleons' Passage.[2] It was the constancy of these east winds, so favorable for navigation to America, but so formidable for the return voyage, that urged the companions of Columbus to mutiny. But it made infinitely easier the path of the great discoverer, as it was a boon to all navigators who followed. In the sixteenth century, the journey from the Canaries to Deseada ordinarily consumed from twenty-five to thirty days.

---

[1] Veitia Linaje, lib. ii, cap. 1, par. 12, 15, 23, 24, 70; cap. 2, par. 43.

[2] In earlier times, a fleet occasionally made San Juan de Porto Rico the first port of call, and thence steered toward the South American mainland. See instructions to Sancho de Biedma, 1550, in A. de I., Patr. 2. 5. 5/13, no. 8, pt. 1.

From Deseada the galleons steered an easy course southwest to Cape de la Vela, and thence to Cartagena, reaching the latter port six or seven weeks after their departure from Spain. Opposite Margarita, an armed patache left the fleet to visit the island and collect the royal revenues, although after the exhaustion of the pearl fisheries the island lost most of its earlier importance. At the same time merchant ships intending to trade on the coasts they were passing either accompanied the patache or sailed alone during the night, and made for Carácas, Maracaibo or Santa Marta, to get gold, cochineal, leather and cocoa. But they were permitted to separate from the convoy only with the license of the general, countersigned by the almirante and the pilot major. And with each were sent instructions indicating the time for rejoining the fleet at Cartagena or Havana, with copies for the governor or audiencia of the port to which they were bound. From Cartagena the galleons continued westward to Nombre de Dios or Porto Bello on the isthmus.

Owing to the ever-present danger from corsairs, the rule was laid down in 1579 that no ship might enter or leave a port in the Indies under cover of darkness, without risk of being fired on by the forts. If a vessel arrived after nightfall, it had to anchor outside and send in word by a pinnace. When a fleet came within sight of the fortress at the mouth of a harbor, the flagship fired one gun if an armada, if a flota two guns, as signal that the approaching ships were friendly. Single vessels also fired two guns on nearing a port, or if without artillery dipped the main-topsail.

The course of the Mexican flota from Deseada was in a general northwesterly direction, passing Santa Cruz and Porto Rico, and sighting the little isles of Mona and Saona, to the Bay of Neyba in Hispaniola, where the ships took on wood and water.[1] Putting to sea again, and circling round Beata and Alta Vela, the fleet sighted in turn Cape Tiburon, Cape de la Cruz, the Isle of Pines, and Capes Corrientes and San Antonio at the west

---

[1] Oppenheim, *The Naval Tracts of Sir William Monson*, ii, pp. 335 ff. Instead of watering in Hispaniola, the fleet sometimes stopped at Dominica, or at Aguada in Porto Rico.

end of Cuba. Meanwhile merchantmen had dropped away one by one, sailing to San Juan de Porto Rico, San Domingo, Santiago de Cuba, and Truxillo and Caballos in Honduras, to carry orders from Spain to the governors, receive cargoes of leather, cocoa, etc., and rejoin the flota at Havana. From Cape San Antonio to Vera Cruz there was an outside or winter route and an inside or summer route. The former lay northwest beyond the Alacran reefs, west or southwest to the Mexican coast above Vera Cruz, and then down before the wind into the desired haven. The summer track was much closer to the shore of Campeche, the fleet threading its way among the cays and shoals, and approaching Vera Cruz by a channel on the southeast.

The general, arrived at Porto Bello or Vera Cruz, exhibited to the colonial authorities his instructions from Spain, and was for the time being subject to the orders of the viceroy or audiencia of that region. When the armada de la carrera sailed to the isthmus, however, its commander took precedence over the president of Panama. The customs officers had full power to visit and inspect the galleons, as they inspected the merchantmen; and if the former carried a part cargo, guards were placed on board, as on merchant vessels, to prevent the secret abstraction of unregistered articles.

The general might require lodgings for his soldiers in the town, and maintain a guard of twenty-five at his own quarters. But at Havana and Cartagena, which were first-class fortresses, it was customary for the governor to furnish a guard of honor from the garrison. If convenient (within twenty or thirty days, according to earlier instructions), the general sent duplicate dispatches in cipher to Spain, one direct and the other via Havana, concerning the state of the country, the amount of treasure to be expected, the prices of merchandise in the colonies, the probable date of departure, etc. And if the flotas wintered in America, word of this decision was forwarded within a month to Seville. A formal report upon the condition of the forts and garrisons of the places visited was likewise prepared for the information of the India Council.

The cost of provisions and other supplies purchased for the homeward voyage was defrayed out of the royal treasure, and the exchequer recouped from the proceeds of the avería in Seville. Under no circumstances might requisitions be made upon the money of private individuals, or upon the Bienes de Difuntos. The crews and armament of merchant ships remaining in the Indies were used to supply deficiencies in the returning fleet, the captains after unlading being required to give particular account of their men, artillery and stores, and strictly forbidden to dispose of any without permission from the general. As unlicensed emigrants often went over in the guise of sailors, the crews were expected to return at the first opportunity, and if they refused were sent back under arrest. Any citizen of the port who bought provisions or arms from the sailors without leave, or who aided or harbored deserters, subjected himself to the general's private jurisdiction.[1] The general, admiral and other warrant officers were from the first forbidden to carry goods to America other than was required for personal use, to own ships in the flota or have any interest in them, to engage in any sort of trade during the voyage, or receive gifts from passengers or merchants. But the enforcement of such rules was rarely attempted, and the extent of these irregular practices was a scandal throughout the sixteenth and seventeenth centuries.

Whatever vessels were in port lading for Spain at the time of the fleet's visit were expected to sail in its company, nor were the authorities permitted to make exceptions to this rule. The object was not only to insure protection against pirates, but to keep information from reaching the outlaws through the mischance of a ship's capture. Indeed frequently when the galleons were in the Indies, all ports were closed by the Spaniards, for fear that precious knowledge of the whereabouts of the fleet and of the value of its cargo might inconveniently leak out to their English, French or Dutch rivals.

The ships at Porto Bello, in view of the prevailing east winds in that region, and the maze of reefs, cays and shoals extending far out to sea from the Mosquito coast, in making their course to

[1] Veitia Linaje, lib. ii, cap. 1, par. 16; cap. 2, par. 45.

Havana first sailed back to Cartagena upon the eastward coast eddy, so as to get well to the windward of Nicaragua before attempting the passage through the Yucatan Channel. They anchored at Cartagena a second time for a week or ten days to receive the king's revenues, when they were rejoined by the Margarita patache and by the merchant ships sent to trade along the Spanish main. From Cartagena the course was northwest past Jamaica and the Caymans to the Isle of Pines, and thence round Capes Corrientes and San Antonio to Havana, a run generally of about eight days. Here the fleet refitted and revictualled, received tobacco, sugar and other Cuban exports, and if not ordered to wait for the Mexican flota, departed for Seville. From New Spain the route to Havana was also an indirect one. As Vera Cruz lay dead to the leeward of Cuba, the fleet sailed north by northeast to about 25 degrees, then steered southeast, and reached Havana in eighteen or twenty days.[1]

If, as sometimes happened, the two fleets were instructed to meet at Havana and return home in company, it was the older rule that the general who arrived first should wait till the middle of June, and if the other appeared within that time, give him at least eight or ten days grace to make whatever dispositions were necessary. But later the sailings became so irregular as to render this detail obsolete. There were also ordinances to the effect that if the Tierra Firme fleet was unable to reach Spain by the latter part of October, it should winter at Cartagena or Havana. But in the seventeenth century they were rarely observed. The necessities of the Spanish exchequer, and the great expense of tying up the ships for five or six months in America, outweighed the supposed dangers of approaching the Spanish coasts in the stormy season. When the fleets sailed together, the commander of the Mexican flota lowered his flag to the general of the galleons or armada de la carrera. If the Tierra Firme fleet was unaccompanied by the galleons, and the two generals were therefore of equal rank, the one who reached Havana first took precedence,

[1] In the first half of the sixteenth century, before Havana became the port of dispatch for returning ships, and when San Domingo was still one of the principal centres of American trade, the route out of the Caribbean was through the Mona Passage between Hispaniola and Porto Rico into the Atlantic.

the other acting as almirante. But these rules touched only matters of navigation, the internal governance of each fleet remaining with the respective commanders.[1]

The course for Spain was from Cuba through the Bahama Channel, northeast between the Virginia capes and the Bermudas to about 38 degrees, in order to recover the strong northerly winds, and then east to the Azores. In winter the fleets sometimes ran south of the Bermudas (the route followed by Columbus and his immediate successors), and then slowly worked up to the higher latitude; but in so doing they often either lost ships on the Bermuda reefs, or to avoid these slipped too far south, were forced back into the West Indies, and missed their voyage altogether. The Bahama strait was one of the most dangerous passages in the journey. It lay in the path of violent hurricanes at certain seasons, and the reefs at the entrance, round the lower part of Florida, bore the significant name of Cabezas de los Martires. At its narrowest point it is only thirty-nine miles wide. Pedro Menéndez de Avilés, shortly after his second voyage, and prior to his establishment of the Spanish settlement at St. Augustine, began to urge upon the king the necessity of ports of refuge near this channel where vessels might put in for repairs. And one of the most powerful arguments for the maintenance of the Florida colony, which was always a drain upon the colonial exchequer, was the rescue of Spaniards cast away in that neighborhood.

At the Azores the general, meeting with his first intelligence from Spain, learned if there were corsairs or hostile squadrons reported in the vicinity, and where on the coast of Europe or Africa he was to make his first landfall. He was usually instructed before reaching the islands to clear out the staterooms and berths of the passengers and put his ships in fighting trim; and with these precautions he made for the port of San Lucar. The Crown was very solicitous that as the fleet approached along the coast of Algarve, no shallop or other small vessel should be permitted to communicate with the shore on any pretext, or any one from shore be allowed to come aboard the ships; the ordinances im-

[1] Veitia Linaje, lib. ii, cap. 1, par. 39, 40, 45, 48.

posing a penalty of 200 stripes and ten years in the galleys for infraction of this rule. On arriving in port, the general was expected to send advice immediately to the Council of the Indies, by the hand of the president of the Casa. But in Veitia Linaje's time, the practice had arisen of dispatching directly to Madrid one of the gentlemen attendant upon the general with the good news of the fleet's return.[1]

The last stage in the general's progress was the "residencia," or judicial inquiry into his acts since the fleet's departure from Spain. The residencia apparently did not become customary till toward the close of the sixteenth century. Thereafter, at the end of each voyage, the commander and his principal subordinates underwent an investigation or scrutiny of thirty days (later often prolonged to six months or more), conducted in secret by a member of the India Council, or more commonly by the president or one of the judges of the Casa. In theory it was a searching ordeal, but from what we know of the irregularities almost universal on the fleets, and the few generals who were brought to account, we may conclude that it was more often an empty formality.

I have followed, with perhaps the same slow pace of the galleons themselves, the India fleets from Seville across the Atlantic to the New World, and back to the quays of the Casa de Contratación.[2] For passengers and sailors it was a long and trying experience. Although they broke the monotony by improvising mimic bullfights, by illuminations, cockfights, shark fishing, and religious festivals, quarters were painfully restricted,

[1] Decrees of 1616 directed that within a month of the return of the fleets to Spain, a dispatch boat be sent to Tierra Firme or New Spain, as the case might be, with word of the safe arrival, dispatches from the court, and private letters. The vessel was sent at the charge of the royal exchequer, and generally permitted to carry some agricultural produce in order to reduce the expense. Veitia Linaje, lib. ii, cap. 21, par. 2.

[2] The principal sources used for this description are the instructions issued to Sancho de Biedma, June, 1550 (A. de I., Patr. 2. 5. 5/13, no. 8, pt. 1), and to Pedro Menéndez de Avilés in 1562 (A. de I., 139. 1. 1, lib. 1); the code of ordinances published in 1597, and used by Veitia Linaje as the basis of chapter 1, book ii of the *Norte;* the "Ordenanzas para las armadas del mar Océano y flotas de Indias," November 4, 1606 (printed by Salas, *Marina Española*, p. 65); and the memoir of MM. Dehalde and de Rochefort to the French king in 1680 (Margry, *Relations et mémoires*, p. 192).

and, after several weeks of sailing, food none of the best. The most striking incidents were the passing of the Canaries, the landfalls in the Windward and Leeward Islands, where the Caribs, if not hostile, came out in canoes to exchange fruits for hardware and trinkets, and the appearance of an occasional corsair, who boldly mingled with the fleet to reconnoitre the convoy, and perhaps snap up a laggard before its fellows could come to the rescue. Alonso Enriquez de Guzman, who in 1535 went out to seek his fortune in Peru, writes in his diary:

> It is now ten days since we have seen land, and we shall consider ourselves lucky if we see it in twenty days from this time. Fortunate are they who now sit down content before their fresh roast meat, especially if a fountain of water flows near their doors. They have now begun to serve out water to us by a measure, and the people on board prefer drinking what is in the ship, to seeing that which is outside. I really believe that there are many here who would be glad to return to Spain, and to have paid their passage without making the voyage.[1]

In the sixteenth and seventeenth centuries, dispatches were carried to and from the Indies, between fleets, on light, swift-sailing caravels of from 60 to 100 tons. Under Philip II the sailings were apparently irregular, but in 1628, in the contract of the Seville merchants with the king for the administration of the avería, it was stipulated that they send four mail boats each year, two to New Spain and two to Tierra Firme, at the pleasure of the president and oficiales of the Casa. This number of regular sailings continued throughout the rest of the century, the business remaining in the hands of the Consulado. After 1664, it seems, a boat departed every three months, going directly to Cartagena for the dispatches from Peru, thence to Havana to pick up those from Mexico and the islands, and back to Spain. It was originally forbidden to carry any merchandise or passengers on these vessels, but the rule was rarely observed.

[1] *Life and acts, 1518–1543* (tr. by Sir C. R. Markham, London, 1862), chap. 36.

## CHAPTER X

### CORSARIOS LUTERANOS

IN the sixteenth and seventeenth centuries corsairs were ever an imminent peril in the India navigation, as they continued to be till the nineteenth on the waters of the Mediterranean and in the Far East. There were always freebooters upon the seas as there were highwaymen upon land. Modern cruisers with rifled guns have eliminated the one, though brigands persist in spite of a twentieth-century constabulary. Something has been said in an earlier connection of the activities of the French on the trade route between Spain, the Canaries and the Azores in the first fifty years after Columbus. They were equally active in the West Indies. Cabot found a French corsair near the Bay of All Saints in Brazil when on his way to the Rio de la Plata in 1526. The ship *San Gabriel* of the expedition of Loaysa to the Philippines had to defend itself against three which attacked it upon the same coast.[1] In July, 1540, an English ship seized a Spaniard laden with sugar and hides near San Domingo. The pirate was wrecked immediately after, close to Cape Tiburón, but the crew put their prisoners ashore and escaped in the prize, leaving behind in their haste their French pilot.[2] The colonial authorities, in reporting the incident, asked the king for two armed galleys to defend their coasts.

A letter dated April 8, 1537, written by Gonzalo de Guzman to the Empress, affords some interesting details of the exploits of an anonymous French corsair in that year. In the previous November this Frenchman had seized in the port of Chagres, on the isthmus of Panama, a Spanish vessel laden with horses from San Domingo, had cast the cargo into the sea and sailed away with the empty ship. A month or two later he appeared off the

---

[1] Fernandez Duro, *Armada Española*, i, 204.
[2] *Colecc. de doc.*, 1st ser., i, p. 572.

coast of Havana and dropped anchor in a small bay a few leagues from the city. As there were then five Spanish ships lying in the harbor, the inhabitants compelled the captains to attempt the capture of the pirate, promising to pay for the vessels if they were lost. Three of about 200 tons each sailed out to the attack, and for several days they fired at the corsair, which, being a caravel of light draught, had run up the bay beyond their reach. Finally one morning the Frenchman was seen pressing with both sail and oar to escape from the port. One of the Spaniards cut her cables to follow in pursuit, but encountering a heavy sea and contrary winds was abandoned by her crew, who made for shore in boats. The other two Spanish ships were deserted in similar fashion, whereupon the French, observing this new turn of affairs, re-entered the bay and easily recovered the three drifting vessels. Two of the prizes they burnt, and arming the third sailed away to cruise in the Florida strait, in the route of ships returning from the West Indies to Spain.[1]

According to Herrera, San German in Porto Rico was sacked in 1540, and La Burburata on the mainland in 1541. In January, 1544, on the day of Santiago, 300 Frenchmen entered the city of Cartagena before dawn, guided by a compatriot who had lived there, overcame the Spaniards after a short defense in which four or five were killed and the governor twice wounded, plundered the place and got 35,000 pesos in gold and silver alone, besides other spoil.[2] The freebooters, however, were not always so uniformly successful. This same band sailed from Cartagena to Havana, but found the inhabitants prepared and retired with the loss of fifteen men. Another party of eighty, who attempted to seize the town of Santiago de Cuba, were repulsed by a certain Diego Perez of Seville, captain of an armed merchant ship then in the harbor, who later petitioned for the grant of a coat of arms in recognition of his services.[3] In October, 1544, six French vessels attacked the settlement of Santa Maria de los Remedios, near Cape de la Vela, but failed to take it in face of the stubborn resistance of the colonists. Yet the latter a few months earlier

[1] *Colecc. de doc.*, 2d ser., vi, p. 22.   [3] *Colecc. de doc.*, 2d ser., vi, p. 23.
[2] Fernandez Duro, *op. cit.*, i, p. 432.

had been unable to preserve their homes from pillage, and had been obliged to flee to La Grangeria de las Perlas on the Rio de la Hacha.[1] The pirates had robbed the churches, and even disinterred the dead in their search for booty. They marched into the country, maimed live stock and cut down the fruit trees and gardens. There is little wonder, indeed, that the defenders were so rarely victorious. The Spanish towns were ill-provided with forts and guns, and often entirely without ammunition or any regular soldiers. The distance between settlements as a rule was great, and the inhabitants, as soon as informed of the presence of the enemy, knowing that they had no means of resistance and small hope of succor, left their homes to the mercy of the freebooters and fled to the hills and woods with their families and most precious belongings. In July, 1548, the prior and consuls of Seville complained that American towns, especially Santa Marta, Cartagena, Nombre de Dios and Havana, were either without protection or their defenses so weak as to be as good as useless. And a letter of September 11 from the authorities at Santa Marta to the Emperor declared that unless a fort and artillery were soon provided, the settlement would be abandoned. The audiencia of San Domingo in March, 1549, urged that small flotillas of caravels be constructed to guard the West Indian coasts. They should be equipped with oars, sheathed with lead, and armed with artillery of brass " pues la de hierro con los soles y la humedad se pierde pronto en Indias." The judges suggested a tax of 1 per cent on all merchandise entering or leaving the colonies to defray the expense.[2]

These appeals, however, met with little response, and West Indian waters were so dominated by Frenchmen that intercolonial trade virtually ceased. In October, 1554, a band of 300 swooped down upon the unfortunate town of Santiago de Cuba, were able to hold it for thirty days, and carried away the value of 80,000 pesos. The following year witnessed an even more remarkable action. In July of 1555, the celebrated captain, Jacques Sore, landed 200 men from a caravel a half league from the city of

---

[1] Marcel, *Les corsaires français au xvi siècle dans les Antilles*, p. 16.
[2] Fernandez Duro, *op. cit.*, i, p. 438.

Havana, before daybreak marched on the town and forced the surrender of the castle. The Spanish governor had time to retire to the country, where he gathered a small force of whites and negroes, and returned to surprise the French by night. Fifteen or sixteen of the latter were killed, and Sore, who himself was wounded, in a rage gave orders for the massacre of all the prisoners. He burned the cathedral and the hospital, pillaged the houses and razed most of the city to the ground. After transferring all the artillery to his vessel, he made several forays into the country, burned a few plantations, and finally sailed away in the beginning of August. No record remains of the amount of the booty, but it must have been considerable. To fill the cup of bitterness for the poor inhabitants, on October 4th there appeared on the coast another French ship, which had learned of Sore's visit and of the helpless state of the Spaniards. Several hundred men disembarked, sacked a few plantations neglected by their predecessors, tore down or burned the houses which the inhabitants had begun to rebuild, and seized a caravel loaded with leather which had recently entered the harbor.[1] It is true that during these years there was almost constant war in Europe between the Emperor and France; yet this does not entirely explain the activity of French privateers in Spanish America, for we find them busy there in the intervals when peace reigned at home. Once unleash the sea dogs, and it was exceedingly difficult to bring them again under restraint.

The adventures of English privateers in Spanish seas in the time of Queen Elizabeth are too well known to merit a repetition of the story here. In the following century, under the first two Stuarts, there was a lull in their activities. James made his peace with Spain in 1604, and the aristocratic freebooters who had enriched themselves by despoiling the Spanish Indies were succeeded by a less romantic but more practical generation which devoted itself to trade and planting. One English captain, however, William Jackson, made a raid in 1642–43 which emulated the exploits of Sir Francis Drake and his contemporaries. Provided with letters of marque from the Earl of Warwick,

[1] *Colecc. de doc.*, 2d ser., vi, p. 360.

Admiral of the Fleet for the Long Parliament, and with duplicates under the Great Seal, he started out with three ships and about 1100 men, mostly picked up in St. Kitts and Barbadoes, and cruised along the Main from Carácas to Honduras, plundering the towns of Maracaibo and Truxillo. On March 25, 1643, he dropped anchor in what is now Kingston harbor in Jamaica, landed about 500 men, and after some sharp fighting and the loss of forty of his followers, entered the town of Santiago de la Vega, which he ransomed for 200 beeves, 10,000 pounds of cassava bread and 7000 Spanish dollars. Many of the English were so captivated by the beauty and fertility of the island that 23 deserted in one night to the Spaniards.[1] Soon thereafter Jackson sailed for England, but was wrecked near Land's End and lost most or all of his booty.

It is a rather remarkable fact that throughout these two centuries, when Spain was so frequently at war with the northern maritime powers, and corsairs swarmed the western seas, the capture or destruction of the treasure fleets, so ardently desired by these intruders, was so rarely accomplished. The "corsarios luteranos," as the Spaniards indiscriminately called them, hovering about the broad channel between Cuba and Yucatan, prowling in the Florida strait or in the waters near the Azores, were the nightmare of Spanish seamen. Like terriers they hung upon the skirts of the great, unwieldy flotas, ready to snatch away any unfortunate vessel which a tempest or other accident had separated from its fellows. But while occasionally they succeeded in cutting off one or two of the Spaniards, they never were strong enough to attempt an entire fleet. Thomas Gage tells us that when sailing in the galleons from Porto Bello to Cartagena in 1637, four privateers hovering near them carried away two merchant ships under cover of darkness. As the same fleet was leaving Havana, just outside the harbor two strange vessels appeared in their midst, and getting to the windward of them singled out a Spanish ship which had strayed a short distance from the rest, suddenly gave her a broadside and made her yield. The vessel was laden with sugar and other goods to the value of 80,000

[1] B. M., Sloane Mss. 793 or 894; Add. Mss. 36,327, no. 9.

crowns. The Spanish rear admiral and two other galleons gave chase, but without success, for the wind was against them. The whole action lasted only half an hour.[1]

It needed a powerful squadron, fitted out with all the resources of a hostile government, to encompass the destruction of the Indian galleons. And this happened but three times, in 1628, in 1656, and in 1657. The first to accomplish it were the Hollanders. In the twelve years' truce of 1609 between Spain and the Netherlands, by which the latter virtually secured that independence for which they had struggled so long, Philip III reserved the right to prohibit trade with his own territories in America, yet declared that he would throw no impediment in the way of Dutch trade with any native states beyond the limits of the Spanish dominions. This was interpreted by the Holland merchants to mean free intercourse with all places in the East and West Indies not in actual possession of the Spaniards. And after several years of discussion, in 1621 was incorporated the Dutch West India Company, so closely identified with the oligarchic mercantile interests controlling the Dutch state as to be virtually a service of the government. As in the same year the Spanish truce expired and hostilities were promptly renewed, the West India Company undertook the colonial end of the struggle. From 1623 onwards it conducted a ceaseless naval war in the transmarine provinces of Spain and Portugal. Within two years the extraordinary number of eighty ships, with 1500 cannon and over 9000 sailors and soldiers, were dispatched to American waters.[2] One of the fleets, composed of 26 ships and 3300 men, in May, 1624, captured San Salvador (Bahia), the principal seat of Portuguese power in Brazil; and although the place was retaken in the following year by Fadrique de Toledo, the Dutch later occupied Pernambuco, and for nearly twenty-five years retained possession of a considerable part of that coast. In 1626 three squadrons were cruising in the Mexican Gulf and off the coast of Florida, in search of the silver fleets; but they either failed to discover their prey, or had not dared attack on account of inferior strength.

[1] Gage, *A New Survey of the West Indies* (ed. of 1655), pp. 199 f.
[2] Blok, *History of the People of the Netherlands*, iv, p. 36.

One was commanded by Piet Heyn, who as vice admiral had greatly distinguished himself at the capture of San Salvador. Heyn, like many another distinguished mariner of that day, had begun his career as a corsair. He had been captured by the Spaniards, and served four years in the galleys; but on recovering his freedom he returned to the "course," and with audacity and good fortune attained to the rank of admiral in the employ of the West India Company. In 1627 he was in command of a squadron which captured a fleet of Portuguese merchantmen laden with sugar and tobacco in the Bay of all Saints; and a year later he appeared in the West Indies again with the design of intercepting the flota from Vera Cruz. With 31 ships, 700 cannon and nearly 3000 men, he cruised along the northern coast of Cuba, and on September 8 fell in with his quarry near Matanzas Bay to the eastward of Havana.

The flota, consisting of thirty merchantmen convoyed by five galleons, had sailed from Vera Cruz on July 21, under command of Juan de Benevides y Bazan, but just outside the harbor had run into a "norther," the flagship being cast ashore and the rest compelled to return to port. On August 8 the fleet set sail again, now reduced to four galleons and eleven merchantmen, with an armament of about 225 brass and iron guns. Meanwhile Heyn had divided his vessels into two squadrons, one entrusted to his vice admiral, Hendrik Lonk, so as to keep watch on all the usual maritime routes; and by the swarm of private interlopers and corsairs he was kept informed of what happened within the extensive zone of operations. From Spanish coasting vessels he learned that news of his presence had spread abroad, and that the fleets were detained in expectation of further orders. But although it was almost September, he kept to his purpose. Removing to a distance from the Cuban coast, beyond the range of the lookouts, he sent out scouts, one of which fell in with the ships of Benevides and accompanied them for a day without being questioned or disturbed. At the same time the two ships from Honduras, deceived by the news of Heyn's disappearance, set out for Havana, found themselves surrounded by part of the enemy near that port, and made vain efforts to escape. One was dismasted by the fire of the Hollanders and forced to surrender, the other was run aground at the entrance to the harbor.

According to Benevides' own story, when the New Spain fleet first sighted the Dutchmen, in a council held aboard the flagship there was a division of opinion. One party was for fighting a way to Havana, the other, supported by Benevides, preferred running into the "Matanzas" River, disembarking the treasure and hiding it in the woods. The latter advice prevailed, and the flagship led the way followed by the rest. But in the twilight it ran aground on an uncharted shoal, and the almiranta and other galleons coming on close behind did the same. Evidently these four armed vessels, which also carried the silver, went ahead leaving the unprotected merchantmen to shift for themselves. In the disorder and confusion the officers called on the general to restore discipline, but his authority was nil. Seeing the Dutch enter and launch boats for an assault, he ordered his people to burn their vessels and make for shore, saving what treasure they could. And he himself, after preparing a mine for the enemy in the poop of the capitana, fled up the river in a shallop to find some one who would carry word of the disaster to the governor of Havana. Of the entire Spanish fleet only three vessels escaped, under cover of night, to the latter port, and most of the rich cargo was diverted into the coffers of the Dutch West India Company. Heyn remained many days at Matanzas transshipping the booty. The four galleons were refloated, and with them and four of the best merchantmen, in which everything of value was gathered, the Dutch admiral sailed through the Florida strait to Europe, arriving in the month of November. The gold, silver, indigo, sugar, and logwood were sold in the Netherlands for 15,000,000 guilders, and the company was able to distribute to its shareholders the unprecedented dividend of 50 per cent.[1]

When the news reached Madrid via the Low Countries, writes Novoa, " atormentó al reino, hizo temblar á los hombres de negocios, y confundió el caudal de todos, poniendo en suma congoja á los mas, no tanto por la faltad que al Tesoro hiciera,

---

[1] Blok, *History of the People of the Netherlands*, iv, p. 37; Fernandez Duro, *op. cit.*, iv, pp. 97-106.

como por la afrenta conque se engrosaban los enemigos para acabarnos de destruir."[1] The general and almirante of the captured flota returned to Spain with the galleons of Tomás de La Raspuru, which had tarried at Cartagena till certain that the seas were free, and on arrival they were immediately arrested and thrown into prison. In the trial the prosecutor for the Crown was the celebrated jurist, Juan de Solórzano Pereira, member of the Council of the Indies and formerly a judge of the audiencia in Lima. In the charge it appeared that Benevides had not obeyed the ordinances or his own particular instructions, that the galleons and merchant ships were so overloaded as to render the artillery of no effect, that the ranks of the soldiers had been filled up with passengers and the general's dependents, that Benevides held no musters or reviews and issued no instructions to his captains, and that neither before nor after entering Matanzas did he make any preparations for defense or offer any resistance.

The almirante's record was a more honorable one. Before entering Matanzas he had prepared his vessel for battle, haranguing the soldiers and offering rewards from his own purse to the bravest. After his ship ran aground, he continued fighting till the enemy boarded and further resistance was useless. Then taking off his habit of Santiago so as not to be distinguished from the sailors, he surrendered and was put on shore by the Dutch with the rest. Benevides, after five years of imprisonment in the castle of Carmona, was executed in Seville. The almirante ended his days in a penal settlement on the African coast.[2]

Juan de Benevides should not be accepted as typical of Spanish admirals and generals in the India navigation. Most of them must have been men of courage and resource, although, as was true in all maritime countries at that time, few were professional seamen. The safety of the treasure fleets was so essential to the solvency of the government, and indeed of the nation, that the council and the merchants between them must have made

---

[1] Novoa, *Historia de Felipe IV*, quoted by Fernandez Duro.

[2] Solórzano Pereira, *El discurso y alegación contra el general D. Juan de Benevides Bazan* (Madrid, 1631).

doubly sure of the commanders they chose. Although shipwrecks were astonishingly frequent, they were usually due to other causes — bad ships, overcrowding, ignorant seamen — rather than to the incompetence of the general. And that so few fleets fell a prey to their numerous foes is no small testimony to the efficacy of the system evolved.

The Dutch not only invaded the West Indies, from the beginning of the century they also harassed the coasts of Chile and Peru. Their exemplar in such enterprises was, of course, Sir Francis Drake, the second circumnavigator after Magellan. He had been imitated in 1587 by Thomas Cavendish, who captured the Manila ship, *Santa Ana*, on the coast of Lower California, and seven years later less fortunately by Richard Hawkins. The first expeditions of the Dutch, in 1598 and 1615, were not very successful, although the latter, commanded by Joris Spilbergen, defeated a small armada sent against it by the Peruvian viceroy, and captured a few merchant vessels which fell in its way. The most remarkable of these Pacific enterprises was fitted out in the spring of 1623. A squadron of eleven vessels (the two largest of 600 tons each) set sail from Holland in April under Admiral Jacques l'Hermite, with the intention of capturing the South Sea fleet conveying the bullion from Callao to Panama, and of establishing a permanent base in some Peruvian port. According to some accounts, l'Hermite expected to win over the negro slaves by offering them their liberty, and to this end carried a large supply of arms and saddles, instead of merchandise for trade as in earlier expeditions to those regions. He took four caravels on the Portuguese coast filled with sugar from Brazil, tarried a month in the Cape Verde Islands for provisions, and then sailed south to Guinea and round Cape Horn to the islands of Juan Fernandez to water and refit. Profiting by the experience of his predecessors, he avoided the coast of Chile, from whose ports advice would have been sent to alarm the entire region, and keeping to the high seas determined to surprise Callao.

The South Sea fleet, however, had departed for the north on May 3, 1624, five days before the Hollanders appeared. Its cargo was an unusually rich one, the accumulation of two successive years, and the Limeños were in the midst of celebrating its dispatch, when news came of a Dutch fleet to the windward preparing to disembark. The colonists were in a panic, and the viceroy, the Marquis of Guadalcázar, had the greatest difficulty in preventing them from fleeing en masse to the interior with their goods and chattels. The enemy landed on the eighth at nightfall, but finding no resistance and fearing an ambuscade, retired to the ships again. On the eleventh they attempted to burn some vessels in the harbor, but were repulsed. They remained in command of the sea, however, seized all vessels that approached, and continued the blockade for five months. In the meantime l'Hermite died of an illness contracted on the voyage, and was succeeded by his vice admiral, Hugues Schapenham. Finally after sacking Guayaquil and destroying a galleon of 500 tons on the stocks, Hugues raised the siege of Callao and returned round the Horn to join the fleet of the West India Company before San Salvador.

In Spain numerous suggestions were forthcoming for averting a repetition of such an enterprise. It was proposed that an armada be sent at once to defend the Pacific coasts, an idea rejected on the score of expense and the risk of capture by the Dutch on the way out. It was suggested that Valdivia be fortified as the only southern port where the Hollanders might be tempted to establish a permanent base; that a watchtower be built on Juan Fernandez, with an advice boat to warn the mainland of the approach of the enemy; and that the sailing time of the South Sea fleet be advanced from May to November, so that the Dutch, who could pass through the strait only from December to March, might have to wait eight or nine months through a southern winter, and far from the base of supplies, for the departure of the treasure to Panama. So far as we know, none of these ideas were acted upon immediately by the government. Apparently at the opening of the year 1625, it was decided to send eight galleons of the armada of Fadrique de Toledo through the strait, but owing to the empty state of the royal exchequer they were never fitted out for the voyage.[1]

[1] B. M., Add. Mss. 13,975, f. 174; Egerton Mss. 320, 321.

In 1638 the Dutch made another desperate effort to intercept the American flotas. Pernambuco they were using as a naval base for operations in the West Indies, and from there Cornelius Joll, one of the most skilful and daring of Dutch captains, sailed with twenty-four ships at the time the fleets were accustomed to join at Havana. He lost several vessels in a hurricane, and did not find the Mexican flota, for unfavorable winds had providentially delayed it at Vera Cruz till news came from Havana of the sighting of the enemy. Similar advice to Cartagena did not arrive in time to prevent the galleons from setting out. They included six men-of-war, and were commanded by Carlos de Ibarra. On August 30 they discovered the Dutch to windward, seventeen ships, and two battles were fought. On the thirtieth the Dutch, counting on superior numbers, tried at once to board, and were shaken off at sundown after eight hours of fighting. The Spanish general was wounded, and the capitana and almiranta badly cut up. But the enemy probably suffered as much, for they did not return to the attack till September 3. After a severe cannonading the Dutch retired again, leaving the galleon, *Carmona*, dismasted and helpless. Ibarra decided to make for Havana at all costs, but when on September 5 he saw the Dutch fleet reenforced to the number of twenty-four, he could not think of risking another encounter, and turning about set his sails for Vera Cruz. One merchantman alone, which out of fear had parted company with the rest on the first day, was captured by the Hollanders. Even the silver on the *Carmona* was rescued, and the hulk floated into a bay on the Cuban coast. Ibarra reached Vera Cruz in safety on September 24, and wintered there with the Mexican flota.[1]

There was great disquiet in Spain when the year 1638 passed without sign or news of the fleets. And although reassuring dispatches eventually arrived from the viceroy in Mexico City, the government had to continue living another year on credit at usurious interest. The united fleets returned by an unusual route, touching neither at Havana nor at the Azores, and entered Cadiz Bay on June 15, 1639, to the great contentment of the realm.

[1] B. M., Add. Mss. 13,975, ff. 242, 244; Fernandez Duro, *op. cit.*, iv, chap. 13.

Most of the Indian fleets at this time were undermanned and underarmed, even when the danger from corsairs and hostile naval squadrons seemed greatest. The galleons which sailed in June, 1625, under the Marquis of Cadereyta, and returning with the flota in November just escaped the English fleet under Wimbledon near Cadiz, was notoriously lacking in armament; and the Casa de Contratación wrote to the Council urging that at least 150 hundredweight of powder be hurried to Havana to supply a suitable defense for the homeward voyage.[1] So, too, the galleons of Ibarra in 1638 were short of men and munitions, although they succeeded in driving off the Dutch. These were days of pessimism and social and political dissolution in the Spanish monarchy. Olivares' attempt to play a grand rôle in European politics was thwarted by the masterly policy of Richelieu, and with defeat abroad there was favoritism, administrative inefficiency and bankruptcy at home. Shipbuilding virtually ceased, and with the maritime losses in Europe and America, the Spanish navy disappeared from the seas. Louis XIII wrote to the archbishop of Bordeaux in May, 1640, doubtless with malicious exaggeration, that Spain's entire naval armament consisted of one vessel hired from the English and another lent by the Duke of Florence.[2] That the armadas de la carrera, though maintained by the Seville Consulado, should be sent out with inferior equipment is therefore not surprising. It is far more a source of wonder that the India fleets continued to sail with any degree of regularity at all. It was probably only made possible by the hiring of foreign-built ships, a practice inconsistent with the ancient policy of the Casa.

In the latter years of Philip IV, and during the reign of the imbecile Charles II, there was no let to this progressive maritime decadence. The Indian fleets decreased in size and frequency, although, whether or not by the intercession of those saints whose protection was so importunately evoked by Spanish seamen, they generally managed to elude their persecutors. The colonies in America continued in a state of military and naval defenselessness, forts without artillery, nominal companies of infantry

[1] B. M., Egerton Mss. 321, f. 27.  [2] Fernandez Duro, *op. cit.*, iv, p. 259.

without soldiers, and the inhabitants more ready to take to the hills and woods than to oppose any resistance to the invader. Indeed, as far back as 1587 the Spanish engineer, Bautista Antonio, had written of the inhabitants of Panama: ". . . forasmuch as the most part of these people are marchants, they will not fight, but onely keepe their owne persons in safetie, and save their goods; as it hath bene sene heretofore in other places of these Indies."[1]

In May, 1655, an expedition sent out by Oliver Cromwell captured Jamaica, the first permanent acquisition by another European power of an integral part of Spanish America. This expedition, consisting of 2500 men and a considerable fleet, set sail from England in December, 1654, with the secret object of "gaining an interest" in that part of the West Indies colonized by the Spaniards. The Protector aimed not only to plant one more colony in the New World, but also to secure a base whence he might dominate the route of the treasure fleets.[2] The commander, General Venables, was not bound by his instructions to any definite plan. It had been proposed, he was told, to seize Hispaniola or Porto Rico or both, after which either Cartagena or Havana might be taken, and the Spanish revenue fleets obstructed. An alternative scheme was to make the first attempt on the Main at some point between the Orinoco and Porto Bello, with the ultimate object of securing Cartagena. Reënforced by some 5000 volunteers from Barbadoes and neighboring islands, the English first attacked the city of San Domingo, where they suffered two shameful defeats from a handful of Spaniards on the 17th and 25th of April. They then sailed to Jamaica, a poor colony sparsely inhabited, and took possession without difficulty on May 11 and 12.

Whatever Cromwell's motives — and there was also something of the Crusader in his character — there could be no adequate justification for this secret attack upon Spain. She had been the first to recognize the Puritan republic, and was willing, and even

---

[1] Hakluyt, *Navigations* (ed. of 1904), x, p. 135.
[2] Exactly similar were the objects of La Salle, twenty-five years later, in urging the colonization of Louisiana at the mouth of the Mississippi.

anxious, to league herself with it. There had been actual negotiations for an alliance, and Cromwell's offers though rejected had never been really withdrawn. Without a declaration of war or formal notice of any sort, a fleet was fitted out to fall unawares upon the colonies of a friendly nation. The attack was inspired by Drake and Raleigh, a reversion to the Elizabethan gold hunt.

The soldiers of the expedition, designed to be kept as colonists in the West Indies, proved to be discouraging material. They were more eager to plunder the Spaniard than to plant corn, and in the war which ensued they were soon given opportunity to try their hand. From July to December of 1655 the English fleet, commanded by Vice Admiral Goodson, was on the coast of the Main between Cartagena and Porto Bello lying in wait for Spanish merchantmen. In October, Santa Marta was taken and sacked, though the booty secured scarcely repaid the powder and shot expended; and six months later Rio de la Hacha suffered a similar fate. In the middle of June, 1656, Goodson had fourteen vessels lying off the Cuban coast near Cape San Antonio, to intercept the galleons or the flota, both of which fleets were then expected at Havana. But his ambition to repeat the achievement of Piet Heyn was not to be realized. The Tierra Firme fleet, he eventually learned, had sailed into Havana on May 15, and on the 13 of July, three days before he appeared off that port, had departed for Spain. Goodson remained on his station, however, till the end of August, watching in vain for the ships from Vera Cruz which, warned in time, had concluded to winter in America.

The two Spanish fleets escaped Goodson only to fall in the way of Admiral Blake's squadrons off the coast of Europe. The Tierra Firme fleet, comprising two galleons, two armed "urcas" or store ships, and three merchantmen, after a voyage of fifty-eight days approached the Andalusian coast in September. Outside Cadiz it was surprised and attacked by three English frigates commanded by Captain Stayner. The capitana was captured with 2,000,000 pesos in bullion, together with the richest of the merchantmen, one urca accidentally caught fire and sank (it was said with 600,000 pesos), and the almiranta, which carried over a million pesos, also burned after a heroic defense of six hours. One urca escaped with the general into Cadiz, and the other two merchant ships succeeded in finding refuge at Gibraltar. The Spanish armament was decidedly inferior to that of Stayner, the four Spanish men-of-war carrying altogether only 104 guns, the three English ships 64, 54, and 52 guns respectively. But the Spaniard's fond belief in the invincibility of his heavy galleons was again rudely shaken.[1]

All the following winter Admiral Blake and his captains remained on their stations blockading the Spanish coast and effectually cutting off communications between Spain and her ultramarine possessions. This winter blockade was a new departure in naval warfare, something which no ships had ever achieved before. Meanwhile the flota, which had lingered in New Spain, arrived without accident at Santa Cruz in the Canaries in February of 1657, where the treasure, registered as 10,500,000 pesos, was disembarked and carried five or six miles into the hills. Blake soon had intelligence of the Spaniards' whereabouts, and on April 13 set sail from Cadiz with twenty-three ships. The harbor of Santa Cruz was strongly protected, with a castle of forty guns at the entrance, and six or seven stone forts connected by three lines of barricade to shelter musketeers. The Spanish vessels were ranged in a half-moon along the shore, as close as possible to the batteries. Fernandez Duro says that there were two galleons, eight merchantmen and a patache. English accounts agree in making the number sixteen. The discrepancy is doubtless accounted for by other vessels not part of the flota. Early on Monday morning, April 20, twelve English frigates led by Captain Stayner ran past the forts, anchored opposite the Spaniards, and by one o'clock had burned or silenced them all. By three o'clock the work of destruction was complete. Blake, meanwhile, with the rest of his ships was engaging the forts near the entrance, and by sundown all the English had succeeded in getting out of the harbor.[2] It was the most brilliant action of the Commonwealth navy, and dealt a blow which was felt on both sides of the Atlantic. Bullion stowed away in the Canary hills was about as useful as in

[1] Firth, *Protectorate*, i, pp. 50–52; Fernandez Duro, *op. cit.*, v, pp. 22 f.
[2] Firth, *op. cit.*, i, pp. 237–258; Fernandez Duro, *op. cit.*, v, p. 24.

the American mines. Spanish finances were disorganized and military operations fatally hampered, while with the destruction of the shipping needed for the next voyage, prices in the colonies rose suddenly for all commodities imported in the European fleets.

In the West Indies, the half-piratical naval war continued. In the autumn of 1658 Colonel Doyley, governor of Jamaica, made a futile effort to intercept the galleons on their course eastward from Porto Bello to Cartagena, and failing his prey, attacked and burned the towns of Santa Marta and Tolu. In the following spring, three frigates were again harrying the South American coast, landing at Cumaná, Coro, and Puerto Cabello, and returning to Port Royal with booty estimated at between two and three hundred thousand pounds sterling.

The war with Spain was essentially a war of the Commonwealth, and with the coming of Charles II into possession of his kingdom in May, 1660, hostilities naturally ceased. The dispatch to Jamaica in 1662 of a new governor, however, Lord Windsor, fortified with instructions " to endeavor to obtain and preserve a good correspondence and free commerce with the plantations belonging to the king of Spain," resorting to force if necessary, did not augur well for the peace. The question of English trade with the Spanish colonies in America had first come to the surface in the negotiations for the treaty of 1604, after the long warfare between Elizabeth and Philip II. The endeavor of the Spaniards to obtain an explicit prohibition of commerce was countered by the English demand for entire freedom. The Spaniards protested that it had never been granted in former treaties or to other nations, or even without restriction to Spanish subjects; but the English commissioners held steadfast, and offered to forbid trade only with ports actually under Spanish authority. A compromise was finally reached in the ambiguous words, " in quibus ante bellum fuit commerciam, juxta et secundum usum et observantiam,"[1] a phrase which appeared again in Cottington's treaty of 1630. Charles II was determined to secure this privilege of free trade with the Spanish colonies, and instructed his succes-

---

[1] Dumont, *Corps diplomatique*, v, 2, p. 625 (art. ix of the treaty).

sive ambassadors at Madrid, Fanshaw, Sandwich, and Godolphin, to press for the concession. Meanwhile, it was made clear to his governors in the West Indies that they were to cajole or frighten the Spanish authorities there into compliance. The efforts of Windsor to come to a " good correspondence " with them were fruitless, and the alternative policy was resorted to. In October, 1662, 1300 men in eleven ships, most of them privateers, sailed from Port Royal under Captain Christopher Myngs, and captured and plundered Santiago de Cuba, the Spanish port nearest to Jamaican shores; and four months later, in February, 1663, a similar fate befell the city of Campeche, on the gulf of that name.

Although the English government, to satisfy the clamors of the Spanish court, wrote letters to Jamaica forbidding such undertakings in the future, subsequent instructions continued to be ambiguous, and the privateers' commissions were not recalled. In October, 1663, a certain Captain Cooper brought into Port Royal two prizes, the larger of which, a ship from Seville, carried 1000 hundredweight of quicksilver for the Mexican mines, besides oil, wine, and olives. Letters from Jamaica in 1664 placed the number scattered abroad in privateering at from 1500 to 2000 men sailing in fourteen or fifteen ships;[1] and the island was soon the principal headquarters for those " buccaneers " whose exploits are perhaps the most characteristic feature of West Indian history in the seventeenth century. Spain was impotent to make their actions a casus belli; and indeed corsairing " beyond the line " had been so customary ever since the days of Charles V that it was scarcely regarded in the same serious light as similar hostilities in Europe. English and French ambassadors at Madrid consistently maintained that the treaties of peace did not extend to tropical America, and Louis XIV, as already related, more than once held the buccaneers as a club over the heads of the Spanish authorities when French participation in the galleon trade was threatened or seriously interfered with.

The buccaneers were most of them in the beginning recruited from the hunters of wild cattle and pigs, who, especially on the

[1] *Calendar of State Papers*, colonial series, v, nos. 744, 765, 786, 812.

northern shores of Hispaniola, gained a rude livelihood by curing the hides, and drying the flesh to supply the needs of passing vessels. When these scattered groups of hunters first appeared we do not know — probably in the first quarter of the seventeenth century. They were mostly English and French, deserters from ships, crews of wrecked vessels, chance maroons, or refugees from the settlements in the Windward and Leeward Islands. A small, rocky island on the northwest coast of Hispaniola, called by the Spaniards Tortuga, offered them a convenient retreat should their neighbors become troublesome, and probably before 1630 it was already one of their headquarters. The island suffered various vicissitudes. It was an English colony under the protection of the Providence Company from 1631 to 1640, and after 1640 in possession of the French. It was attacked by Spanish forces from San Domingo five times between 1630 and 1654, and each time but one the inhabitants momentarily driven out. After a temporary English occupancy in 1656–60, the island became definitely French, was ceded in 1664 to the new French West India Company, and became the centre whence radiated the colonization of the important French dependency of Saint Domingue.

Until about 1650 buccaneering in the West Indies was more or less accidental, occasional, in character. In the second half of the century, after the capture of Jamaica, came the period of leaders like Mansfield, Morgan, and de Grammont, the heyday of this piratical fraternity. Then they usually sailed under commissions, real or pretended, from the authorities at Jamaica or Tortuga, set aside a tenth of the profits for the governor, and sometimes as much to pay the English admiralty dues. Or, when their prizes were unauthorized, they withdrew to some secluded coast to make a partition of the booty, and on their return to port eased the governor's conscience with politic gifts.

It was the Spanish coast towns on the Caribbean and the Gulf of Mexico which suffered most from the buccaneers' activities. For them the record was a terrible one. Between the years 1655 and 1671 alone, the corsairs had plundered eighteen cities, four towns and more than thirty-five ·villages — Cumaná once,

Cumanagote twice, Maracaibo and Gibraltar twice, Rio de la Hacha five times, Santa Marta three times, Tolu eight times, Porto Bello once, Chagres twice, Panama once, Santa Catalina twice, Truxillo once, Campeche three times, Santiago de Cuba once, and other towns and villages in Cuba, Hispaniola and Central America for thirty leagues inland innumerable times. And this tale of robbery and outrage does not embrace the expeditions against Porto Bello, Campeche, Cartagena and other Spanish ports made after 1671. The Marquis of Barinas in 1685 estimated the losses of the Spaniards at the hands of the buccaneers since the accession of Charles II to be 60,000,000 crowns; and these figures covered merely the destruction of towns and treasure, without including the loss of merchant ships and frigates.[1] The most celebrated of the expeditions was of course that which, under Henry Morgan, captured and sacked the city of Panama in January, 1671. It was by such means, coupled with the trade of the interloper, that the fountains of Spanish-American commerce were dried up, not by the destruction of the silver fleets.

The English policy of "forcing a trade," however, proved a complete failure, and after 1670 was definitely abandoned for one of conciliation. On July 18 of that year, just a month before Morgan sailed from Jamaica for Panama, a treaty was concluded at Madrid by Sir William Godolphin for "composing differences, restraining depredations, and establishing peace" in America. No trading privileges in the West Indies were granted by either Crown, but the king of Spain for the first time acknowledged the sovereignty of the English king over all islands, colonies, etc., in the New World then in his possession, and the ships of either nation, if in distress, were promised entertainment and succor in the ports of the other.[2] Thereafter, although an occasional colonial governor found his cupidity too strong for him, the buccaneers were driven more and more into open piracy. There were from the beginning reasons which made it dangerous to treat the freebooters too curtly. Privateering maintained a great number

---

[1] Fernandez Duro, *op. cit.*, v, p. 310.
[2] Record Office (London), State Papers. Spain, vol. 57, f. 76; vol. 58, f. 27.

of seamen in Jamaica, by whom the island was protected in the event of a war, without the immediate need of a naval force. If denied the freedom of Jamaican ports, they resorted to the islands of other nations, especially Tortuga, and became a potential danger instead. An exactly analogous situation confronted the French governors of Saint Domingue, and although " the course " was also prohibited by Louis XIV a few years later, not till the end of the century did this irregular mode of warfare disappear from the French Antilles.

Armed vessels to protect the coasts of America are mentioned from the early days of Spanish occupation. But they were never maintained with the consistency and regularity which the ever-present peril demanded. As early as April, 1513, a royal cédula to the officials of the Casa de Contratación bade them send two caravels to guard the coasts of Cuba.[1] Later, in the thirties and forties, when French corsairs became so fatally active in the West Indies, there were repeated and urgent requests from the colonial authorities to furnish ships for their defense. In 1537 one of the oficiales reales, Diego Cavallero, wrote to the king urging that three caravels, well armed, sheathed with lead, and each carrying fifty men, be sent to ply continuously along the northern shores of Cuba and Hispaniola.[2] In July, 1543, the president and judges of the audiencia at San Domingo begged for two galleys and a brigantine, to scour the seas in conjunction with two other vessels supplied by the colony. And similar representations were made in 1547 and 1549.[3]

Early in 1552, as related in a previous chapter, the Crown decided for the moment to dispense with convoys for the merchant fleets, and depend on two armadas with headquarters one at Seville and the other at San Domingo, to keep the paths of navigation clear of pirates. A small armadilla was in the same year got ready in Hispaniola, consisting of three armed vessels and a patache, and carrying 300 men; but soon after putting to sea it was wrecked on the shores of the island by a terrific hurricane, and 130 men drowned. Its commander was Cristobal Colon, grand-

---

[1] *Colecc. de doc.*, 2d ser., vi, p. 3.  [3] *Ibid.*, vol. xxv, nos. 8, 11, 12, 13.
[2] N.M.C., vol. xxi, no. 10.

son of the discoverer.[1] Another small squadron equipped in Spain for the protection of Hispaniola was not allowed to sail till three years later. In 1555 it departed under command of Juan Tello de Guzman, five vessels ranging from 60 to 250 tons, returned within a year and went out again in 1557 in convoy of one of the fleets. Soon after it was dismantled at San Domingo, the ships sold and the men dispersed. In 1568 we hear that Pedro Menéndez de Avilés, adelantado of Florida and scourge of the French Protestants there, was in the Indies with a fleet of galleons for coast-guard duty. But it is evident that his squadron was really the armada de la carrera. In 1570 he returned from America escorting the two fleets of New Spain and Tierra Firme, he was performing a similar duty in 1571–72, and in the years 1573–74 he was apparently policing the seas between Andalusia and the Azores.

Up to this time the defense of the American coasts seems usually to have been left to the armadas de la carrera, which sometimes tarried in the West Indies to hunt out intruders, but more generally were called upon for convoy duty back and forth across the Atlantic. After the death of Pedro Menéndez in 1574, it came to be recognized that such measures were inadequate. The galleons were too heavy to pursue the lighter, swifter vessels of the corsairs, and their presence in the Indies too irregular and uncertain. The depredations of the freebooters suffered little interruption. In 1575, therefore, it was proposed in the Council that two groups of oared galleys be permanently maintained in colonial waters, one with headquarters at Cartagena, to watch the coast from Honduras to the Windward Isles, the other stationed about the four larger islands of Porto Rico, Hispaniola, Cuba, and Jamaica, cruising also along the shores of Yucatan, and in the Florida strait as far as Cape Hatteras. Each group was to consist of two galleys and a pinnace, the former lateen-rigged vessels of 300 tons each propelled by both sail and oar, with a bank of 20 oars to a side, and carrying 50 seamen and 150 soldiers. Four large guns were to be placed in the prow, and two in the stern, with a broadside of eight smaller pieces.[2] This type of ship, of

---

[1] N. M. C., vol. xi, no. 35.   [2] Fernandez Duro, *op. cit.*, ii, pp. 473, 475.

very light draught, was found by long experience to be the most efficient for such service, and was revived for use against the buccaneers just a century later. How soon the scheme was put into practice is uncertain. In 1578 we hear of two galleys and a sloop being sent out to Cartagena, in 1582 of two more for the defense of Hispaniola, and in 1586 of four galleys, two for Hispaniola and two for Tierra Firme, their predecessors having been cast away in a storm. In the latter year a pair was equipped for headquarters at Havana, and the cost of their upkeep settled upon the Mexican treasury. Such small flotillas came to be known specifically as the "armadas de barlovento," or windward squadrons.

In the early years of the seventeenth century, an armada of four galleons of 400 to 500 tons burden and two pataches was urged in the Council of the Indies as a means of stopping the illicit traffic of the Dutch and English with the Spanish Main. The idea was not accepted, perhaps because of the expense, and in 1613 or 1614 was brought forward again, with presumably no better success.[1] A much more elaborate scheme was proposed in 1633: that "guardacostas" be built and maintained in the colonies, four for Cartagena, four for New Spain, two apiece for Santa Marta, Carácas, Porto Rico, San Domingo, and Havana, and one for Rio de la Hacha, Maracaibo, Cumaná, Margarita, Jamaica, and Honduras. The cost was reckoned at 250,000 ducats. Not till the following decade, apparently, was an armada de barlovento actually reëstablished, composed of twelve ships and two pataches, and supported by colonial funds. It retained its identity only a few years, till 1647, when it was diverted to other uses, first to convoy the fleets back to Spain, and then to reenforce the royal navy.[2]

Although the Council often discussed the reconstituting of the squadron, for another fifteen years the seas and coasts of Spanish America were left exposed to the tender mercies of the corsairs. In 1662–63, with the new dangers arising from the English occupation of Jamaica, the construction of an armada de barlovento became more pressing; and in the following year, after an elabo-

---

[1] B. M., Add. Mss. 13,975, ff. 27, 245.
[2] Veitia Linaje, lib. ii, cap. 5, par. 4.

rate report on the state of the Indies and the best means of defending them, a squadron was created of six small men-of-war and one caravel, under command of Agustín de Diustegui.[1] But as happened so frequently before, the exigencies of the government at home led to its incorporation in the royal navy, and not till June, 1667, was it finally dispatched to its original destination, now reduced in number to five ships.

Although the raids of Mansfield and Morgan in Central America, and the visits of the Frenchman, l'Olonais, to Maracaibo, had redoubled the clamors of the colonists for protection, when the fleet actually appeared the viceroy of Mexico complained that the ships were too large and too expensive for pursuing buccaneers among the channels and cays where they were accustomed to hide. And in 1668 the two heaviest returned to Spain with the king's revenues of that year, leaving three behind with the almirante, Alonso de Campos. It was this emasculated armada which was destroyed by Morgan at the entrance to Lake Maracaibo in 1669. The viceroy sent the unfortunate admiral a prisoner to Spain, although the parsimony of the viceroy was the true cause of his mischance. Alonso, however, was exonerated by the Junta de Guerra, and indeed commended for his valor.[2] Five years later, according to Fernandez Duro, there were again three armadas de guarda on the coasts of America, one at Cartagena, another at Porto Bello, and a third in the Gulf of Campeche.[3]

Squadrons for the protection of American commerce were the occasion for introducing several new taxes into Spanish America. In May, 1627, the Crown requested the two viceroyalties to join in a "unión de las armas católicas" for maintaining the forces of the monarchy. They were asked to contribute for fifteen years an annual subsidy of 600,000 ducats, with which to construct fifteen galleons and three patapes, some to cruise continuously in the Atlantic from the English Channel to Gibraltar, the rest to convoy the flotas and protect the coasts of the West Indies. Mexico was to provide 250,000, Peru the remainder. The colonists agreed

---

[1] Veitia Linaje, lib. ii, cap. 5, par. 4; B. M., Add. Mss. 13,992, f. 134.
[2] Veitia Linaje, lib. ii, cap. 5, par. 8, 9; Fernandez Duro, *op. cit.*, v, p. 171.
[3] *Ibid.*, p. 181.

on condition that the impost should cease the moment its proceeds were applied to any but the original purpose; but the condition was not observed by the Crown, and the tax was renewed every fifteen years till the middle of the eighteenth century. It was apparently collected as a tax on sales, and called the Derecho de Union de Armas.[1]

Ten years later, in 1636, the government began to treat for another impost in support of an armada de barlovento. The viceroy of New Spain, the Marquis of Cadereyta, received orders to build and keep at sea a fleet of fourteen vessels, and to suggest to the colonists that privileges and concessions might be forthcoming if they lent their aid. The Mexicans offered to contribute 200,000 pesos a year as long as the armada was used for the protection of New Spain and the islands, reserved the right to decide whence the money should come, and presented a long list of demands upon the king's favor. Among other things, they asked for entire freedom of trade with Peru (it had been prohibited in 1634), a double " permiso " of exchange with the Philippines, perpetual encomiendas of Indians, and restrictions upon the increase of monasteries and the acquisition of property by the Church. The viceroy, in December, 1637, agreed to the conditions relative to the administration of the tax, but reserved the rest for royal approval. The Mexicans soon discovered that they had repeated the fatal Castilian mistake of permitting supply to precede redress, and secured few if any of the privileges asked for. The 200,000 pesos were obtained by raising the alcabala from 2 to 4 per cent, and like the derecho de union de armas became a perpetual contribution. In the eighteenth century these two taxes with the alcabala were combined in a 6 per cent impost on sales.[2]

[1] B. M., Add. Mss. 13,975, f. 27: "Representación del ayuntamiento de México sobre . . . alcabalas," 1753. Of the 250,000 ducats assigned to the northern viceroyalty, Guatemala contributed but 4000, which is sufficient commentary on the relative wealth and resources of Mexico and Central America. These 4000 ducats were to be raised by a tax on certain imports and exports, and any deficit met by an increase of the alcabala. Milla and Gomez Carillo, *América Central*, ii, p. 269.

[2] B. M., Add. Mss. 13,975, f. 27; Solórzano, *Política Indiana* (ed. Valenzuela, 1776), lib. vi, cap. 8, par. 20.

It is worthy of note that till the last quarter of the seventeenth century the Spanish government consistently refused to issue letters of marque to privateers to retaliate upon the English, French, and Dutch in the West Indies. Such a recourse would probably have been the most efficacious against the buccaneers, as well as most economical, for it would have filled the American seas with armed vessels without the expenditure of a ducat from the royal coffers. But it was bitterly opposed by the Casa de Contratación and the merchants of Seville, for fear that such commissions would lead to an infringement of the commercial monopoly. In the year 1666, in view of the decay of the Spanish marine, one of the councillors of the Almirantazgo, or mercantile gild, of Flanders sought permission on certain conditions to send privateers from Flemish ports to the Indies to punish buccaneers and defend the coasts of Spanish America. And in 1669 analogous proposals were made by certain "armadores" belonging to the seaport towns of Biscay. They offered to sail with six or eight ships to America, provided they might also dispatch annually two supply ships for the fleet of 400 tons each, partly laden with merchandise and exempt from registration or the payment of duties in Spain or the colonies. The fleet was to be disposed of in the Indies at the end of the year, and another of equal size sent out to take its place. The ulterior purpose of such a scheme was too transparently obvious to escape the suspicious eyes of the judges of the Casa, and the offer was refused, as was that of the Flemish Almirantazgo.[1]

In the end, the importunate representations of the authorities in America overcame the scruples of the India Council, and in February, 1674, an ordinance appeared providing for the issue of letters of marque under very liberal conditions. Periaguas, or small, flat-bottomed galleys, were to be constructed for use in shoal waters. They were to be ninety feet long, and from sixteen to eighteen wide, with a draft of only a foot and a half, and were to be equipped with a long gun in the bow and four smaller pieces in the stern. They were to be propelled by both sail and

[1] Veitia Linaje, lib. ii, cap. 5, par. 11–20.

oar, and to carry one hundred and twenty men.¹ Their activities became very annoying to English interlopers, especially to the logwood cutters in the Gulf of Campeche; but as the logwood trade was itself irregular, and English pirates still remained abroad in spite of their disavowal by the government, there was little just ground for complaint.

[1] A. de I., 139. 1. 16, lib. 41, p. 324; Fernandez Duro, *op. cit.*, v, p. 181.

# CHAPTER XI

## SHIPS AND NAVIGATORS (I)

VESSELS plying in the India navigation had, in theory, to be of Spanish ownership and construction and manned by Spanish seamen. The requirement of Spanish ownership, or at least of immediate Spanish possession, was from the time of Philip II with fair consistency lived up to. The other conditions were probably never seriously enforced. During the reign of the Emperor, when colonial trade was free to non-Spaniards, it is natural to suppose that India ships were owned and manned by Germans and Italians who took advantage of this liberty. Indeed, in days when the merchant so often sailed as master or captain of his own vessel, freedom to trade and freedom to navigate could with difficulty be kept distinct and separate. And from the beginning foreigners naturalized by long residence in the peninsula enjoyed the twofold privilege. We read in Hakluyt that in the flota of 1555 a certain Robert Tomson sailed in a ship belonging to John Sweeting, an Englishman settled and married in Cadiz, and commanded by his English son-in-law, also resident in Cadiz, named Leonard Chilton.[1] And in 1562 another Anglo-Spaniard, Roger Bodenham, residing with a wife in Seville, accompanied the fleet of Pedro Menéndez de Avilés as master of a London ship of 160 to 180 tons, named the *Barke Fox*.[2]

In Charles' later years, however, when he was pressed to debar all but Spanish subjects from this commerce, exclusion from navigation was a logical and necessary consequence; for the employment of foreign ships and masters would have involved their participation in trade, if only to the extent of the freights collected and the incidental profits of ship's officers. It would also have left wide open a door for the entrance of unlicensed strangers

---

[1] Hakluyt, *Navigations* (ed. of 1904), ix, p. 341.
[2] *Ibid.*, p. 359. The freights both ways amounted to over 13,000 ducats.

## SHIPS AND NAVIGATORS 259

into the colonies. The return to greater strictness probably dates from the year 1538, for a cédula of December 6 reads:

> Nuestros oficiales que residis en la ciudad de Sevilla en la casa de la contratacion delas Indias . . . por si y en su nombre de todos los mercaderes y tratantes en las nuestras Indias, me han hecho relacion, que a nuestro servicio y al bien de los dichos sus partes y de todos los tratantes en las dichas Indias convenia que de aqui adelante ningun estrangero destos reynos anduviesse en la navegacion de las dichas nuestras Indias, porque por experiencia avia parecido los daños que se avian seguido . . . vos mando que de aqui adelante no consentais ni deis lugar que ningun estrangero destos nuestros reynos ande en la navegacion de las nuestras Indias, ni los dexais ni consintais passar a ellas por marineros, ni por otro ningun oficio. Y . . . que ningun maestre ni otra persona los passe ni traiga en su nao, so pena de cien mil maravedis.[1]

Foreigners not subjects of the Emperor were of course from the first prohibited from owning India ships, except by special dispensation of the Crown.

The condition that India vessels be of Spanish construction probably goes back to the time of Ferdinand and Isabella, for like their Tudor contemporaries they were greatly interested in the increase of shipbuilding and the creation of a mercantile marine. As early as 1498 they had offered an annual premium to those who built and maintained ships of 600 tons or over.[2] In 1500 Spaniards were forbidden to lade in foreign bottoms if native vessels were available, and in the following year they were enjoined, under severest penalties, not to sell or hypothecate their own ships to strangers, even if the latter were naturalized subjects.[3] It is very likely, however, that some of the vessels which sailed in the earlier expeditions to the New World were of Genoese or other foreign build; and from the time of Philip II the inclusion of such ships in the flotas was not uncommon.

As the Crown always reserved the right to grant particular licenses to foreign vessels, whether for lack of native ships or to fill its exchequer, it was without doubt the chief offender against the spirit of the earlier ordinances. Although the prohibitions

---
[1] Encinas, i, p. 441.
[2] *Recop.*, lib. vii, tit. 10, ley 3. In the reign of Philip II bounties were given for vessels of 300 tons and over.
[3] *Ibid.*, ley 6.

were frequently renewed, especially toward the end of the century, as frequently they were rendered of no effect. In 1562, as we have seen, Roger Bodenham was master of an English ship in the fleet of Pedro Menéndez de Avilés. A royal cédula of May, 1571, expressly stated that "urcas esterlinas" and "filibotes" might be admitted to the India navigation, if a sufficient number of Spanish vessels was not to be had; and in 1599 the trade with Hispaniola was declared open to these foreign-built ships, provided they were owned and manned by Spaniards and sailed with the New Spain fleets.[1] In 1608 the Council of the Indies pressed upon the king the objections to these innovations; and five years later, in a decree of March, 1613, the Duke of Lerma resolved upon the punctual observance of the ancient rules of the Casa, so that native builders might be encouraged and protected.[2] Yet, owing to the progressive decay of the Spanish merchant marine consequent upon the disastrous wars of the seventeenth century, and the more rapid progress of other nations, notably the Dutch and English, in the art of ship design, most of the merchant vessels composing the India fleets came from foreign yards. By 1662 the Council had sought refuge in a philosophical resignation worthy of the situation. It laid down the broad principle that in pursuing the public weal account must also be taken of the exigencies of the moment. There were occasions when it was necessary to disregard the strictest of laws. Now without doubt many things had changed since the formulation of the ordinances respecting American commerce. And when the merchants of Seville, therefore, demanded licenses which were contrary to the law, the Council found itself obliged by the very force of circumstances to consent; for it was necessary above all else to maintain relations between Spain and the Indies, or see the bonds dissolved which bound the colonists to the mother country and to the Holy Catholic Church.[3]

It was just as impossible to shut out foreign sailors and soldiers from the India navigation, when foreign ships had to be hired and Spanish seamen were insufficient to man the fleets. In the middle of the sixteenth century, with the change in royal policy which

---

[1] Antuñez y Acevedo, p. 44.     [2] *Ibid.*, p. 43.
[3] A. de I., 153. 6. 19. Consulta of June 17, 1662.

excluded non-Spaniards more strictly from the colonies, they were also forbidden to serve on Atlantic ships. But the prohibition was not applied to able-bodied seamen already so employed, for fear that they might be dispersed and carry their knowledge of Spanish America to other lands. Even so partial a restriction, however, soon broke down. A royal decree of January, 1590, admitted any strangers of Roman faith, save only the English; another of April, 1595, admitted as masters or pilots in the New Spain fleet all but the English, French, and Dutch; and similar decrees are frequent in the first half of the following century.[1]

Even in local, intercolonial trade in the New World, a parallel situation was soon apparent. From a cédula to the viceroy of Peru, dated July, 1572, we gather that the employment of foreigners as masters and pilots for vessels on the Pacific was already necessary, for lack of competent Spaniards. A large bond (4,000 to 50,000 pesos), however, was required, and none were permitted to return to Europe without special royal license, because with their knowledge they were in a position to guide corsairs to those regions.[2]

Atlantic ships in the first fifty years after the Discovery were astonishingly small, probably rarely exceeding 200 tons burden. Indeed at that time the mariners of Cantabria, the best in Spain, considered a vessel of 200 tons the prototype of the ship of the period, whether for war or for trade. Such was certainly the opinion of Alonso de Chaves, pilot major of the India House and one of the most learned Spanish navigators of his day. For discovery and exploration, where capacity was not a desideratum, a vessel of 100 tons was preferred, and most of the ships so employed were apparently of about that size. Of the three vessels of Columbus, only the largest was of 120 to 130 tons, a clumsy boat almost as broad as long, built with one deck, high poop and forecastle and three masts, two with square sails, the mizzenmast lateen-rigged. The other ships were tiny, open caravels of 40 and 50 tons respectively, decked only at the extremities. Columbus' flagship on the second voyage was said to be of 400 tons, but the

---

[1] Encinas, i, pp. 459, 461.   [2] *Ibid.*. p. 451.

other sixteen vessels comprising the squadron must have been very much smaller. In 1495 the Crown contracted with Juanoto Berardi, a Florentine resident in Seville, for the hire of twelve ships to be freighted for the Indies on the king's account. The combined tonnage was to be only 900.[1] The ordinances of July 14, 1522, governing the armament and inspection of India vessels, fixed the minimum size at 80 tons;[2] and as late as the reign of Philip IV trading ships of 100 tons or even less frequently made the voyage to minor colonial ports. A cédula of March, 1609, however, decreed that no ship of less than 200 tons should be admitted to the American flotas.[3]

Spaniards in the early sixteenth century and even before had certainly been constructing sailing vessels of larger capacity, as were other maritime peoples of western Europe.[4] Ferdinand and Isabella, as we have seen, offered bounties for ships of 600 tons and over. In 1493 a squadron got together in Biscay, apparently for Columbus' second voyage, consisted of a carrack of over 1000 tons (perhaps of Genoese origin), and four ships ranging from 150 tons to 450. But the armada was sent instead to the coast of Granada to transport Muley Boabdil, last of the Moorish kings, and his companions to Africa.[5] From the middle of the sixteenth century, larger vessels in the India navigation were not uncommon. A cédula issued in May of 1557 specifically excluded those exceeding 400 tons, and three years' grace were allowed to Spaniards employing ships above this maximum to withdraw them from the American trade.[6] The chief reason for the limitation was without doubt the difficulty presented by the sand bar at San Lucar, which vessels of over 200 tons were unable to negotiate without transshipping part of their cargo; and from 1560 on-

[1] *Viajes*, ii, p. 169.
[2] *Colecc. de doc.*, 2d ser., ix, p. 143.
[3] Veitia Linaje, lib. i, cap. 24, par. 5.
[4] James IV of Scotland had four ships in his navy, the *Mitchell, Margaret, James*, and another, of 300 tons each. And the *Regent*, built for Henry VII in 1487–90, was probably of 600 tons burden. *Letters and Papers of the Reign of Henry VIII*, i, no. 3359; ii, no. 3330; Oppenheim, *Naval Accounts and Inventories*, p. xxi.
[5] *Viajes*, ii, pp. 79, 81.
[6] Veitia Linaje, lib. ii, cap. 6, par. 12.

wards in the records of the Casa petitions from masters for permission to make this transshipment become increasingly frequent. In the reign of Philip II, Juan de Escalante de Mendoza regarded the ship of not over 500 tons as the ideal for a man-of-war,[1] and the galleons which crossed to the Indies probably rarely surpassed that capacity. As mentioned before, Atlantic ships, whether of war or of trade, were limited by a cédula of December, 1628, to a displacement of 550 tons; yet in the later seventeenth century galleons of 700 and even 1000 tons were not unusual.

Vessels which crossed the Atlantic were of several quite distinct classes. The use of the galley had begun to diminish in Castile early in the fifteenth century, and virtually disappeared in the sixteenth, although in Aragon, with its Mediterranean commerce, this type persisted for a much longer time. The early trans-Atlantic ships were caravels, light boats with somewhat finer lines, and at most a single deck. Ordinarily provided with lateen sails, they were faster and sailed closer to the wind than the larger, heavier "nao," which carried a square rig and topsails. There were two kinds of caravel, the Portuguese, equipped exclusively with lateen sails and employed by the intrepid mariners who first explored the west coast of Africa to the Cape of Good Hope; and the Castilian, which often combined a square-rigged foremast with lateen-rigged main and mizzenmasts. Later, however, almost any vessel of about 100 tons, whatever its nautical characteristics, was designated a caravel.

The common type of Atlantic ship from the middle of the sixteenth century was the "galeon." It was apparently longer and narrower than the medieval tub called the "nao," but shorter, broader and higher than the galley, from which it derives its name; and in the endeavor to increase capacity, it was developed into a notoriously unseaworthy vessel. Constructed with keel and beam in the proportion of three to one or less, and with towering "castles" at either extremity, its sailing qualities were of the very worst. It had one or two decks, depending upon its size, although in the later seventeenth century galleons of three decks were built for purposes of war.

[1] *Itinerario de Navegación*, 1575.

There were also " urcas " or storeships, slow, extremely short and round, and flat-bottomed, constructed entirely with a view to capacity, rigged like a ship, but an easy prey to contrary winds and useless for defense against a foe. In the seventeenth century great Portuguese carracks were likewise occasionally found in the American fleets. Numerous kinds of smaller vessels, flyboats (filibotes), pinks (pingues), polacres (polacras), tartans (tartanas), bilanders (balandras), pinnaces (pinazas), and sloops (barcos), some of foreign origin, others Spanish, ranging from 40 to 150 and sometimes 200 tons, were not infrequently used for trading voyages, but more commonly as advice boats in the fleets, where they were known generically as " pataches."

The mariners most closely associated with the progress of Spanish naval construction in the sixteenth century were the brothers Alvaro and Alonso Bazan, and the adelantado of Florida, Pedro Menéndez de Avilés. Alvaro Bazan was the first to employ in the India navigation large galleons of his own propriety for the transport of merchandise and treasure.[1] He invented a new type of galleon, and imitated from the Genoese and Venetians the galleas or " galeaza," for the building of which he obtained the exclusive concession in February, 1550. Bazan was required to supply within two months six galleons of a combined displacement of at least 2000 tons, three of the newer sort and three of the older. He was then to begin the construction of six galleases, three to take the place of the three old-type galleons, and complete them as soon as possible; so that in the end there might be three newly constructed armadas of two galleases and a galleon each. These armadas were apparently to sail to Vera Cruz, Nombre de Dios and San Domingo respectively. They were given the monopoly of carrying the king's treasure from the Indies, might lade whatever articles private merchants chose to entrust to them, and were subject to the ordinary rules governing the American trade. But they were not obliged to escort other ships, being free to come and go independently of other sailings. The king promised to contribute 1800 quintals of artillery and as much of munitions, Bazan furnishing all the rest of the equip-

---

[1] Fernandez Duro, *Armada Española*, i, p. 327.

ment. He also contributed 3200 ducats for each voyage, but reserved the right to requisition any or all of Bazan's vessels for other services. Bazan was granted the title of captain general in the India navigation for fifteen years, and if he died in the meantime leaving a son of age, the latter might inherit the distinction.[1] There was much opposition to these terms from the Consulado, and also in the Council of the Indies, chiefly because of the exemption from convoy duty, but the contract was confirmed, and Bazan's patent as captain general issued on August 1, 1550.[2]

The galleas was an attempt to unite the conditions of the galley and the sailing ship to produce a vessel larger and faster than either. It carried three lateen-rigged masts, and like the galleon high castellated structures at each end. The oars were long and heavy, from twenty-five to thirty-two on a side, and propelled by six or seven men apiece. But this type never superseded the galleon, for it possessed the virtues of neither of its progenitors. Its sail area was smaller, and the supplementary oars proved useless except in the smoothest weather. It was also more expensive to maintain, and in the words of Fernandez Duro served " mas de buen parecer en los puertos que de desempeño en la mar."[3] Four galleases were included in the Great Armada of 1588.

With the increase in size of ocean-going vessels came the necessity of changing rules of construction and the theories underlying them. Pedro Menéndez de Avilés seems to have been the first to conceive the idea of lengthening the keel in relation to the beam, and in the late sixties constructed on the island of Cuba several ships embodying this innovation, which he called " galeoncetes." The idea was encouraged by the brothers Bazan, but met with opposition from the older, more conservative builders. As the galeoncetes were very good sailors, however, and experience proved their seaworthiness, the king later ordered eight to be built on the coasts of Biscay.[4] This was the first step in the evolution of the frigate, which in the second half of the seventeenth century became an accepted type in all the navies of western

---

[1] *Colecc. de España*, i, p. 265.
[2] N.M.C., xxi, nos. 21, 29; Fernandez Duro, *op. cit.*, i, p. 440.
[3] *Ibid.*, iii, p. 184. [4] *Ibid.*

Europe. The short, deep, tub-like ship of the sixteenth century gradually evolved into a longer vessel of lighter draft, lower freeboard and finer lines at bow and stern. Especially after the lesson of the Great Armada, the Spaniards began to imitate the construction of their English rivals. In the time of Philip III, ships were built of 500 tons which drew less water than the older galleons of 250 or 300, and therefore able to enter the Guadalquivir at high tide. But it must be admitted that the improvements came very slowly, and were confined rather to men-of-war. In respect to merchantmen the Spaniards' ideal, even into the age of the Bourbons, was capacity, and their ships in point of design remained far behind those of the rest of Europe. In 1618 the Crown published an elaborate set of ordinances for the construction of Spanish vessels, whether for the king or for private individuals, in which every detail was prescribed with the nicest exactness.

The largest and best ships of the Castilian kingdom were built in the Biscay provinces, and from the beginning the Crown, and the Andalusian merchants it patronized, resorted there for vessels and stores to make up the India fleets. The forests of the south were mostly of pine, while the rugged mountains of Galicia and Asturias furnished an abundant supply of oak and other desirable hardwoods. Bazan's galleases were constructed in Biscay, and so long as Spain retained the vestige of a marine, the prosperity of the northern yards was an especial care of the government. After 1593, indeed, ships of Andalusian origin were forbidden to enter the American navigation, as vessels of war or as merchantmen, for, the cédula declared, as they were made of unseasoned pine, on the voyage bolts loosened, planks were sprung, and the vessel frequently lost.[1] It was the custom, however, after a ship had been launched, to send it to the Guadalquivir to be fitted out and the upper works completed with Andalusian woods.

The building of ships in the colonies seems at first to have been prohibited, or at least restricted. Columbus and his companions, it is true, put together a caravel named the *Santa Cruz* in Hispaniola in 1496, the first naval construction by white men in the

[1] *Recop.*, lib. ix, tit. 30, ley 21.

New World. And later, during the Admiral's absence in Spain, two others were built under the direction of Bartholomew Columbus, to facilitate communication between the coastal settlements.[1] But after that there is no mention of shipbuilding in the West Indies for many years. In 1516, as related in an earlier chapter, the Hieronymite governors of the Indies were instructed to allow settlers in Cuba to build and own vessels for trade with the other colonies; but the concession apparently was not published, for two years later, in response to a petition of proctors from the island, a cédula to the local governor, Diego Velazquez, permitted the construction of ten vessels, none of more than 100 tons burden. And the decree specifically states that such construction had hitherto been forbidden.[2] We have no record that the inhabitants made use of the privilege, and doubtless in the early sixteenth century, at least, most of the larger vessels came from Spain.

Only on the Pacific was shipbuilding then an active and important industry, for there from Balboa's time caravels and brigantines had to be constructed for the task of exploration which terminated in the conquest of Peru. In 1533 there were over thirty vessels reported in the South Sea, all built upon its shores. The largest, the " capitana " of the adelantado Alvarado, was said to be of 300 tons, but most were of only forty or fifty.[3] Fray Antonio de Valdiviedo, bishop of Nicaragua, in a letter to the Council of the Indies in 1545 describing the advantages of the province for shipbuilding, added that " cada dia se hacen buques ";[4] and the celebrated expedition of Legaspi to the Philippines in 1564–65 was made in vessels entirely constructed and equipped on the shores of New Spain. A letter from Panama in August, 1590, mentioned some ten large ships in the harbor, the heaviest of 500 tons; and in 1607 the audiencia of that city informed the king that two or three vessels were built there every year, ranging from 60 to 175 tons.

[1] Cappa, *Estudios críticos*, x, pp. 7 f.
[2] *Colecc. de doc.*, 2d ser., i, pp. 69, 85.
[3] N. Y. Public Library, Rich Collection, ii. Lic. Espinosa to the Empress, Oct. 10, 1533.
[4] Cappa, *op. cit.*, x, p. 37.

At the same time, 1590, there was great activity in the yards at Havana, the chief shipbuilding centre of the West Indies. The impetus given to the industry by Menéndez de Avilés had never quite been lost, and small vessels of the type he originated continued to be constructed there, often to serve as auxiliaries to the Seville fleets. In the latter part of the century, moreover, when the flotas no longer sailed regularly every year, the king's revenues were often carried to Spain in these lighter vessels of American build. Especially was this true after the fatal expedition against England, when with the destruction of Spanish shipping and the penury of the treasury, Philip was constrained to turn to the colonies for vessels to make up the loss. Fleets sailed without convoy, and were sometimes armed in the Indies for the homeward voyage. In 1590 six galeoncetes or frigates were under construction at Havana, and foundries established for the manufacture of artillery. The royal treasure was apparently brought to Havana in caravels from Vera Cruz and Nombre de Dios, and there placed on the frigates for transmission to Spain. In 1591 orders were sent for the building of six more ships of the same type; and it was in this year also that the Crown transferred to the Consulado the responsibility of maintaining an armada for the American flotas.[1] All of these Cuban vessels seem to have been of smaller tonnage than the usual Spanish galleons. By a cédula of June, 1638, ships constructed in Havana, Campeche, San Domingo, Porto Rico, and Jamaica were accorded all the privileges enjoyed by those constructed in the Peninsula; and ten years later this order was extended to vessels built anywhere in the Indies.[2]

One disadvantage with which the colonial shipbuilders had to contend was the lack of cordage, tackle, and hardware, most of which had to be brought out from Spain, even to the carpenters' tools. It was an unfortunate consequence of the policy of prohibiting in America the production of such articles, and sometimes made the cost of construction almost double that in the Peninsula.

[1] Fernandez Duro, *op. cit.*, ii, pp. 483 ff.; Hakluyt (ed. of 1904), x, pp. 158–161.
[2] Veitia Linaje, lib. ii, cap. 6, par. 6.

In the sixteenth century the Crown possessed no navy in the present understanding of that term, no ships of its own expressly designed for war and for the other services to which a modern navy lends itself. Under the early Hapsburgs, all vessels were more or less suited to all requirements of war and trade. All carried some armament as a precaution against the insecurities of the sea, all were fit for fighting. The distinguishing feature of men-of-war lay in the soldiers and additional artillery with which they were supplied. The policy of encouraging shipbuilding by offering bounties for vessels over a certain tonnage, besides helping commerce, largely obviated in those days the maintenance of a royal marine; for upon these vessels the government had the first claim in time of need. The Spanish kings, when they undertook a maritime enterprise, embargoed and hired such merchant ships as they immediately required. Or, if there was call for a permanent service of some sort, this too was adjusted by means of a contract with private individuals to arm and maintain the ships for a fixed sum; or the king paid so much per ton for the hire alone of the ships, which sailed under command of their owners, but were armed and manned at the charge of the royal exchequer. Under such a system, nobles, landowners, and even bishops used their capital in the constructing and arming of vessels, whether for service in Europe or for the armada de la carrera de las Indias.

This plan may have been advantageous in the beginning, for it at least spared the finances of the king. Under Philip II it was already becoming an anachronism. Yet in spite of the complaints of merchants, shipowners, and deputies of the Cortes, the custom of embargoing private ships continued, to the detriment of fishing and trade. Indeed Philip, though engaged in a titanic struggle with the young and vigorous maritime peoples of the north, displayed an indifference, or even antipathy, toward everything connected with the sea, which was one of the unpardonable mistakes of his policy. Arsenals and stores were neglected, no attempt was made to obtain a permanent royal marine. And with the constant requisitions, as shipowners and crews were ill-paid, and often made to wait years for the wages due them, the merchant marine too suffered a rapid decline. The lack of Spanish ships had then to be made up from abroad, by hiring from the French, Italians or even the rebel Dutch. Sometimes contracts were made for entire squadrons, with admiral, captains and crews complete, and often on conditions which had been denied to native seamen. Of the armament of eighty-four vessels gathered at Ferrol in 1597 under command of the Adelantado of Castile, sixty-four were of foreign construction.[1]

In the two succeeding reigns, spasmodic efforts were made to remedy this state of affairs. Philip III, by entrusting the general control of naval matters to the Admiral, Diego Brochero, did much to remove the disdain formerly attaching to service on the sea. Brochero was given a seat in the Council, and by the ordinance of November, 1606, " para las armadas del mar océano y flotas de Indias," introduced reforms which attempted to restore some order and system, especially in the American fleets. Under Philip IV, the construction of ships by private initiative in Cantabria was stimulated by the renewal of earlier privileges, such as exemption from the alcabala for vessels of more than 200 tons; and measures were taken for the installation of hospitals, and the general improvement of conditions for the sea-faring population. The period from the beginning of the reign to 1635 was in fact one of considerable shipbuilding activity, but the industry was again ruined by the debacle at the close of Olivares' administration. In the sixties, the government, at the end of its resources and desirous of creating a new fleet, used the asiento of negroes as a means of reviving naval construction. In a contract concluded with two Genoese bankers, Grillo and Lomelin, the latter agreed to build in Biscay ten ships of a tonnage prescribed by the Crown — either vessels for the royal fleet at thirty-one ducats silver per ton, or galleons for the India navigation at a rate to be decided upon later. The cost of these ships was to be deducted from the 300,000 pesos which the asentistas paid into the exchequer as duty on the negroes they imported into the colonies. They engaged, moreover, to deliver five hundred negroes a year

[1] Fernandez Duro, *op. cit.*, iii, p. 180.

during the term of the contract to arsenals and shipyards in the Indies, the proprietors of these yards to pay the duty on each negro but devote it to the construction of vessels for the government, at a fixed rate of fifty-one ducats silver per ton. Grillo and Lomelin secured the privilege of carrying to the colonies the necessary hardware and other ship's stores, a valuable concession seeing that the American provinces were dependent for such things upon the mother country.[1]

Owing to endless quarrels and misunderstandings between the king and the asentistas, the clauses regarding naval construction were never carried out; and a few years later the Crown was in such dire straits for money that it consented to a new contract in which this prime consideration was allowed to fall from sight altogether. With the accession of the imbecile Charles II, although interest in maritime affairs was by no means dead, owing to the absolute lack of resources shipbuilding in Spain slowly disappeared; and finally in 1688, with the complete paralyzation of work in the yards, the offices of Superintendent, Inspector, and Comptroller of Construction for the king were suppressed.[2] Veitia Linaje wrote in 1672, when describing the duties of the president of the Casa:

> Uno de los principales cuydados del Presidente, ó por mejor dezir el principalissimo, es el de los aprestos de las Armadas, y Flotas en que cada dia se necessita mas de major provedencia, respecto de la falta de Vaxeles, pertrechos, y Oficiales, que ordinariamente se padece, y de esto ultimo mas en los tiempos presentes que en ninguno de los pasados: con lo qual suele tambien concurrir la penuria de dineros, y el necessitarse de buscarlos prestados, y fiados los bastimentos; con que es una continua tarea de fátigas la desta puesto.[3]

From the beginning the Crown prescribed in minute detail the equipment, arming, provisioning, lading, and manning of all vessels sailing to the New World. This far-reaching official control was common to Barcelona, Venice and other cities of the medieval Mediterranean, and may have represented a Catalan influence in American maritime legislation. The first set of ordinances relating specifically to such matters was probably that of July 14,

---

[1] Scelle, *La traite négrière*, i, pp. 521 f.    [2] *Ibid.*, v, p. 88.
[3] Veitia Linaje, lib. i, cap. 3, par. 22.

1522. Every ship of 100 tons was obliged to carry at least fifteen mariners including a gunner, eight "grumetes," or apprentices, and three "pajes," or ship's boys, all the men being provided with a corselet or breastplate and other armor. The vessel must also have a battery of four large iron guns and twenty-four swivel guns ("pasavolantes" and "espingardas"). For each large gun there were to be supplied three dozen shot, and for each of the pasavolantes six dozen, with molds and lead to make bullets for the espingardas. There were likewise required two hundredweight of powder, ten crossbows with eight dozen arrows, four dozen short lances, eight long pikes and twenty shields. Other vessels were to carry a similar armament proportionate to their size and capacity, but apparently ships much larger than 100 tons were not then contemplated.[1] None of this equipment might be sold or left in the Indies, the value of whatever was unaccounted for when the vessel returned being deducted from the wages or other profits of the master. An examination of the actual outfit of various India ships between 1520 and 1530 shows that each mariner carried a sword, which with his armor was sometimes at his own expense, and that vessels besides an assortment of crossbows were occasionally provided with a few muskets. Generally there were about two dozen rounds for each type of weapon.

A much more elaborate code of rules was promulgated in September, 1534, for the remedying of certain abuses growing out of the negligence or avarice of shipmasters.[2] As old and worn-out vessels, unfit for a long voyage, were frequently brought to Seville to be employed in the colonial trade, thereafter no ship, unless it was new, might lade for America without first being careened,[3] calked, and repaired to the satisfaction of the officers of the Casa. Pilots and masters had to be native Spaniards, and examined for

---

[1] *Colecc. de doc.*, 2d ser., ix, p. 143.

[2] *Ibid.*, 1st ser., xxxii, p. 492.

[3] It seems that vessels when careened were not always drawn up on shore, but often by a manipulation of ballast turned over in the water far enough to uncover the keel itself. It was a delicate operation, in which the careneros of Seville were reputed very skilful. As Spanish methods of calking were extremely thorough, and labor and materials high, the process was apt to be a tedious and expensive one. In the first half of the seventeenth century, carpenters and calkers were paid from 8 to 10 reals a day besides their board.

the particular voyage they intended to make before the pilot major of the India House; and it was significantly stated that no one might lend to vessels cables, arms, casks, tackle, etc., to be displayed to the Casa's inspector and left behind after he had gone. Sailors, too, who appeared at the inspection but did not sail were threatened with dire penalties. On the voyage, the upper deck and principal cabins had to be kept free of merchandise so as to avoid overloading, only provisions, artillery and passengers' chests being permitted above board; while minute regulations were laid down for the stowage of cargo in the superstructures fore and aft. Thirty passengers was the maximum for a ship of 100 tons, and captains were forbidden to demand more money of them than had been agreed upon before embarkation. The daily rations for each person were one and one-half pounds of bread, two pints of drinking water (and another for bathing), and two pints of wine, which, the ordinance adds, " es la ración ordinaria." The code contains nineteen clauses in all, most of which reappeared in the ordinances of the Casa of 1552.

It seems that the master mariners of Seville protested to the Council of the Indies against some of the rules as unreasonable; wherefore in the following August a royal decree was dispatched to the Casa modifying and explaining certain of them. Among others, the clause requiring the careening of old ships before receiving permission to lade for the colonies was temporarily suspended, for lack of " instrumento y aparejos para ello." The accommodations at Seville were still inadequate for a trade of which it enjoyed the exclusive monopoly.

In February, 1552, when, as related before, it was for the moment decided to abolish convoys and arm all ships against possible foes, a new set of ordinances appeared, by which India vessels were grouped in three general classes according to size, 100–170 tons, 170–220 tons, and 220–320 tons. One hundred tons was fixed as the minimum for a trans-Atlantic voyage. The provisions of these ordinances may, for greater ease of comprehension, be presented in tabular form:

ROYAL ORDINANCES OF FEBRUARY 13, 1552, REGARDING THE ARTILLERY, MEN, ARMS AND MUNITIONS TO BE CARRIED ON SHIPS SAILING TO AND FROM THE INDIES [1]

| | Tonnage of vessels | 100–170 tons | 170–220 tons | 220–320 tons |
|---|---|---|---|---|
| Crew | Mariners | 18 | 28 | 35 |
| | Gunners | 2 | 4 | 6 |
| | Apprentices | 8 | 12 | 15 |
| | Cabin-boys | 2 | 4 | 5 |
| Artil'y Brass | Demiculverins | .. | 1 | 1 |
| | Sacres | 1 | 1 | 2 |
| | Falconets | 1 | 1 | 1 |
| Artil'y Iron | Lombards | 6 | 8 | 10 |
| | Versos | 12 | 18 | 24 |
| Small arms and armor | Arquebuses | 12 | 20 | 30 |
| | Crossbows | 12 | 20 | 30 |
| | Pikes | 24 | 36 | 48 |
| | Half-pikes | 144 | 180 | 240 |
| | Lances | 180 | 240 | 360 |
| | Shields | 12 | 18 | 24 |
| | Breastplates | 12 | 18 | 24 |
| | Helmets | 20 | 25 | 30 |
| | Powder | 9 cwt. 1 quart. | 14 cwt. 2 quart. | 18 cwt. 3 quart. |
| | Balls | 50 each for the falconets; 20–30 for other guns. | | |

Each vessel was to carry a netting which in time of action might be drawn over the decks from bow to stern to intercept dropping missiles; and also waistcloths to be rigged up so as to prevent boarding, and provided with openings for the discharge of bows, arquebuses and the smaller artillery. There must be a complete equipment of ramrods, carriages for guns, molds for making lead bullets, etc., and a special chamber in the bow below decks for the storage of powder.

The demiculverins, sacres and falcons [2] were brass guns of comparatively small calibre, and very long, from 25 to 40 times the diameter of the muzzle. The demiculverins, as a rule individually named, weighed between 3000 and 4000 pounds. They fired a ball weighing from 7 to 12 pounds, and had a point blank range of about 1000 paces. They were the largest pieces commonly found on ships in the India navigation in the sixteenth century. Sacres weighed from 1700 to 2400 pounds, and used a 5 or 6 pound

[1] N. M. C., xxi, no. 30.
[2] Though called falconetes in the ordinances, it is evident from their weight that the larger falcons were meant.

ball with a range of 900 paces; the 1alcons, from 700 to 900 pounds, fired a 2 to 4 pound ball about 700 paces. To discharge these cannon was used an amount of powder about equal to the weight of the shot, or if it was very fine powder, about one half that amount. The other artillery mentioned were smaller, iron guns, the lombards being comparatively short, large-bore pieces of rather primitive construction, the versos and pasavolantes very long and light, mounted on swivels and firing a 4 to 8 ounce ball.[1]

Iron artillery, unless new, was often of little effective use, the persons most injured being those serving the guns. And in the second half of the sixteenth century the armament of Spanish vessels was almost entirely of brass. Crossbows, too, a relic of the Middle Ages, were soon entirely superseded by the more effective arquebus. In a cédula of June 24, 1573, the factor of the Casa was instructed to keep in the Atarazanas or arsenal at least 200 pieces of artillery; and by another of August 11, he was further ordered to have on hand 1500 arquebuses, 50 corselets, 1500 helmets, 200 hundredweight of powder, 500 pikes, 1000 half-pikes, 200 halbards and partizans, and 300 dozen lances.[2]

With the increase in the capacity of ships came also an increase in the number and calibre of their guns. Yet even in the seventeenth century artillery on the American fleets was comparatively small, firing balls not exceeding thirty pounds in weight, although the capitanas and almirantas sometimes mounted as many as fifty cannon ranged in several tiers. The tradition, indeed, kept

[1] Arántegui y Sanz, *Apuntes históricas*, pp. 313 ff.; Fernandez Duro, *Disquisiciones náuticas*, vi, pp. 449, 483, 500.
We also hear of falconetes, weighing 600 lbs., and firing balls of from $1\frac{1}{2}$ to 2 lbs.; and medio-sacres, of 1,000 to 1,400 lbs., firing balls of $2\frac{1}{2}$ or 3 lbs. Full-sized culverins fired a shot weighing from 14 to 25 lbs., but were in the sixteenth century considered rather too long and heavy for ships. There was also another series of guns called cañones, which differed from those mentioned above in being shorter and heavier. The largest weighed 5,500–6,000 lbs. and used about a 40 lb. shot. The smaller cannon were called medios or pelicans, tercios and cuartos, according to their calibre. Still heavier guns, found only occasionally mounted in fortresses, and some firing missiles of 100 lbs. or more, were called basilisks (*basiliscos*). Artillery pieces longer or shorter than the length customary for their particular type were usually called bastards.

[2] Veitia Linaje, lib. i, cap. 13, par. 7.

alive by the Mediterranean wars with Turks and Barbary pirates, persisted too long on the Atlantic that artillery was but a supplementary arm, a preliminary to boarding and hand-to hand combat. It was an error for which the Spaniards paid dear in their conflicts with the Dutch and English, especially in 1588 and after. The armament of the galleons was distributed on the two sides of the upper deck, and in the larger vessels on the second deck as well. On the superstructures fore and aft were other pieces, some discharged through portholes as bow or stern chasers, others fired on the broadside, but also if necessary used to command the rest of the vessel amidships.

Although the government, after the promulgation of the rules of 1552, returned to the system of convoyed fleets, these rules continued in force for merchant vessels sailing to the New World, were incorporated with the general ordinances of the Casa de Contratación, and republished with them from time to time. Already in 1557, however, it was found necessary to take further precautions against the dangerous practices of Spanish ship owners. A cédula of May 5 relates that instead of the best vessels being sent to America, as so long and difficult a voyage required, the contrary was usually the case; that ordinarily Spanish ships were first dispatched to the Levant and elsewhere, and only when they were superannuated and their timbers sprung were they brought to Seville to be sold for the India trade; and as many ships sailing to the Caribbean were discarded there, the matter of age was regarded by the purchasers as of little moment. Other shipowners, the cédula continues, rebuilt their vessels, adding a larger superstructure to a short keel so as to increase the storage capacity, sometimes by as much as a third. Such ships, being extremely topheavy, were bad weather boats, and carried artillery with difficulty, while at the same time, not having a spread of canvas commensurate with the increased burden, they were very slow sailers. To remedy this state of affairs, the decree instructed the visitadores or inspectors, together with the captain general of the fleet, to examine the staunchness and the scantlings of each vessel, permit no " edificios " to be added above what was necessary, and give their approval to no old ships, or indeed to any which had seen more than two years' service. They were, moreover, to allow no mariners to sail in the ships unless they had been examined in the duties of their respective offices, or had served three years as grumete or apprentice, and no passengers to embark as members of the crew.[1]

From this time forward, ships might not be sent to the Indies to be abandoned there without special permission from the Crown; and in 1584 orders were issued that a vessel might remain in America only if the general of the fleet gave his assent, based on the testimony of six pilots or masters that the case was unforeseen and unpremeditated. In any event, masters and sailors had to return immediately to Seville. But to favor those whose ships were worn out in the colonial service, the practice arose of admitting at least one such vessel to each of the fleets, provided it was of Spanish construction. It was also sometimes found convenient to use the crew, artillery, and other equipment of discarded ships to reënforce the rest of the fleet on the homeward voyage.

When the *Recopilación* was published in 1681, of course vessels had vastly increased in size and innovations and improvements appeared in armament and construction. Law 30 of section 30, book 9, of this collection, therefore, while again repeating the old rules of the time of Charles V and Philip II, declared that in the future they should serve merely by way of a guide to what was reasonable and convenient in the light of later changes.

In the expedition of Pedrarias Dávila to Tierra Firme in 1514, for the first time the hulls of vessels were protected by a sheathing of lead from the devastations of the teredo or shipworm, which had worked such havoc on Columbus' fourth voyage. An order to Pedrarias from Valladolid, August 7, 1513, directed him to purchase " dos carabelas, que sean nuevas, las cuales fareis enforrar de la manga abajo, de plomo."[2] On the caravel, *Santa Catalina*, of his fleet, 35 hundredweight of lead were used; on another caravel in the same year, 40 hundredweight; and on a smaller, $27\frac{1}{4}$. Navarrete says that there is no earlier Spanish record of this practice.

[1] Encinas, iv, p. 152.  [2] A. de I., 109. 1. 5.

The inventor of the device may have been a certain Antonio Hernandez, for in a decree of July, 1514, he was appointed " emplomador de naos," with a salary of 25,000 maravedis. De Solis wished to take him along on the voyage to La Plata in 1515, but was not permitted, for the daily need there was of him at the Casa de Contratación.[1] Apparently sheets of lead were later often replaced by thin plates of copper, but the practice of sheathing cannot have been universal. In 1554 the Consulado was urging the king to order the Mexican viceroy to see that ships at Vera Cruz were not delayed there by lawsuits and appeals, since every year " se comen alli de broma (teredo) ocho ó diez naos," and those which returned were often in so bad a state as to founder on the voyage.[2]

On Spanish vessels in the sixteenth and seventeenth centuries the customary rations to sailors and soldiers included biscuit, wine, salt pork and fish, beans and peas, oil, vinegar, rice, and sometimes cheese or beef. There survives in the Archivo de Indias an interesting document[3] giving an estimate of the provisions and munitions needed for the armada which accompanied the fleet of Pedro de las Roelas to America in 1563. There were only two ships to the armada, a capitana and an almiranta, both of them merchantmen part of whose tonnage was reserved for the accommodation of soldiers and extra artillery. The estimate included provisions for only the general, admiral and seventy soldiers, gunners and officers added to the vessels' regular crews. It was reckoned that half the number, accompanying the general to Tierra Firme, would require rations for eight months, the other half, going with the admiral to Vera Cruz, for sixteen months.[4] The paper is especially valuable in that it gives the whole amount of each article required, the cost per unit, and the daily rations. In tabular form it appears on pages 279 and 280.[5]

[1] *Viajes*, i, p. cxxvii; Puente y Olea, *Los trabajos geográficos de la Casa de la Contratación*, p. 137.
[2] *Colecc. de doc.*, 1st ser., iii, pp. 513–520.   [3] A. de I., 30. 3. 1.
[4] The early ordinances of the Casa, in 1510, required every vessel returning from the New World to carry provisions for eighty days, to preclude any excuse for calling at another port before coming to Seville.
[5] It is interesting to compare prices as estimated in this report of 1563 with prices 44 years earlier, when Magellan was preparing his celebrated expedition, and

## SHIPS AND NAVIGATORS

STATEMENT OF THE PROVISIONS, MUNITIONS, ETC., NECESSARY FOR THE ARMADA OF PEDRO DE LAS ROELAS, 1563–64

| Provisions | Amount | Cost per unit | Whole cost | Daily rations |
|---|---|---|---|---|
| Ordinary biscuit | 373 cwt. 25 lbs. | 2 ducats per cwt. | 279,937 maravedis | 1½ lbs. daily per person |
| White biscuit for the general and admiral.. | 10 cwt. | 36 reals per cwt. | 12,240 " | |
| Wine | 1642 arrobas [1] | 250 maravedis per arroba | 410,500 " | ½ azumbre [2] daily per person |
| Beef | 7488 libretas [3] (for 3 months) | 15 maravedis per libreta | 112,320 " | 1 libreta per person 2 days in the week, Sundays and Thursdays |
| Salt fish | 99 cwt. 84 lbs. | 20 reals per cwt. | 67,888 " | 1 libra carnicera [4] to every 3 persons 4 days in the week |
| Salt pork | 18 cwt. 72 lbs. | 2500 maravedis per cwt. | 46,800 " | ½ libreta per person 1 day in the week |
| Beans and peas | 31 fanegas,[5] 3 almudes | 16 reals per fanega | 17,000 " | ½ almud to 15 persons, 3 days in the week, half beans, half peas |
| Rice | 3 cwt. 74 lbs. | 40 reals per cwt. | 5,094 " | 1 lb. to 10 persons, 1 day in the week |
| Cheese | 14 cwt. 4 lbs. | 2500 maravedis per cwt. | 35,100 " | 2 oz. per person on beef and pork days |
| Oil | 54 arrobas | 1 ducat per arroba | 20,250 " | ½ azumbre monthly per person |
| Vinegar | 172½ arrobas | 4 reals per arroba | 23,460 " | 1 arroba monthly to 5 persons |
| Garlic | 300 strings | 1 real per string | 10,200 " | |

[1] Arroba = 3½–4 gals.  [3] Libreta = troy lb.  [5] Fanega = 1.6 bushels = 12 almudes.
[2] Azumbre = 3½–4 pints.  [4] Libra carnicera = 36 oz.

with others in 1586, submitted by the Marquis of Santa Cruz in his estimates of the probable cost of the Great Armada:

|  | 1519 | 1563 | 1586 |
|---|---|---|---|
| Biscuit (per cwt.) | 170 maravedis | 750 maravedis | 612 maravedis |
| Salt Pork (per cwt.) | 770 " | 2500 " | 2380 " |
| Beans and Peas (per fanega) | 162 " | 444 " | 340 " |
| Rice (per cwt.) | 485 " | 1360 " | 1500 " |
| Cheese (per cwt.) | 940 " | 2500 " | 2380 " |
| Oil (per arroba) | 302 " | 375 " | 306 " |
| Vinegar (per arroba) | 13 " | 136 " | 148 " |
| Gunpowder (per cwt.) | 2084 " | 4125 " | 5100 " |
| Lead (per cwt.) | 722 " | 1125 " | 1020 " |

These data are of course too meagre to permit of any generalizations as to the rise of prices in the sixteenth century. According to this table, most articles appear to have become from two to three times dearer. Only olive oil remained nearly stationary.

The figures for 1519 were taken from *Viajes*, iv, pp. 162 ff.; those for 1586 are found in Fernandez Duro, *La armada invencible*, i, pp. 274 ff.

STATEMENT OF THE PROVISIONS, MUNITIONS, ETC., NECESSARY FOR THE ARMADA OF PEDRO DE LAS ROELAS, 1563-64

| Munitions, etc. | Amount | Cost per unit | Whole cost |
|---|---|---|---|
| | | | Maravedis |
| Arquebuses | 50 | 1½ ducats each | 28,125 |
| Coarse powder for 8 pieces of artillery | 20 cwt. | 11 ducats per cwt. | 82,500 |
| Fine powder for arquebuses | 3 cwt. | 17 ducats per cwt. | 19,125 |
| Cannon balls | .... | .... | 12,000 |
| Lead for shot for the arquebuses | 2 cwt. | 3 ducats per cwt. | 2,250 |
| Match for arquebuses and artillery | 4 cwt. | 9 ducats per cwt. | 13,500 |
| Tallow candles | 4 cwt. | 2,200 maravedis per cwt. | 8,800 |
| Wax torches for ship's lantern | 2 cwt. | 9,000 maravedis per cwt. | 18,000 |
| Medicines | .... | .... | 30,000 |
| Flags and drums for the general and admiral | .... | .... | 22,500 |
| Royal standard | .... | .... | 22,500 |
| Water casks | 30 | 33 reals each | 33,660 |
| Barrels and other articles | .... | .... | 75,000 |
| Cordage and timber | .... | .... | 30,000 |

Just a century later, in 1665, a royal decree prescribing the daily rations on the armada de barlovento, then preparing for American waters, provides a schedule remarkably like that of 1563. The daily portion of wine per person was reduced to about half, and there was no salt beef, but in its place there were more frequent rations of bacon and rice:

| | |
|---|---|
| Biscuit | 24 ounces every day |
| Wine | 1 cuartillo every day |
| Fish | 8 ounces 4 days in the week |
| Salt Pork | 8 ounces 3 days in the week |
| Peas and Beans | 2 ounces 4 days in the week |
| Rice | 1½ ounces 3 days in the week |
| Oil | 1½ ounces every day |
| Vinegar | ⅙ cuartillo every day |
| Cheese | small amount each week[1] |

The rations on a ship in the India fleets twenty years later, at least as Alvarez Osorio would have arranged them according to his *Discourses* published in 1686, are more meagre. There were to

[1] Veitia Linaje, lib. ii, cap. 5, par. 22.

be only twelve ounces of biscuit provided daily, and six ounces of codfish or salt pork. The other portions were about the same as earlier. The Consulado in the sixteenth century was sometimes given a voice in these dispositions respecting provisions, etc. In the seventeenth century, such matters were administered solely by the Casa de Contratación.

Presuming that a ship was of Spanish ownership and origin, a license from the Casa was also requisite for every voyage made to the New World; which license, according to the ordinances of September, 1534, might be granted only after an inspection of the vessel as to its age, tonnage, and fitness for a long sea journey. The license prescribed the maximum amount of freight and number of passengers which might be carried, this information being likewise included in the ship's register, so that customs officers in America could take cognizance of any excess. The penalty in 1552 was fixed at 10,000 maravedis fine for every ton of freight and each passenger above the maximum, besides forfeiture of the excess cargo.[1] In the beginning a license could be denied to no one who fulfilled the requirements laid down by the Crown. Any vessel properly equipped and laded might depart alone or with the fleets as the rule might be. But at least as early as 1582 the number of ships sailing in each fleet was settled by the Casa in consultation with the prior and consuls of the merchants (after 1642 also with the gild of mariners); and this would seem to imply that thereafter the licenses issued each year were more or less limited in number. It also meant that the choice of vessels rested with the officers of the Casa, an invidious privilege bound to cause heartburnings and bitter complaints among masters and owners less favored than the rest. So much time was consumed apparently in the discussion and justification of such cases that in 1601 the election of ships was transferred to the Council of the Indies, the Casa sending to Madrid a descriptive list of eligible vessels found in the Guadalquivir. It had always been customary to remit to the council a report of the ships which the president and jueces had chosen. But the council, too, soon found the selec-

[1] *Ord. of the Casa*, 1505, no. 22; 1510, no. 31; 1552, no. 155.

tion of merchantmen too embarrassing a task, and in September, 1613, shifted the responsibility back to the Casa. Licenses to "navios de registro," however, i. e., to vessels permitted to sail to West Indian islands and ports outside the beaten track of the fleets, had until 1642 always to come from the king or the Council of the Indies.[1]

The limitation in the tonnage of the fleets and the resulting competition made inevitable sooner or later the formulation of a body of rules governing the admission or exclusion of merchant ships; rules which offer an excellent example of the meticulous character of Spanish mercantile and maritime regulations. To encourage shipbuilding in the peninsula, one third of the tonnage of the flotas was reserved to those who had constructed the ships they owned. If there was competition among these "fabricadores," or among those eligible for the other two thirds, the preference was given to vessels which fulfilled most closely the specifications issued from time to time by the government.[2] If ships were equally eligible in these respects, those were preferred which possessed seniority of arrival at the port of San Lucar; and among the latter, vessels constructed in Biscay had preeminence over those built in other parts of the kingdom or in the Indies. That a ship was equipped with artillery of brass also gave it a prior claim over others of greater seniority, or the fact that its owner had served the king for six years in the royal armadas.[3]

The Crown frequently conceded to particular individuals or corporations special permission (licencias de privilegio) to send a ship with the American flotas; and these licenses became so numerous that in 1625 an order appeared allowing only one such

[1] Antuñez y Acevedo, pp. 53-55; Veitia Linaje, lib. ii, cap. 6, par. 3; *Recop.*, lib. ix, tit. 42, ley 1.
After 1582 the jueces oficiales were assisted in their examination of eligible vessels by the general or the almirante appointed for the fleet, the capitan de la maestranza, and sometimes by the visitadores.

[2] Rules for the measurement or gauging of ships were published by the government in 1613, and in 1620 an official ship-gauger or "arqueador" was appointed for the Casa with a salary of 20 escudos a month. See *Recop.*, lib. ix, tit. 28, leyes 23-25.

[3] Veitia Linaje, lib. ii, cap. 6, *passim*.

vessel to accompany each of the fleets, the licenses being honored in the order of their date of issue. After 1647, when the Consulado was granted a perpetual license of this nature in return for constructing twelve galleons for the royal service, there were generally two privileged vessels in each of the fleets. But the tonnage of these ships was always deducted from the whole tonnage assigned for that particular year.

Most of these rules became more or less obsolete as the number of native ships decreased, and greater and greater dependence was put on those of foreign construction; for it was to encourage and favor Spanish ships and shipbuilding that they were in the first place directed. Owners of foreign-built vessels which were admitted to the India navigation enjoyed the same privileges and immunities conceded to the mariners' gild of Seville.

It is likely that in the beginnings of Spanish colonial commerce freight contracts were not subjected to royal regulation, but were fixed by custom or governed by the ordinary forces of supply and demand among masters and shippers.[1] The first attempt at interference is said to have been made in April, 1572. In response to complaints from the Consulado of the excessive rates demanded by Biscayan shipowners in the fleet then preparing for New Spain, the Council of the Indies ordered the Casa's officers to have American freight charges immediately reduced to schedule on the basis of the rates in previous fleets.[2] If the decree was intended to

---

[1] At the beginning of the sixteenth century, from 100 to 110 maravedis per ton per month were paid for the hire of ships. At the close of the reign of Charles V the rates customarily paid by the Crown for vessels employed in the armadas were as follows:

| | |
|---|---|
| While being fitted out in the river at Seville .................... | 110 maravedis per ton per month. |
| On a voyage to the Azores ........ | 130 " " " " " |
| On a voyage to the Indies ......... | 140 " " " " " |

As prices of ship's stores, however, had risen 10 per cent in the previous decade, the oficiales of the Casa suggested to the king that these rates be made more generous. A. de I., Patr. 2. 5. 1/14, ramos 18, 23; *Viajes*, ii, pp. 81–86; Fernandez Duro, *Armada Española*, i, p. 352.

[2] Antuñez y Acevedo, pp. 169 f. Apparently the schedule was made the same for Seville, San Lucar, and Cadiz.

inaugurate a new policy, it was in force only a short time; for in the ordinances regulating the dispatch of flotas issued in January, 1582, the king specifically states that in view of the increased cost of ship's stores it is his wish that the schedules for freight rates for the time being be discontinued. That they were not renewed for a considerable period may be inferred from a report of the India House to the Council in 1615. The Mexican colonists in that year petitioned the Council to publish a fixed freight charge for carrying their products from Vera Cruz to Spain, and the officials of the Casa, in reply to a request for information, recommended that, as it was not the custom to regulate rates on outbound vessels, it would be well to maintain the same rule for the return voyage.[1] In conformity with this opinion, a cédula was issued by the king in December of the same year. Sometime in the seventeenth century, however, the practice of 1572 was reëstablished, for in Veitia Linaje's day a flat rate of fifty-eight ducats silver per ton was in force, fourteen paid in advance at Seville and forty-four on arrival in the Indies.[2] Finally, in the *Recopilación* of 1681 we find codified the decree of December, 1615, again leaving freights both at Seville and in the Indies to be regulated by the operation of supply and demand.[3]

The Castilian ton or "tonelada" was equal in weight to twenty quintals or hundredweight, and in Spanish vessels of the sixteenth and seventeenth centuries was estimated to represent a space of something over fifty-six cubic feet.[4] By an ordinance of 1543 was minutely prescribed what weight and bulk of each article of common export to America might be stowed in the space of a tonelada, and this schedule was posted, with other important rules, on a tablet on the walls of the Casa. But in the seventeenth century such regulations had disappeared, the calculation of these

---

[1] Veitia Linaje, lib. ii, cap. 16, par. 2.   [2] *Ibid.*, par. 3.
[3] *Recop.*, lib. ix, tit. 31, ley 6. By a law of 1592 it was forbidden to all officials connected with the Casa, from the president down, under heavy penalties, to compel shipmasters to accept consignments of freight, or interfere in any way with their entire liberty of action.
[4] "... siendo cada tonelada el tamaño de dos pipas, 6 el de ocho codos cubicos medidos con el codo Real lineal de 33 dedos, de los que una vara Castellana tiene 48. ..." Veitia Linaje, lib. ii, cap. 15, par. 2.

details being left to individual arrangement between master and shippers.[1]

As it was customary to receive the major part of the freight charges on delivery in the Indies, in order to meet the heavy expense incidental to a long voyage across the Atlantic shipowners and masters found it necessary to negotiate loans (bottomry bills) on the security of their vessels, sometimes with obligation to repay to correspondents in the colonies. Motives of honesty were no more compelling in the sixteenth century than in the twentieth, and as the organization of the business world was much simpler then than now, opportunity for fraud was all the greater. From the very outset of the American trade, shipmasters made these financial transactions the occasion for dishonest dealings, either misrepresenting the value or proprietorship of the vessel, or borrowing several times over on the same security. As early as 1507, the officials of the Casa were obliged to issue an order that all masters, before obtaining advances of money, present themselves at the Casa with information as to the ownership and capacity of their ships, so that the Oficiales might determine their value and the amount which could safely be secured upon them. Record of the transactions was thereafter kept in the Casa's books, for the information of any who cared to see. The penalty for disobedience was forfeiture of interest in the vessel, a fine of 100 ducats in gold, and obligation to repay twice the sum unlawfully borrowed. If a money lender disregarded the terms of the ordinance, his contract was unenforceable in any court of law. The rule was republished in March, 1509, when its provisions were extended to merchants who took up money on goods shipped to America. A receipt for the sums borrowed had also to be deposited with the contador of the Casa.[2]

After 1587 loans on ship bottoms were registered before the prior and consuls, and limited to one third the value of the vessel. In 1621 the limit was raised to two thirds. But it mattered little what the rules were, if they were not observed. Much larger amounts were negotiated without license from the Casa or the

[1] Veitia Linaje, lib. ii, cap. 16, par. 2–8.
[2] *Viajes*, ii, p. 320; *Colecc. de doc.*, 2d ser., v, p. 101.

Consulado, sometimes to double the worth of the ship involved. And to escape the letter of the law, the notes were worded as a simple promise to pay, although it was understood that the ship was the security. It seems that in the seventeenth century this practice was quite open, with the knowledge of the Consulado, business men declaring that within the legal restrictions few vessels could sail. And occasionally a master was found who considered it more profitable to lose his ship than repay the money secured upon it. But if, as Veitia Linaje declares, freights earned on a voyage to America were often greater than the value of the vessel, and as the purpose of the two-thirds rule was merely to protect the creditors, these irregularities were probably less dangerous than might at first sight appear. In cases of bankruptcy, however, loans made with the license of the prior and consuls were given precedence over any others.

Marine insurance is an institution much older than the discovery of America, and was from the first applied to equalize the dangers and losses of the long trans-Atlantic voyage. The business was under the immediate supervision of the Consulado of Seville, half of whose ordinances relate to its regulation; but as elsewhere in Europe it was conducted by brokers (corredores de seguros) who acted as intermediaries between insurer and insured. The broker obtained upon the policies (polizas) the signature of merchants or bankers who were ready to take a risk, with the amount each ventured, and guaranteed their signature with his own; and he kept a complete record of each policy which passed through his hands. But no broker might assume any risks for himself or for another, directly or indirectly, under penalty of 30,000 maravedis fine and exclusion from his profession.

The hull of a ship might be insured to two thirds of its value for the outbound voyage, and for the return to such amount as the prior and consuls indicated. But artillery, rigging, and freight receipts might not be included without invalidating the policy; and if money was borrowed on the vessel, that amount was deducted from the insurable value. By decrees of 1587 and 1588, the maximum for ship insurance was reduced from two thirds to one third.[1] Yet merchandise, curiously enough, might be secured to its full value and including the cost of the policy, provided the goods were registered in the ship's papers.

A few of the more general rules it may be of interest to note here. Insurance ran from the moment the merchandise was embarked on barges for transfer to vessels in the harbor, and ended only when the goods were placed safely on shore at the termination of the voyage. Premiums had to be paid within three months of the signing of the policy, or the latter was void; but should all or part of the goods insured fail to be shipped, the owner might recover his premium if he made claim within fifteen days. Marine policies were in every case limited to a period of two years, and any claims for loss or damage had to be presented within that time. But if a ship and its cargo completely disappeared, after the lapse of a year and a half the owner or consignees might present claims for payment.[2]

Before a vessel was allowed to depart from Cadiz or San Lucar, altogether three visitations or inspections were necessary; one, already alluded to, prior to lading for the voyage, another held generally after the lading was completed, and a third just before the ship put to sea. When the India House was founded, these examinations were made by the three jueces oficiales together or more probably in rotation.[3] But very soon special officers were employed to assist in such duties. The first time we hear of a visitador is in a cédula of December, 1518, which ordered the salaries enjoyed by Diego Rodriguez Cómitre and Bartolomé Diaz as "visitadores de naos" to be continued to them. The office therefore existed before 1518. In another decree, of August, 1522, visitadores are mentioned again, as forbidden, with the jueces of the Casa, to own or have any interest in ships engaged in commerce with America.[4] To secure the observance of the many rules and restrictions applied to the colonial trade, everything

---
[1] Veitia Linaje, lib. ii, cap. 19, par. 4.
[2] Of premiums returned, the insurer always retained ½ per cent. See Appendix XI.
[3] *Ord. of the Casa*, 1510, nos. 9, 31.
[4] Veitia Linaje, lib. i, cap. 24, par. 2.

depended on the zeal and intelligence displayed in the preliminary inspections. The visitadores, consequently, were supposed to be men of capacity and experience in the structure, repair and careening of vessels, as well as versed in all that pertained to the lading and dressing of cargoes. Their position was always regarded as one of distinction, and in the minutely graded order of precedence maintained by the Casa on all occasions, they ranked with the prior and consuls of the merchant gild. Like most other offices in Hapsburg Spain, however, theirs was sold as a life tenure to the highest bidder, the proprietors being allowed to nominate to the Casa deputies to serve for them. Two continued to be the number of visitadores till 1670, when a third was added.

By 1552 the personal intervention of the jueces oficiales in these inspections had become somewhat limited. The first examination was conducted by one or both of the visitadores, who sent to the Casa in writing a report of the size and quality of the vessel, and the alterations or repairs proposed to make it acceptable for the voyage.[1] At the same time they received an oath from the master that he would take on board no priests, friars or other persons unless they possessed a license from the Crown or from the India House; and they indicated what stores and duplicate equipment, such as tackle, spars, sails, anchors, cables, etc., must be procured for the journey.

Till 1553 the second examination was the business of the contador of the Casa, made on personal application of the owner or master when the ship was laded and ready to drop down the river. The contador had any excess cargo disembarked, and inspected the crew, artillery, munitions, provisions and other appointments of the vessel to see that the ordinances and the visitadores' instructions had been complied with.[2] After 1553, with the increased draft of Atlantic ships, and the gradual silting up of the river, it was usually necessary to complete the lading and hold the second examination at San Lucar; and as the contador was prevented by his other duties from travelling to that port, the inspection devolved upon the visitadores.[3] Moreover it was soon found

[1] *Ord. of the Casa*, 1552, no. 153.
[2] *Ibid.*, no. 156.
[3] Antuñez y Acevedo, p. 77.

physically impossible, in the short time commonly given to these inspections, to examine the nature, quantity and quality of all the provisions on board, many of which were sealed in casks or stowed away in different parts of the ship. For these reasons, doubtless, there was later introduced the practice of accepting a detailed statement, signed and sworn by the master, mate and steward, of the food and other stores on hand. The master also took another oath to the effect that everything declared belonged to the ship, and would be carried on the voyage, and that he would receive no more cargo or any prohibited articles or persons. Indeed, so far as was humanly possible, this harassed mariner was allowed no loophole of escape. In the seventeenth century, the second visitation was apparently made immediately after the vessel had been careened and renovated, and before lading, and only then were directions given as to the artillery and other equipment.[1]

The third inspection, at San Lucar just before sails were hoisted and the ship put to sea, although of a general character, covering everything attended to at the first and second, was particularly directed to the cargo, to detect any smuggled or prohibited merchandise. It was conducted by the visitadores, or if an entire fleet was preparing, by one of the jueces oficiales in his turn, assisted by the visitadores. They were authorized to compel the master to unship at his own expense, and in their presence, anything carried contrary to rules and instructions; and if the same or any other articles were taken aboard after this final visitation, they were forfeited to the royal exchequer.[2] The inspectors were forbidden to pass any vessel till the last iota had been complied with, even if it involved the loss of the voyage, nor were they permitted to accept a master's promise in lieu of immediate performance.

When, in the event of overloading, it was necessary to choose which shipments should remain on board, those laded at Seville were preferred to those laded at San Lucar, and of goods from the same place, that belonging to passengers to that shipped by merchants. Seville goods, unless unregistered or otherwise confiscate,

---

[1] Veitia Linaje, lib. i, cap. 24, par. 9.
[2] *Ord. of the Casa*, 1552, no. 187.

were sent back to the Casa de Contratación to be delivered to the owners at their expense.[1]

The third examination was also extended in 1569 to ships of the armada, because of the growing practice of concealing merchandise upon them, the owners or factors sailing as soldiers or in some other official capacity. Inspection was especially needed in the years when, according as the policy of the Casa fluctuated one way or the other, the convoys were forbidden to carry any registers at all. But there is every indication that it remained little more than a formality.

The visitadores received a salary per diem, apportioned among the masters or owners of the ships examined, as well as the hire of a sloop they employed in going about the harbor; but they were forbidden to accept, or the masters to offer, any collation, gift or other perquisite in addition to the legal remuneration.[2] A testimonial of the inspection was inserted in each ship's register, and guards were detailed to remain on board till the vessel reached the open sea. In Veitia Linaje's time this practice had fallen into abeyance, except for ships of the armada, having proved, as this same writer declares from his own experience, utterly futile to accomplish the purpose intended. For usually the men so employed secured their place through influence, and not on their character or reputation; wherefore they were easily suborned and became merely the instruments for more extended fraud.[3]

After 1565 the captain general of the fleet was expected to be present at the last visitation, but the rule came to be disregarded in the seventeenth century. When a president was set over the Casa de Contratación, he, too, frequently went down to San Lucar for the dispatch or reception of the fleets, either alone or with the juez oficial whose turn it was to be there. But we are told that this duty was always regarded by the officials of the India House as one of the most onerous connected with their institution.

Except for a score of years after 1588, the visitadores of the Casa were also charged with the examination of ships sailing from

---

[1] *Ord. of the Casa*, 1552, nos. 186, 188, 192.  [2] *Ibid.*, nos. 189, 195.
[3] Veitia Linaje, lib. ii, cap. 1, par. 13.

Cadiz, one of them making the journey to that city whenever his services were called for. From 1588 to 1610 there was a separate inspector appointed for the sister port, but after 1610, although the Cadiz Juzgado repeatedly urged its claim to independence in this regard, the Council never saw fit to renew the concession. Inspection of merchantmen in colonial ports belonged to the treasury officers, or oficiales reales, sometimes aided by a deputy of the local governor or by the fiscal of the audiencia.

The regular duties of the visitador extended only to the dispatch of fleets and navios de registro to the New World. When a returning fleet dropped anchor at San Lucar (or in earlier years before Seville itself), one of the jueces oficiales, accompanied by the clerk of registers with copies of the papers sent on the outward voyage, went down to the port to receive it and visit each of the ships;[1] and no person, whether sailor, soldier or passenger, might leave, or any articles be disembarked, till this formality was accomplished. The visitadores, however, as experienced in these matters, were sometimes deputed to advise in the examination. This was intended to be of the most inquisitorial character. Not only was there search for unregistered, or fraudulently registered, bullion and other precious commodities; not only was there verification of the muster sheets, and of the artillery and other appointments of each vessel, to see that they corresponded with the requirements originally set at the departure from Spain; but, according to the ordinances of 1552, each mariner and passenger was to be approached separately and made to wear if he had in any way contravened the host of regulations touching the India navigation, or knew of any one who had. Within the scope of this cross-examination were included smuggling, false registry, blasphemy, gambling, lechery, failure to have a license, concealment of Indian servants or slaves or unlicensed

---

[1] *Ord. of the Casa*, 1510, no. 9; 1552, nos. 211–215.

Till the middle of the seventeenth century, the same official went to meet the returning fleet who had dispatched it to the Indies. In the sixteenth century, he received for this 5 ducats a day, in the seventeenth, 6 ducats. If the president went down to inspect the fleets, he was paid 12 ducats. His expenses, with constables, notaries, a skiff to go about in the harbor, etc., amounted to another 16 or 18 ducats, a very heavy charge.

negroes, deaths en route and disposition of the belongings of the deceased, whether the master had called at or delivered goods to forbidden ports, had borrowed equipment for the time of inspection, carried a full quota of seamen, etc. The juez oficial also inquired of the crews what wages were still owing them, and ordered payment by the master of the vessel within three days. Finally, when the inspection was completed, guards were stationed on each of the ships to prevent the secret abstraction of contraband articles which had escaped the judge's eyes.

Although returning fleets were consistently forbidden to put in at Cadiz, a member of the Casa was occasionally sent there to compel ships for any reason appearing in that port to pass on to San Lucar, or if they were in no condition to go further, to receive and examine them there. From Cadiz bullion was not carried overland to the Casa de Contratación, but by sea on sloops to San Lucar, and thence up the Guadalquivir to Seville. Even in time of war, when there was always danger of the presence of enemy ships outside, transport overland was prohibited, either the "barcos de plata" being convoyed by men-of-war along the coast, or the remission of bullion suspended till peace returned.[1] At San Lucar the treasure was transshipped to large river boats called "gavarras," the chests and bars from each galleon being kept carefully distinct and separate.

Most of these rules had taken shape before the close of the reign of Charles V, and they were with wearisome monotony recalled to the attention of the king's officers in repeated decrees of the sixteenth and seventeenth centuries. Yet in no matter supervised by the India House was fraud more common or more disastrous than in this of the equipment, gauging, and lading of ships in the American trade. Multiplication of precautions, piling Pelion upon Ossa, had no appreciable effect. Generals, masters, passengers, sailors and merchants found a common interest in rendering the laws nugatory, and members of the Casa and even of the Council of the Indies must frequently have had a hand in their irregular practices. Atlantic vessels, whether merchantmen or men-of-war, were frequently so embarrassed with goods and pas-

[1] Veitia Linaje, lib. i, cap. 9, par. 20.

sengers that it was scarcely possible to defend them if attacked. Shipmasters hired anchors, cables, provisions and especially artillery,[1] to make up the required equipment, and men to fill the muster rolls, against the time when the visitadores came on board, getting rid of both men and stores immediately after. Merchant ships were so feebly manned, owing to the excessive overcrowding, that it was all they could do to withstand the least spell of bad weather, let alone outmanoeuvre a swift-sailing privateer.

Foreigners remarked upon this early in the sixteenth century. The Italian traveller, Benzoni, writes in his *History of the New World:*

> ... the principal reason of the French getting so many of the ships belonging to the Spaniards was the avarice of the owners; for on quitting Spain, such was their avidity to fill up with merchandise and passengers, that they did not put the due number of guns on board, in case they had to defend themselves if attacked by an enemy's ship; nor even the number ordered by the Council of the Indies. ... The Council, moreover, appointed certain commissaries to take special care by going to San Lucar, to visit the ships when they were about starting, and ascertain whether they were provided according to the orders issued. But the captains of the ships, by putting a piece of gold into the hands of the commissaries, made them say that all was right; and with this arrangement they went away to Seville, waited on their superiors at the Contract office, and swore to God that everything was in perfect order, and that the ship, whatever it might be, was equal to fighting against four French vessels. In this way three or four Spanish ships used to start, though the best of them carried only two or three iron guns, half eaten through with rust, and one keg of indifferent powder. On their return, if a little French galleon (galleoncette) well-armed happened to meet a ship, even of 1500 or 2000 " salme " (about three or four hundred tons) they attacked her without the least fear, knowing how ill Spanish ships were provided. ...[2]

Another consequence of the utter disregard of rules and regulations was the frightful prevalence of shipwreck. Advance in nautical knowledge and experience, improvements in the art of shipbuilding, seemed to make little difference. From beginning to end, the passage to and from America on a Spanish vessel was

---

[1] As early as 1507, a decree had to be issued forbidding any one to lend or rent to shipmasters arms, munitions, etc., for the visit of the Casa's officials, under penalty of forfeiture of the articles involved. *Colecc. de doc.*, 2d ser., v, p. 101.

[2] Benzoni, *History of the New World*, tr. by W. H. Smyth. (Hakluyt Soc., ser. i, no. 21.)

a hazardous undertaking. The chances seemed nearly even that the passenger would either fail to reach his destination, or arrive only after enduring all the terrors and vicissitudes of the deep. One wonders, sometimes, that Spaniards entrusted their goods or their persons so readily to unseaworthy boats, inadequately manned and equipped. The wonder grows when we recollect that the harbors of Cadiz, San Lucar and Vera Cruz offered little more protection from wind and storm than the open sea, and that West Indian hurricanes were as fatal to shipping then as now. The explanation is probably to be found, as Benzoni suggests, in the avarice as well of the merchant exporter as of the shipmaster. It was a great lottery, this American commerce. Both preferred to take a long chance, with the prospect of enormous winnings.

The toll, however, was a terrible one. To cite but a few instances in the period following 1550, when the India navigation was well organized: four vessels were wrecked upon the shores of Florida in 1554. In 1555 the flagship of Cosme Rodriguez Farfan was cast away on the Andalusian coast. His fleet had been scattered by a storm in the West Indies, and three ships driven into San Juan de Porto Rico. In 1556 an armada of three was sent to San Juan under Gonzalo de Carvajal to collect the bullion from these ships, and on the return two of the three were wrecked on the coast of Portugal. In 1563 were destroyed by a storm seven vessels of the flota lying in the harbor of Nombre de Dios. And in the same year, of the Vera Cruz fleet five were cast away on the dangerous reefs in the Gulf of Campeche. Two vessels of the Tierra Firme squadron were lost in a hurricane in 1564, and several upon the island of Dominica three years later. Four ships of the New Spain flota were wrecked on the Tabasco coast in 1571, and five more in 1572. In 1581, on the voyage to Nombre de Dios, one ship sank in the Caribbean Sea, and two more off the coast of Spain on the homeward journey; while in 1590 fifteen vessels of the flota of Antonio Navarro were destroyed by a "norther" in the harbor of Vera Cruz and two hundred men drowned. In the following year the flagship of the New Spain flota went down in a storm with all on board, and sixteen of the fleet were stranded on the island of Tercera in the Azores. The difficult sand bar across the mouth of the river at San Lucar also provided its quota of disasters. The flagship and two other vessels of the Mexican fleet were wrecked there as they were departing in 1579, and another vessel of the same fleet in 1580. In 1587 six ships from Tierra Firme were cast away on the bar as they tried to enter, but the crews and the treasure were saved. In the harbor of Cadiz, fifteen were driven ashore in a terrible storm, just as the fleet was about to sail in 1563, and a similar accident occurred there eleven years later, in 1574.

In the seventeenth century conditions scarcely improved: in 1600 a galeon de Indias was wrecked upon Cape St. Vincent, and another in 1601; in the latter year fourteen at the entrance to Vera Cruz in a sudden norther, one thousand men perishing and two millions lost in merchandise; in 1603 the flagship and two others of the New Spain fleet on the island of Guadaloupe, with the loss of another million in cargo, and a vessel of the same fleet on the coast of Hispaniola on the return voyage; in 1605 four galleons of the armada of Luis de Córdoba on the coast of Cumaná near Margarita; in the next year several more vessels of a flota commanded by the same general, in which the latter was lost and millions of treasure; in 1607 two galleons of the Mexican flota in which perished the general and six hundred men; in 1608 the flagship of Juan de Salas Valdés in the Azores; the flagship of the same general in 1609, and in 1610 that of the Tierra Firme fleet; in 1614 a Tierra Firme galleon on the voyage to Spain, and seven vessels bound for Vera Cruz near Cape Catoche; etc.[1]

As an example of what the American flotas had to anticipate if they fell in the way of a West Indian hurricane, may be cited the experiences of the summer of 1622. The Mexican fleet of that year, commanded by Francisco de Sosa, with Antonio Liri as almirante, was ill-omened from the start, for it lost its flagship and another large vessel while sailing out from San Lucar. Putting to sea from Vera Cruz on June 7, it took forty days to reach Havana on account of storms and contrary winds. But this was

[1] Many of these data were taken from the lists of shipwrecks published as appendices to volumes ii and iii of Fernandez Duro's *Armada Española*. But the entire accuracy of these lists is questionable.

only a prelude to what it experienced after emerging from the Bahama Channel. There the fleet was dispersed by a hurricane, some of the ships dismasted, others filled with water, and one broken to pieces altogether with the loss of ninety men.

This New Spain fleet, however, encountered only the edge of the storm. The galleons from Tierra Firme emerged from the port of Havana for Spain on September 4. They consisted of seventeen vessels convoyed by a squadron of eight men-of-war and three pataches, the armada commanded by Lope Diaz de Armendariz, Marquis of Cadereyta, with the distinguished mariner, Tomás de La Raspuru, as almirante. Shortly after they put to sea, the cyclone burst upon that region with extraordinary fury. About Havana itself many houses were overthrown and plantations destroyed. But the fleet was struck by the storm in the most dangerous part of the Channel, where there was no room to manoeuvre. Of the convoy, the galleon, *Santa Margarita*, was driven upon the Martires and instantly went to pieces; the almiranta, *N. Señora de Atocha*, foundered; the *N. Señora del Rosario* was cast away upon the island of Tortuga, and one of the pataches upon reefs in the same neighborhood. Four of the seventeen merchantmen sank, and only four of the rest remained with their masts standing. More than a thousand men were drowned, including the commander of the flota, Pedro Pasquier, and the loss of bullion and merchandise was reckoned at over four million pesos. The ships which survived made their way as best they could back to Havana, and wintered there, as there were not sufficient stores for the repair of so great a catastrophe.[1] The hurricane also struck a small armada of guardacostas, and wrecked the flagship and two other vessels.

When news of the disaster reached the Spanish court, the government, acting with unwonted promptness, ordered three galleons to the island of Madeira to rescue the almiranta from New Spain reported there in a sinking condition, and the squadron of Antonio Oquendo to carry spars and cordage for the refitting of the shattered fleets; while other men-of-war under Fadrique de Toledo and Juan Fajardo were sent to cruise near Cape

[1] Fernandez Duro, *op. cit.*, iv, pp. 40 f.

St. Vincent for Dutch and Barbary ships reported as sailing to that coast.

One of the principal reasons, doubtless, why these disasters assumed such alarming proportions was the lack of good sailors and pilots. In spite of the regulations, crews were recruited with men of every sort and condition, who used this means of crossing over to and remaining in the Indies without encountering the emigration laws, and whose gross ignorance placed the ship in jeopardy with every passing squall. When the flotas arrived at their American destination and the hatches were opened, frequently the sailors could not be compelled to unlade the merchandise, all immediately deserting the ships, or even, it is said, setting fire to the cargoes to render their escape more certain.

## CHAPTER XII

### SHIPS AND NAVIGATORS (II)

IN describing the organization of the Casa de Contratación, something was said of that institution as a hydrographic bureau and school of navigation. The Casa very early had its own pilots and cosmographers, as well as a professor of cosmography, and created a technical office where charts were designed or authenticated for use by Spanish seamen.

The great need of a nautical school was emphasized in the cédula of instructions to Americo Vespucci, the first pilot major, in August, 1508, a few months after his appointment. Very few mariners at that date could have any real knowledge of the Atlantic route or of the American coasts, and the sailing of ignorant pilots resulted not only in the loss of ships and the discouragement of trade, but also in the confusion of nautical knowledge through the reporting of false or inaccurate observations. The instructions read as follows:

> Por cuanto á nuestra noticia es venido, é por experiencia habemos visto que, por no ser los pilotos tan expertos como seria menester, é tan estructos en lo que deben saber, que les baste para regir é gobernar los navios que naveguen en los viajes, que se hacen por el mar Occéano á las nuestras Yslas é Tierra firme, que tenemos en la parte de las Yndias, é por . . . no tener fundamento para saber tomar, por el cuadrante é astrolabio, el altura, ni saber la cuenta dello, les han acaecido muchos yerros, é las gentes que, debajo de su gobernacion navegan han pasado mucho peligro, de que nuestro Señor ha seydo deservido, é en nuestra hacienda é de los mercaderes, que allá contratan, se ha recibido mucho daño é pérdida, é para remediar lo susodicho . . . mandamos que todos los pilotos de nuestros reinos é señorios . . . que quisieran ir por pilotos en la dicha navegacion, sean instruidos é sepan lo que es necessario saber en el cuadrante é astrolabio, para que junta la plática con la teórica se puedan aprovechar dello en los viajes que hicieren en las dichas partes, é que, sin lo saber no puedan ir en los dichos navios por pilotos, nin ganar soldadas por pilotage, ni los mercaderes se puedan concertar con ellos para que sean pilotos, ni los maestres los puedan recibir en los navios, sin que primero sean examinados por Vos, Mérigo Vespuchi Nuestro Piloto mayor é les sea dada por Vos carta de examinacion é aprobacion, de como saben cada

uno dellos lo susodicho, con la cual carta mandamos que sean tenidos é recibidos por pilotos espertos doquier que la mostraren . . . Vos mandamos que les enseñeis en vuestra casa en Sevilla á todos los que lo quisieren saber, pagandovos vuestro trabajo.[1]

The extent of the theoretical knowledge of masters and pilots who conducted vessels to and from the Indies is also revealed in a memorial presented by the pilot major in 1512, saying that a certain Juan Rodriguez Sardo, although of practical experience as an American pilot, should be given a term of six months in which to learn the use of the quadrant or the astrolabe. The oficiales of the Casa agreed, but permitted him to make one more voyage, for which it seems he was already prepared, without knowing how to make observations of the sun.[2] In view of this primitive state of nautical science among Spanish mariners, it is surprising that so many fleets, like those of Ovando, Diego Columbus, Pedrarias Dávila, etc., as well as single ships licensed or unlicensed, should have made voyages with comparatively little mishap. Without instructions or a great deal of experience, they sailed everywhere, skirting unknown capes and bays, which they described and crudely located for the benefit of those who followed after in the same course.

The pilot major was, therefore, in the beginning a teacher, who conducted a school at his own residence in Seville and received fees from his students. He himself also examined candidates for the profession of pilot, and granted the necessary certificate, without the interposition of any higher official. No pilot might sail in that capacity to the Indies without first passing this examination, even though he had fulfilled similar requirements elsewhere.[3] It is clear that such extensive power might become a source of abuse. As the Casa possessed no monopoly of the teaching of cosmography and map making, the examiner might be tempted to look with especial leniency on candidates who had come to him for instruction; or he might charge excessive fees for the examination. It seems that in 1534 Sebastian Cabot was accused of some

---

[1] Puente y Olea, *Los trabajos geográficos de la Casa de la Contratación*, p. 65; *Viajes*, iii, p. 299.

[2] Fernandez Duro, *La Armada Española*, i, p. 120.

[3] *Ord. of the Casa*, 1552, nos. 135, 143.

such practices. A royal cédula of March 14 of that year instructed the Casa:

> que fagais ynformacion, e sepais qué derechos son los quel dicho Sebastian Caboto a llevado, e lleva por el exámen de los dichos Pilotos, e cómo e de qué manera los a examinado e examina, e qué delyxencias son los que face en los tales exámenes . . .;[1]

but as nine months later Cabot was still superintending these examinations, the charges were evidently unsubstantiated. However, ordinances were enacted by Charles V toward the end of his reign forbidding the pilot major to teach the science of navigation and the use of nautical instruments, on pain of ten ducats fine and the exclusion of his pupil from examination for two years. He was at the same time ordered to exact no fees from candidates, or receive victuals or gifts of any kind.[2] In the meantime what instruction was given at the Casa was necessarily transferred to the cosmographers, till in December, 1552, a regular chair in cosmography was created.[3]

By the year 1552, moreover, the examinations were no longer conducted by the pilot major alone, but with him were associated the cosmographers of the Casa and a number (at least six) of experienced pilots chosen from among those who happened at the moment to be in Seville. Each was duly sworn to give a faithful decision, and a majority vote of those present was sufficient to warrant the issue of a certificate.[4] After September, 1604, one of the jueces oficiales presided at the examination instead of the pilot major. Each candidate was required to give evidence beforehand, supported by four witnesses, that he was a native or naturalized Spaniard, at least twenty-four years of age, of good character and lineage, and of at least six years' experience in the navigation to America. For the last qualification, two of the

---

[1] *Colecc. de doc.*, 1st ser., xxxii, p. 479.

[2] Reissued as nos. 130, 132, and 143 of the ordinances of 1552.

[3] Between 1596 and 1612, however, the professorship of cosmography was united with the office of pilot major in the person of Rodrigo de Zamorano.

According to Veitia Linaje, in the later sixteenth century there was a second pilot major for the examination of navigators to the Rio de la Plata. But the office evidently was not long continued. Lib. ii, cap. 11, par. 2; cap. 12, par. 19.

[4] *Ord. of the Casa*, 1552, nos. 128, 139.

witnesses had to be pilots who had sailed in the same ship with him. The information was given in the presence of the pilot major (and later the deputies of the mariners' gild), and read before the assembled examiners prior to the opening of the examination.[1] The candidate was tested, so far as maritime geography was concerned, for a particular route previously indicated, such as to Tierra Firme, or to New Spain, or to the Rio de la Plata, and if he chose later to serve as pilot in another region, had to be examined a second time. The pilot major and cosmographers might ask as many questions as they liked, the visiting pilots were limited each to three. If a candidate was rejected, he might not come up for reëxamination without first making another voyage to the Indies, and an additional voyage was also required of the successful candidate before he was permitted himself to act as an examiner.[2] The examinations were held within the walls of the Casa, generally on a holiday (in the seventeenth century, in the hall assigned to the Consulado).

As was the case with every other department of the Casa's activities, these examinations were not conducted in the spirit intended by the Crown. Already in 1534, as we have seen, an inquiry was made into the official behavior of Sebastian Cabot. In August, 1547, the Emperor wrote to Cabot reiterating that no unnaturalized foreigners be admitted; for, he continued, he understood that the pilot major examined any one who presented himself, foreigner or native, without insisting on any of the conditions prescribed.[3] A short time after, in 1551, a letter from a Sevillan pilot, Alonso Zapata, to Dr. Hernan Perez, one of the Council of the Indies who had been to Seville as inspector or visitador of the Casa, charged still more serious irregularities.[4] The acting pilot major, Diego Sanchez Colchero, an old man of

---

[1] *Ord. of the Casa*, 1552, nos. 135, 136; A. de I., 146. 1. 9, lib. ii, fol. 55 (testimony of the pilot major, Alonso de Chaves, 1561).
It seems that while Spain and Portugal were united, Portuguese pilots who held a certificate from their Crown were admitted to examination in Seville for employment in the negro slave traffic between Guinea and the West Indies.
[2] *Ord. of the Casa*, 1552, no. 140.
[3] Encinas, i, p. 457.
[4] A. de I., 153. 1. 8.

over seventy, was reputed to receive "gifts" which blinded him to discrepancies in the candidate's statements. Pedro de Medina, another of the examiners, shared the bribes with him. Alonso de Chaves, cosmographer of the Casa, was aware of the evil, but maintained a neutral attitude, declaring that he could do nothing to remedy the situation. On the one hand, he refused to have part in any information to the king, on the other, he withheld his vote from every candidate who presented himself. Sancho Gutierrez, a very young man, tried to follow an honest course, but all the others were against him. In another letter to Dr. Perez, Zapata says that in Portugal any pilot or master who lost his ship through his own ignorance or negligence was deprived for a time of his certificate, and he urges that the same custom be followed in Spain.

Instructions from Dr. Perez himself to the Casa, in October, 1551, shed further light upon the matter. He relates that money was received not only for the examinations, but for accepting witnesses who testified to the fitness of the candidates; that the latter were informed beforehand of the questions which would be put to them; that in the preceding two years between thirty and forty foreigners had been admitted as pilots or masters; and that in the same time over twenty-five vessels had been lost with crews and cargoes. He also cites the instance of a certain Alejo Alvarer of the port of Ayamonte, who paid sixteen ducats for his examination. This state of affairs probably suffered little permanent improvement, for in 1561 the Crown, having been warned by the fiscal of the Council that many Portuguese and other foreigners were admitted, appealed to the Casa again for information and advice.[1] In spite of the ordinances, it was the custom toward the close of the sixteenth century for each successful candidate to give a present to the pilot major and the professor of cosmography of two or three ducats "para guantes y gallinas."[2]

Apparently it was the unsatisfactory state of nautical instruction at Seville which prompted Prince Philip to establish a special chair in cosmography. Pedro de Medina, in dedicating his

---

[1] Encinas, i, p. 459; A. de I., 146. 1. 9, lib. ii, fol. 55.
[2] Hakluyt (ed. of 1904), xi, p. 451.

*Arte de navegar* to Philip in 1545, had justified his treatise on the ground that as " pocos de los que navegan saben lo que á la navegación se requiere, la causa es porque ni hay maestres que lo enseñen ni libros en que lo lean."[1] And Martin Cortes in his *Breve compendio de la esfera y de la arte de navegar*, printed six years later, complains that " pocos ó ningunos de los pilotos saben apenas leer, y con dificultad quieren aprender y ser enseñados."[2] From now on, instead of private teaching by the pilot major or the cosmographers in their own houses, there was to be a regular course of lectures given in the Casa under its official direction.[3] Thereafter no one might be admitted to examination unless he had attended the lectures for a year, or at least had covered the greater part of the subjects taught. But this minimum was evidently found too extended for candidates many of whom were already of considerable practical experience. Besides, it kept them too long out of employment on the sea. At any rate the strict intentions of 1552 were soon relaxed. In 1555 the term of instruction was reduced to three months, and in 1567 to two months. And by an order from the Council in 1568, the two months were interpreted to include all holidays falling within that period.[4]

The course prescribed in 1552 may bear quotation from the original cédula:

... lo que el dicho bachiller Hierónymo de Chaves ha de leer en la dicha cathedra ... es los siguiente.

Primeramente ha de leer la sphera:[5] ó á lo menos los dos libros della primero y segundo.

Ha de leer assimismo, el regimiento que tracta del altura del Sol y como se

[1] Fernandez de Navarrete, *Disertación sobre la historia de la náutica*, p. 156.
[2] *Ibid.*, p. 164.
[3] In 1622 the lectures were transferred to the quarters in the Merchants' Exchange occupied by the Mariners' Gild.
[4] Veitia Linaje, lib. ii, cap. 11, par. 15. In the sixteenth century there were two sessions, morning and afternoon, of two hours each.
[5] Perhaps the *De Sphaera Mundi* of Joannes de Sacro Bosco, a thirteenth century professor of mathematics at Paris. It was a treatise on spherical astronomy, based upon Ptolemy and the Arab commentators, first printed in Ferrara in 1472, and running through 24 editions before 1500. It continued to be a favorite text book in Spain for the teaching of astronomy and cosmography till the middle of the seventeenth century.

sabra, y la altura del Polo, y como se sabe: y todo lo demas que paresciere por el dicho regimiento.[1]

Ha de leer assimismo el uso de la carta, y como se tiene de echar punto en ella: y saber siempre el verdadero lugar en que esta.

Ha de leer tambien el uso de los instrumentos y la fábrica dellos, porque se conozca en viendo un instrumento si tiene error.

    Los instrumentos son los siguientes.
        Aguja de marear
        Astrolabio
        Quadrante
        Ballestilla.[2]

De cada uno destos ha de saber la theórica y prática: esto es la fábrica y uso dellos.

Ha de leer assimismo como se han de marcar las agujas, para que sepan en qualquiera lugar que estuvieren, quanto es lo que el aguja les nordéstea o noruéstea en el tal lugar: porque esta es una de las cosas mas importantes que han menester saber, por las equaciones y re(s)guardos que han de dar quando navegan.

Ha de leer assimismo, el uso de un relox general diurno y nocturno, porque les sera muy importante en todo el discurso de la navegacion.

Ha de leer assimismo, para que sepan de memoria ó por escripto en qualquiera dia de todo el año, quantos son de luna: para saber quando y á qué hora les sera la marea, para entrar en los rios y barras, y otras cosas á este mismo tono que tocan á la prática y uso.

In fifty years the science of navigation was still scarcely advanced beyond the stage reached in the time of Columbus. The elements of spherical astronomy, the use of the astrolabe, quadrant and cross-staff, some knowledge of the variations of the compass and a fairly good table of the sun's declination, a sandglass and a sundial, and perhaps a very incorrect chart — such was the professional outfit of the skilled mariner in the sixteenth century. The equipment of the majority of pilots was doubtless much slighter. Nautical science seems practically to have sprung into being with the sudden efflorescence of commercial and geographical activity among the Portuguese in the fifteenth century. Prince Henry, called The Navigator, is given credit for having

[1] The *Regimiento* of Pedro de Medina?
[2] The astrolabe was employed for observing the meridian altitude of the sun in determining differences of latitude. The quadrant and ballestilla (cross-staff or Jacob's staff) were used for nocturnal observations, to secure the altitude of the polestar. All these instruments had been known since the thirteenth century, but the cross-staff was not in common use among mariners till the middle of the sixteenth century. Columbus used only the astrolabe and the quadrant.

brought together and systematized the knowledge then obtainable. John II, whose reign began in 1481, followed up the good work, appointing a commission in 1484 or 1485 which calculated new solar tables, simplified the astrolabe for use by mariners, and laid down rules for determining latitude by these means from the meridian altitude of the sun. But there matters rested for nearly a century, till astronomers and sailors outside the Iberian peninsula took up the great problems associated with the progress of navigation. Spanish cosmographers, some connected with the India House, wrote many treatises — Pedro de Medina, Martin Cortes, Alonso de Chaves, Rodrigo Zamorano, etc. — but the first two at least still used the astronomical system of Ptolemy; and although Philip III in 1598 offered a reward of one thousand crowns for the discovery of a method of finding longitude at sea, that problem remained a mystery until the eighteenth century. Compasses were small, of the simplest form imaginable, and corrected so as to make the terrestrial pole coincide with the magnetic. And calculation of latitude by means of the astrolabe on the unsteady platform of a ship was so uncertain that an error of four or five degrees was not unusual.

The offices of pilot major and professor of cosmography were filled by competition. When a vacancy occurred, a proclamation was posted by order of the Council, in Seville, at the universities of Salamanca, Valladolid and Alcalá, and also in the Andalusian ports of Cadiz, San Lucar, Santa Maria, and Ayamonte, where it might come to the notice of practical navigators as well. But it was rare that mariners were found who combined with practical experience the theoretical and mathematical knowledge necessary for these posts. The competition was in the hands of the president and jueces of the Casa, and they transmitted a report to the Council, with whom in consultation with the king lay the final decision.[1] The same formalities were observed in choosing a cosmógrafo fabricador, except that the proclamations were posted only in Seville and at the court, for the peculiar skill required of him was not taught at the universities or acquired by familiarity with the sea.

[1] Veitia Linaje, lib. ii, cap. 11, par. 8.

From the beginning, one of the duties of the pilot major and his associates was to set down on maps and charts the results of geographical discovery and exploration in the New World; both those of official expeditions organized by the State, and those made by private navigators and explorers, who on their return to Seville were obliged to inform the Casa of their newly-acquired maritime knowledge. The pilot major had also to enter in a book a list and description of the islands, shoals, harbors, etc., with their position and distances, based upon the information so obtained. And as doubtless many mariners in the seaports of Andalusia made a living by the drawing and sale of nautical charts, in order to avoid the errors arising from too great a multiplication of such maps, Americo Vespucci was instructed to create an official pattern or Padrón Real. This standard map was to include "all the lands and islands of the Indies till now discovered and belonging to our kingdoms and lordships," and no pilots were permitted to employ any other under penalty of fifty doubloons. A later cédula provided that at the beginning of each year, or oftener if necessary, a conference be held of the pilot major, cosmographers, and others skilled in cartography, to discuss new geographical data, and the expediency of inserting them in the Padrón Real.[1]

As regards the elements out of which this first model was constructed, they were without doubt borrowed from maps then current in Spain, and not the result of any special surveys. But there were also configurations furnished by the royal pilots and cosmographers and derived from their own stock of information, especially if these men were of foreign experience, like Vespucci, Cabot, Ribero, and others.[2] In any case, the Padrón Real did not greatly improve matters. The knowledge of those to whom it was entrusted was at best scant enough, and there is also evidence that they were negligent in their duties. Clandestine charts, moreover, probably often counterfeiting the Padrón, were still made and sold by unauthorized pilots, which introduced new

[1] *Viajes*, iii, p. 300; *Ord. of the Casa*, 1552, no. 126.
The requirement to keep a log or journal to be delivered to the officials of the Casa seems later to have been disregarded.
[2] Harrisse, *John Cabot*, p. 73.

sources of error and even differences in graduation. In October, 1526, therefore, Fernando Columbus, son of the Discoverer, in the absence of Cabot in America was entrusted with the construction of a new map for the Casa de Contratación. It was to appear in three forms, as a sailing chart, a universal geographical map or "mapamundi," and a globe or "sphera." With him were associated first the Portuguese, Diego Ribero, and later Alonso de Chaves; and he was instructed to secure the aid and advice of all those versed in nautical science he could find. Over a hundred, it seems, were called upon to contribute to the undertaking.[1] Alonso de Chaves, however, was the cartographer who really did Fernando's work. In spite of this display of solicitude by the government, for nine years the royal order remained unfulfilled. At last, in May, 1535, the Empress Isabella, then governing Spain in the absence of her husband, recalled the project to Fernando's attention, and bade him see that the map was executed at once.[2] The task was probably completed in the following year, and although no copy of the new Padrón has come down to us, it is identified with the map of Alonso de Chaves, of 1536, described by the historian Oviedo.[3]

In July, 1512, Andrés de San Martin and Juan Vespucci, the latter a nephew of the first pilot major, and both recently appointed pilots to the king, were conceded the privilege of taking copies of the Padrón Real and selling them to mariners at a tariff fixed by the Casa.[4] And after their time the concession was doubtless extended to others in the same position. But there is no evidence that the Casa had a monopoly of chart or instrument making, although the pilot major was accused of arbitrarily refusing to approve maps and instruments made outside, so as to compel all to come and buy there.[5] Certainly when the general ordinances of 1552 were published, no restrictions were contemplated. Indeed by this time the pilot major, as he was forbidden to give nautical instruction, was also debarred from selling charts or instruments within the city of Seville, whether his own or those

[1] Puente y Olea, *op. cit.*, pp. 308 ff.; Harrisse, *op. cit.*, p. 74, note 2.
[2] *Colecc. de doc.*, 1st ser., xxxii, p. 512.   [3] Lib. xxi, cap. 10.
[4] Puente y Olea, *op. cit.*, p. 283.
[5] Harrisse, *Discovery of North America*, pp. 264 f.

made by others, under penalty of paying double the price received. But he might construct them for himself or to sell outside the city, or make globes and other objects not used in navigation.[1] No map made by private persons might be sold or used without first being brought to the Casa to be corrected in accord with the Padrón, and no instrument without being authenticated and receiving the stamp of official approval; the dies being kept in a special coffer with two keys, one held by the pilot major and the other by one of the cosmographers. The latter met once, and later twice, a week to attend to this business, and after 1565 two other pilots were chosen each year by the president and jueces to assist them. When maps or instruments constructed by the cosmographers themselves were presented for examination, the makers of course had no voice in the decision. If an astrolabe or quadrant was rejected, it was broken up, and hopelessly inaccurate maps or compass cards were cut in pieces and retained by the Casa to prevent their being used.[2] Veitia Linaje, however, says that in his day nautical instruments were generally manufactured by the cosmógrapho fabricador, and the chart was that which had been standardized and printed by the pilot major, Sebastian de Ruesta.[3] The earlier rule, therefore, respecting the sale of maps by the pilot major was evidently in abeyance, although it was reprinted in the *Recopilación* of 1681.

With a school of navigation established so early at Seville, one would expect from the Spaniards a considerable contribution in the course of the sixteenth century to the progress of nautical science. Something was accomplished in a practical way. The sheathing of vessels with lead may have been original with the Spaniards, who first tried it out in 1514. Diego Ribero is said to have been the inventor of metal pumps, lighter in weight and more efficient than the older ones of wood. In 1526 he was promised a pension of 60,000 maravedis a year, in addition to his salary as cosmographer, as soon as the merits of his invention were substantiated, with the exclusive privilege for twelve years

---

[1] *Ord. of the Casa*, 1552, no. 131.
[2] *Ibid.*, no. 141; Veitia Linaje, lib. ii, cap. 11, par. 19.
[3] Veitia Linaje, lib. ii, cap. 11, par. 20.

of furnishing such pumps to Spanish ships. The invention was not finally accepted by the Casa till October, 1533, just after Ribero's death.[1] The pumps weighed between 300 and 400 pounds for a vessel of 100 to 120 tons, but owing principally, perhaps, to the cost, they did not supersede those of wood for a long time. Navarrete would also have us believe that a primitive steamboat was invented by a certain Blasco de Garay in 1543, and given a successful trial at Barcelona.[2] However, the tale of what was actually accomplished scarcely rises to our anticipations. Spaniards on the other hand, as already intimated, were very active in publishing treatises and compendiums on practical navigation which, while useful and translated into foreign tongues, did not advance the science very far beyond the stage arrived at by the Portuguese at the close of the fifteenth century.

Of the earliest navigators connected with the Casa, Juan de la Cosa, surnamed El Vizcaino, was perhaps the most distinguished. Sailing in 1492 as master of Columbus' flagship, of which he was also the proprietor, and appointed by the Discoverer " maestro de hacer cartas " for the second voyage, in 1500 he was the author of the first map showing the coasts of America, a chart doubtless made on his return from the voyage of 1499–1500 as pilot of the expedition of Ojeda. And as his name appears on the books of the treasurer of the Casa in the very year of its foundation, before any other mariner of importance, he may perhaps be considered its first cartographer. Peter Martyr, one of the most trustworthy of contemporary witnesses, says that the navigators of the day valued his maps above all others. He accompanied Ojeda on his second expedition to Tierra Firme in 1509–10, and was killed by Indians in a skirmish on the seashore near Cartagena.[3]

Another of the earliest pilots celebrated for his skill as a hydrographer was Andrés de Morales. He sailed with Columbus on one of his voyages, probably the third, was pilot for Rodrigo de Bastidas in 1500–02, accompanied La Cosa in 1504–06, and remained for a number of years a resident of San Domingo. He

---

[1] Fernandez de Navarrete, *Disertación sobre la náutica*, pp. 360–365.
[2] *Viajes*, i, p. cxxvii.
[3] Harrisse, *Discovery of North America*, p. 711; Fernandez de Navarrete, *Biblioteca maritima*, ii, p. 208.

was employed by Governor Ovando to explore and map the coasts of the Antilles, and his charts at the time Diaz de Solis was pilot major seem to have been accepted at Seville as the best and most accurate then obtainable. Endowed with a profound gift of observation, he was the first to deduce the theory of ocean currents in the Atlantic, which contributed so much to render easy the navigation to and from the West Indies. According to Harrisse, in November, 1515, he was appointed royal pilot to the Casa.[1]

The first modern treatise on navigation, and the first geographical description of the New World, were written by a Spaniard, Martin Fernandez de Enciso. Enciso, a native of Seville, was already settled in San Domingo and had acquired wealth as a lawyer in 1509. In that year he joined fortunes with Alonso de Ojeda, bringing succor to the latter's colony in Tierra Firme, of which he was appointed alcalde mayor; and after Ojeda's death, he was distinguished as one of the founders of La Antigua del Darién. Deprived of his authority by Balboa, he returned to Spain in 1512 to lay complaint before the king, going back with Pedrarias Dávila two years later as alguacil mayor of the colony. The date of his second return to Europe is uncertain, but in 1519 he published in Seville his *Suma de geografía* dedicated to the new sovereign, Charles V.[2] Enciso's object in writing the work was to give pilots and other mariners sufficient geographical and astronomical information to enable them to continue the task of discovery; and in this endeavor he was the first to gather together the rules, precepts and observations which became the basis of all other works of that nature for a century or more.

The next important nautical treatise was that of Pedro de Medina, one of the examiners connected with the India House. His *Arte de navegar*, published at Valladolid in 1545, with the sanction of the pilot major and cosmographers of the Casa, was a methodical compilation of the principal cosmographical knowledge of the time as applied to practical navigation. It was trans-

---

[1] Puente y Olea, *op. cit.*, pp. 280–282; Fernandez de Navarrete, *Biblioteca maritima*, i, p. 88.

[2] Nicolás Antonio, *Bibliotheca Hispana Nova*, ii, p. 101. Later editions appeared in Seville in 1530 and 1546.

lated into Italian, French, Flemish, and English, and, though severely criticized by foreign writers later in the century, ran through many editions and continued to be used as a textbook in France for nearly a hundred years. To facilitate and simplify the instruction of pilots at Seville, in 1552 he published a compendium of the larger work under the title *Regimiento de navegación*, and in 1561 with the same object wrote a *Suma de cosmografía*, which still remains in MS.[1]

English mariners preferred to Medina the *Breve compendio de la esfera y de la arte de navegar* of Martin Cortes, which, though written contemporaneously, was not printed till 1551, at Seville. It was translated into English by Richard Eden, at the suggestion of Stephen Borough who had just returned from Spain, and was published in London at the expense of the Merchant Adventurers Trading to Russia, in 1561. Cortes' work was in many ways superior to that of Medina, not only in clarity and precision of exposition and arrangement, but also in depth and originality of thought. His most notable contribution was that of supposing the phenomenon of variation in the mariners' compass to be produced by a magnetic pole distinct from the terrestrial, an idea which became the basis for the investigations of a long line of distinguished mathematicians and observers from that day to this. But Cortes, like Medina, still followed the astronomical system of Ptolemy, although Copernicus had been dead eight years.

One of the most distinguished cosmographers of the India House, though less widely known abroad because his writings were never printed, was Alonso de Santa Cruz. We first hear of him as royal treasurer of the expedition of Sebastian Cabot which sailed ostensibly for the Moluccas in 1526. In 1536 he gained his connection with the Casa de Contratación, and three years later was lecturing on cosmography and astronomy before the Emperor at the court. In 1545 he went to Lisbon, to study the charted water routes to the East Indies, and to learn from Portuguese pilots the variations of the magnetic needle in the eastern seas. Conscious of his abilities and attainments, and of the scientific

[1] Fernandez de Navarrete, *Disertación*, pp. 156-162.

services he might render, he urged Philip II in 1557 to make him a Councillor of the Indies, though, it may be added, without success. Later however, probably in 1563, he was appointed cosmographer major to the king. He dedicated the greater part of his life to the study of magnetic variations, and to the contriving of a mode of finding longitude. He was the first in Europe to conceive and attempt to carry out the idea of magnetic ocean charts, a task not satisfactorily achieved till a century and a half later; and he also in a measure anticipated the solution of the problem of constructing spherical maps. Indefatigable in his scientific labors until his death in 1572, he was remembered as the greatest adept in the theories of navigation that Spain ever had.

A notable Spanish work of the later sixteenth century is the *Itinerario de navegación* of Juan de Escalante de Mendoza, written about 1575. The principal object of Escalante was to explain the sailing routes between Spain and the ports and islands of North America, with a description of the latter, and of the winds, currents, storms and other ordinary phenomena of navigation. But in the course of his work, which is thrown into the form of a dialogue, he manages skillfully to introduce a great deal of information respecting the construction, manning, provisioning, etc., of ships, the conditions of naval war, and much about nautical theory and practice.[1] The book, therefore, becomes a sort of encyclopedia of American navigation, the sum of the maritime knowledge of that day, and of considerable importance for naval history. Escalante entered very early upon a seafaring life, under the patronage of an uncle who was a ship captain of Seville. At eighteen he already commanded a vessel of his own in the Honduras trade, and gained a reputation especially for his skill in combating pirates in the West Indian seas. His *Itinerario*, although representing the result of twenty-eight years of experience, receiving the encomiums of the best cosmographers and mariners, and approved and commended by the Council of the Indies, was forbidden by the Council to be printed, on the pretext that foreign foes might thus secure pre-

---

[1] Fernandez de Navarrete, *Disertación*, p. 240. The Itinerario has been printed by Fernandez Duro in *Disquisiciones náuticas*, vol. v.

cious knowledge of Spanish seas and sailing routes. A petition to be reimbursed for the 10,000 ducats he had spent in its composition was also denied, and not till forty-eight years later, long after the author was dead, was the manuscript finally returned to his son with license to print, although pirated and erroneous copies had been allowed to appear in the meantime. Escalante died as captain general of the Tierra Firme fleet in 1596.

A *Compendio del arte de navegar*, published in 1581 by Rodrigo Zamorano, professor of cosmography in the Casa and later its pilot major — an elementary work by one who, although trained as a mathematician, had no experience of the sea — because concisely and clearly written was adopted and followed for many years as a textbook in Spanish schools. But a truly important work was the *Regimiento de navegación y de la hidrografía*, published by Andrés Garcia de Céspedes, cosmographer major to the king, in 1603. Printed by royal order, it was a register of sorely needed reforms in Spanish hydrography and instrument making which Céspedes had undertaken in conjunction with the best pilots of Seville in 1596. His treatise marked a considerable advance over earlier Spanish productions of this character. Its author was well abreast of the scientific knowledge of his day, was distinguished as a mathematician and astronomer, and also contributed to the development of artillery and hydraulics in his own country. This *Regimiento* definitely superseded among intelligent men the books of Medina and Cortes, and fixed for the rest of the seventeenth century the science of navigation in Spain.[1]

At the same time among Spanish seamen there seems to have been little improvement in intelligence or skill. Obsolete authors were still expounded in the schools, and as late as 1634 the king ordered the cosmographer major to lecture at Court on the treatise of Sacro Bosco! Abuses in the examination of pilots at Seville continued. A short course of two months' instruction in the compendium of Zamorano was not calculated to turn out capable navigators, and the pretext of a scarcity of mariners was insufficient excuse for such precipitation. There can be little doubt but

---

[1] Fernandez de Navarrete, *Disertación*, pp. 271-275.

that many secured certificates from the pilot major with no examination at all, while others bought them in the open market, substituting their own names for those originally inserted. Nautical instruments too were carelessly manufactured by unskillful workmen, and charts remained primitive and inexact, because of the lack of intelligent application and of theoretical knowledge in those charged with the examination and correction of both. The general ignorance and inefficiency of Spanish pilots, therefore, was not greatly relieved. They displayed a repugnance to new ideas, and an affection for traditional and faulty methods, which accounts for many of the disasters in the American navigation in that era.

On each of the India fleets there was, in addition to pilots for individual ships, a pilot major for the entire squadron. The pilot major of the galleons, or more correctly, of the Armada de la Carrera de las Indias, was held to be of superior rank and dignity to his confrère of the flotas, and seems to have been always an appointee of the Crown, usually for life, the appropriate candidates being nominated by the Casa to the Council of the Indies.[1] He was consulted by the captain general regarding the choice of pilots for the almiranta and other galleons, and on all occasions when important decisions were taken respecting the course or disposition of the fleet. The pilots major of the flotas were till the middle of the seventeenth century selected by the captain general for each voyage, with the approval of the Council; but in Veitia Linaje's time their position in point of dignity and manner of appointment was assimilated to that of the pilot major of the galleons.[2]

As for the commanders of individual vessels in the fleets, they fell into two classes, pilots and masters. Upon the pilot alone devolved the navigation of the ship, from the moment it left port until it arrived at its destination, and through the "contremaestre" or mate he communicated his orders to the crew. In port his duties were ended.[3] But the head of the ship was the master, the

---

[1] Veitia Linaje, lib. ii, cap. 12, par. 1.  [2] *Ibid.*, par. 4.
[3] There were local pilots to guide vessels over the bar at San Lucar, and into the harbor of Cadiz, their examination and appointment resting with the municipal authorities of Seville and Cadiz respectively.

"patronus" of the Consulato del Mar and earlier medieval maritime law. He equipped and provisioned it, received the freight payments, engaged and paid the pilot and crew, in short was the business manager; but except to indicate the ship's general course and direction, he was not supposed to interfere with its practical navigation. He was frequently proprietor or part proprietor of the vessel, as in earlier times in the Mediterranean he had always been. In any case, he represented the partners or associates who owned it. These latter might themselves be merchants, or engaged solely in the business of building and running ships — "armadores," as they were called in Spain. After 1534 masters had also to pass an examination, not only in the elements of navigation, but in everything pertaining to the governance of a ship, its manning and accoutrement.[1] But by decrees of 1582 and 1586 a shipowner who was his own master was excused from the examination, and later any master, if he carried with him on the voyage two pilots, in case one was incapacitated by illness or other accident. An earlier law, of July, 1573, on the other hand, declared that the grade of pilot included that of master; consequently any one who possessed a pilot's certificate might exercise a master's functions, provided he had at least an eighth part interest in the vessel.[2]

The commander of a ship in the armada was called "captain," as his duties were almost exclusively of a martial sort, to have charge of the soldiers and gunners, and direct operations in case of attack. And apparently any shipowner might obtain from the general of the fleet the title of captain, if he accompanied his vessel and served without pay. The distinction carried with it various privileges, among others immunity from imprisonment for debt.

According to the ordinances of 1552, masters had to furnish security to the amount of 10,000 ducats silver, that they would faithfully observe the rules and instructions given them by the judges of the Casa, and would render a true and just account of all merchandise, coin, bullion, etc., received in the ship, in

[1] *Ord. of the Casa*, 1552, no. 145.
[2] Veitia Linaje, lib. ii, cap. 7, par. 30; cap. 8, par. 8.

case of default they or their sureties being responsible for the loss involved.¹ They were also bonded for various other amounts, added from time to time, and equalling altogether 8100 ducats: that their ships would be ready for lading on the date prescribed (1564, 2000 ducats); that they would carry no unlicensed passengers (1604, 1000 ducats); that they would settle their accounts with shippers or consignees within four months of the completion of the contract (1000 ducats), and present a certificate of quittance at the Casa within two months more (1604, 100 ducats); and that they would not call at any forbidden port, or on the return voyage put into the Bay of Cadiz (4000 ducats). These combined were called the securities "de penas pecuniarias," and to them was added a general clause holding the master responsible for any amount in a suit brought by the Casa for failure to meet the requirements set at the official inspection of the ship.² Similar sureties were apparently demanded by the oficiales reales in colonial ports of masters sailing to Spain.

With the gradual rise of prices in Spain in the sixteenth century, there seems to have been little corresponding increase in the wages paid to Spanish seamen. The common sailor or soldier in 1550 as in 1500 was paid on an average about thirty maravedis a day, or something over two ducats a month, in addition to food and drink, reckoned at twelve maravedis, or a ducat a month extra. Judging from the code of ordinances issued for the fleets in 1633, in the seventeenth century seamen's wages had risen considerably. Each mariner in the armadas was to receive four escudos four reals a month, or about fifty-one maravedis a day. The remuneration of captains and pilots in the armadas shows a more rapid and striking increase. At the opening of the sixteenth century pilots received from 1000 to 2000 maravedis a month, depending on the size of the ship. Fifty years later they were getting from 1500 to 3750 maravedis (four to ten ducats), and in the seventeenth century about twenty escudos or 7000 maravedis. The pilots major who sailed on the flagship, being

[1] *Ord. of the Casa*, 1552, no. 160.
[2] Veitia Linaje, lib. ii, cap. 8, par. 10–12.

the oldest and most experienced of their profession, often commanded from 50 to 100 per cent more. Captains of large vessels (300 to 400 tons) paid in the time of Columbus at the rate of 30,000 maravedis (80 ducats) a year, received from 50,000 to 100,000 maravedis (133 to 266 ducats) in 1550, and from 126,000 to 168,000 maravedis (360 to 480 escudos) in 1633. Commanders of smaller ships (100 tons and under) were paid correspondingly less; in 1500, from 15,000 to 20,000 maravedis a year, in 1633, about 65,000 maravedis. The aristocratic generals of the India fleets, from Blasco Nuñez Vela in 1537 to the close of the reign of Charles V, received six ducats a day, or at the rate of something over 2200 ducats a year. In the time of Philip II they frequently were given an " ayuda de costa " of 500 ducats on the completion of their voyage. In the seventeenth century they were paid 4000 ducats, and the almirantes 2000 ducats.[1]

|  |  | 1500 | 1550 | xvii Cent. |
|---|---|---|---|---|
| Seamen.... | per month | 2½ duc. | 2½ duc. | 4 esc., 4 reals |
| Pilots...... | "    " | 2⅔–5⅓ " | 4–10 " | 20 escudos |
| Captains... | per year | 80 " | 133–266 " | 360–480 " |
| Generals... | "    " | 133 " | 2,200 " | 4,000 ducats |

Till late in the sixteenth century at least, crews were hired on shares, as had been the common practice in Europe throughout the Middle Ages. Each person connected with the vessel, from the owner to the ship's boy, was assigned a certain proportion of the proceeds of the freights and other profits of the voyage. Each therefore had a direct interest in the success of the undertaking. In Veitia Linaje's time this was no longer the custom, the amount of wages, as in modern practice, being specifically agreed upon beforehand. It appears that under the earlier system the proprietor and the crew each chose a representative, these two together computed the gross receipts, and after deducting certain general liabilities (including 2½ per cent called " quintaladas," distributed in special rewards to mariners who had performed unusual services), divided the net proceeds into three parts, two going to the owner and one to the crew. This latter portion was divided in turn into so many shares, each able-bodied seaman

[1] See Appendix X.

receiving one share, each grumete or apprentice two-thirds of a share, and each ship's boy one-fourth. Apparently an analogous system was still in vogue on Portuguese vessels in the sixteenth century. There the unit of reckoning was again the common sailor. Two grumetes were equal to one sailor, and three boys to one grumete. The boatswain and quartermaster were each reckoned as one and one-half sailors, and the calker, carpenter, steward, barber-surgeon, chaplain, etc., as two sailors.[1]

This practice was a survival of the primitive maritime partnerships or fellowships which, owing to the expense and risks of shipbuilding and seafaring adventure, had been the rule among all early maritime peoples. In the beginning no sharp distinction had existed between shipowner, sailor, and merchant; as we see in the eleventh century Laws of Amalfi, where all on the vessel appear as partners in the undertaking, trade either on their own or to the common account, and have an active voice in the governance of the ship. With the development of a money economy, the appearance of a capitalistic class, and the increased division of labor, the sailors became hired men, the merchant and the "armador" followed two distinct callings and there appeared the "patronus," corresponding to the Spanish master of the sixteenth century. Community of interests and of authority in large measure disappeared. Yet the wages of the sailor continued to bear a direct relation to the prosperity or failure of the voyage, it is possible that under certain circumstances the crew had to be taken into consultation, and they seem to have retained the right to carry a limited quantity of goods for their own private trade and profit. Indeed as late as 1644, seamen and soldiers on the galleons were conceded the privilege of embarking free of duties a certain number of jars of wine for sale in the colonies; the first pilot, 250 jars; the ensign, 200; the second pilot and the chief gunner, 150 each; the sergeant and the storekeeper, 100 each; the dispenser, the water bailiff, and each corporal, 50; each sailor 34, each gunner 25, and each grumete 10.[2]

[1] Whiteway, *Rise of the Portuguese Power in India*, p. 44.
[2] Veitia Linaje, lib. ii, cap. 12, par. 20; Schmoller, "Die Handelsgesellschaften des Mittelalters und der Renaissancezeit," in *Jahrbuch für Gesetzgebung . . . des Deutschen Reiches*, 2d ser., xvii, 1, pp. 4-14.

The prudent and Catholic Philip II in 1582 published an order that no mariner or soldier should receive wages or rations until he showed a certificate that he had been shriven by one of the numerous friars appointed to hang about San Lucar at the time the fleets were preparing to sail. But this was a precaution not generally enforced.[1]

One of the ordinances of 1552 forbade masters to engage, or in any manner entice away, sailors or officers who had already signed for another vessel. Mariners who "jumped" their contracts were punished with twenty days imprisonment and a fine double the sum of their wages on the prospective voyage; offending masters were mulcted 10,000 maravedis, half of which went to the plaintiff. If a sailor received any money from a master as a retainer, it was to be interpreted as a contract.[2]

In theory seamen at the end of the voyage could not claim a settlement of their pay unless they remained with the ship until she was laid up in her mooring berth. But as a matter of fact it was so difficult to keep them on board after the long absence from home, that they were generally released at once, with a slight reduction from their wages to defray the cost of mooring and unrigging the vessel.

Among the medieval gilds in Seville, there was one of the owners and masters of Andalusian ships, called the gild or "colegio" of the Comitres, among whose functions was that of policing the river, and maintaining order among the shipping. There was also a gild or college of Biscayan pilots established at Cadiz, the origin of which was declared to be so ancient " que de tanto tiempo acá que memoria de hombres non es en contrario," as we learn from a royal cédula of March, 1500, confirming its ordinances and privileges. It had its consul, elected each year, and a private jurisdiction over its own members and affairs. Its pilots conducted to the north of Europe the carracks and galleys which called at Cadiz on their way from the Levant.[3] Doubtless in imitation of these organizations, there arose in the middle of the sixteenth century, probably after the accession of Philip II,

---
[1] Veitia Linaje, lib. ii, cap. 2, par. 49.   [2] *Ord. of the Casa*, 1552, no. 147.
[3] Fernandez de Navarrete, *Disertación*, p. 357.

a "cofradía," brotherhood or gild, of shipowners, masters and pilots engaged in the India navigation. A few years later a hospital was founded for old or infirm mariners, and the constitution and ordinances for the administration of the two, hospital and cofradía, received the king's sanction in March, 1569. The entire foundation was named the Universidad de los Mareantes de Sevilla, within which were comprehended not only shipowners, masters and pilots, but also quartermasters or mates, boatswains, sailors and grumetes. But the governing body was the original cofradía, composed only of those first mentioned, who had passed the Casa's examinations.[1] The eldest son, unless he entered the Church, inherited the right of admission to the fraternity on the death of his father.

To provide funds for this corporation, a sum equal to the fourth of the wages of an able-bodied seaman was withdrawn from the total wages and profits of every ship sailing between Spain and America, even if the master or owner was not a member of the cofradía. If we may judge from a cédula of November, 1605, by that time this fourth part had been increased to a half; and finally in 1608, as noted in an earlier chapter, there was substituted a new method of payment, in the form of a tonnage tax of one and one-half reals on every ton of vessels departing for the colonies from Seville, Cadiz or the Canary Islands.[2] In addition, each pilot on returning from America was expected to contribute two ducats, and on every ship was a box or chest to receive money for the Mariners' Hospital. These resources were employed not only to defray administrative expenses, and the cost of festivals and other corporate celebrations such as were common to all craft gilds in those days; with them succor was extended to mariners robbed by corsairs, ransoms were made up to rescue others from captivity in Barbary, poor members who had fallen into the debtors' prison were assisted, or dowers provided for their daughters.

The gild elected each year, usually after the return of the galleons and flota, three officials, a mayordomo and two diputados,

---

[1] A. de I., 138. 3. 18; Veitia Linaje, lib. ii, cap. 7, par. 2, 4, 5.
[2] *Ibid.*, par. 7, 13, 16.

as they were afterwards called, each with a salary of 12,000 maravedis. They had to be over thirty years of age, were not reëligible, and in order to avoid the possible absence of a majority of the board were chosen from among those members who had retired from active sea life. One of the jueces oficiales presided at the elections, and each year had to visit the hospital and review the financial accounts. As the ostensible object of the mariners in organizing the gild was to enable them to communicate to the king suggestions for the improvement of the India navigation, and needless to say of their position in it, they were allowed to appoint and maintain at the court or elsewhere proctors and solicitors to represent their interests, or send their own members for the purpose. Those belonging to the cofradía were the recipients of numerous exemptions and privileges in the course of the sixteenth and seventeenth centuries, some of which have already been alluded to. Among other things, they were excused from the quartering of soldiers and "huéspedes" in their houses, from military service on land, from municipal office unless they desired it, and from the payment of "pechos, pedidos y moneda forera." They were permitted to carry arms, and employment on the sea was declared in no wise to prejudice their claims to "hidalguía." Those who had been in the India navigation for twenty years continued to enjoy these privileges in their retirement.[1]

The Universidad de Mareantes had its headquarters across the river from Seville in the suburb of Triana, where lived most of the seafaring population. Its earliest residence, including the hospital and a chapel, was situated on the river bank almost opposite the historic Torre del Oro and the quays of the Casa de Contratación.[2] It was under the peculiar patronage of an ancient image of the Virgin called "Nuestra Señora del Buen Aire," and of the saints Andrew and Peter. It is said that on the façade of the chapel facing the river was a high balcony with an altar, which could be discerned from all sections of the port, and where each morning, as the altar was illumined by the first golden rays of the sun, the sacrifice of the Mass was celebrated by an officiating priest.

[1] Veitia Linaje, lib. ii, cap. 7, par. 29, 33.   [2] Puente y Olea, *op. cit.*, p. 367.

The project of a college or asylum at Seville for the orphan sons of Spanish seamen was frequently suggested, first, it seems, by the Duke of Medina Sidonia in the latter part of the sixteenth century. In 1607 it was urged by the Mariners' Gild, and again in 1627. Following a favorable report from the Casa, a decree for the foundation of the institution was issued in 1628. And to provide funds, the king shortly after granted a perpetual "licencia de privilegio" to send a ship with every other fleet to the West Indies. But in 1638, when some 8000 ducats had been collected, and they were about to build next to the hospital, the Crown took the money to help defray the expense of dispatching the galleons; and in 1647 the privilegio was permanently transferred to the Consulado. The idea apparently remained in abeyance till 1665, and not till sixteen years later was the College of Pilots of San Telmo created by royal decree, but at the charge of the Mariners' Gild. In 1734 a splendid edifice was erected on the Seville side of the river, in which over a hundred orphan boys received a home and nautical instruction. This building in the nineteenth century became the residence of the Duke and Duchess of Montpensier, was bequeathed by the Duchess to the archbishopric of Seville, and is to-day a seminary for priests. But over the high altar of the chapel of this palace of San Telmo still presides Nuestra Señora del Buen Aire, patroness of the ancient mariners of Seville.

# APPENDICES

## APPENDIX I

### The Casa Lonja

The Casa Lonja, or Exchange, of Seville, in which is located to-day the Archivo de Indias, was originally the headquarters of the Consulado. The idea of erecting such a building first appeared in the time of Philip II. In the autumn of 1572 an agreement was entered into by the king and the prior and consuls of Seville for the construction of an edifice where merchants could congregate to negotiate their affairs. Till then they had been accustomed to use the cathedral for this purpose, to the scandal of the community. The site chosen lay just south of the cathedral, on ground occupied by the smithy of the Alcázar, part of the Mint, and several minor streets and private properties. The architect eventually selected was Juan de Herrera, responsible also for the design of the Escorial. Philip II offered to advance 5,000 ducats to begin the work.

As the Consulado was empowered to levy an excise to defray the cost of the structure, in January, 1573, $\frac{1}{3}$ per cent was imposed on merchandise and other articles entering or leaving the city by land or water, and on all money exchanges at the fairs. Royal and ecclesiastical property, plate and bullion from the Indies, and the produce of farms and estates of Sevillan citizens, were exempt. Later the tax oscillated between $\frac{1}{3}$ per cent and $\frac{1}{2}$ per cent, and it remained a permanent contribution long after the building was finished.

It seems, however, that for some reason or other, for a decade at least the "derecho de Lonja" was not collected, nor construction begun. A cédula of the summer of 1582 again ordered the work to be undertaken. Perhaps part of the difficulty lay in the importunities of the Crown for money. In 1590 the prior and consuls lent Philip 50,000 ducats out of the receipts from this and other tolls, and in 1592 another 18,000. In 1601 the building was still far from complete. Witnesses testified that the second story was lacking, and the structure open to the sky. If merchants did come there to trade, they were driven out by the rains in winter, and in summer by the sun, and resorted again to the neighboring cathedral. Even after the Lonja was finished, in 1606, it was difficult to compel merchants and notaries to leave their accustomed places for the new Exchange.

(A. de I.: 140. 3. 9, año 1614; 151. 2. 9, años 1591–1611.)

## APPENDIX II

"Libro de Situados," or Salaries and Pensions Paid out of the Funds of the Casa de Contratación

| Office | Remarks | Year | Salary |
|---|---|---|---|
| President of the Council of the Indies | Count of Osorno | 1535 | 300,000 mrs. |
| Admiral of Castile | Fernando Enriquez | " | 270,000 |
|  | Simon de Alcazaba | " | 100,000 |
| Fiscal (of the Council?) | ........ | " | 100,000 |
|  | Juan de Tavera | " | 75,000 |
| Secretary to H. M. for colonial affairs | Francisco de los Cobos | " | 50,000 |
|  | Rui Falero | " | 50,000 |
|  | Francisco Falero | " | 50,000 |
| Secretary to H. M. | Juan de Samano | " | 40,000 |
| Treasurer of the Casa | (1504, 100,000 mrs.) | " | 120,000 |
| Comptroller of the Casa | " | " | 120,000 |
| Factor of the Casa | " | " | 120,000 |
| Pilot major of the Casa | (1508, 75,000 mrs.) | " | 100,000 |
| Judge of the Casa at Cadiz | ........ | " | 60,000 |
| Pilot of the Casa | (1512, 20,000 mrs.) | " | 30,000 |
| Cosmographer | ........ | " | 30,000 |
| Visitador | ........ | " | 12,000 |
| Porter | (1511, 5,000 mrs.) | " | 10,000 |
| Counsellor | (1518, 3,000 mrs.) | " | 6,000 |
| Relator | ........ | 1543 | 30,000 |
| Assessor | ........ | 1543 | 10,000 |
| Receptor de averías | (1552, 75,000 mrs.) | 1568 | 90,000 |
| Auditors of the Tribunal de la Contaduría | (paid from the avería) | 17 cent. | 187,500 |
| Jueces letrados | (200,000 mrs. from the avería) | " | 300,000 |
| President of the Casa | (paid from the avería) | " | 750,000 |

Sources: A. de I., 2. 3. 2/3; 2. 3. 6/7, ramo 1; 40. 3. 1; 46. 1. 1/51, no. 2; 139. 1. 4, lib. 1, f. 144; lib. 3. f. 200; 139. 1. 5, lib. 7, f. 101. *Viajes*, vol. iii, pp. 297, 298.

# APPENDIX III

### Avería Collected on the Cargoes of the India Fleets, 1537-61

| Fleet of | Receipts | | | Expenditures |
|---|---|---|---|---|
| | On Exports | On Imports | Total | |
| Blasco Nuñez Vela 1537–38.......... | .... | .... | .... | 12,712,600 |
| Bartolomé Carreño 1552–53.......... | .... | .... | 21,385,408 | 21,296,610 |
| Juan Tello de Guzman 1553–54.......... | .... | 18,240,309 | .... | .... |
| Pedro Menéndez de Avilés 1555–56.... | 18,883,562 | 12,830,741 | 31,714,303 | 37,613,525 |
| Pedro de las Roelas 1557–58.......... | 17,483,018 [1] | 15,597,136 | 33,080,154 | 30,639,576 |
| Pedro de las Roelas 1559–60.......... | 1,274,408 | 10,444,272 | 11,718,680 | 10,922,179 |
| Pedro Menéndez de Avilés 1560–61.... | .... | 12,050,987 | .... | .... |

[1] Of this figure, 9,214,666 maravedis represented a loan from bankers in advance for fitting out the fleet.

RATE OF THE AVERÍA PAID ON ARTICLES IMPORTED FROM THE INDIES, 1557-64

| Repartimiento de la Avería cobrada del oro y plata y otras cosas que vinieron en la flota de: | Pedro de las Roelas. 1557-58. A. de I., 36. 4. 4/10 | *Ibidem* (segunda viaje). 1559-60 A. de I., 36. 4. 4/10 | *Ibidem* (tercera viaje) 1563-64 A. de I., 30. 3. 1 |
|---|---|---|---|
| Por cada peso de buen oro, en oro ó en plata....... | 17 maravedis | 10 maravedis | oro 4¼ maravedis plata 3¾ |
| Por cada peso de tipuzque. | 10½ | 6 | 2⅓ |
| Por cada marco de plata que no venga reducido en pesos de oro.......... | 85 | 50 | 19 |
| Por cada marco de tejuelos á 75 mrs. que es 15 mrs. cada peso............. | 15 | 8 | 3 |
| Por cada marco de perlas comunes.............. | 210 | 150 | 70 |
| Por cada marco de cademilla | 562½ | 400 | 270 |
| Por cada marco de avemarias | 421½ | .... | .... |
| Por cada marco de aljofar.. | 843 | 560 | .... |
| Por cada marco de topos.. | 126 | 80 | .... |
| Por cada marco de bromas y grançones............. | 64 | 43 | .... |
| Por cada arroba de grana.. | 600 | 280 | 90 |
| Por cada cuero vacuno (y que los cueros de tenera paquen cada dos tanto como uno)........... | 13½ | 10 | 7 |
| Por cada caxa de azucar .. | 487½ | 272 | 150 |
| Por cada quintal de sebo que está avaliado á 5 pesos.. | 85 | .... | .... |
| Por cada quintal de sarsaparilla que está avaliado á 10 pesos.............. | 170 | .... | .... |
| Por cada saca de lana, á 3 pesos................. | 51 | .... | .... |
| Por cada quintal de palo de guayacan que está avaliado á 8 reales........ | 10½ | .... | .... |

## APPENDIX IV

RECEIPTS OF THE TREASURERS OF THE CASA DE CONTRATACIÓN, 1503-90

| Year | Maravedis | | Pearls | | | | | Brazil wood | | Guañines (base gold) | | |
|---|---|---|---|---|---|---|---|---|---|---|---|---|
| | From the Indies | From other sources | | | | | | | | | | |
| 1503 | 2,995,217½ | 1,002,800½ | marcs | onz. | och. | tom. | gr. | cwt. | lbs. | marcs | onz. | och. |
| 1504 | 18,756,736 | 432,624 | 19 | 7 | 1 | 2 | 9 | 1,866 | 78½ | 13 | 1 | 4 |
| 1505 | 22,784,787 | 463,385 | | | | | | | | | | |
| 1506 | 15,527,291 | 4,989 | | | | | | | | | | |
| 1507 | 21,204,675 | 1,342 | | | | | | | | | | |
| 1508 | 17,671,681½ | 898,415½ | 18 | 1 | 2 | 0 | 0 | | | | | |
| 1509 | 25,958,530½ | | ........ | | | | | 731 | 10 | | | |
| 1510-11 | 24,061,232½ | | | | | | | | | pesos | tom. | gr. |
| 1511 | 21,742,410 | | ........ | | | | | 584 | 93 | 1,277 | 5 | 10 |
| 1512 | 33,801,175½ | | 211,277 maravedis in value | | | | | 1,193 | 25 | | | |
| 1513 | 33,706,806 | | 3 sacks | | | | | 593 | 88 | 232 | 0 | 0 |
| | | | marcs | onz. | och. | tom. | gr. | | | | | |
| 1514 | 23,264,835 | | 13 | 1 | 4 | 3 | 6 | 220 | 0 | 5,337 | 4 | 0 |
| 1515 | 26,928,065 | | 12 | 6 | 1 | 0 | 0 | 23 | 75 | | | |
| 1516 | 13,148,222 | | 48 | 7 | 6 | 1 | 2 | 638 | 50 | | | |
| | | | and 5 " barruecos " | | | | | | | | | |
| 1517 | 24,524,250 | | 16 | 4 | 5 | 3 | 0 | | | | | |
| | | | and 4 " perlas gruesas " | | | | | | | | | |
| 1518 | 45,852,352 | | 309 | 6 | 1 | 2 | 6 | | | | | |
| | | | and 615 " perlas escogidas " | | | | | | | | | |
| 1519 | 24,178,692½ | | 34 | 0 | 0 | 0 | 0 | | | | | |
| 1520 | 13,151,781 | | 162 | 0 | 3 | 0 | 0 | | | | | |
| 1521 | 2,214,833½ | | ........ | | | | | 2,429 | 50 | | | |
| 1522 | 8,333,516 | | | | | | | | | | | |

# APPENDIX IV

| Year | Maravedis | Pearls, etc. | Guañines, gold dust, etc. |
|---|---|---|---|
| 1526 | 15,330,147 | | marcs onz. och. tom. gr. |
| 1527 | 25,723,190½ | marcs onz. och. tom. gr. | 1    3    5    4    6 |
| 1528 | 38,693,961½ | 185   4   0   1   7 | (gold dust) |
| 1529–30 | 48,521,305 | and 380 pearls unweighed | and 45 pesos, guañines |
| 1530 | 13,940,630½ | | |
| 1531 | 25,818,771 | | marcs onz. och. tom. gr. |
| 1532 | 16,106,109 | | 132   5    3    2    0 |
| 1533 | 31,658,681 | marcs onz. och. tom. gr. | (gold dust) |
| 1534 | 28,782,325½ | 1,329   4   5   2   0 | 99,832 pesos, 1 tom., 6 gr. |
| 1535 | 119,283,851 | and 1,969 pearls unweighed | (guañines) |
| 1536 | 39,689,245½ | | 8,081 marcs, 7 och. (base silver) |
| 1537 | 321,915,017 | | |
| 1538–39 | 371,223,461 | | |
| 1539 | 85,392,082 | 562 emeralds | |
| 1540 | 76,160,626 | | |
| 1541 | 19,673,537 | | |
| 1542 | 16,192,989 | | |
| 1543 | 215,680,975 | | |
| 1544 | 54,756,205 | | |
| 1545 | 122,830,523 | | |
| 1546 | 60,693,821 | | |
| 1547 | 7,330,388 | | |
| 1548 | 40,797,420 | | |
| 1549 | 55,846,613 | | |
| 1550 | 62,259,077 | | |

| Year | Maravedis | Year | Maravedis | Year | Maravedis |
|---|---|---|---|---|---|
| 1551 | 847,485,902 | 1565 | 163,348,000 | 1578 | 789,621,000 |
| 1552 | 116,784,094 | 1566 | 100,584,000 | 1579 | 494,739,000 |
| 1553 | 250,197,059 | 1567 | 433,836,700 | 1580 | 646,692,000 |
| 1554 | 522,426,218 | 1568 | 473,322,000 | 1581 | 600,460,000 |
| 1555 | 479,661,402 | 1569 | 398,294,700 | 1582 | 622,974,500 |
| 1556 | 278,379,998 | 1570 | 381,729,000 | 1583 | 957,143,000 |
| 1557 | 722,427,066 | 1571 | 374,067,500 | 1584 | 458,290,000 |
| 1557–59 | 1,390,611,253 | 1572 | 257,662,000 | 1585 | 820,313,000 |
| 1560 | 268,000,000 | 1573 | 268,886,000 | 1586 | 239,190,000 |
| 1561 | 291,524,000 | 1574 | 322,634,700 | 1587 | 1,774,276,000 |
| 1562 | 103,331,000 | 1575 | 292,885,500 | 1588 | 990,090,000 |
| 1563 | 201,391,500 | 1576 | 142,000,000 | 1589 | 731,332,000 |
| 1564 | 103,841,500 | 1577 | 395,501,000 | 1590 | 591,430,000 |

Figures for 1503–14 were obtained from A. de I., 39. 2. 1/8.
" " 1515–22 " " " " 39. 2. 2/9.
" " 1526–29 " " " " 2. 3. 1/2.
" " 1530–37 " " " " 2. 3. 2/3, and 39. 3. 3/1.
" " 1538–40 " " " " 2. 3. 4/5.
" " 1541–46 " " " " 2. 3. 6/7.
" " 1547–52 " " " " 2. 3. 7/8.
" " 1553–57 " " " " 2. 3. 9/10.
" " 1557–59 " " " " 2. 3. 16/17.
Figures for 1560–90 were obtained from a Muñoz MS. in the Rich Collection, vol. iv, New York Public Library.

# APPENDIX IV

Receipts for 1508 close Dec. 10; those for 1509 begin Dec. 11, 1508.

In the annual statements of the treasurer, the distinction between receipts from the Indies and from other sources is not continued after 1508. Among the former are included the fare of passengers and freight receipts from vessels belonging to the Crown; also remittances to cover the value of Spanish coin sent to Hispaniola for use in the new colony.

Receipts for 1510 close March 3¹, 1511; those for 1511 begin April 1.

Treasurer's accounts for the years 1523–1525 are missing.

Receipts for 1526 begin with July.

Receipts for 1529 close August 11, 1530; those for 1530 begin August 12.

The large receipts for 1535 were due in part to the gold and silver brought from Peru by Hernando Pizarro in Feb., 1534, but not charged to the treasurer till Jan.–Feb., 1535. This amounted to:

gold: 49,897,224 maravedis;
silver: 5,378,221½ maravedis.

The receipts also included 22,500,000 maravedis sequestered from the bullion arriving from America on the account of private individuals.

The large receipts for 1537 were due to the sequestration by the Crown of 800,000 ducats which arrived on four vessels from Tierra Firme (Peru) in 1535, but which were not charged to the treasurer till July, 1537. The actual proceeds were apparently 293,161,373 maravedis.

The receipts also include 4,500,000 maravedis advanced by bankers on royal treasure expected from America.

In addition to the figures given in this table, there were charged to the treasurer by his auditors for the years 1530–37, 53,334,574 maravedis, received from Francisco de Alcazaba, "tesorero de la casa de moneda de Su Magestad," from Juan Suarez de Carvajal of the Council of the Indies, from Juan de Enciso, Diego de Ayala and others, on various accounts, some of it apparently money sequestered by the king.

Receipts for 1538 run over into April, 1539. They include the treasure brought back on the armada of Blasco Nuñez Vela, as follows:

on the king's account: 279,926,184 maravedis;
sequestered: 86,984,777 maravedis.

The receipts also include 4,312,500 maravedis borrowed from bankers.

Receipts for 1539 include 2,063,000 maravedis advanced by bankers, and 8,140,000 maravedis from the royal treasury.

Receipts for 1543 include the treasure brought from the Indies in the fleet of Martin Alonso de los Rios.

The large receipts for 1545 were due in part to the seizure of 180,000 ducats in India goods and bullion from a fleet of 9 vessels which arrived from New Spain in Nov., 1544.

Receipts for 1546 include 1,875,000 maravedis advanced by bankers.
" " 1547 " 3,000,000 " " "
" " 1548 " 1,321,500 " " "
" " 1550 " 9,375,000 " " "
" " 1551 " the treasure brought back on the fleets of Pedro de la Gasca (arrived Sept., 1550) and Sancho de Biedma (arrived July, 1551):

Gasca: 567,372,527 maravedis;
Biedma: 149,024,324 maravedis.

Other noteworthy remittances in this year were:

From Mexico: 42,186,665 maravedis;
From Peru: 78,255,937 maravedis;
From Honduras: 8,706,557 maravedis.

Receipts for 1552 include 5,250,000 maravedis advanced by bankers.
" " 1553 " 1,987,500 " " "

No comments are offered for the years following 1560 because of lack of opportunity to examine the accounts in detail.

## APPENDIX V

### Remittances of Bullion from New Spain, 1522–1601

"Relacion de la Plata Reales oro Joias que se allevado a su magestad desta nueva españa a los Reinos de Castilla desde el año de mil y quinientos y veinty dos que fue rrecien descubierta y ganada esta tierra hasta el año presente de mil y quinientos y noventa y nueve ques quando este memorial se haze," etc. Brit. Mus., Add. Mss. 13,964, f. 196.

| Year | Pesos | Tom. | Gr. | Year | Pesos | Tom. | Gr. |
|---|---|---|---|---|---|---|---|
| 1522 | 52,709 | 4 | 9 | 1558 | 313,543 | 1 | 0 |
| 1523 | no se llevo nada | | | 1559 | no se llevo nada | | |
| 1524 | 99,264 | 5 | 8 | 1560 | 268,702 | 5 | 2 |
| 1525 | 30,886 | 0 | 0 | 1561 | 252,937 | 4 | 2 |
| oro en oja | 1,838 | 2 | 0 | 1562 | 284,857 | 5 | 0 |
| oro en joyas | 1,592 | 0 | 0 | 1563 | 315,218 | 1 | 2 |
| oro sin ley | 1,145 | 2 | 0 | 1564 | 333,209 | 7 | 1 |
| 1526 | 20,387 | 1 | 1 | 1565 | 424,409 | 0 | 1 |
| oro sin ley | 5,542 | 0 | 0 | 1566 | 480,597 | 4 | 3 |
| 1527 | 47,505 | 6 | 7 | 1567 | 517,394 | 4 | 1 |
| oro sin ley | 16,049 | 4 | 0 | 1568 | 931,463 | 2 | 0 |
| oro en joyas | 1,130 | 0 | 0 | 1569 | 338,737 | 4 | 11 |
| 1528 | 33,015 | 3 | 6 | 1570 | 811,484 | 2 | 0 |
| oro sin ley | 16,558 | 0 | 0 | 1571 | 704,383 | 4 | 10 |
| 1529 | no se llevo nada | | | 1572 | 684,052 | 0 | 10 |
| 1530 | 20,142 | 4 | 6 | 1573 | 690,076 | 5 | 5 |
| 1531 | 24,971 | 4 | 1 | 1574 | 685,629 | 3 | 4 |
| 1532 | 40,927 | 7 | 1 | 1575 | 641,276 | 4 | 8 |
| 1533 | 40,272 | 5 | 6 | 1576 | 934,391 | 4 | 11 |
| 1534 | 104,440 | 2 | 9 | 1577 | 1,111,202 | 5 | 9 |
| 1535 | 16,250 | 0 | 0 | 1578 | 937,002 | 3 | 10 |
| 1536 | 32,500 | 0 | 0 | 1579 | 835,304 | 7 | 0 |
| 1537 | 33,108 | 6 | 6 | 1580 | 734,285 | 2 | 11 |
| 1538 | no se llevo nada | | | 1581 | 521,883 | 4 | 8 |
| 1539 | 65,407 | 7 | 0 | 1582 | 582,293 | 4 | 7 |
| 1540 | 132,996 | 1 | 0 | 1583 | 775,483 | 7 | 1 |
| 1541 | 16,599 | 3 | 0 | 1584 | 835,720 | 6 | 4 |
| 1542 | 113,240 | 3 | 0 | 1585 | 880,474 | 7 | 7 |
| 1543 | 50,524 | 4 | 0 | 1586 | 1,114,588 | 2 | 7 |
| 1544 | 164,136 | 3 | 5 | 1587 | 1,852,078 | 2 | 8 |
| 1545 | 26,483 | 4 | 7 | 1588 | 1,042,000 | 0 | 0 |
| 1546 | no se llevo nada | | | 1589 | 791,797 | 5 | 0 |
| 1547 | 20,497 | 6 | 9 | 1590 | 1,038,675 | 4 | 9 |
| 1548 | 115,996 | 9 | 0 | 1591 | 1,043,377 | 2 | 5 |
| 1549 | no se llevo nada | | | 1592 | 784,000 | 0 | 0 |
| 1550 | 236,344 | 3 | 4 | 1593 | no se llevo nada | | |
| 1551 | 61,635 | 3 | 1 | 1594 | 1,136,114 | 5 | 9 |
| plata baxa | 1,253 marcos | | | 1595 | 945,712 | 1 | 8 |
| 1552 | no se llevo nada | | | 1596 | 899,386 | 0 | 4 |
| 1553 | 165,039 | 0 | 0 | 1597 | 1,311,053 | 7 | 3 |
| 1554 | 165,636 | 0 | 10 | 1598 | 1,100,000 | 0 | 0 |
| 1555 | 207,118 | 4 | 2 | 1599 | 1,474,406 | 0 | 0 |
| 1556 | 433,914 | 2 | 7 | — | | | |
| plata baxa | 1,113 marc., 4 onz. | | | 1600 | 1,500,000 | 0 | 0 |
| 1557 | 167,078 | 2 | 3 | 1601 | 1,527,000 | 0 | 0 |

The figures for the years 1541–50 have been taken from the Ternaux-Compans table printed by Soetbeer. The copyist of the British Museum manuscript evidently substituted in these years figures belonging to the following decades.

The figures for 1600 and 1601 were added in a later hand.

## APPENDIX VI

### Royal "quinto" of the Silver extracted from Potosí, 1556–1640

"Razon que halla Juan de Echavarria, official mayor de la real contaduria y caxa desta villa imperial de Potossi, de la plata que se a presentado á quintar en ella y derechos que se an cobrado para Su Magestad desde 4 de Febrero de 1556, que ay libros y quenta dello en la dicha contraduria, hasta fin del pasado de 1640." Brit. Mus., Add. Mss. 13,976, f. 405.

The royalties were
- "derecho de ensayador, fundidor y marcador" . 1 %
- "quinto" (one-fifth of the remainder) . . . . . 19 $\frac{4}{5}$%
- total . . . . . . . . . . . . . . . . . . . . 20 $\frac{4}{5}$%

By a royal cédula of July 8, 1578, the "derecho de ensayador" etc. was raised to 1½%, the quinto being levied as usual on the remainder, making a total of 21$\frac{1}{5}$%.

The figures for 1585 are partly under the old system, partly under the new, the cédula apparently being first sent to New Spain and later extended to Peru.

| Year | Amount of silver registered | | | Royalties | | |
|---|---|---|---|---|---|---|
| 1556 | 1,339,975 pesos | 1 tom. | 4 gr. | 278,714 pesos | 6 tom. | 8 gr. |
| 1557 | 1,392,893 | 1 | 1 | 289,721 | 7 | 2 |
| 1558 | 1,150,597 | 1 | 4 | 239,324 | 1 | 9 |
| 1559 | 1,120,865 | 5 | 7 | 233,140 | 0 | 7 |
| 1560 | 1,136,911 | 4 | 0 | 236,477 | 4 | 9 |
| 1561 | 1,205,963 | 3 | 7 | 250,840 | 3 | 7 |
| 1562 | 1,268,769 | 0 | 0 | 263,903 | 7 | 8 |
| 1563 | 1,337,689 | 2 | 8 | 278,239 | 3 | 0 |
| 1564 | 1,177,727 | 2 | 9 | 244,967 | 2 | 4 |
| 1565 | 1,545,727 | 6 | 6 | 321,511 | 3 | 0 |
| 1566 | 1,444,858 | 7 | 8 | 300,530 | 5 | 4 |
| 1567 | 1,240,005 | 7 | 9 | 257,921 | 2 | 4 |
| 1568 | 1,183,340 | 4 | 1 | 246,342 | 6 | 10 |
| 1569 | 1,129,414 | 6 | 5 | 234,918 | 2 | 3 |
| 1570 | 967,572 | 3 | 7 | 201,255 | 0 | 7 |
| 1571 | 791,380 | 3 | 2 | 164,607 | 1 | 10 |
| 1572 | 643,678 | 4 | 8 | 133,885 | 1 | 3 |
| 1573 | 698,393 | 6 | 5 | 145,265 | 7 | 2 |
| 1574 | 932,824 | 1 | 10 | 194,027 | 3 | 4 |
| 1575 | 1,229,245 | 5 | 8 | 255,683 | 1 | 0 |
| 1576 | 1,618,889 | 2 | 6 | 336,766 | 2 | 10 |
| 1577 | 1,128,837 | 4 | 6 | 242,798 | 1 | 9 |
| 1578 | 2,454,122 | 0 | 0 | 510,457 | 3 | 0 |

| Year | Amount of silver registered | | | Royalties | | |
|---|---|---|---|---|---|---|
| 1579 | 3,243,479 pesos | 3 tom. | 5 gr. | 674,643 pesos | 5 tom. | 10 gr. |
| 1580 | 3,535,706 | 2 | 0 | 735,426 | 7 | 3 |
| 1581 | 3,795,980 | 1 | 6 | 789,563 | 7 | 0 |
| 1582 | 4,051,596 | 6 | 0 | 842,732 | 1 | 0 |
| 1583 | 3,631,150 | 7 | 8 | 755,279 | 3 | 3 |
| 1584 | 3,613,699 | 3 | 9 | 751,649 | 3 | 11 |
| 1585 | 4,472,646 | 1 | 2 | 943,895 | 0 | 0 |
| 1586 | 4,355,960 | 2 | 11 | 900,920 | 7 | 4 |
| 1587 | 3,576,929 | 7 | 8 | 758,309 | 1 | 3 |
| 1588 | 4,204,997 | 2 | 10 | 891,459 | 3 | 6 |
| 1589 | 4,575,915 | 0 | 9 | 970,094 | 0 | 0 |
| 1590 | 4,149,342 | 4 | 7 | 879,660 | 5 | 0 |
| 1591 | 4,557,533 | 1 | 4 | 966,197 | 0 | 3 |
| 1592 | 4,603,991 | 6 | 0 | 976,046 | 2 | 0 |
| 1593 | 4,636,695 | 6 | 0 | 982,979 | 4 | 0 |
| 1594 | 4,093,675 | 7 | 2 | 867,859 | 2 | 4 |
| 1595 | 4,542,073 | 2 | 5 | 962,919 | 4 | 4 |
| 1596 | 4,282,366 | 4 | 10 | 907,861 | 5 | 10 |
| 1597 | 3,955,022 | 4 | 4 | 836,464 | 6 | 3 |
| 1598 | 3,823,642 | 4 | 0 | 810,612 | 1 | 9 |
| 1599 | 3,886,847 | 1 | 9 | 824,011 | 4 | 11 |
| 1600 | 3,788,981 | 4 | 5 | 803,264 | 0 | 9 |
| 1601 | 4,309,513 | 6 | 7 | 913,616 | 7 | 6 |
| 1602 | 4,431,035 | 4 | 11 | 939,379 | 4 | 5 |
| 1603 | 4,315,395 | 4 | 9 | 914,863 | 6 | 11 |
| 1604 | 3,868,327 | 2 | 10 | 820,085 | 3 | 2 |
| 1605 | 4,470,394 | 3 | 8 | 947,723 | 5 | 0 |
| 1606 | 4,185,526 | 6 | 4 | 887,331 | 5 | 6 |
| 1607 | 4,126,253 | 1 | 8 | 874,765 | 5 | 6 |
| 1608 | 3,501,562 | 0 | 7 | 742,331 | 1 | 4 |
| 1609 | 3,303,780 | 4 | 1 | 700,401 | 3 | 9 |
| 1610 | 3,324,329 | 2 | 8 | 704,757 | 6 | 7 |
| 1611 | 3,789,050 | 4 | 2 | 803,278 | 5 | 7 |
| 1612 | 3,878,448 | 1 | 4 | 822,231 | 0 | 1 |
| 1613 | 3,502,901 | 2 | 2 | 742,615 | 0 | 7 |
| 1614 | 3,703,415 | 6 | 9 | 785,124 | 1 | 4 |
| 1615 | 3,950,523 | 6 | 7 | 837,511 | 0 | 5 |
| 1616 | 3,668,140 | 0 | 1 | 777,645 | 6 | 4 |
| 1617 | 3,126,591 | 7 | 0 | 662,837 | 3 | 0 |
| 1618 | 3,095,475 | 1 | 0 | 656,240 | 5 | 10 |
| 1619 | 3,233,965 | 1 | 10 | 685,600 | 5 | 1 |
| 1620 | 3,119,786 | 0 | 10 | 661,394 | 6 | 3 |
| 1621 | 3,206,254 | 0 | 0 | 679,725 | 6 | 10 |
| 1622 | 3,188,629 | 0 | 0 | 675,989 | 2 | 10 |

## APPENDIX VI

| Year | Amount of silver registered | | | Royalties | | |
|---|---|---|---|---|---|---|
| 1623 | 3,160,745 pesos | 5 tom. | 8 gr. | 670,078 pesos | 0 tom. | 9 gr. |
| 1624 | 3,194,978 | 2 | 9 | 672,307 | 7 | 7 |
| 1625 | 2,989,100 | 3 | 5 | 633,689 | 2 | 4 |
| 1626 | 3,015,568 | 7 | 10 | 639,300 | 5 | 0 |
| 1627 | 3,145,209 | 6 | 8 | 666,784 | 3 | 10 |
| 1628 | 3,419,494 | 7 | 5 | 724,932 | 7 | 5 |
| 1629 | 2,839,464 | 5 | 0 | 601,542 | 4 | 0 |
| 1630 | 2,806,673 | 5 | 0 | 595,014 | 6 | 8 |
| 1631 | 3,112,210 | 0 | 0 | 639,788 | 5 | 2 |
| 1632 | 2,812,858 | 0 | 6 | 596,325 | 7 | 4 |
| 1633 | 2,944,397 | 4 | 0 | 620,800 | 3 | 9 |
| 1634 | | | | 608,344 | 2 | 2 |
| 1635 | 2,765,314 | 2 | 0 | 585,449 | 0 | 9 |
| 1636 | 4,155,708 | 6 | 7 | 881,010 | 2 | 2 |
| 1637 | 3,493,056 | 4 | 0 | 740,527 | 7 | 10 |
| 1638 | 3,425,448 | 7 | 8 | 726,195 | 1 | 6 |
| 1639 | 3,292,281 | 6 | 8 | 697,963 | 6 | 0 |
| 1640 | 2,854,020 | 7 | 7 | 605,052 | 3 | 6 |
| Totals [1] | 256,114,187 | 1 | 6 | 54,056,108 | 7 | 1 |
| Totals in pesos of 8 reals.. | 400,178,417 | 3 | 8 | 84,462,670 | 1 | 0 |

[1] The totals are slightly inaccurate, but are the figures given in the manuscript.

## APPENDIX VII

VALUE IN MARAVEDIS OF THE ROYAL TREASURE ON THE PRINCIPAL FLEETS RETURNING FROM THE INDIES BETWEEN 1538 AND 1556

| Fleet of | Blasco Nuñez Vela, 1538 | | Martin Alonso de los Rios, 1543 | | Pedro de la Gasca, 1550 | |
|---|---|---|---|---|---|---|
| | Gold | Silver | Gold | Silver | Gold | Silver |
| New Spain | .... | 58,852 | 25,282,272 | 93,570,946 | | |
| Peru | 90,709,562 | 125,345,027 | 41,962,771 | 50,260,330 | | |
| Tierra Firme | 4,782,541½ | 13,085,297 | | | | |
| Guatemala | 5,542,010 | | | | | |
| Honduras | | | | | | |
| New Granada | 29,865,023 | | | | | |
| West Indian Islands | 8,476,669 | | 4,950 | | | |
| Pearls | | 78,000 | | 3,454,108 | | |
| Miscellaneous | | 1,983,202 | | 375,000 | | |
| Private bullion sequestered for the king's use | | 87,284,888 | | | | |
| Totals | 366,909,185½ maravedis | | 214,910,377 maravedis | | 567,372,527 maravedis | |

| Fleet of | Sancho de Biedma, 1551 | | Francisco de Mendoza, 1552 | | Bartolomé Carreño, 1553 | |
|---|---|---|---|---|---|---|
| | Gold | Silver | Gold | Silver | Gold | Silver |
| New Spain | 7,390,409 | 28,932,955 | .... | .... | .... | 133,613,952 |
| Peru | 46,494,256 | 54,344,316 | 22,246,912 | 209,722,152 | 54,819,877 | 97,301,289 |
| Tierra Firme | 4,719,168 | | | | | |
| Honduras | 5,683,312 | 1,460,108 | 6,155,050 | 1,778,909 | 165,036 | |
| New Granada | | | | | | |
| West Indian Islands | | | | | | |
| Pearls | | | | | | |
| Miscellaneous | ..... | | ..... | | 249,000 | |
| Private bullion sequestered for the king's use | ..... | | ..... | | 224,853,710 | |
| Totals | 149,024,324 maravedis | | 239,903,023 maravedis | | 511,002,864 maravedis | |

## APPENDIX VII

VALUE IN MARAVEDIS OF THE ROYAL TREASURE ON THE PRINCIPAL FLEETS RETURNING FROM THE INDIES BETWEEN 1538 AND 1556

| Fleet of | Cosme Rodriguez Farfan, 1555 | | Diego Felipe, 1555 | |
|---|---|---|---|---|
| | Gold | Silver | Gold | Silver |
| New Spain | .... | 11,308,943 | .... | 44,069,091 |
| Peru | 7,250,964 | 67,532,892 | | |
| Tierra Firme | | | | |
| Honduras | | | | |
| New Granada | 117,591 | | | |
| West Indian Islands | | | | |
| Pearls | | | | |
| Miscellaneous | 92,884,737 | | 98,894,426 | |
| Private bullion sequestered for the king's use | 39,065,511 | | 86,068,172 | |
| Totals | 218,160,638 maravedis | | 229,031,689 maravedis | |

| Fleet of | Alvar Sanchez de Avilés, 1556 | | Pedro Menéndez de Avilés, 1556 | |
|---|---|---|---|---|
| | Gold | Silver | Gold | Silver |
| New Spain | .... | .... | .... | 132,428,423 |
| Peru | 83,018,815 | | | |
| Tierra Firme | 960,480 | 644,839 | | |
| Honduras | 3,104,428 | 3,913,896 | | |
| New Granada | 27,212,242 | | | |
| West Indian Islands | .... | 4,118,646 | | |
| Pearls | 6,594,619 | | | |
| Miscellaneous | 1,242,075 | | 4,343,228 | |
| Private bullion sequestered for the king's use | 600,146,021 | | | |
| Totals | 867,727,712 maravedis | | | |

Fleet of Blasco Nuñez Vela, 1538.
    Figures obtained from A. de I., 2. 3. 4/5.
    "Miscellaneous" includes a gold nugget weighing over 28 marcs, and valued at 611,501 maravedis.
Fleet of Martin Alonso de los Rios, 1543.
    Figures obtained from A. de I., 2. 3. 6/7.
Fleet of Pedro de la Gasca, 1550.
    Figures obtained from A. de I., 2. 3. 7/8.
    The source of the bullion was unspecified in the accounts. The fleet consisted of seven vessels from Nombre de Dios, and practically all the treasure must have come from Peru.

# APPENDIX VII

Fleet of Sancho de Biedma, 1551.
    Figures obtained from A. de I., 2. 3. 7/8.
    Most of the gold and silver from Peru had originally been shipped with Pedro de la Gasca in 1550. The vessel was cast away 25 leagues from Nombre de Dios, but the treasure was salved and reshipped with Biedma.
    One of Biedma's vessels was lost on the homeward voyage by fire, and none of the treasure saved.

Fleet of Francisco de Mendoza, 1552.
    Figures obtained from A. de I., 2. 3. 9/10.

Fleet of Bartolomé Carreño, 1553.
    Figures obtained from A. de I., 2. 3. 9/10.

Fleet of Cosme Rodriguez Farfan, 1555.
    Figures obtained from A. de I., 2. 3. 9/10, and 39. 3. 5/3.
    "Miscellaneous" comprised the gold, silver and pearls recovered from a ship of Farfan's fleet which was lost on the coast of Zahara. Some of the treasure belonged to private individuals, but being unidentified was taken by the Crown.

Fleet of Diego Felipe, 1555.
    Figures obtained from A. de I., 2. 3. 9/10.
    "Miscellaneous" represents part of the bullion saved from the wreck of a fleet of three vessels on the Florida coast in the previous year. There were recovered 64,914 marcs of silver and 35,061 pesos of gold, altogether about 153 million maravedis.

Fleet of Alvar Sanchez de Avilés, 1556.
    Figures obtained from A. de I., 2. 3. 9/10.

Fleet of Pedro Menéndez de Avilés, 1556.
    Figures obtained from same source as above.

## APPENDIX VIII

REGISTERED VESSELS SAILING TO AND FROM THE INDIES, 1504-55

| Year | Outgoing | Returning | Year | Outgoing | Returning |
|---|---|---|---|---|---|
| 1504 (from Aug. 14) | 3 | .. | 1530 | 79 | 33 |
|  |  |  | 1531 | 54 | 33 |
| 1506 | 22 | 12 | 1532 | 45 | 39 |
| 1507 | 32 | 19 | 1533 | 60 | 37 |
| 1508 | 46 | 21 | 1534 | 86 | 35 |
| 1509 | 21 | 26 | 1535 | 81 | 47 |
| 1510 | 17 | 10 | 1536 | 84 | 67 |
| 1511 | 21 | 13 | 1537 | 42 | 28 |
| 1512 | 33 | 21 | 1538 | 63 | 41 |
| 1513 | 31 | 30 | 1539 | 69 | 47 |
| 1514 | 30 | 46 | 1540 | 79 | 47 |
| 1515 | 33 | 30 | 1541 | 71 | 68 |
| 1516 | 42 | 10 | 1542 | 86 | 64 |
| 1517 | 63 | 31 | 1543 | 72 | 56 |
| 1518 | 51 | 47 | 1544 | 22 | 54 |
| 1519 | 51 | 41 | 1545 | 97 | 38 |
| 1520 | 71 | 37 | 1546 | 79 | 65 |
| 1521 | 33 | 31 | 1547 | 83 | 75 |
| 1522 | 18 | 25 | 1548 | 89 | 73 |
| 1523 | 41 | 13 | 1549 | 101 and (2) | 73 and (2) |
| 1524 | 60 | 10 | 1550 | 85 " (2) | 72 " (7) |
| 1525 | 73 | 37 | 1551 | 78 | 84 " (4) |
| 1526 | 59 | 37 | 1552 | 72 | 53 " (8) |
| 1527 | 68 | 41 | 1553 | 47 | 32 " (7) |
| 1528 | 55 | 17 | 1554 | 3 | 24 " (11) |
| 1529 | 62 | 42 | 1555 | 65 | 44 " (15) |

## REGISTERED VESSELS SAILING TO AND FROM THE INDIES

Outgoing vessels, 1548–55

|        | New Spain | Tierra Firme | Honduras  | Cape de la Vela | San Domingo | Puerto de Plata | Havana | Santiago de Cuba | Puerto Rico | Burburata | Rio de la Hacha | Rio de la Plata | Unspecified |
|--------|-----------|--------------|-----------|-----------------|-------------|-----------------|--------|------------------|-------------|-----------|-----------------|-----------------|-------------|
| 1548   | 21        | 50           | 4         | 1               | 10          | 2               | ..     | ..               | 1           | ..        | ..              | ..              | ..          |
| 1549   | 25        | 48           | 1 and (2) | 3               | 16          | ..              | 1      | 1                | 2           | ..        | ..              | ..              | 4           |
| 1550   | 21        | 33           | 6         | 1               | 16 and (1)  | 1               | 1      | ..               | 3 and (1)   | ..        | ..              | 3               | ..          |
| 1551   | 22        | 30           | 9         | 1               | 10          | 1               | ..     | 1                | 4           | ..        | ..              | ..              | ..          |
| 1552   | 19        | 33           | 2         | 1               | 13          | 2               | ..     | ..               | 1           | ..        | ..              | ..              | 1           |
| 1553   | 9         | 25           | 5         | 1               | 4           | ..              | ..     | 1                | 1           | 1         | ..              | ..              | ..          |
| 1554   | 1         | 2            | ..        | ..              | ..          | ..              | ..     | ..               | ..          | ..        | 1               | ..              | ..          |
| 1555   | 20        | 37           | 2         | ..              | 5           | ..              | ..     | ..               | ..          | ..        | 1               | ..              | ..          |
| Totals | 138       | 258          | 29 and (2)| 8               | 74 and (1)  | 6               | 2      | 3                | 12 and (1)  | 1         | 1               | 3               | 5           |

The figures in these tables were secured from a volume in the Archivo de Indias (30. 2. 1/3) entitled: "Libro de registros de las naos que han ido y venido á las Indias desde el año de 1504 en adelante." It seems to be a sort of index or calendar of the registers which passed through the Casa de Contratación. Whether the list is complete or not there is no means of knowing.

The figures in parenthesis represent vessels wrecked, abandoned at sea or in some port before reaching their destination, or captured by corsairs. They probably include only those whose registers were saved and returned to Seville, and are noted in the "Libro de registros" only for the later years.

## REGISTERED VESSELS SAILING TO AND FROM THE INDIES

### Vessels returning, 1548–55

| | New Spain | Tierra Firme | Honduras | Cartagena | Cape de la Vela | San Domingo | Puerto de Plata | Monte Cristi | Havana | Santiago de Cuba | La Yaguana | Puerto Rico | Jamaica | Unspecified |
|---|---|---|---|---|---|---|---|---|---|---|---|---|---|---|
| 1548 | 8 | 20 | 5 | | | 26 | 4 | | 3 | | 4 | 3 | | |
| 1549 | 8 and (2) | 33 | 4 | 1 | | 23 | | | | | 1 | 3 | | |
| 1550 | 8 and (1) | 18 and (2) | 2 | 2 | 1 | 23 and (1) | 6 | | 5 | 1 | | 6 | | |
| 1551 | 12 and (1) | 24 | 5 | | | 27 and (1) | 1 and (2) | (2) | 3 | 1 | 1 | 4 | 1 | 3 |
| 1552 | 8 and (2) | 16 and (3) | 3 and (1) | 1 | | 14 and (2) | 2 | 1 | 2 | | | 5 | | 1 |
| 1553 | 4 and (1) | 6 and (2) | 1 and (1) | | | 15 and (7) | 1 and (1) | (1) | 2 and (1) | | | 2 | | |
| 1554 | | 2 and (2) | 1 | | | 16 and (1) | 1 and (1) | 1 | 1 | | | 1 and (1) | 1 | |
| 1555 | 5 and (5) | 7 and (8) | 1 | | | | 4 | | 1 | | 3 | 6 | 1 | (1) |
| Totals | 53 and (12) | 126 and (17) | 22 and (2) | 4 | 1 | 159 and (12) | 19 and (4) | 3 and (3) | 17 and (1) | 2 | 9 | 30 and (1) | 3 | 4 and (1) |

## APPENDIX IX

### WAGES ON VESSELS IN THE INDIA NAVIGATION. SIXTEENTH CENTURY

| | Almiranta *San Nicolás* of an armada guarding the Spanish coasts in 1543 against French corsairs | Carrack *Santa María* of the same armada (A. de I, 40. 3. 1/13) | Similar Spanish vessel in the year 1544 (*ibidem*) | Armada of Sancho de Biedma, 1550–51 (A. de I, 30. 3. 2) | Armada of Pedro de las Roelas, 1563–64 (A. de I, 30. 3. 1) |
|---|---|---|---|---|---|
| General | ........ | ........ | ........ | ........ | 1,875 ducats per year |
| Almirante | ........ | ........ | ........ | ........ | 1,000 ducats per year |
| Capitán | 4,166 maravedis per month | ........ | ........ | 100,000 maravedis per year | ........ |
| Maestre | 6 ducats per month | ........ | ........ | 110–180 ducats per voyage | ........ |
| Piloto | (2) 10 and 4 ducats per month | 10 ducats per month | ........ | 8 ducats per month | 8 ducats per month |
| Escribano | 4 ducats per month | 6 | 5 ducats per month | 12 | 8 " |
| Médico | ........ | 4 | ........ | 6 | ........ |
| Boticario | 4 ducats per month | 4 ducats per month | 5 ducats per month | 6 | 6 ducats per month |
| Alguacil | 5 | ........ | ........ | ........ | ........ |
| Alférez and Trompeta | ........ | 6 | ........ | 6 | 6 " |
| Caporal | ........ | 4 | ........ | ........ | ........ |
| Sargento | ........ | ........ | ........ | ........ | 4 " |
| Pífaro and Atambor | ........ | ........ | ........ | ........ | 4 " |
| Artillero | 4½ ducats per month | 4 ducats per month | 5 ducats per month | 4 ducats per month | 4 " |
| Condestable | ........ | ........ | 6 | 5 " | 5 " |
| Soldado | 2 ducats per month | 2 ducats per month | ........ | 2 " | 2 " |
| Marinero | ........ | ........ | 2½ ducats per month | 3 escudos per month | ........ |
| Grumete | ........ | ........ | ........ | 2 " | ........ |
| Page del general | ........ | 1 ducat per month | ........ | 2 ducats per month | ........ |
| Capellán | ........ | 4 | 5 ducats per month | 2 " | 20.450 maravedis per voyage |
| Contramaestre | 4 ducats per month | ........ | 5 " | ........ | ........ |
| Carpintero | 4 " | ........ | 5 " | ........ | ........ |
| Calafate | 4 " | ........ | 5 " | ........ | ........ |

# APPENDIX IX

SCHEDULE OF MONTHLY WAGES ON A GALLEON OF 500 TONS IN THE ARMADA REAL — XVII CENTURY?

From a "Diálogo anónimo entre un vizcaíno y un montañes sobre construcción de naves," printed by Fernandez Duro in *Disquisiciones Náuticas*, vol. vi, pp. 156–157.

| | | Escudos | | | Escudos |
|---|---|---|---|---|---|
| Gente de guerra | Capitán............ | 40 | Gente de mar | Capellán........... | 12 |
| | Alférez............ | 15 | | Guardián.......... | 11 |
| | Sargento........... | 11 | | Cirujano........... | 8 |
| | Cabos de esquadra (5) | 8 | | Condestable........ | 8 |
| | Tambores (2)....... | 6 | | Artilleros (28)...... | 6 |
| | Pífaro............. | 6 | | Trompeta.......... | 6 |
| | Abanderado........ | 4 | | Dispensero......... | 6 |
| | Mosqueteros (40).... | 6 | | Alguacil de agua.... | 6 |
| | Arcabuceros (54).... | 4 | | Escribano de raciones. | 6 |
| Gente de mar | Maestre de nao..... | 25 | | Carpinteros (2)..... | 6 |
| | Maestre de jarcia... | 20 | | Marineros (36)...... | 4 |
| | Maestre de raciones.. | 20 | | Grumetes (15)...... | 3 |
| | Piloto ............ | 20 | | Pajes (8)........... | 2 |
| | Contramaestre ..... | 15 | | | |

## APPENDIX X

### Ordinances of the Consulado of Seville Relating to Marine Insurance

Otro si, por quanto vna las cosas mas necessarias para el trato de la mercaduria, y para la conseruacion della es la antigua costumbre, que en todos cabos se guarda, de assegurarse vnos mercaderes á otros las mercaderias que cargan, y los nauios en que las lleuan: lo qual si cessasse diminuyrian mucho los tratos: porque no auiendo asseguradores, no auria quien osasse cargar y osasse auenturar á perder todo lo que cargasse. Y por esto conuiene que aya muchos asseguradores, que asseguren á otros lo que cargare. Y que entre los cargadores y asseguradores aya mucha verdad y llaneza, y que no cesse de auer los dichos asseguradores como de presente ha commençado a cessar. Y que los asseguradores esten verdaderamente seguros: y que los asseguradores no reciban engaño en pagar lo que no deurian pagar, por los engaños q̄ se suelen hazer, y en el viaje delas Indias lo suele auer muy mayores, por ser nauegaciō mas apartada destos reynos. Y por euitar en alguna manera parte de estos dichos negocios, y por dar ocasion á q̄ aya personas q̄ asseguren á otros las haziēdas que cargaren, para que el trato y commercio se estienda mas: de hazer las ordenanças siguientes.

Que todas las personas que firmaren riesgos de yda ó venida de Indias, que pusieren en el renglon que firman por fulano, ó por comission, ó por comissiones: que primero que firmen ninguna poliça, muestren los poderes que tuuieren ante el prior y consules: los quales los examinen si son bastantes: y siendolo le den licēcia que firme por ellos: y no lo siendo, que no pueda firmar el q̄ tuuiere los dichos poderes por nadie, sin estar aprouado por el dicho prior y consules: so pena que cada vez que firmare tenga veynte mil marauedis de pena, la mitad para la camara, y la mitad para costas del consulado. Y si los poderes fueren bastantes y dieren la dicha licencia, que dé vn traslado de todos ellos ante vn escriuano de la casa.

Que por quanto muchas poliças de seguros se pierden, de lo qual las partes reciben daño por no auer registros. Ordenamos que de aqui adelante los corredores que hizieren las tales poliças, las hagan conforme á las ordenanças, y tengan libro en que assienten la poliça que hizieren dende el principio hasta el fin de ella con el dia y mes y año en que se

## APPENDIX X

firmare cada firma: y quién la firmó, y qué cātidad: y qué precio: sopena, que el que lo contrario hiziere pague de pena veynte mil marauedis: la tercia parte para la camara de su Magestad, y tercia para gastos del consulado, y tercia para el denunciador: y quede priuado de su officio: esto demas del interesse de la parte.

Y porque muchos asseguradores se mueren, ó se van ó ausentan, y para cobrarse los daños y auerias que ay en las poliças que han firmado, es menester reconoscer las firmas. Ordenamos, que de aqui adelante estando la poliça firmada del corredor que la hizo, y dando en ella fé como la vido firmar á las personas en ella contenidas: y estando escripta en su libro: sea visto las tales firmas estar reconoscidas, para poderse executar, ó embargar los que las firmarē: como si estuuiessen reconoscidas por ellos: y ansi sirua para los muertos y ausentes, solamente para el dicho effecto de execucion, ó embargo: sin que por esto quede reconoscida para el negocio principal.

Que nīgun corredor pueda firmar riesgos por si ni por otra persona: sopena de perdimiento de su officio. Y q̄ ninguna persona pueda firmar riesgos por ningū corredor, sopena de treynta mil marauedis cada vez que los firmare: tercia parte para la camara de su Magestad, tercia parte para los gastos del consulado, tercia parte para el denunciador.

Que ninguna persona pueda assegurar de yda ni venida á las Indias sobre los fletes ni artillerias, ni aparejos de ninguna nao, sopena que que el seguro de lo que sobre ello se hiziere sea ninguno: y que el assegurador no sea obligado á pagarlo aunque se pierda: agora sea en poliça, agora en confiança. Pero permitese, que se pueda assegurar las dos tercias partes de qualquier nao, ó nauio: y caxco del solamente, conforme á la ordenança de yda á las Indias: lo que verdaderamente valiere y no mas. Y este seguro se haga en poliça á parte, y no juntamente con mercadurias. Y si de venida se quisieren assegurar, puedan assegurar lo que tuuieren de licencia del dicho prior y consules. Y si algun maestre, ó señor de nauio tomare dineros á cambio, ó hiziere escriptura de deudo que deua, que el acreedor corra el riesgo sobre el tal caxco y aparejos, y fletes, q̄ tanto menos se assegure el maestre, ó señor del nauio, del valor del caxco.

Otro si, por quanto quando algū seguro se haze, despues de perdida de alguna nao, siempre se tiene por cierto que el que se asseguró sabia la perdida quando se hizo assegurar. Porende ordenamos, que si algunos se asseguraren despues de la perdida de la nao ó naos, ó la perdida vuiere sido en lugar que á legua por hora por tierra lo pudiera saber el assegurado: que en tal caso, que el seguro sea ninguno, y los asseguradores no sean obligados á pagar la perdida: solamente buelvan el premio que recibieren, deteniendo el medio por ciento. Y si el seguro fuere en qualquier, q̄ no sean obligados á correrlo en otra nao.

Que quando alguna nao de yda ó de venida á Indias, no se supiere della despues de partida del puerto de donde saliere y tomo carga, en vn año y medio dende el dia que se partio: que esta nao sea tenida y tengan por perdida: y se pueda cobrar el riesgo de ella, haziendo dexacion en los asseguradores, y dando los recaudos necessarios.

Que quando alguna mercaduria de yda ó de venida se assegurare, tassandola, por pacto espresso en algun precio senalado, sea y se entienda entrar en aquel precio el coste principal, y el seguro y todas las costas.

Que quando algun riesgo vuiere sobre qualquier cosa que se aya echado á la mar por beneficio de todos: ó si se descargare de la nao para poder passar algunos baxos deste rio, ó de otra qualquier parte, y en esto vuiere algun riesgo, sea y se entienda que es aueria gruessa, y que lo han de pagar la nao y el flete y todas las mercaderias que lleua dētro: con tanto que no aya sido la ocasion forçosa, y no tenga en ello culpa el maestre.

Que qualquiera persona que por si, ó por otra persona se assegurare de yda ó de venida á Indias, sea obligado de pagar el premio del tal seguro dētro de tres meses despues que se firmare de contado, ó en blanco, sin que se le pida: y sino le fagare dentro de los tres meses como dicho es, si algun riesgo vuiere despues, el assegurador no sea obligado á pagarlo: y en los dichos tres meses, y despues el dicho assegurador pueda pedir el premio al assegurado, y sea obligado á luego pagarselo.

Y si alguna persona se vuiere assegurado de aquí á las Indias, y por alguna causa no cargasse la cargazon, y parte della en la nao que estuuiere assegurado: que para que le restituyan lo que vuiere dado del premio del seguro, sea obligado á pedirlo y hazerlo saber al assegurador, ó asseguradores, quinze dias despues de salida la nao de San Lucar. Y si ansi no lo hiziere, despues no lo pueda pedir, y pierda el premio que vuiere dado.

Que en qualquier manera que se deshaga qualquier poliça de yda ó venida á Indias, por no correr el riesgo: el assegurado pague medio por ciento al assegurador de todo lo que se deshiziere.

Que todo lo que se cargare en este rio de Guadalquiuir para Sanlucar de Barrameda, y alli sea y se entienda que se carga en esta ciudad de Seuilla, aunque la poliça no lo declare, y lo que fuere en barcos para

## APPENDIX X

lleuarlo á las naos, ansi mismo lo han de correr los asseguradores, aunque en la poliça no lo diga.

Que todas las poliças que se hizieren de yda á las Indias, si se assegurare más summa de lo que vale la cargazō, los asseguradores postreros vayan fuera: no ganando ni perdiendo, sino su medio por ciento del deshazerse. Y los demas asseguradores corran la carga con todos sueldo á libra: y entiēdese ser los postreros asseguradores, los postreros firmados en la poliça, aunq̄ aya otros aquel mesmo dia.

Y entiendese, que en todas las mercaderias, oro, y plata, y otras cosas que se registraren en el registro del rey, á la yda en esta ciudad de Seuilla, y en otras partes donde se cargaren las naos: y á la venida, en qualquiera parte de las Indias donde se hiziere el registro: sea auido por parte la persona á quien vinieren consignadas las tales mercaderias, oro, ó plata, ó el que lo cargare en el registro cobrar la perdida y aueria que vuiere: y hazer la dexacion con la persona que asseguró. No embargante que las tales mercaderias no sean de la persona á quien vuieren consignadas. Esto se ha de entender y entiende sin perjuyzio, conforme á la ordenança cinquenta y cinco, so la pena della.

Que todas las poliças que se hizieren de venida de qualquier parte de las Indias á estos reynos: assi sobre mercaderias como sobre oro, y plata: assi en qualquier nao, como en nao nōbrada: sea y se entienda q̄ han de estar corridas dentro de dos años, desde el dia que se firmare: y sino fueren corridas lo que assi se asseguró, ó quedare alguna parte dello por correr: q̄ la poliça sea en si ninguna: y quede deshecha para lo que faltare por correr el riesgo, sino fueren de acuerdo de ambas las partes. Y de lo que se deshiziere, los asseguradores bueluan el precio de lo que recibieren, tomando el medio por ciento.

QUE si alguna perdida ó aueria vuiere en lo assegurado de yda ó venida á Indias: que el cargador, ó dueño della sea obligado á notificar los asseguradores que ay la tal perdida ó aueria dentro de dos años de la firma: y que si no lo notificare, que despues no le pueda pedir en ninguna manera. Y que si notificaren que ay perdida ó aueria, tengan otros dos años de tiēpo para traer los recaudos para cobrar la dicha perdida ó aueria. Y si dentro de quatro años despues de la firma de la poliça no pidierē la dicha perdida y aueria, y truxeren los recaudos: que despues no la pueda pedir ni cobrar, y los asseguradores queden libres.

Que qualquiera persona que hiziere seguro de venida de Indias, assi en nao nombrada como en qualquiera, sea obligado á poner en la poliça del tal seguro, antes que firme algun assegurador, si tiene hecha otra poliça de venida aquí ó en otra parte, y de que suma es, y lo que le falta de correr de la tal poliça. Y si ansi no lo hiziere, que qualquier cosa que viniere de las dichas Indias á la persona que ansi se asseguró, sin dezir lo que mas tenia assegurado, sea y se entienda venir para en cuenta de cada poliça que tenga hecha, aunque sea dos otras poliças que en cada vna lo ganē los asseguradores todo, en pena de auerse assegurado, sin dezir lo que passaua: y si perdida vuiere, la paguen solamente los primeros asseguradores, y son los primeros aseguradores los primeros en tiēpo, aūque aya vna poliça en qualquiera nauio, y otra nao nōbrada, si la en qualquiera fuere primero, se ha de correr primero, aunque no quede que corra los de la nao nombrada.

Que ninguna mercaderia que se asseguarre de venida de Indias pueda auer aueria de daño ni falta que trayga la tal mercaderia. Y si algun daño ó falta vuiere, ha de ser á cargo del cargador, y no del assegurador: sino fuere solamente aueria gruessa de echazon: que esta tal ha de ser á cargo de los aseguradores por su parte: conforme á la ordenança de arriba numero treynta y seys.

Que en todas las poliças de venida de Indias, sobre oro y plata, y perlas, y mercaderias, no se pueda assegurar el costo del seguro.

Que si alguna nao de venida de Indias se perdiere cō oro ó plata, ó perlas, ó se descargare en algū puerto, por no estar la nao para nauegar: de suerte q̄ verdaderamēte todo el oro y plata y perlas q̄ este en saluo para poderse traer á esta ciudad q̄ los dueños del tal oro ó plata ó perlas, no pueda hazer dexaciō de ello á los seguradores, diziendo q̄ vuo naufragio, y que se descargó la nao por no estar para nauegar sino que aya de esperar á q̄ se cargue en otro nauio ó nauios: y q̄ venga ó verdaderamente se pierda: y en tal caso los aseguradores han de pagar todas las auerias, costos y gastos que se hizieren en poner el dicho oro y plata y perlas en cobro, y cargarlo en otros nauios, y traerlo á esta ciudad, y corran el riesgo en la nao ó naos que se tornare á cargar aunque sean passados los dos años.

Que quando alguna mercaderia de yda ó de venida se descargare en algun cabo, ó se mudare de vna nao en otra, ó otra cosa semejante que sea por cosa que los seguradores sean obligados á pagar al cargador todas las costas gastos, dadiuas, y rescates que se hizieren en beneficio de la hazienda, por cuenta y juramento del cargador, ó de la persona que lo gastare: solamēte sin mas recaudos. Y si los aseguradores se sintieren por agrauiados despues de auer desembolsado las dichas costas, sean recebidos á pruena y se verifique.

Que en qualquier cabo de Indias que se cargare oro ó plata, y si pusiere en el registro, lo que costó hazer de mal oro bueno, ó de mala plata labrada, que esta tal demasia no la corrē los asseguradores. Y si perdida ó aueria vuiere, no han de pagar mas de lo que verdaderamente montan los pesos de oro ó plata que vienen.

Que quando alguna nao llegare á algun puerto de yda ó venida á Indias: y por la justicia, ó por el pueblo, ó por otra persona le fuere tomada por fuerça alguna mercaderia sin pagarsela, que los asseguradores se la paguen por el coste, dando los recaudos de como se la tomaron para que la puedan pedir.

Entiendese, que las fees de los registros de venida de Indias son y han de ser las verdaderas cargazones: Y por los mesmos dias que se registraren sea entēdido, que aquel dia se cargan: no embargante que la mercaderia se aya cargado antes, ó se cargare despues. Por manera que el dia del registro sea dia de carga, y siempre prefiera el primero registro al segūdo, aunque el segūdo sea cargado primero.

Y porque suele auer riesgo en las mercaderias de Indias mientras estan cargando en los puertos antes que se registren: y el que las carga las podia cargar por cuenta de más de vna persona, y despues atribuyr el registro á quien quisiere: sea y se entiēda, que qualquiera que cargare qualquiera mercaderia, el dia que la cargare la manifieste ante el escriuano de los registros: y diga lo que carga, y por cuenta de quien, en el entretanto que se haze el registro, y la firma el mercader: y que esta manifestacion valga tanto como el registro para cobrar de los asseguradores la perdida q̄ vuiere. Y dōde no vuiere manifestaciō ante el escriuano de los registros de lo q̄ se carga, y por cuēta de quien, que los seguradores no corran el riesgo sobre ello.

Y quanto á las mercaderias q̄ se cargaren en los puertos de España para las Indias, mientras no se estuuieren registradas antes que los dichos nauios partan: que si algun riesgo vuiere, que el libro del escriuano se entienda ser registro, y con el y con el juramento del cargador se puedan cobrar, como si estuuiessen registradas: y faltādo el libro del escriuano, lo aya de prouar con testigos.

Que en qualquiera manera de yda ó venida á Indias, aya perdida de nao, ó naufragio della, ó descarga de mercaderias por no poder estar la nao para nauegar: q̄ en tal caso los cargadores puedā hazer dexaciō en los asseguradores de todas las mercaderias, oro, ó plata que fueren ó vinieren registradas solamēte, y cōstādo de la perdida ó naufragio ó descarga, q̄ los asseguradores sean obligados á desembolsar luego por mādamiento del prior y consules todo lo q̄ vuieren segurado, sin q̄ del dicho mādamiento de desembolso aya lugar apelaciō ni otro remedio alguno, sino ante todas cosas desembolsen y pōgan en poder de los asseguradores la cantidad que ansi seguraren: dādo primeramente fiança los asseguradores, que si paresciere no ser bien cobrados, bolueran lo que recibieren con treynta y tres por ciento de interesse.

Entiendese, que la nao no está para nauegar, quando se haze dexacion ante la justicia, y la justicia da licēcia para descargarla, y verderamente se descarga, y queda allí la mercaderia sin tornarse á cargar en la mesma nao: en tal caso, trayendo testimonio de esto y en cuyo poder quedó la hazienda, se podra hazer la dicha dexacion, y cobrar de los dichos asseguradores: pero tornadose á cargar en la dicha nao, no se ha de poder hazer dexacion, sino cobrar las costas de los seguradores. Esto se entiēde, no acaesciendo lo susodicho en el puerto donde se carga la tal mercaderia porque descargandose en el dicho puerto donde se cargó, aunque se aya descargado por mandamiento de la justicia, no se ha de hazer dexacion de las dichas mercadurias, sino el cargador ha de poner cobro en ellas, y los seguradores le ha de pagar las costas, y mas fletes si vuiere y corriere el riesgo en el mesmo nauio ó en otros donde se tornare á cargar.

Que quando alguna persona estuuiere assegurado de venida de Indias, y quisiere cobrar alguna perdida por carta misiua de su factor, ó de la persona que lo embiare ó cargare, sin mostrar fé del registro, que lo pueda hazer: con tanto que dé fianças, que dentro de dos años despues de la sentencia traerá la fé del registro, y la presentará ante prior y consules, sin que se le pida ni requiera: y si no la truxere, que passando el dicho tiempo, como depositario boluerá luego lo que cobró, con mas los treynta y tres por ciento del interesse, si el assegurado los quiere cobrar.

Que no se pueda hazer ninguna poliça de seguro de yda ni de venida á Indias sobre oro y plata y mercaderias que no vayan ni vengan registradas en el registro del rey: y que la poliça que de otra manera se hiziere pública ó en confiança, sea en sí ninguna. Y que aūque aya perdida, los asseguradores no sean obligados á pagarlo.

Que los seguros que se hizieren sobre esclauos, ó sobre bestias se aya de declarar en la poliça, como son sobre ellos, y de otra manera no lo corren los asseguradores. Y q̄ si alguna bestia se echare en la mar, q̄ no se pueda echar por aueria gruessa, sino que lo paguen los asseguradores.

Que todo lo que se assegurare, ansi de yda como de venida á Indias, sea y se entienda estar assegurado, cōforme á la poliça general que está puesta en estas ordenanças: y conforme á estas ordenanças, que no se pueda assegurar de otra manera, ni renunciar la dicha poliça ni parte della: ni estas ordenanças ni alguna della: so pena, que si alguna persona lo hiziere pague cincuenta mil maravedis de pena, la mitad para la camara de su Magestad, y la otra mitad para gastos del consulado, y que todavia se entienda estar el dicho seguro hecho conforme á la dicha poliça, y conforme á estas ordenanças.

### Poliça General de Yda á Indias

In Dei Nomine, Amen. Otorgamos y conoscemos, los q̄ aqui baxo firmaremos, que asseguramos á vos fulano, sobre qualesquier mercaderias, cargadas por vos ó por otra qualquier persona ó personas por vos: y tambien vos asseguramos sobre todas las costa y costas de este seguro; las quales dichas mercaderias van registradas en el registro del Rey y á riesgo de fulano, en tal nao nombrada tal, maestre fulano, ó otro qualquiera que vaya por maestre en la dicha nao. Y assi cargada la dicha mercaderia en la dicha nao, siga su presente viage con la buena ventura hasta tal puerto de las Indias: y alli sea llegada á buē saluamēto, y las mercadurias descargadas de la dicha nao en qualquier barco ó barcos, hasta ser descargadas en tierra en buen saluamento. Y es condicion, que la dicha nao pueda hazer y haga todas las escalas que quisiere y por biē tuuiere, asi forçosas como voluntarias, entrando y saliendo en qualquier puerto ó puertos: dando y recibiendo carga, no mudando viage, sino fuere por juntarse con alguna compañía.

Y si riesgo ó daño vuiere, dezimos, q̄ trayendolo por certificacion, hecha con parte ó sin parte, ó por persona q̄ no sea parte, hecha en el lugar donde se perdiere la nao, ó en otra qualquier parte: que passados los seys meses, contados desde el dia que la poliça de asseguro se firmare, pagaremos llanamente, y desembolsaremos luego ante todas cosas, y depositaremos en poder del cargador, ó persona que se haze assegurar todo lo que vuieremos firmado: ó la parte que del daño nos cupiere á pagar, con tanto que nos deys finaças llanas y abonadas, para que si fuere mal pagado, nos lo boluereys con treynta y tres por ciento.

Y si la nao no paresciere, se entiēde que hemos de pagar dentro de vn año y medio que la nao vuiere salida del puerto, y no paresciere dentro del dicho año y medio. Y el año y medio se ha de contar dende que la nao sale del puerto, y no dende que la poliça se firma.

Y entiendese que lo hemos de correr los primeros y postreros á sueldo á libra, hasta la contidad que monta la cargazon, y los demas de lo que montare la cargazon han de yr fuera conforme á la ordenança.

Y de esta manera y con estas condiciones somos contētos de correr el dicho riesgo. Y para ello obligamos nuestras personas y bienes, y damos poder cumplido á los juezes de la casa de la contratacion desta ciudad de Seuilla, y á otras qualesquier justicias de estos reynos: para que nos lo hagan cumplir: y renunciamos nuestro proprio fuero y jurisdiccion y la ley si conuenerit, y sometemonos al fuero y jurisdiccion de los dichos juezes officiales, y á todas las otras justicias, y al prior y consules que son ó fueren de aquí adelante de la vniuersidad de los mercaderes tratantes en las Indias desta ciudad de Seuilla, para que por todo rigor de derecho, asi por via executiva como en otra qualquier manera nos compelan y apremien á lo ansi guardar y cumplir como si fuesse juzgado y sentenciado por sentencia diffinitiua dada por juez competente en contraditorio juyzio: y por nos y por cada vno de nos consentida y passada en cosa juzgada.

### Limitaciones de la Poliça Passada: y Declaracion Della

Y Entiendese, que en diziendo mercaderias todo genero de mercaderias, excepto bestias y esclauos, caxcos y aparejos, y fletes, y artilleria de naos, que como diga mercaderia, no ay cosa exceptada sino las susodichas.

Y entiendese, que se corre el riesgo dende el punto y hora que las mercadurias se commençaron ó commençaren á cargar dēde tierra en el puerto de las muelas del rio de Guadalquiuir desta ciudad de Seuilla en la dicha nao. Y si las dichas mercadurias ó qualquier dellas se lleuare en qualquier barco ó barcos á la d̄ha nao se corre el dicho riesgo, estando la nao en qualquiera parte de este rio hasta Sanlucar, y correse el riesgo en el dicho barco ó barcos, hasta q̄ la mercaduria esté cargada dentro en la dicha nao: y aūque se cargue de esta manera se entiende que es cargada en este rio y en este puerto.

Y donde dize la poliça, hasta ser descargadas en tierra en buen saluamento, se pone esta declaracion: y hasta entōces corre el riesgo sobre el assegurador. Y siendo el riesgo para nueua España, entiēdese que han de correr los dichos asseguradores el riesgo hasta que las mercadurias sean descargadas en sant Iuan de Lua en barcos, y las lleuen á la Veracruz, y alli sean descargadas en buen saluamento.

Y entiendese, que las naos que fueren á la Isla de sant Iuan, que puedan hazer escalas con ellas si quisieren, en qualesquier puerto ó puertos de las Islas de Canaria, y en otros qualesquiera, como no mude viage. Y la nao que fuere á qualquier puerto de la Isla Española, se entienda, que pueda hazer escala, y dar y recebir carga en qualesquier puerto ó puertos de las Islas de Canaria, islas de sant Iuan de Puerto rico, sant German, y otros puertos de la dicha isla Española. Y la nao que fuere al nombre de Dios, pueda hazer escala en los dichos puerto ó puertos de las islas de Canaria é islas de sant Iuan Puerto rico, y sant German: y en qualesquier puerto ó puertos de la isla Española, y en el cabo de la vela, y Iamayca, y sancta Martha, y Cartagena. Y la nao que fuere á Cuba pueda hazer escala en las dichas islas de Canaria y san Iuan, y isla Española. Y la que fuere al cabo de Honduras pueda hazer escala en las dichas islas de Canaria, san Iuan y isla Española, y en la isla de Iamayca, Cuba y Hauana. Y la nao que fuere á la nueua España, pueda hazer escala en las dichas islas de Canaria, y sant Iuan y sant German, y isla Española, y isla de Cuba. Y si alguna nao fuere á otros puertos de las Indias, pueda hazer escalas conforme á estas que estan dichas las q̄ fueren en el camino del puerto adonde fuere a descargar.

Y entiendese, que la nao que fuere por su volūtad a las islas de Caboverde, y en las poliças de seguro que se hizieren no se pusiere y declarare que lo tal es mundāça de viage: y si se perdiere la nao, que el assegurador no ha de pagar cosa ninguna, agora se pierda ó roben la nao antes de llegar á las dichas islas de Cabo verde, ó despues.

Entiendese, q̄ quāto al costo y valor de la mercaduria, se ha de creer por solo juramento del cargador sin mas diligencia.

El qual seguro se entiende de mar, y viento, y fuego, y de enemigos y amigos, y de otro qualquier caso q̄ acaezca ó acaescer pueda, excepto de barateria de patron, o mācamiento de la mercaduria.

Y entiendiese, que si necessario fuere traspassar la mercaderia de vn nauio en otro, ó de otro en otro: assi en mar como en puerto: y descargar la mercaderia en tierra, y tornarla á cargar en el nauio ó nauios donde fuere, ó en otros qualesquier caxco ó caxcos, que lo puedan hazer sin que pare perjuyzio al que se haze assegurar. Y todas las costas que se hizieren pagaremos nos los asseguradores: quier vayan en saluo las mercaderias ó no. Y si algun caso acontesciesse, damos licencia al cargador, ó á la persona que de la mercaderia lleuare cargo, para que el le pueda poner la mano, y beneficiarla, ni más ni menos que si no estuuiesse assegurada.

# INDEX

Acapulco, 145, 146, 149, 184.
Acosta, José de, 161, 193.
Acuerdo de hacienda, 89.
Acuña, Dr. Alberto de, 45 n.
Admirals, of Castile, 6 n., 41 n.; of the flotas and armadas, *see* Almirantes.
Admiralty, court of, in Andalusia, 26, 41 n.
Admiralty dues, 6 and n.
Aduana, *see* Customhouses.
Aduanilla, 135.
Africa, trade with, 5 n., 25, 69.
Agente solicitador of the Casa, 57 n.
Agriculture in Spanish America, premiums for, 106; encouraged by the Crown, 124, 125; backwardness of, 131–133.
Aguila, Pedro de, 9.
Albert and Isabel, archdukes of Flanders, 129.
Alcabala in Andalusia, administration of, 48; colonial trade exempt from, 6; colonial trade subject to, 83, 84.
Alcabala in the colonies, 106, 137, 255.
Alcaide y guarda mayor of the Casa, 33 n., 55, 56.
Alcázar Real of Seville, residence of the Casa, 25.
Alguacil mayor of the Casa, 54–56.
Alguaciles of the Casa, 44, 54.
Alguaciles of the Consulado, 44.
Almaden quicksilver mine, 51, 158, 159, 161.
Almagro, Diego, 100.
Almiranta, 79, 222.
Almirantazgo, *see* Admiralty dues.
Almirantazgo (mercantile gild of Flanders), 256.
Almirantes of the flotas and armadas, 75, 206, 217, 218, 317.
Almojarifazgo, *see* Custom duties.

Almojarifes, 86.
Alvarez Osorio y Redin, Miguel, cited in text, 56, 63, 119, 138, 217.
Amalfi, Laws of, 318.
Amalgamation of silver ore, 51, 158, 160.
America, discovery of, xi f.; *see also* Columbus; early descriptions of, xviiif., 310, 312.
Amilivia, Domingo Alonso de, 69, 70.
Ampies, Juan de, 22 n.
Andagoya, Pascual de, 192.
Andalusia, corsairs on the coasts of, 16, 70; merchants of, 65, 81, 172.
Annuities issued by the Crown, 80 n., 135, 169–172, *passim.*
Antioquia, 188.
Antonio, Bautista, 244.
Antwerp, 24, 25 n.
Aragonese in America, 96–98.
Aranda, Count of, 196.
Araya, salt pans of, 119.
Arca de tres llaves, *see* Casa de Contratación of Seville — coffers.
Archivo de Indias (Seville), xv, xviii.
Archivo histórico-nacional (Madrid), xv.
Arcos, Duke of, 70.
Arica, 189 n.
Armada de la carrera de las Indias, 69, 70, 202, 204, 209, 210, 252.
Armada, of the South Sea, 83 n., 152, 189, 240, 241; of 1588 against England, 90, 161 n., 266, 268; del mar océano, 218 n.; de barlovento, *see* Fleets, coast-guard, in the colonies. *See also* Convoys.
Armadores, 315.
Arqueador of the Casa, 282 n.
Arriaga, Luis de, 24.
Arribadas maliciosas, 139.
*Arte de navegar*, of Pedro de Medina, 310.
Artillero mayor of the Casa, 50.

Artillery, administration of, 30, 49, 50, 56, 57, 79; description of, 274, 275 and n.; school, 50.
Asesor of the Casa, *see* Juez asesor.
Asesor of the Consulado, 44.
Asiento of the avería, *see* Avería.
Asiento of negroes, *see* Slave trade.
Asistente (chief justice) of Seville, 40, 41.
Astrolabe, 304, 305.
Asylum, right of, 43 n.
Atarazanas of Seville, residence of the Casa, 25; warehouse of the Casa, 31 n., 49, 99.
Atarazanas (arsenal) of the Casa, 49, 50.
Atrato River, 193, 194.
Audiencias, relations of, with the colonial exchequer, 89, 93.
Ausentes y depósitos (unclaimed or sequestered property), 31 n., 33 n., 48, 52.
Avería, 13, 54, 55, 60 n., 61 n., 67-82, 202-206, *passim*, 327; administration of, 51-53, 58 n., 69, 70, 72-75; rate of, 65, 69, 72, 73, 76-78, 79 n., 83 n., 328; assessment of, 72-74; exemptions from, 74 and n., 75 and n.; contribution to, by passengers on the galleons, 76; asiento of, with the Seville merchants, 78-80; vieja, 80 and n.; abolished on cargoes from America, 80, 81; gruesa, 82 n.; in Peru, 83 n.; del camino, 183.
Avilés, 15.
Azogues, 162.
Azores, corsairs about the, 68-71, 202, 228.

Badajoz, Alonso de, 157, 158.
Badoero, Andrea, 163.
Bahama channel, 228.
Balearic Islands, 135; admitted to colonial trade, 98 n.
Bankruptcies, 44, 79, 80, 82.
Barbadoes, 118, 235.
Barbary coast, *see* Africa.
Barcelona (Spain), 15, 40.
Barinas, Marquis of, 143, 152 and n., 250.
Barratry, 41.
Barrionuevo, Francisco de, 182.

Basilisks, 275 n.
Bastidas, Rodrigo de, 24, 309.
Bayona, 15, 17 n.
Bazan, Alonso, 264.
Bazan, Alvaro, 264, 265.
Benevides y Bazan, Juan de, 237-239.
Benzoni, Girolamo, quoted, 293.
Berardi, Juanoto, 262.
Biedma, Sancho de, 211.
Bienes de difuntos, 31 and n., 33 n., 48, 52; depository-general of, 48.
Bilbao, 15, 16.
Biscay provinces, trade of, 15-17, *passim*, 153, 154; shipbuilding in, 266, 270. *See also* Bilbao, Coruña, etc.
Biscayan pilots, gild of, 319.
Blackmail of foreigners in the colonies, *see* Foreigners.
Blake, Admiral Robert, 13, 245, 246.
Boabdil, Muley, 262.
Bodenham, Roger, 258, 260.
Bonds required of those connected with colonial trade. *See* Casa de Contratación of Seville; Fleets, officers of; Masters of ships.
Book of Registers, 16, 18.
Books, export of, to the colonies restricted, 135, 136, 152.
Borough, Stephen, 39, 311.
Bottomry bills, 285, 286.
Bounties to shipbuilders, 68, 259 and n.
Brazil, 116, 147; trade with the Rio de la Plata, 117, 140-143.
Brazilwood, 31.
Breda, siege of, 171.
Bretons in the Canaries, 19.
*Breve compendio de la esfera y de la arte de navegar*, of Martin Cortes, 311.
Bristol, merchants of, 19.
Briviesca, Jimeno de, 21 and n.
Brochero, Diego, 270.
Brokers, insurance, 286.
Buccaneers, 114, 194, 195, 248-251. *See also* Corsairs.
Buenos Aires, trade with, 87 n., 117, 118, 140-143, 162.
Bullion, export of, to the colonies forbidden, 26, 134.

# INDEX

Bullion, American, xii, xxi, 31 n., 34, 51, 70, 82; amounts remitted to Spain, 13, 162–171, 246, 336–338; export to foreign countries, 13, 64, 113, 114 and n., 145, 177, 178; seized by the Crown, 24, 169–174; unregistered, 30, 31, 62–65, 81; captured by corsairs, 69, 70, 83 n.; shipped on men-of-war, 72, 79, 206 and n., 220 n.; transport from Cadiz to Seville, 292; disposal of, in Spain, *see* Bullion merchants. *See also* Mines, Quinto.
Bullion merchants, 174–176.
Burgos, consulado of, *see* Consulado.

Cabot, Sebastian, 36–39, *passim*, 299–301, 306, 311.
Cabrera, Amador de, 160 and n.
Cadereyta, Marquis of, 65, 243, 255, 296.
Cadiz, 5, 6 n., 7, 9–17, 53, 58, 64, 74 n., 82, 84, 86, 108; visitador, 9, 291; Juzgado de Indias, 10–12, 14–16, 42.
Calatrava, military order of, 159.
Calero, Alonso, 191.
Callao, 83 n., 85, 145, 149, 150, 184, 189 and n., 240, 241.
Campeche, 87 and n., 248, 250.
Campos, Alonso de, 254.
Canal, inter-oceanic, 190–197.
Canary Islands, 68, 69, 86, 97, 110, 113, 125 n., 219, 223; trade of, with America, 18–20, 25; emigration from, to America, 98 n., 125.
Cañones, 275 n.
Capitán y superintendente de las maestranzas, 49.
Capitana (flagship of the fleets), 79, 222.
Captains in the armadas, 75, 217, 315, 317.
Captains general of the flotas and armadas, 75, 206, 217–219, 222, 225, 226, 239, 240, 290, 317; residencia of, 229.
Carácas, 87 n.
Carácas Company, *see* Guipuzcoa, Company of.
Caravels, 212, 263.
Cardona, Nicolás de, 24, 151.

Careening of ships, 49, 272 n., 273.
Caribbean Sea, *see* West Indies.
Carracks, xi, 68, 264.
Carreño, Bartolomé, 71, 77, 169, 170, 211.
Cartagena (Spain), 15, 17.
Cartagena de Indias, 81, 87, 107 n., 138, 139, 151, 188–190, *passim*, 232, 244, 250, 252.
Cartography of America, 306–308, 309, 310, 314. *See also* Cosmographers of the Casa.
Carvajal, Andrés de, 32.
Carvajal, Gonzalo de, 294.
Casa da India (Portugal), 23.
Casa de Contractación of Coruña, 25 n.
Casa de Contratación of Seville, establishment of, 3, 7; relations with Cadiz, 9–15; relations with the Canaries, 17–20; ordinances, xvii, 21, 22, 24, 25, 28–34; duties of its officials, 22, 29 ff.; records, 25, 30, 31 n., 52 n.; residence, 25, 26; judicial power, 29, 39–43, 57, 58; office hours, 29, 33 and n.; correspondence, 30, 31 n., 33 n., 34; order of voting, 30 n.; coffers, 31 n., 52 n., 74, 75, 93; prison, 32; chapel, 32 and n., 55; privileges and exemptions, 33; clerical staff, 33 and n.; leave of absence, 33 n.; bonding of its officers, 34 n., 48, 56; officers forbidden to trade, 34; salaries, 35, 38, 80 n., 95, 326; hydrographic bureau and school of navigation, 35–39, 298–308; cartography, 36; threatened removal from Seville, 41, 98; increase of personnel, 56; faults of administration, 56, 73; connivance of officials in frauds, 67; receipts, 164–167, 170, 171, 329–331. *See also* Comptroller; Factor; Jueces oficiales; Pilot-major; President; Treasurer; etc.
Casa de fundición, 155, 157.
Casa Lonja, xv, 325.
Casas, Bartolomé de las, 107.
Casas de Contratación in America, 26–28.
Castellanos, firm of, 175.
Castellanos de Espinosa, Juan, 48.

# INDEX

Castilian monopoly of American trade, 26, 97, 98.
Castilla del Oro, 131, 157.
Castillo, Pedro de, 10 n.
Castrillo, Garcia de Avellaneda, Count of, 33 n., 55.
Cateau Cambresis, Peace of, 77.
Catherine de Medici, 77.
Catholic Kings, xviii, 3, 21, 22 n., 26, 28, 40, 55, 83, 97, 105, 126, 134, 155, 259.
Cavallero, Diego, 251.
Cavalli, Marino, 163.
Cavendish, Thomas, 140, 240.
Cebú, 144.
Centeno, José, 14.
Chagres River, 181-184, *passim*, 191, 192, 196.
Chagres (town), 250.
Chambers of the Casa, 58.
Charles II (of Spain), xviii, 243, 271.
Charles II (of England), 247, 248.
Charles III (of Spain), xv, 20, 143, 196.
Charles V, emperor, xviii, 8, 25 n., 26 n., 35, 37 and n., 42, 43, 69, 71, 83, 92, 107, 124, 125, 137, 159, 166, 190-192, 203, 258; freedom of trade under, 13, 15-17, 98-101; freedom of emigration under, 96; seizure of American bullion by, 169, 170, 172; wars of with Francis I, 16, 69, 71, 170.
Charts, nautical, *see* Cartography.
Charts, magnetic, 312.
Chaves, Alonso de, 37 and n., 261, 302, 307.
Chaves, Jerónimo de, 38, 303.
Chile, copper production in, 155 and n.
Chilton, Leonard, 258.
China, trade of Spanish America with, 145-149.
Chroniclers of America, early, xviii f.
Church in Spanish America, 130-133, 255.
Cifuentes, Count of, 40.
Cimaroon Indians, 183.
Clifford, George, *see* Cumberland, George Clifford, Earl of.
Cloth industry in Spanish America, *see* Textile industry.

Coatzacoalcos River, 190.
Cobos, Francisco de los, 42.
Cocoa, 27, 119, 149 n., 150.
Collections of colonial documents, printed, xvi f.
Colmenar de Arenas, 70 n.
Colon, Cristobal, 251.
Colonial policy and administration, *see* Spain; Spanish America.
Columbus, Bartholomew, 267.
Columbus, Christopher, 3, 7, 19, 21, 22, 24, 27, 40, 59, 68, 105, 125 n., 261, 266, 309; capitulations of, with the Crown, 4, 5 n., 6 n.; profits of, 4, 6 n.
Columbus, Christopher (grandson of above), *see* Colon, Cristobal.
Columbus, Fernando, 37 n., 92, 307.
Comitres, gild of the, 319.
Compass, mariner's, 305, 311, 312.
*Compendio del arte de navegar*, of Rodrigo Zamorano, 313.
Composiciones, cédulas generales de, 111.
Compradores de oro y plata, *see* Bullion merchants.
Comptroller (contador) of the Casa, 21, 26 n., 33, 34 n., 49, 52, 59, 60 n., 69, 288.
Comptrollers, royal, in the colonies, 4, 27, 63 n., 88.
Comuneros, insurrection of the, 98 n.
Condamine, Charles-Marie de la, 195.
Constables — *see* Alguaciles.
Consulado of Burgos, 40, 41, 43.
Consulado of Seville, xvii, 25 n., 43-45, 47, 72, 73, 78, 79, 108, 109, 136, 137, 142, 150, 169, 171, 175, 203, 204, 214, 268, 281, 286, 325.
Consulados in the colonies, 45 and n., 136.
Contador, *see* Comptroller; Diputado contador de averías; Tribunal de la contaduría.
Contarini, Gasparo, 163.
Contraband trade, 18-20, 62-67, 77, 78, 80, 86, 94, 143, 215-217; at Cadiz and San Lucar, 111-115; in the colonies, 115-121, 149, 150, 152, 212.
Contremaestre, 314.
Conversos excluded from the colonies, 104, 105.

Convoys of the merchant fleets, 16, 49, 51, 53, 67, 84, 201 ff.; size of, 71, 78, 79 and n., 202, 206, 210; carry merchandise, 72, 79, 206, 209, 215–217; devoted to other uses, 82; soldiers on, 206, 219, 220. *See also* Armada de la carrera de las Indias; Avería; Ships.
Cooper, Captain (buccaneer), 248.
Copper, 155 and n.; sheathing for ships, 278.
Córdoba (Argentina), 142.
Córdoba, Luis de, 295.
Coreal, François, 188.
Coro, 101, 247.
Corral, Miguel del, 195.
Corredores de seguros, *see* Brokers, insurance.
Correo mayor, *see* Postmaster-general.
Corsairs, 13, 68, 189, 202, 231 ff.; French, 16, 68–71, 76, 77, 231–234; English, 77, 116, 231, 234, 235, 248–251; Dutch, 171, 240, 241.
Cortés, Hernando, 21, 70, 190, 191, 204 n.
Cortés, Martin, son of Hernando, 126.
Cortés, Martin (cosmographer), 311.
Cortes of Castile, 127, 130, 172, 173, 178, 197.
Coruña, 13, 15, 16, 17 n., 25 n., 98.
Cosa, Juan de la, 36, 309.
Cosmographers, of the Casa, 36–38, *passim*, 300–302, *passim*, 306, 308–314, *passim*; of the Council of the Indies, 38 n.
Cosmographer major to the king, 312, 313.
Cosmography, professor of, at the Casa, 38, 300 n., 302–305.
Cottington, Sir Francis, 247.
Cotto, Francisco, 36.
Cotton fabrics imported from the Orient, 145.
Council of the Hacienda, 95.
Council of the Indies, xv, xvii, 9, 11, 17, 19–21, 38 n., 41–45, *passim*, 46, 54, 55, 67, 75, 87, 93, 95, 101, 108, 109, 120, 135, 140, 176, 196, 214, 217, 218, 281, 282.
Cramer, Agustín, 195.

Criminals transported to America, 105.
Cromwell, Oliver, 194, 210, 244, 245.
Cross-staff, 304 n.
Crown, trade with the colonies, 4, 5, 22–24, 29, 31; revenues from America, 47 and n., 56, 95, 162–167, 169, 336–338; dependence on foreign bankers, 67, 99, 100; subsidies to, from the merchants, 171; monopoly of quicksilver, *see* Quicksilver; seizure of bullion, *see* Bullion.
Cruces, *see* Venta Cruz.
Cruzada, Santa, 58.
Cuba, 69, 87 n., 124, 125 and n., 155.
Cuesta, Miguel de la, 182.
Culverins, 275 n.
Cumaná, 85 n., 87 and n., 118, 139, 247, 249.
Cumanagote, 250.
Cumberland, George Clifford, Earl of, 77, 82, 116.
Cunega, Felix de, president of San Domingo, 120.
Curaçoa, 118.
Currents, Atlantic ocean, 310.
Customhouses established in America, 4, 27.
Custom duties, in the colonies, 6, 84, 85, 137; in Andalusia, 48, 65, 81, 83–86; appraisal of, 85, 88–92, 136; *see also* Contraband trade; Registration.

Dampier, William, 185.
Darién, Gulf of, 192, 194; province of, 106, 195. *See also* Tierra Firme.
Dávila, Pedrarias, 24, 180, 277, 310.
Demiculverins, 274.
Deputy auditor of the avería, *see* Diputado contador.
Derecho de extrangería, 88.
Derecho de lonja, 325.
Derecho de toneladas, *see* Tonnage dues.
Derecho de union de armas, 254, 255.
Desaguadero de Nicaragua, *see* San Juan River.
*De Sphaera Mundi*, 303 n.
Diaz, Bartolomé, 287.
Diaz Pimienta, Francisco, 120.

## INDEX

Diaz de Pisa, Bernal, 63 n.
Diaz de Solis, Juan, 24, 36, 37, 278.
Diezmo, of bullion, 157.
Diputado contador de averías, 51–53, 75.
Dispatch boats to the colonies, 223, 229 n., 230. *See also* Pataches.
Diustegui, Agustín de, 254.
Doria, J. Andrea, 206 n
Doyley, Edward, 247.
Drake, Sir Francis, 10, 77, 82 and n., 182, 210, 240.
Dutch trade with Spanish America, xxi, 63, 114 n., 117–119, 129, 236.
Dutch West India Company, naval war of, in America, 236–238, 240–242.

East Indies, search for a strait to, 36, 37, 190; trade with, *see* Casa de Contratación of Coruña; Portugal.
Eden, Richard, 311.
Egues, Diego de, 13.
Ehinger family, of Constance, 99.
Ehinger, Ambrosius, 99.
El Dorado, 101.
Elizabeth of Valois, 77.
Emigration to the colonies, 5, 15, 96 ff., 132; confined to Castilians, 96, 97; inducements offered for, 105–107; illicit, 109–111, 136. *See also* Licenses; Registration.
Emigration from the Antilles to the mainland, 107.
Encinas, Diego de, xvi, 15.
Enciso, Diego de, 182.
England, trade with Spanish America, 19, 63, 114 n., 116, 247, 248, 250; naval war with Spain, 244–247; treaties with Spain, 247, 250.
Enriquez, Fernando (Admiral of Castile), 6 n.
Enriquez de Guzman, Alonso, 183 n., 230.
Escalante de Mendoza, Juan de, 263, 312, 313.
Escribano, de nao, *see* Ship's clerk; de armadas, 49, 74, 75; de registros, 63.
Escribano mayor of the Casa, 54 n.
Espingardas, 272.

Essex, Robert Devereux, Earl of, 82.
Estrées, Jean, comte d', 115 n.
Examination of mariners, 36, 273, 277, 299–302, 315.
Exchange, merchants, of Seville, *see* Casa Lonja.
Exchequer, colonial, 27, 30, 92–95; royal, 34, 43, 52, 78, 81, 82, 95, 108.
Exchequer officials in the colonies, *see* Oficiales reales.

Fabricador de instrumentos, 38, 305.
Factor of the Casa, 21, 26 n., 33, 34 n., 47, 48–51, 53, 75, 176, 275.
Factors, commercial, 102 n.; royal, 4, 22 and n., 23, 25, 27.
Fairs, Castilian, 24, 177.
Fajardo, Juan, 296.
Falconetes, 275 n.
Falcons (artillery), 274, 275.
Falero, Francisco, 38, 39.
Falero, Rui, 38, 39.
Fanshaw, Sir Richard, 248.
Felipe, Diego, 211.
Ferdinand III, 8.
Ferdinand V, 22, 23, 28, 29, 35, 36, 41, 68, 96–98, 104, 108, 125.
Ferdinand VII, 197.
Ferdinand and Isabella, *see* Catholic Kings.
Fernandez de Enciso, Martin, 310.
Fernandez de Navarrete, Martin, xv, xvi.
Fernandez de Navarrete, Pedro, 164.
Fernandez de Oviedo y Valdés, Gonzalo, 96.
Fernandez de Santillan, Felipe, 161.
Firearms, export of, to the colonies forbidden, 134, 135.
Fiscal of the Casa, 53, 57 and n.
Flanders trade, 12, 15, 19, 129.
Fleets, American, return to other ports than Seville, 13, 14; establishment of system of, 16, 71, 166, 201–207; equipping and provisioning of, 49, 50, 75, 79, 83, 243; officers of, 60, 219–221; size of, 71, 73, 201, 205, 211–215, 237, 245, 246, 281, 296; winter in America, 80, 207, 208; time of sailing, 90, 207–209;

# INDEX

value of bullion on, 165-171, *passim*, 336-338; route of, 203, 204, 223-228; description of voyage of, 222-230; instructions, 222-229, *passim;* destroyed by enemies, 236-239, 245, 246; decline of, *see* Trade. *See also* Armada; Avería; Convoys; Ships.
Fleets to guard the American coasts, 202, 204, 233, 251-255. *See also* Armada de la carrera de las Indias.
Florence, 24.
Flores, Alvaro de, 13.
Florida, 139, 228.
Florin, Jean, 70 and n.
Fonseca, port of, 184.
Foreign capitalists in Spain, 177-179; clergy excluded from the colonies, 111; goods in the colonies, *see* Contraband trade; ships, *see* Ships.
Foreigners in the colonies, 102, 110, 151, 186; fined by the Crown, 110, 111; in colonial navigation, 38, 39, 258-261, 302.
Foreigners in colonial trade, *see* Contraband trade.
Foreigners in the slave trade, 109.
Foreigners, naturalization of, 18, 107-109.
Fourquevaux, M., 169.
Francis I, wars of, *see* Charles V.
Freight rates, 283, 284; receipts exempt from avería, 74, 75 n.
French trade with Spanish America, 19, 63, 66, 114 and n., 116.
French West India Company, 249.
Frigates, 265.
Fugger, Anton, 99.
Fugger, Jacob, 98.
Fuggers, mining concessions to, in Spain, 47 n., 159-161; contract for the colonization of Chile, 99, 100.

Gage, Thomas, 188-190, *passim*. 235.
Galeoncetes, 265, 268.
Galicia, *see* Biscay provinces.
Galindez de Carvajal, Dr. Lorenzo, 34, 35.
Galisteo, Manuel, 196.
Galleas, 264, 265.

Gallego, Vasco, 36.
Galleons, xi, 213, 263, 264.
Galleys, xi, 252, 253, 263.
Galvao, Antonio, 192.
Gama, Vasco da, 23.
Gaona, Bernardino, 182.
Garay, Blasco de, 309.
Garcia, Miguel, *see* Garcia Torreño, Nuño.
Garcia de Céspedes, Andrés, 313.
Garcia de Hermosilla, Juan, 184.
Garcia de Loaysa, Francisco, 42 n.
Garcia Torreño, Nuño, 36, 37 n.
Gasca, Pedro de la, 166, 167.
Gasca de Salazar, Diego, 46.
Gavarras, 292.
General average, *see* Avería gruesa.
Genoese merchants in Spain, *see* Italian merchants.
German capitalists in Spanish America, *see* Fuggers; Welsers.
German merchants in Portugal, 23.
German miners in Spanish America, 99.
Gibraltar (Spain), 13, 14.
Gibraltar (Venezuela), 87, 250.
Gijón y León, Manuel, 197.
Gild, *see* Consulado; Mariners' gild.
Gipsies excluded from the colonies, 104 n., 110.
Gobernador of the armadas, 219, 220.
Gobierno (ship), 220.
Godolphin, Sir William, 248, 250.
Gold, *see* Bullion.
Gomera (Canary Islands), 19.
Gonzalez Dávila, Gil (historian), quoted, xii, xiii.
Gonzalez Dávila, Gil (explorer), 191.
Gonzalez de León, Sebastian, 50.
Goodson, Vice Admiral Sir William, 245.
Grammont, Sieur de (buccaneer), 249.
Grand Canary, 19, 20.
Grenville, Sir Richard, 77.
Grillo, Domingo, 270, 271.
Grimaldi, firm of, 177.
Grumetes, 272, 277.
Guadalcanal, silver mine of, 47 and n., 159.
Guadalcázar, Marquis of, 241.

# INDEX

Guards on merchant ships, to prevent fraud, 225, 290, 292.
Guatemala, restrictions on trade with, 126, 146, 150; proposed trade route through, 184, 185.
Guayaquil, 149 n., 150, 184, 241.
Guerra y de Cespedes, Francisco de la, 152.
Guevara, Antonio de, 49.
Guinea, trade with, 5 n., 60 n.
Guipuzcoa, Company of, 119, 138.
Gumiel, Nuño de, 21 n.
Gutierrez, Sancho, 302.
Gutierrez Flores, Dr. Pedro, 10 n.
Guzman, Gonzalo de, 231.

Hacienda real, *see* Exchequer, royal.
Hampton, Thomas, 116.
Hardware, importation of, into the colonies, 124, 135 n., 268, 271.
Haro, Luis de, 55 n.
Haros, firm of, 177 and n.
Havana, 87 and n., 139, 189, 244; attacked by corsairs, 68, 234; port of call for the fleets, 71, 72, 139, 201, 203, 207 and n.; shipbuilding at, 268.
Hawkins, John, 19, 77, 82, 116, 204 n., 210.
Hawkins, Richard, 240.
Hawkins, William, 116.
Hawks, Henry, 127.
Henry II (of France), 71.
Henry VII (of England), 22.
Henry, the Navigator, Prince, 304, 305.
Heretics excluded from the colonies, xii, 104, 105, 107.
Hermite, Jacques l', 240, 241.
Hernandez, Antonio, 278.
Hernandez Franco, Bartolomé, 60 n.
Herrera, Juan de, 325.
Heyn, Pieter Pieterzoon, 171, 237, 238.
Hieronymite governors of the Indies, 9, 106, 124, 267.
Hispaniola, 5, 6, 22 n., 40, 102, 116, 124, 125, 139, 155, 156, 158, 163, 244, 249 petitions from, 9, 26, 97, 104, 106, 233, 251; secures special privileges, 11, 18, 85 n., 87 and n.; population declines, 106, 107 n. *See also* San Domingo.

Honduras, 87 and n., 139, 150, 157, 204; proposed trade route through, 184, 185.
Honduras, Company of, 138.
Honduras Ships, 79, 207 n., 237.
Horses, export of, to the colonies forbidden, 134, 135.
Hospital for mariners at Seville, 320, 321.
Howard, Lord Charles, of Effingham, 82.
Huancavélica, mines of, 156, 160, 161.
Humboldt, Alexander von, cited in text, 123, 132, 156, 197.
Hungary, quicksilver from, 51.
Hydrographic Office (Madrid), xv.

Ibarra, Carlos de, 242, 243.
India House, *see* Casa de Contratación of Seville.
Indians, tribute from, 27, 92; exploitation of, 128, 132, 133; permitted to develop mines, 156 and n.
Indies, *see* East Indies; Spanish America.
Indultos, 65, 66, 113, 114.
Industries, colonial, Spanish policy regarding, 123, 125–130.
Informers, 31, 61 and n.
Inquisition, 105, 135.
Inspection of ships and cargoes, 11, 12, 16, 29, 30, 61, 281, 282 n., 287–292.
Insurance, marine, 41, 286, 287, 344–353.
Inter-colonial trade, *see* Custom duties; Peru.
Interlopers, *see* Contraband trade.
Intestates in the colonies, *see* Bienes de difuntos.
Iron, imported into the colonies, 135 n., 155.
Isabella, queen of Castile, 3 n., 4, 28, 96, 97. *See also* Catholic Kings.
Isabella (wife of Charles V), 307.
Isasaga, Pedro Ochoa, 21 n., 28, 29.
Istapa, port of, 184.
Italian merchants in Spain, xxiv, 8, 114 n., 178 n.; in Portugal, 23.
*Itinerario de navegación*, of Juan de Escalante de Mendoza, 312.

## INDEX

Jackson, William, 234, 235.
Jalapa, 204 n.
Jamaica, 139, 196, 235, 247–251, *passim;* Cromwell's expedition against, 194, 244, 245.
James I (of England), 234.
Jeréz de la Frontera, 108.
Jettison, 82 n.
Jews excluded from the colonies, 104, 105.
Joanna, queen of Castile, 3, 28, 40, 41, 98.
John II (of Castile), 156.
John II (of Portugal), 305.
Joll, Cornelius, 242.
Juan Fernandez (island), 240, 241.
Judge of the avería, 73, 74 n.
Jueces de registros (Canary Islands), 19, 20.
Jueces letrados of the Casa, 57, 58.
Jueces oficiales of the Casa, 27, 42. *See also* Comptroller; Factor; Treasurer.
Jueces oficiales supernumerarios, 55.
Juez asesor of the Casa, 57.
Juez conservador of the Lonja, 55.
Juez de alzadas, 44, 45 n.
Junta de guerra y armadas de Indias, 218, 221.
Jurisdiction of the Casa, *see* Casa de Contratación of Seville.
Juros, *see* Annuities.
Juzgado de Indias, *see* Cadiz.

La Antigua del Darién, *see* Santa Maria del Darién.
Labat, Jean-Baptiste, 121.
La Guayra, 87 and n., 119, 139.
Laisa, licentiate, 126.
La Palma (Canary Islands), 19, 20.
La Plata, audiencia of, 93.
La Raspuru, Tomás de, *see* Raspuru.
Laredo, 15.
La Salle, Robert Cavelier, Sieur de, 244 n.
La Serna, Fernando de, 182.
Laws of the Indies, *see* Recopilación.
Lead sheathing for ships, *see* Sheathing.
Lepe, Diego de, 5.
Lerma, Francisco Gomez de Sandoval, Duke of, 260.

Letrados of the Casa, 42 and n., 57.
Letters of marque, issued by Spain, 256.
Licenses to go to the colonies, 5, 33 n., 34, 101–104; to return to Spain, 102 n.; to trade with the colonies, 97, 109; for ships, 18, 259, 281–283.
Lima, 95, 107 n., 132, 188; Portuguese in, 117.
Lira, Manuel de, 138.
Liri, Antonio, 295.
Lisbon, 13, 23, 25 n., 117.
Logwood cutters, 257.
Lombards (artillery), 275.
Lomelin, Ambrosio, 270, 271.
Longitude, problem of finding, 305, 312.
Lonja, *see* Casa Lonja.
Lonk, Hendrik, 237.
Lopez, Gregorio, 201.
Lopez de Gómara, Francisco, cited in text, 163, 192.
Lopez de Legaspi, Miguel, 144, 146, 267.
Lopez de Recalde, Juan, 21 n., 69.
Lopez de Roelas, Diego, 202.
Lopez de Valdenebro, Rui, 192.
Lopez de Villalobos, Rui, 144.
Louis XIII (of France), 243.
Louis XIV (of France), 114, 115 n., 248, 251.
Louisiana, 244 n.

Madeira, 68, 69.
Maestres de plata, 220 and n.
Maestro de hacer cartas, 36.
Magellan, Ferdinand, 25 n., 38, 39, 144, 190.
Magellan, strait of, voyage via, 25 n., 98, 138, 144, 180.
Magnetic pole, 311.
Malaga, 13, 15–17, *passim.*
Mancera, Marquis of, 152.
Manifestación, 66, 114.
Manila, 144–149, *passim.*
Manoel (king of Portugal), 23.
Manrique, Pedro, 69.
Mansfield, Edward (buccaneer), 249, 254.
Maps and map-making, *see* Cartography; Cosmographers of the Casa.
Maracaibo, 87 n., 119, 235, 250.

Margarita, 79, 87, 139, 189, 224.
Mariquita, 188.
Mariners' gild of Seville, 86, 88, 216, 281, 301, 320–322. *See also* Comitres.
Mariners' wages, *see* Wages.
Mariners' hospital, *see* Hospital.
Married men emigrating to the colonies, 102 n., 151.
Martinique, 118.
Martyr, Peter, 163, 309.
Masters of ships, 24, 25 and n., 60 n., 62, 314, 315; bonds of, 59, 103, 315, 316. *See also* Mariners' gild.
Matanzas, 237, 238.
Matienzo, Dr. Sancho de, 21 and n., 33 n.
Media anata, 87, 88.
Medina, Bartolomé de, 158.
Medina, Fernando de, 35.
Medina, Pedro de, 302, 304 n., 310, 311.
Medinaceli, Duke of, 70, 152.
Medina Sidonia, Duke of, 70, 322.
Medio-sacres, 275 n.
Mendoza, Pedro de, 100 n.
Menendez de Avilés, Pedro, 77, 211, 217, 228, 252, 264, 265.
Mercado, Diego de, 194.
Mercantilism in Spain, 123–130.
Merchant Adventurers Trading to Russia, 311.
Merchants' gild of Seville, *see* Consulado.
Mercury, *see* Quicksilver.
Metedores, 112 n.
Mexico, *see* New Spain.
Mexico City, 89, 95, 107 n., 149.
Mines in the colonies, 5, 155–157.
Mint of Seville, 66, 174, 176.
Mocenigo, Andrea, 163.
Moluccas, trade with, 25 n., 98, 145, 181.
Monasteries in Spanish America, 131, 132.
Moncada, Dr. Sancho de, 164.
Monopoly of trade, *see* Crown; Seville; Trade.
Montealegre, Marquis of, 210.
Montejo, Francisco de, 184.
Moors, *see* Moslems.
Morales, Andrés de, 309, 310.
Morgan, Henry (buccaneer), 187, 194, 249, 250, 254.

Moslems excluded from the colonies, 104, 105, 107, 134, 135.
Munibe, Andrés de, 55.
Munitions for the fleets, 49, 50, 79.
Muñoz, Juan Bautista, 196, 197.
Myngs, Christopher, 248.

Nao, 263.
Naturalization, *see* Foreigners, naturalization of.
Nauerre, M. de la, 196.
Nautical instruction, *see* Cosmography, professor of; Pilot major.
Nautical instruments, *see* Astrolabe; Compass; Cross-staff; Quadrant.
Nautical instruments, making of, 36, 38, 307, 308, 314.
Nautical science in Spain, xxii, 299, 304, 305, 308–314.
Navarrese admitted to colonial trade, 98 n.
Navarro, Antonio, 294.
Navidad, 146.
Navigation to the Indies, *see* Fleets.
Navio del Oro, 189.
Navios de registro, 87, 88, 213, 282.
Navy, *see* Ships-of-war; Armada.
Negroes, *see* Slave trade.
Nelson, Horatio, 196.
Netherlands, *see* Dutch trade; Flanders trade.
Nevis, 119.
New Christians, *see* Conversos.
New Galicia, 185.
New Granada, 65, 81, 161, 166. *See also* Cartagena de Indias.
" New Laws " of Charles V, 92, 202.
New Spain, 65, 69, 81, 82, 89, 94, 106, 125 n., 157, 166, 212, 254; fleets to, 79, 203–214, *passim;* textile manufactures of, 126, 127; remittances of bullion, 166 n., 167 n., 207, 332; price of quicksilver in, *see* Quicksilver; trade with Peru, *see* Peru; trade with the Philippines, *see* Philippine Islands.
Nicaragua, 157, 184.
Nicaragua canal route, *see* Canal, interoceanic.

## INDEX

Nicaragua, Lake, 189, 191, 193, 194, 196.
Niño, Alonso, 5.
Niño, Andrés Garcia, 36.
Nombre de Dios, 85, 151, 181, 182 n., 184, 185, 201.
*Norte de la contratación de las Indias*, xvii, 3, 11, 55.
Notaries, *see* Escribano.
Novoa, Matías de, quoted, 215, 238.
Nuestra Señora del Buen Aire, 321, 322.
Nueva Córdoba, 87.
Nuñez de Balboa, Vasco, 180, 190, 310.
Nuñez de Castro, Alfonso, cited in text, 167.
Nuñez Vela, Blasco, 71, 77, 165, 170, 202.

Oficial mayor, 33 n., 34 n.
Oficiales reales, 27, 59, 60 n., 61 n., 63 and n., 88, 89, 92, 291; relations with the executive authorities, 93–95.
Oidores of the Casa, *see* Jueces letrados.
Ojeda, Alonso de, 5, 24, 309, 310.
Olivares, Gaspar de Guzman, count of, *and* duke of San Lucar, 35, 54 and n., 55 and n., 214, 243.
Olive, cultivation of, in Peru, 126.
Olonais, l' (Nau, Jean-David), 254.
Oñate, Count of, 35.
Oquendo, Antonio, 296.
Oran, 14, 37, 103.
Orchandiano, Domingo de, 21 n., 33 n.
Ordas, Diego de, 190.
Ordinances of the Casa, *see* Casa de Contratación of Seville.
Ordnance, *see* Artillery.
Ortiz de Matienzo, Pedro, 9, 10.
Ovando, Nicolás de, 6, 7, 22 n., 26, 27, 97, 104, 310.

Pacific Ocean, navigation of, 144; search for a strait to, 190, 191; shipbuilding on the shores of, 267.
Padrón real, 306–308.
Pagador de averías, 51.
Palos, 7.
Panama city, 93, 107 n., 126, 145, 146, 147, 151, 180–190, 250.
Panama, isthmus of, highway across, 180–186, *passim;* canal through, *see* Canal, inter-oceanic.
Panuco, 184.
Papagayo, port of, 194.
Pasavolantes, 272, 275.
Pasquier, Pedro, 296.
Passengers on ships to the colonies, 76, 219 and n., 273. *See also* Registration.
Pataches, 78, 79, 204, 210, 264.
Paternalism of the Spanish crown, 123, 124.
Paterson, William, 195.
Patronus, 315, 318.
Payta, 149 188, 189.
Pearls, 47 and n., 79, 165 and n., 186, 189.
Penalties for infraction of rules governing the colonial trade, 13, 14, 31, 34 n., 61, 62, 65, 80, 103, 108, 136, 139, 222, 229, 281, 285, 286.
Penas de casados, 102 n.
Perez, Diego, 232.
Perez, Dr. Hernan, 44, 301, 302.
Periaguas, 256.
Perico, harbor of, 187.
Pernambuco, 236, 242.
Peru, 24, 58 n., 65, 71, 81, 82 and n., 85, 93, 94, 157, 166, 168, 212, 254; trade with New Spain, 111, 146, 147, 149, 150, 187, 255; Central America, 126, 150, 152; the Orient, 145, 146; Spain, 188–190; via Buenos Aires, *see* Buenos Aires; production of wine, 125, 126, 129; textiles, 127–129; quicksilver, *see* Huancavélica; remittances of bullion, *see* Bullion; Crown; privateers on coasts of, 195, 240, 241.
Philip I (of Spain), 28, 29, 36.
Philip II (of Spain), 11, 17, 19, 24, 38, 44–46, 56, 57, 72, 73, 77, 85 n., 86, 90, 101, 108, 111, 116, 126, 127, 137, 156, 160, 166, 173, 192, 193, 203, 259, 269, 325.
Philip III (of Spain), 87, 132, 171, 194, 236, 270, 305.
Philip IV (of Spain), 53–55, 78, 171, 243, 270.
Philippine Islands, trade with, xxi, 111, 143–149, 255.

Pilot major of Castile, 35–38, 298–302, 305–308.
Pilot major of England, 39.
Pilot major of the fleet, 219, 224, 314, 316.
Pilots, 314–316, *passim;* royal, 36, 37.
Pinelo, Francisco, 21 and n.
Pinzón, Vicente Yañez, 5, 24, 36.
Pirates, *see* Corsairs.
Pizarro, Gonzalo, 166.
Pizarro, Hernando, 168.
*Pole Star of American Trade, see Norte de la contratación de las Indias.*
Popayan, 188.
Population of colonial cities, 107 n.
Port Royal (Jamaica), 247, 248.
Portazgo, *see* Admiralty dues.
Porto Bello, 79, 91, 138, 185, 188–190, 194, 250.
Porto Rico, 11, 82, 87 and n., 124, 139, 156, 244.
Ports of entry in Spanish America, 138.
Portugal, xi, xxiii, 13, 23, 25 n., 39, 68; trade with the Spanish colonies, 66, 113, 116, 117.
Portuguese in Spanish America, 104, 105, 110.
Portuguese mariners in Spain, 39.
Postmaster-general of the colonies, 34, 35, 52.
Potosí, 110, 160, 161, 166, 181, 189 n., 333–335.
Precious metals, *see* Bullion.
President of the Casa, 12, 33 n., 46, 47, 53, 54, 58.
Prices in the colonies, 91, 137, 186 n., 214, 278 n., 279, 280.
Prior and consuls of the Seville merchants, 43, 44, 62, 73, 74, 78, 281, 285, 325.
Privateers, Spanish, in the West Indies, 256, 257.
Prizes at sea, 69, 222 n.
Proctors from the colonies in Spain, 40, 97, 139.
Prohibited articles in colonial trade, 26, 134–136.
Providence, Old (island), 120, 250.
Provisioning of the fleets, *see* Fleets.

Puebla de los Ángeles, 107 n., 127.
Puerto Cabello, 119, 247.
Puerto de Caballos, 184, 207 n.
Pumps, marine, 308, 309.
Purveyor-general of fleets and armadas, 49, 50 and n., 75.
Purveyors of the avería, 79, 80.

Quadrant, 304 n.
Quicksilver, supply of, to the colonies, 50, 51, 74 n., 157–162; produced in America, 155, 160; obtained from Germany, 159, 160, 162; price of, 161, 162.
Quintaladas, 317.
Quintanilla, Jorge, 193.
Quinto, of bullion, 64, 92, 156, 157, 333–335; of pearls, 165 n.
Quito, 189, 195.

Rancherías, 189.
Raspuru, Tomás de la, 13, 166, 169, 171, 239, 296.
Reader of the Casa, 57 n.
Receptor de averías, 51, 53 and n., 74, 75.
*Recopilación de leyes de los reynos de las Indias,* xviii.
*Regimiento de navegación,* of Pedro de Medina, 311.
*Regimiento de navegación y de la hidrografía,* of Andrés Garcia de Céspedes, 313.
Registers of ships, 11, 15, 18, 25, 33 n., 59, 60 and n., 63 and n., 64, 88, 89, 103, 168, 281, 290.
Registration in colonial trade, 4, 5, 7, 14–16, 25, 27, 29, 59–67, 102, 105; abolished for goods from America, 80, 81; frauds in, *see* Contraband trade.
Registros sueltos, *see* Navios de registro.
Relator, *see* Reader.
Revenues from America, *see* Crown.
Rhodes, law of, 82 n.
Ribera, P. Henriques de, 167 n.
Ribero, Diego, 36, 37 n., 39, 306, 307, 308, 309.
Richelieu, cardinal, 210, 243.
Rio de la Hacha, 77, 85 n., 87, 119, 139, 245, 250.

# INDEX 369

Rio de la Plata, 37, 100 n.; contraband trade on, *see* Buenos Aires.
Rios, Martin Alonso de los, 71, 76, 165.
Rios, Pedro de los, 180, 182.
Rodriguez Cómitre, Diego, 287.
Rodriguez de Fonseca, Juan, 3, 21, 40.
Rodriguez de Valdes y de la Banda, Diego, 141.
Rodriguez Farfan, Cosme, 64, 201, 211, 294.
Rodriguez Sardo, Juan, 299.
Roelas, Pedro de las, 77, 211.
Rouen, 24.
Royal monopoly of trade, *see* Crown.
Royalties on mines in the colonies, 156, 157. *See also* Quinto.
Ruesta, Sebastian de, 308.

Saavedra Ceron, Alvaro de, 191.
Sacres, 274.
Sacro Bosco, Joannes de, 303 n., 313.
Sailing routes, *see* Fleets.
Sailors, *see* Mariners.
Saint Domingue, 249, 251.
St. Kitts, 118, 119, 235.
St. Martin (island), 120.
St. Vincent, Cape, 13, 68, 69, 70 and n., 202.
Sala de justicia, of the Casa, 57, 58.
Salas Valdés, Juan de, 295.
Sale of public offices, 54, 56, 94, 151, 218, 288.
Salinas, Marquis of, 214.
Sanchez Colchero, Diego, 301.
Sanchez de la Parra, Miguel, 110.
Sanchez de la Tesorería, Juan, 97.
San Domingo, city of, 9, 68, 99, 106, 107 n., 116, 139, 201, 202, 244.
Sandoval, licentiate, 202.
Sandwich, Edward Montagu, Earl of, 248.
San Gabriel (Rio de la Plata), 142.
San Juan de Ulua, *see* Vera Cruz.
San Juan River (Nicaragua), 184, 189, 191, 193, 194.
San Lucar de Barrameda, 7, 11, 14, 58, 86, 110; delays at, 8, 10, 72, 73, 208, 213, 262.

San Martin, Andrés de, 36, 307.
San Miguel, gulf of, 180.
San Salvador (Brazil), 236.
San Sebastian, 15.
Santa Catalina, *see* Providence, Old.
Santa Cruz, Alonso de, 311, 312.
Santa Cruz (Canary Islands), 13, 18, 246.
Santa Cruz (West Indies), 120.
Santa Fé de Bogotá, 95, 188.
Santa Maria (Azores), 70.
Santa Maria del Darién (La Antigua), 180, 310.
Santa Marta, 87 and n., 233, 245, 247, 250.
Santander, 13.
San Telmo, College of, 88, 322.
Santiago de Cuba, 68, 107 n., 139, 203, 232, 233, 248, 250.
Santiago de la Vega (Jamaica), 235.
Saragossa, treaty of (1529), 25 n., 144.
Schapenham, Hugues, 241.
Schmidt, Ulrich, 100 n.
Seigniorage, 175.
Serreno, Juan, 36.
Seville monopoly of colonial trade, 7 ff., 82, 91, 103, 136, 137, 153, 256.
Sharpe, Bartholomew, 194, 195.
Sheathing of ships, 277, 278, 308.
Shipbuilding, in the colonies, 124, 266–268, 271; in Spain, 263–266, 269–271.
Ship captains, *see* Masters.
Ships, size of, 8, 71, 79, 201, 212, 213, 261–263; by law, of Spanish ownership and construction, 26, 258–260; foreign-built, in colonial trade, 88, 243, 259, 260, 270, 283; sail without convoy, 202, 205, 206; armament of, 209, 272, 274–276, 280; superannuated, in colonial trade, 211, 272, 276, 277; overloading of, 216, 217, 239, 276, 293; manning of, 272, 274, 293, 297; rations on, 273, 278–281; election of, for the fleets, 281, 282; disregard of ordinances relating to, 292, 293; loans on security of, *see* Bottomry bills; bounties for building of, *see* Bounties; inspection of, *see* Inspection; insurance of, *see*

Insurance, marine; sheathing of, *see* Sheathing; construction of, *see* Shipbuilding.
Ship's clerk, 24, 25 and n., 31, 59, 60 n., 63 n.
Ships-of-war, hired by the Crown, 206, 269–271.
Shipwrecks, 293–297.
Silks, manufactured in New Spain, 126, 127; imported from China, 145.
Silver, *see* Bullion.
Simancas, archives at, xv, xviii.
Slave trade, negro, 26, 99, 118, 119, 134, 135, 140, 141, 270, 271.
"Sloop trade," 121.
Smuggling, *see* Contraband trade.
Sociedad de los Amigos de Madrid, 197.
Solicitors of the Casa, 42 n.
Solórzano Pereira, Juan de, 45 n., 137, 239.
Sore, Jacques, 233, 234.
Soria, Juan de, 7.
Soriano, Michel, 163.
Sosa, Francisco de, 295.
South Sea, *see* Pacific Ocean.
Spain, colonial policy, xii, 96, 123–134, 153; decline of, xxiii, 47, 63, 127, 153, 154, 243, 270, 271; imperialism of, 178, 179; navy of, *see* Ships-of-war.
Spanish America, civilization of, xii f., 130–134; administration of, 3, 21, 22, 92–95, 150–152; military defencelessness of, 233, 243, 244.
Spice trade, 23, 180, 181. *See also* Moluccas.
Spilbergen, Joris, 240.
Stayner, Sir Richard, 245, 246.
Storekeeper of the Casa, 50, 52.
Suarez de Carvajal, Juan, 46.
Subsidies of the Seville merchants to the king, 171, 172, 325.
Sugar, 11, 19, 124, 125 and n.
*Suma de cosmografía*, of Pedro de Medina, 311.
*Suma de geografía*, of Martin Fernandez de Enciso, 310.
Sumptuary laws in the colonies, 131.
Sweeting, John, 258.

Tabasco, 87 n.
Tehuantepec, isthmus of, 190, 192, 195.
Tello de Guzman, Juan, 202, 203, 211, 252.
Tenedor de bastimentos, *see* Storekeeper of the Casa.
Tenerife, 18–20, *passim*.
Tercio de galeones, 219, 220.
Teredo (shipworm), 277.
Textile industry in the colonies, 124, 126–129.
Textiles imported from the Orient, *see* China.
Thirty Years' War, 210, 214.
Tiepolo, Niccolò, 163.
Tierra Firme, fleets to, 72, 79, 80, 203–214, *passim*; canal through, *see* Canal, inter-oceanic. *See also* Nombre de Dios; Panama; Porto Bello.
Tithes, ecclesiastical, 106, 131.
Tobacco, 119, 129.
Toledo, Fadrique de, 119, 171, 236, 296.
Toledo, Francisco de, 93, 126–128, 151, 152, 183.
Tolu, 247, 250.
Tomson, Robert, 258.
Tonelada, 284 and n.
Tonnage dues, 86–88.
Tordesillas, treaty of (1494), 148.
Torres, Francisco de, 36.
Tortuga (off Hispaniola), 120, 249, 251.
Trade with America, a monopoly of Spain, xii, 26, 96–98, 101, 107, 108, 153; *see also* Crown; Seville; decline of, 12, 129, 147, 153, 187, 213–215, 243; foreigners in, *see* Contraband trade; Ships.
Trading companies, exclusive, 137, 138.
Treasurer of the Casa, 21, 26 n., 33, 34 n., 47–49, 52 n., 95.
Treasurers, royal, in the colonies, 4, 27, 30, 88.
Treasury officials in the colonies, *see* Oficiales reales.
Treatises on navigation, *see* Nautical science.
Triana, 86, 321.
Tribunal de la contaduría, of the Casa, 52, 54 n., 95; in the colonies, 95.

# INDEX

Trinidad, 87 and n., 139.
Truxillo (Peru), 189.
Truxillo (Honduras), 235, 250.
Tuna fisheries of Andalusia, 25 n.

Unión de las armas católicas, 254, 255.
Universidad de los Mareantes de Sevilla, see Mariners' gild.
Urcas, 213, 264.
Urdaneta, Andrés de, 144.
Ursua, Pedro de, 13.

Vaca de Castro, Cristobal, 165.
Valdivia, 241.
Valdiviedo, Antonio de, 267.
Valle de la Cerda, Luis, 163.
Veedor, de fundiciones y rescates, 27 n.; de la artillería, 50 n.; on the fleets, 74, 75, 220.
Veitia Linaje, Joseph de, xvii f.; cited in text, 3, 11, 15, 18 n., 64–66, 76, 78, 79, 82 n., 91, 96, 113, 114, 161, 205, 308.
Velasco, Diego Ferdinand de, 194.
Velasco, Luis de, 128.
Velazquez, Diego, 267.
Velvets, see Silks.
Venables, General Robert, 244.
Venezuela, 85 n., 155, 189; trade with the Dutch, 118, 129. See also Guipuzcoa, Company of; Welsers.
Venice, Sebastian Cabot's relations with, 37.
Venta Cruz, 182–185, *passim*.
Vera Cruz, 28, 77, 79–81, 89, 138, 162, 204 and n., 207.
Verrazano, Giovanni da, 70.
Vespucci, Américo, 35–38, *passim*, 298, 306.
Vespucci, Juan, 36, 37 n., 307.

Viceroys in America, relations of, with the exchequer, 93–95.
Vigo, 13.
Villars, Marquis of, 114.
Visitadores, 287–291.
Vitoria, fray Francisco de, 140.

Wages of Spanish seamen, 63, 74, 316–319, 342, 343.
Welsers, in American trade, 98, 100 n., 158, 165 n.; colonization of Venezuela by, 99–101.
West Indies, poverty of the settlements in, 83, 85 n., 124, 125; colonized by English, French, and Dutch, 118–120; trade with, 138–140; English naval war in, 244, 245, 247; corsairs in, see Buccaneers; Corsairs.
Windsor, Thomas, Lord, 247, 248.
Wine, export of, to the colonies, 10, 19, 40, 124, 125, 217 n., 318; duties on, 84 n., 85; production of, in Peru, see Peru.
Woad, 106.
Women, emigration of, to the colonies, 102 n., 111, 151.
Wool exported from Peru, 182. See also Textiles.

Ximenes de Cisneros, cardinal, 106.
Xuarez de Castillo, Pedro, 76.

Yucatan, 139.

Zamorano, Rodrigo de, 300 n., 313.
Zapata, Alonso, 301.
Zipangu, xii.
Zultepeque, silver mines of, 100.